FITLY FRAMED TOGETHER

THE HUMAN BODY

Mike Culpepper

WESTBOW
PRESS®
A DIVISION OF THOMAS NELSON
& ZONDERVAN

WestBow Press books may be ordered through booksellers or by contacting:

WestBow Press
A Division of Thomas Nelson & Zondervan
1663 Liberty Drive
Bloomington, IN 47403
www.westbowpress.com
1 (866) 928-1240

Scripture taken from the New King James Version®. Copyright © 1982 by Thomas Nelson. Used by permission. All rights reserved.

Scripture taken from the King James Version of the Bible.

ISBN: 978-1-9736-6213-6 (sc)
ISBN: 978-1-9736-6214-3 (hc)
ISBN: 978-1-9736-6212-9 (e)

Library of Congress Control Number: 2019906701

Print information available on the last page.

WestBow Press rev. date: 6/6/2019

I am most grateful to God for my life and abilities and opportunities He has given me. He gave me good parents. I dedicate this book to my dad, Milton (MI) Culpepper, Jr. as a memorial to his life and meaning to me. He was the biggest fan of my previous book, *Fitly Framed Together: The Bible,* and I truly miss his humor and fatherly advice.

... I have created him [man] for my glory, I have formed him; yes, I have made him.

—Isaiah 43:7

CONTENTS

LIST OF FIGURES

The illustrations shown in the Figures listed below and depicted throughout the text were done by the author and his granddaughter, Jennifer Lee.

PREFACE

People need to know about God ... and man's relationship with Him. Eternity is a long time! Too often, people will act and talk as if they understand the nature of God, but in fact, they do not have a clue. People may even display a belief in God, yet in their convictions, they do not relate to Jesus or most any concepts of the Bible for that matter. The Scripture tells of the creation. God created the heavens and the earth (Genesis 1:1). God created the realm of spiritual beings such as angels, cherubim and seraphim. But God also created the realm of the physical, including the creation of man. Whether this creation was "instantaneous" or developed over a period of time is a discussion for other times. The purpose of the Bible is not to explain "how" God created the spiritual and physical. Scripture simply begins with the supposition that a physical realm was indeed created and that man was included in that creation and that God did it.

Over sixty years ago I began a journey of life. Included has been a diverse and fulfilling assortment of education and life experiences. Even as a young child I can remember reflecting and contemplating nature, how it seemed everything works together as one, as part of God's creation. As I grew older, I was equally amazed at how the human body works. I studied the sciences including Biology, Chemistry and Physics throughout my undergraduate and graduate studies, but began to focus my attention on the human body, including Anatomy, Exercise Physiology, Kinesiology and Biomechanics.

As my research, teaching, and coaching career unfolded, I began to see how the nature and form of God is in His creation of man. I began to see how God's Word through Scripture reflected His attributes as the sole designer, architect and redeemer of His creation. In my previous book, *Fitly Framed Together: The Bible* (WestBow Press, 2013), I described how the Bible came to be and how it can be shown that it is indeed a Godly writing and that it was God breathed and that it was indeed fitly framed together. In similar fashion, as one studies the human body, a similar connection can be seen with the human body. Just as God was able to "fitly frame" the Bible in the way He did, He did the same thing to the human body. Thus, the title of this book, *Fitly Framed Together: The Body*.

I have traveled world-wide coaching sports teams and teaching Human Anatomy and Physiology, Kinesiology, Biomechanics and other related courses. In each endeavor, I have instructed and showed how the body moves so efficiently and how it can perform at such elite levels. The human form and design exceed ordinary comprehension. I am always amazed when I watch a science-fiction movie. In many cases it depicts an "alien" as more intellectually superior and advanced and more technically refined than humans. In addition, movie makers portray an "alien" in a most unusual or hideous form, and in most cases, it is vastly more "superior". However, it is the human body that is in fact superiorly advanced. The anatomy that the human body presents is most advanced, indeed. There are many anatomy books, written at all levels for different degrees of study, including commentaries and learning guides.

A purpose of this book is not dissimilar to any other anatomy book. It will indeed examine human anatomy as can be described in anatomy books used in college courses. But the major purpose of this "anatomy" book is not just to echo information that can be found in other human anatomy and physiology books. It is the intent to reflect God's nature in His ultimate creation, man.

Using my knowledge and background in anatomy, physiology, and human performance, and my reflections on Scripture, it is my desire to best condense and comment on the anatomy and physiology associated with his creation. Thus, the similar title to my previous book.

In this undertaking, I have observed some specific examples of human anatomy and have researched Scripture. I have included knowledge and application of human anatomy and physiology and in the process describing the very nature of God, as shown in His creation of man.

Of course, the belief is that if the Bible is undeniably the Word of God, then what it says is meaningful and very important. The Bible says that God created man in his own image. He created male and female (Genesis 1:27). Therefore, a study of human anatomy of this sort is logical and can be very meaningful. However, even those who do not believe in the Bible or Jesus or otherwise does not subscribe to the notion of the Bible as being God's Word, one can still find this particular book interesting.

It is the intent of this writing to illustrate that the human body was put together in such a way as to claim that it is the created work of God, not necessarily because we have anatomy that can be described and studied, but *how* it is put together. The human body is truly "Fitly Framed Together", just as the Bible was put together. In this text, I have utilized the New King James Version (Thomas Nelson, 1994) for biblical references, trying to centralize on a most accurate and popular version of the Bible. The author gratefully acknowledges HarperCollins Christian Publishing for their permission to use this version of the Bible.

As architects, engineers, and construction workers design, build, and put together bridges and buildings—and these structures stand firm—so it is with the body. It is literally designed and put together by God Himself and it stands firm. The human body has the framework and fabric showing that it is indeed *Fitly Framed Together.*

Mike Culpepper

Mike Culpepper
Author

CHAPTER 1

AN INTRODUCTION

By faith we understand that the worlds were framed by the word of God, so that the things which are seen were not made of things which are visible. – Hebrews 11:3

The above Scripture describes a unique paradox of our universe—and of humankind's existence. It is stating that this vast universe with the galaxies, stars, planets, earth, and humans—everything we know of and see—was created by something that we cannot see. However, everything we can see is not eternal. At some point, when the "end of time" comes, all physical things that can be seen will pass away and cease to exist, whereas the spiritual things, which cannot be seen, are eternal.

There is little doubt of the enormity of the universe. One can estimate that there are more than 100 billion galaxies. It can also be estimated that an average galaxy may have as many as 100 billion stars (our own Milky Way galaxy may have as many as 400 billion). But even if we take a conservative approximation and say there are 100 billion galaxies with 100 billion stars in each, then there are more than 1×10^{22} stars. This can be quickly estimated by multiplying 1×10^{11} (100 billion galaxies) times 1×10^{11} (100 billion stars per galaxy) which equals 1×10^{22} stars in the universe. That is 10,000,000,000,000,000,000,000,000 or ten sextillion stars! A high-end estimate could be 200 sextillion. A reasonable estimate as to the number of stars in the universe, then, could be 100 sextillion. The number of grains of sand on the earth has been estimated to be around 5 sextillion.[1] Thus, it can be estimated that there are about twenty times more stars in the universe than grains of sand on the earth. That is an enormous universe!

In addition, the atom is considered the basic unit of structure and function of all physical matter in the universe. Atoms consist of subatomic particles called protons, electrons, and neutrons. There are 100 billion atoms in a single drop of water. If an atom were as large as the head of a pin, then all the atoms in a grain of sand would fill a cube one mile on each side. But there are actually other elementary and intermediate mass and force "particles" including, but not limited to, mesons, baryons, hadrons, bosons, quarks, pions, gluons, leptons, and photons, not to mention their shadow antiparticles, such as antiquarks. All matter and substance of this great universe consist of these elementary particles. A greater understanding of these basic matter and "force" particles helps to explain matter and forces in the universe.

However, the part of the universe that we can actually "see" accounts for only about 5 percent of the total universe. Dark matter makes up about 25 percent, and dark energy accounts for 70 percent of the rest of the universe. Particle physicists are only just now beginning to grasp the vastness and incalculability that is the characteristic of our universe.

Considering all the stars and the expanse and enormity of the universe, one might consider that there could be life elsewhere. However, NASA has yet to find any other place in the universe where life can exist. Nestled within the vast expanse of the universe, only our earth has been found to support life. And certainly, the earth is full of life. Scientist have estimated that there are nearly 9 million species of life on earth, though some have said it could be upward of 50 million. The latter scientists figure we have only accounted for less than 20 percent of all the species on this planet.[2]

The opening words of the Bible are "In the beginning (time), God created the heavens (space) and the earth (matter)" (Genesis 1:1). From a science perspective, that means time and space came into existence, as well as matter. God created an enormous spiritual (nonphysical) realm that has no time or physical limits. But He also created a vast physical universe, including earth, that is bound by time and space. And then God filled the earth with all its life forms. "Indeed My hand has laid the foundation of the earth, and My right hand has stretched out the heavens; when I call to them, they stand up together" (Isaiah 48:13).

In my previous book, *Fitly Framed Together: The Bible*, the number three was described as spiritual trinity—the completeness and fullness of God (God the Father, Son, and Holy Spirit). God has three major attributes. These include omniscience (all knowledge), omnipresence (ever present, everywhere), and omnipotence (all powerful). Thus, the number three represents the very essence of God. It is interesting that when considering time, space, and matter, the three components of the physical world, each can be divided into three facets. For example, with time, there are the past, present, and future. With space, there are length, width, and depth (height). Concerning matter, scripture describes this. "There are three that bear witness on earth, the spirit, the water and the blood; and these three agree as one" (1 John 5:8). Thus, God the Father, Son, and Holy Spirit are manifest in the physical creation of the world.

However, in all that creation, something was missing. It was man! Considering the entire universe and all the life on earth, God wanted to create a life-form that was above all. He wanted something unique and special. And each individual human who has walked upon this planet is special. What began in the book of Genesis is developed throughout the Bible and is fulfilled in the book of the Revelation. It gives us an insight into why God would create a physical realm, including man.

Since the creation, consider the number of humans who have been born. It has been estimated that 105 billion humans have lived on earth, and no two individuals have ever been alike![3] Even "identical twins" are never exactly alike. Mathematically, taking all factors into consideration, the probability of you being born at all is 1 in $10^{2,685,000}$![4] This probability would be equivalent to, say, 2 million people, each with a 3 trillion-sided dice, and if they all roll the dice at once, every single dice lands on the same number! In effect, the chance your being born was basically zero. From the beginning of time until the end of time, you are special; there have been none like you. You are a miracle indeed!

In His Image

The Bible clearly states that God is "Spirit." "God is Spirit, and those who worship Him must worship in spirit and truth" (John 4:24). And both scripture and reason should support the fact that the God of all creation cannot be limited to a physical body. "But will God indeed dwell on the earth? Behold, heaven and the heaven of the heavens cannot contain You" (1 Kings 8:27).

However, the Bible also states that at the beginning, man was created in the image of God. "So God created man in His own image; in the image of God He created him, male and female He created them" (Genesis 1:27). The Bible also states, "He (man) is the image of the invisible God, the firstborn over all creation" (Colossians 1:15). Now if man is in the image of God, but Got is spirit and even invisible, how is it that man has a physical body that can be seen and felt whereas God does not? Or does God literally have "body parts" like man?

If one studies scripture, one may find that, although God may not have a physical body, the Bible clearly discloses how God revealed Himself in human form through Jesus. "In the beginning was the Word, and the Word was with God, and the Word was God. He was in the beginning with God … and the Word became flesh and dwelt among us" (John 1:1–2, 14). Thus, God did take on the physical form of a man through Jesus Christ. Jesus was fully God, yet He was also fully man.

> Let this mind be in you which was also of Jesus Christ, who being in the form of God did not consider it robbery to be equal with God, but made Himself of no reputation, taking the form of a bondservant, and coming in the likeness of men, and being found

in appearance as a man, He humbled Himself and became obedient to the point of death, even the death of the cross. Therefore God also has highly exalted Him and given Him the name which above every name .... (Philippians 2:5–9)

The salvation message of scripture is that as physical man sinned, death entered the world. Death can be defined as eternal separation from the living God. Hell! And as sin occurred, there must be a payment for sin. It did cost something! When Adam and Eve sinned in the Garden, God had to kill an innocent animal for clothing, to cover the nakedness of Adam and Eve. Innocent blood was shed as a result of man's sin. This sin cost an innocent life.

Of course, humans could not and cannot repay this cost. Only perfect, innocent blood could atone for our sin. This payment could only come from the perfect God! Only God could pay that infinite price for the atonement and redemption of our sin. Thus, He became flesh (as Jesus), lived a perfect, innocent (human) life, and shed His (physical, human) blood and died as payment for our sins so that the consequences of sin and death could be overcome. Only God was able to accomplish that, and He was willing to do just that. And in doing so, He was able to demonstrate His love, grace, and power and illustrate His glory in doing just that! Thus, God the Father (Spirit) gave Himself God the Son (physical, human) Jesus as a ransom for our sins. And He continually gives us God the Holy Spirit to "live" in us and through us as His creation and work of His glory. Jesus, the incarnate of God, will be discussed later.

Although God is spirit and not confined to a physical body, time and space, there are numerous scriptural references to God as having "human form body parts" in a symbolic manner. Since man is physical, we can understand "physical things" better than we can understand "spiritual things". Thus, there are numerous scriptural references, figuratively and metaphorically illustrating attributes and characteristic of God the Father, in a way physical, mortal man can understand.

We read early in the Scriptures that, "God said, 'Let there be light'" (Genesis 1:3). Does that mean God has vocal chords? We also read, "Behold the name of the Lord comes from afar ... His lips are full of indignation, and His tongue like a devouring fire" (Isaiah 30:27). In addition, "Who is the wise man that may understand this? And who is he to whom the mouth of the Lord has spoken, that he may declare it?" (Jeremiah 9:12). Lips, mouth, tongue? All physical attributes of man yet used to illustrate the work of God. In describing His glory, God Himself said this in Exodus 33:20–23, "But He (God) said, you cannot see My face; for no man shall see me and live ... So it shall be, while My glory passes by, that I will put you (Moses) in the cleft of the rock, and will cover you with my hand while I pass by. Then I will take away My hand you shall see My back; but my face shall not be seen." Other examples of using physical body parts to describe the characteristics of God include:

Arm – "... I am the Lord; I will bring you (Hebrews) out from under the burden of the Egyptians. I will rescue you from their bondage, and I will redeem you with an outstretched arm and with great judgments" (Exodus 6:6).
Eye – "I (God) will instruct you and teach you in the way you should go. I will guide you with My eye" (Psalm 32:8).
Ear/Hand – "Behold the Lord's hand is not shortened, that it cannot save; nor His ear heavy, that it cannot hear" (Isaiah 59:1).
Heart – "Yes, I (God) will rejoice over them (Israel) to do them good, and I will assuredly plant them in this land, with all My heart and with all my soul" (Jeremiah 32:41).

These are but a few examples of the Bible using human anatomical parts to better explain and illustrate the characteristics and workings of an almighty, omnipotent God. And as it describes the physical, it serves to illustrate the finite to the infinite, from the physical to the spiritual.

Throughout the years there have been many philosophical discussions as to who man is, and what was the point of his creation and existence. Even the Bible presents its discourse on the "Doctrine of Man". "When I consider Your heavens, the work of your fingers, the moon and the stars, which You have ordained, what is man that You are mindful of him, and the son of man that you visit him? For you have made him a little lower than the angels and have crowned him with glory and honor. You have made him to have dominion over the works of Your hands. You have put all things under his feet ..." (Psalms 8:3–6).

The Bible says that man was created by God. "So God created man in his own image; in the image of God He created him; male and female He create them" (Genesis 1:27). "And the Lord God formed man of the dust of the ground and breathed into his nostrils the breath of life; and man became a living being" (Genesis 2:7). The Hebrew word for "formed" (which can also be used for "fashioned") is Yatsar, which means coming from to be distressed, as a potter "forms" something from a "blob", or disorganized (distressed), formless, pile of clay. Thus, something that was originally unorganized and "formless", was shaped, or "formed" into something that had a specific and unique shape. And the object that was "formed" into a specific shape, was formed for a purpose, such as a potter shapes clay to make a bowl or pitcher, which have specific purposes, based on their shapes.

Scripture also says that everything was created by Him and for Him. Man was created for a purpose and that this should be recognized. "Every one who is called by my name: Whom I have created him for my glory; I have formed him; yes, I have made him" (Isaiah 43:7). "I will praise you, for I am fearfully and wonderfully made" (Psalm 139:14). In other words, all of creation was created by God, but it was created with a divine purpose, including man.

It could be said that the richest man in the world could support and supply the needs of all the birds for only three days. Scripture states that if God takes care of the sparrow, how much more he takes care of man. "Are not two sparrows sold for a copper coin? And one of them shall not fall on the ground apart from your Father's will. Do not fear therefore; you are of more value than many sparrows" (Matthew 10:29, 31).

In the book of Nehemiah in the Bible, we find the story about Nehemiah. In this story, the Jews had returned home from their Babylonian captivity 142 years earlier. But after a period of time, there developed chaos and turmoil as the Jews floundered and were unable to complete a successful campaign of rebuilding and resettling. The city walls and buildings had been neglected and dilapidated. Nehemiah had arrived in Jerusalem to help the Jews rebuild the wall around that ancient city. Through the leadership of Nehemiah, the people did rebuild the wall of Jerusalem. This is but one of the countless examples that are found in the Bible that give accounts of greed, controversy, complacency and self-centeredness that led to ruin and rebuilding.

But, in the original creation, including the creation of man, there was no "greed" or "controversy". There was no "rebuilding". There was creation from nothing by God! And man was the centerpiece of it all. It was not even the heavenly creatures of seraphim, cherubim or angels. It was man! Yet these biblical stories depict God's love and grace, and how He uses people (man) for His purposes. As awestruck as we may be in viewing the universe and abundance of life on Earth, it is man that best demonstrates the glory and greatness of God. Even the gospel of Christ is more than just an account of His birth, life, crucifixion and resurrection. It is a human nature story that includes love, death, marriage, birth, sadness, deceit, faithfulness, happiness, and more. It includes all the human nature characteristics we are familiar with. It helps us to better understand just who and what God is.

Each word of the Bible was written as God's message to His people, to enlighten us so that we may be more aware of who we are and who God is, and our relationship with Him. Many of us have experienced chaos and turmoil and have parts of our lives that are neglected and dilapidated. Yet, our "walls" can be made whole again and we can live in peace and security. Certainly, how these conditions occur, and better, yet, how these conditions can be corrected, is of vital importance. In studying the Bible, we can truly enhance our lives and enlighten ourselves to establish a closer relationship with our creator.

God did create the spiritual world. But He also created the physical world. It can be discussed as to why God did such a thing. In creating the physical, God was better able to present Himself and His character. Thus, in understanding God's nature, it would only seem logical that after the fall of man and sin and death entered the world, that "… God demonstrated his own love toward us, in that while we were still sinners Christ died for us" (Romans 5:8). And it is certainly through the analogies and metaphors that are illustrated in Scripture that God is more able to describe His nature.

Man was made in God's image, "… in the image of God He created man" (Genesis 1:27); was made upright, "Truly, this only I have found, that God has made man upright" (Ecclesiastes 7:29); is endowed with intelligence, "And have put on the new man, who is renewed in knowledge according to the image of him that created him" (Colossians 3:10); is superior to animals, "Do not fear therefore; you are of more value than many sparrows" (Matthew 10:31); and is given wide dominion, "And God blessed them and said unto them be fruitful and multiply; fill the earth and subdue it: and have dominion over the fish of the sea and over the fowl of the air, and over every living thing that moves upon the earth" (Genesis 1:28). The human body was built by God, made of matter, and created for His service.

Paul says in 1 Corinthians 6:19, "What? Do you not know that your body is the temple of the Holy Spirit who is in in you, whom you have from God, and you are not your own?" Thus, our bodies are an intended creation of God, made in His image and for his purpose. And as a reflection of God our bodies are indeed a place of prayer, a place of power and a place of worship. It literally becomes a dwelling place for its creator.

In Matthew 21:12–15 we find the following story. "Then Jesus went into the temple of God and drove out all those who bought and sold in the temple, and overturned the table of the money changers, and the seats of them that sold doves. And he said to them, 'It is written, My house shall be called a house of prayer, but you have made it a den of thieves.' Then the blind and the lame came to him in the temple; and he healed them. But when the chief priests and scribes saw the wonderful things that He did and the children crying out in the temple, and saying, 'Hosanna to the Son of David', they were indignant."

The Hebrews "wandered" in the wilderness for forty years, and we know that the purpose of the tabernacle represented the dwelling place of God and thus a place of prayer, power, and worship throughout this time. During the existence of Israel as a nation the temple (known as "Solomon's temple") represented the dwelling place of God and thus a place of prayer, power and worship. After the crucifixion of Jesus, the body became the dwelling place of God and thus a place of prayer, power and praise (worship). Therefore, we know that God not only dwells "within the hearts of men", but in reality, we become "one with God" as He rules our lives.

In this biblical account by Matthew, Jesus showed the purpose of the temple. The purpose of *power, prayer* and *praise* (worship) is illustrated in this story. And in doing so, Jesus used this story to demonstrate the purpose of the physical body it paralleled the purpose of the temple. Just as the tabernacle and "Solomon's Temple" were built for their purpose of *power, prayer* and *praise* (worship*),* so too, the body was created in the mind of God as a body of *power, prayer,* and *praise* (worship).

The physical healing of the blind and the lame demonstrated the *power* in the temple. Jesus said that the temple was a place of *prayer.* And the result was *praise* (in the temple). As the physical temple of God ("Solomon's Temple") demonstrated a place of communication with God through prayer, and where power and praise can also be found, so it is with the body. It was created for similar purposes. Unlike spiritual angels, man is physical, but he can still fellowship and communicate with God through prayer and can validate God's power through the physical body and of course can show praise from Whom all blessing flow.

A name for God, Elohim is actually a plural noun. These are three attributes of the person of God; God the Father, God the Son, and God the Holy Spirit. Like myself where I have several attributes of my person. I am a son, a husband and father (and grandfather, brother, cousin, etc.) and each has a specific identity and function. God, the Father, is the essence of God (Jehovah) as demonstrated in the Old Testament as the creator and living God. God, the Son (Jesus), is the essence of God as demonstrated in the New Testament as Jesus takes away the sins of man. God the Holy Spirit is the essence of God as demonstrated in our lives today. The Holy Spirit inhabits the lives of each believer. As we "see" each part or essence of God we can better "interpret" and understand God.

Man, being created in the image of God has similar tripartite attributes., and can be described as a body, a soul, and a spirit. Man is certainly made up of physical material, and the body can be seen and physically touched. But man is also made up of immaterial aspects which are intangible. These include the soul and spirit, which include intellect, will, emotion, conscience. These immaterial characteristics exist beyond the physical lifespan of the human body, and distinctly separate mankind from the rest of creation. **Figure 1-1** illustrates the relationship of the body, soul and spirit as they make up the complete man.

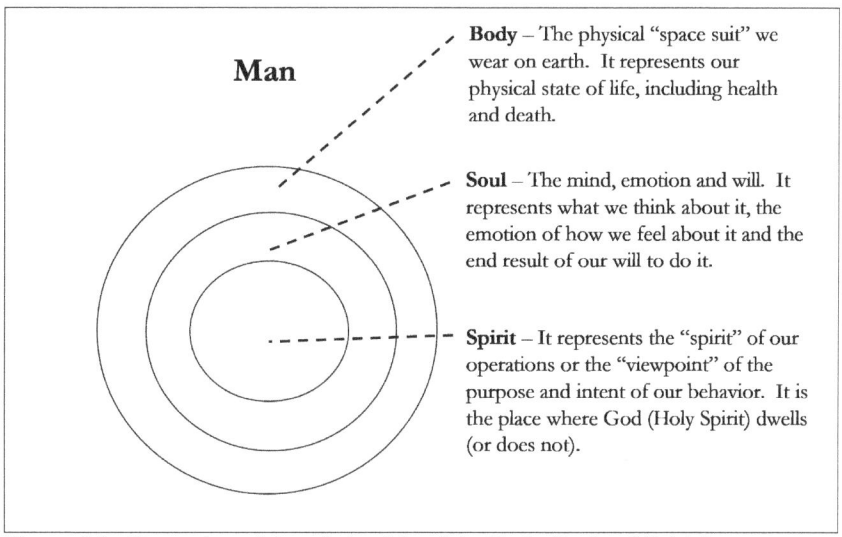

Figure 1-1. Illustration of the relationship of the Body, Soul and Spirit in man.

The body (flesh) is the essence of man in sin. Sin can easily overtake the flesh. "Watch and pray, that you do not enter into temptation: the spirit indeed is willing but the flesh is weak" (Matthew 26:41). There are many "parts" of the body, each with a specific function. And if a single part fails, the body suffers and may even perish. The body will be the focus of this text.

The soul is the mind, emotion and the will of a person. You think about it (mind). You feel like it (emotion). You will do it (will). The soul is the essence of man through creation by the Father. "And God formed man of the dust of the ground and breathed into his nostrils the breath of life; and man became a living being" (Genesis 2:7).

God, the Holy Spirit, is the essence of God in man through His Spirit. "And it shall come to pass afterward that I will pour out my spirit upon all flesh; and your sons and daughters shall prophesy, and your old men shall dream dreams, your young men shall see visions" (Joel 2:28). It is in the spirit where the Holy Spirit of God can exist and reside. "Behold. I stand at the door and knock: if any man hears My voice, and opens the door, I will come in to him, and dine with him, and he with Me" (Revelations 3:20). The spirit part of man is the animating force that makes the body alive. It is that part of man where the Holy Spirit can direct and lead the will of man (soul) to do the will of God.

However, we are also physical and have a physical body with a will of our own. It guides and directs our physical desires such as eating, drinking, seeking shelter, etc. But it also can lead us to other behavioral actions driven by our carnal desires of lust, anger and greed. The Bible seems to link the soul and the spirit together into what it refers to the "heart". "Watch over your heart with all diligence, for from it flow the springs of life" (Proverbs 4:23). One can follow the flow from the spirit (whether God is there or not), to the soul (whether God is at the center of our thoughts and actions), to the body (certainly our actions can affect our physical bodies such as drugs, alcohol or careless activities).

Thus, we can certainly make mindful decisions based on our own desires, which are established from our thoughts, which come from our physical upbringing and life in general, but we can also be influenced by the very nature of God through the spirit. It is interesting that Paul used this body, soul, spirit relationship as he wrote his letter to the Thessalonians. "Now may the God of peace Himself sanctify you completely; and may your whole spirit, soul, and body be preserved blameless at the coming of our Lord Jesus Christ" (1 Thessalonians 5:23).

Scripturally speaking, God used the physical to display His purpose and glory. Even from Adam (and Eve) to Abraham, the physical human lineage continued through Isaac and Jacob, all the way to Jesus (Jewish or Hebrew lineage) for displaying His love, grace and mercy, and redemptive power through Jesus as a savior from our sins. He did not choose the great dynasties of Egypt or the powers of Babylon, Persia, Greece or Rome from which to present the message of the Scripture. He chose Israel, who came into existence through the calling of Abraham, Isaac, and Jacob. This calling and development can be described in the first five books of the Bible. The rest of the Old Testament gives us a timeline of actions and activities of the nation of Israel, and gives us insight as to how the physical man in the physical world interact with an almighty, righteous, spiritual God. Readers of Scripture recalling the accounts and events of the Jews can show three reasons why God identified a people like Israel.

First, to show how people discern important matters and issues of physical life accurately. Some people do it better than others, but at some point, we all fail.

Second, to show that God can indeed establish an intimate relationship with others. He established an intimate relationship with the Hebrews. Thus, in viewing this intimate relationship, it can be shown that God, whether with Old Testament Hebrews or in modern times through the Holy Spirit, a Holy, omnipotent, righteous God desires and can establish an intimate relationship with His ultimate creation, man.

Third, to show that, although man's behavior is depraved and goes against God, man can also reflect the high moral standards and the high righteous character of God. The nation of Israel, as presented in Scripture, reflects the high righteousness character of God and the high moral standards it represents. Story after story, episode after episode, the moral character and direction of God can be seen.

There are no compromises with God. Although in today's changing world, it may seem that the fabric of morality is constantly changing. But the Bible gives evidence that the "rules" or concepts of righteous morality does not change. "For we know that the law is spiritual, but I am carnal ...." (Romans 7:14). The physical analogies of physical man to a spiritual God is presented throughout Scripture.

Man

In 1953 James D. Watson and Francis H.C. Crick announced the discovery of the double helix structure of the DNA molecule. This Watson and Crick model of the DNA molecule has become a mainstay on the study of general biology, anatomy, physiology, genetics, and just about every other biological discipline. The DNA molecule has been described as the "secret of life", and literally determines all structures and functions of all living things, including man. A human DNA molecule is the main part of the cell nucleus. If this molecule were stretched out it would be approximately three feet long.[5] There are between 50 and 100 trillion cells in a mature human body.[6] You can do the math! Three feet per cell, times 50 trillion cells, equal 150 trillion feet of DNA. If we divide this by 5,280 feet (the length of a mile), we would get approximately 30 billion miles of DNA in each human body! This is equivalent to 165 trips to the sun AND back!

"But now, O Lord, you are our Father; We are the clay, and you our potter; and all we are the work of Your hand" (Isaiah 64:8). And what a creation we are!

In a life of 72 years, an average person:

- will sleep 21 years and be awake 51 years,
- will consume 45,000 pounds of food/liquids (52 million calories),
- will take 380 million breaths (6.5 million cubic feet of air),
- will walk 125,000 miles (half way to the moon);

and our:

- feet will strike the ground (or surface) 180 million times,
- heart will beat 2.7 billion times,
- heart will pump 45 million gallons of blood,
- kidneys will "purify" 11 million gallons of blood and make 9,000 gallons of urine,
- body has over 60,000 miles of blood vessels,
- lungs have a surface area that could cover a full-length basketball court.

An average automobile has a gasoline tank to receive gasoline as its only fuel. Most other fuels like diesel fuel, kerosene or cornstarch that goes into the "gas tank" will render the car helpless. Humans, however, have a digestive system that can receive many types of "fuel" and convert it the one source of energy we need. An automobile needs an air filter replacement every four months. However, humans do not have a replaceable air filter but we do have specific anatomy to meet that need. Automobiles have a suspension system that accommodates mobility yet stability. But even this cannot compare to that of the anatomy of the human foot. The heart is a pump made of muscle. Have you ever had a "pulled" muscle, became tired and fatigued, or had sore muscles after an exercise that needed rest? Skeletal muscles may be subject to these physical parameters, but the heart can never rest. Never! It cannot "rest" nor can it tolerate a strain or "tear". Thus, it must have some special traits of anatomy.

There are countless accounts of tremendous feats of physical performance, especially in the sports arena, including individuals that have run in the Boston Marathon over fifty times. Some individuals over the age of seventy have run the 26-mile 300-yard course in three hours. (I do not believe I could run this distance in three weeks, much less three hours!) Consider the fingers, which may seem fragile. They are uniquely designed to play the piano or violin in a delicate and subtle fashion yet are also used to lift and hold heavy objects or used to beat or pound objects in a more harsh and unforgiving fashion.

In the book *Fitly Framed Together: The Bible,* it was presented that the Bible was intentionally constructed and written the way it was (by God). It was written for a particular purpose with a particular message. So to, the human body is "Fitly Framed Together". It was created and is constructed the way it is for a particular purpose. There are analogies of study in Scripture that can help us better understand God, the role of the Church, and our individual place and purpose in His physical creation.

> For the equipping of the saints for the work of the
> ministry, for the edifying of the body of Christ: till we
> all come in the unity of the faith, and of the knowledge

of the Son of God, unto a perfect man, to the measure of the statue of the fullness of Christ: that we should no longer be children, tossed to and fro, and carried about with every wind of doctrine, by the trickery of men, and cunning craftiness of deceitful plotting, but speaking the truth in love, may grow up into him in all things, which is the head, even Christ: from whom the whole body joined and knit together by what every joint supplies, according to the effective working by which every part does its share, causes growth of the body for the edifying of itself in love. (Ephesians 4:12–16)

Sixty-five percent of the body by weight is water. If a gallon of water weighs seven pounds, then a person weighing 160 pounds would consist of 104 pounds of water, or rather, fifteen gallons of water with "stuff" mixed in. In the science of Chemistry, there are 109 known chemical elements (stuff). Yet 99.85% of this fabulous human body is made of chiefly eleven chemical elements. These include Carbon, Hydrogen, Oxygen and Nitrogen (CHON), accounting for 96%, and Calcium, Phosphorus, Potassium, Sodium, Sulfur, Chlorine and Magnesium accounting for another 2.5%. The remaining 0.15% is made up of approximately fifty other elements.

As humans, we ascribe value to various things in our lives. We give value to gold, silver, diamonds. We place value on our homes and automobiles, and we even place value on our pets. Yet these have no intrinsic value to God. If the human body could be "melted down" and sold for these elements as listed above, it would be worth approximately $5.40 based on today's commodities market. In other words, it could be said that the human body is "made up of" fifteen gallons of water with $5.40 worth of "stuff" mixed in it. In this regard, the "value" of a human is not much. However, a human is more valuable than $5.40 worth of elements mixed in fifteen gallons of water. In fact, a human life is beyond setting a price for it. It is priceless. It is of infinite worth! Or is it?

Many people do not place any value on human beings. In America alone, over 17,000 murders and non-negligent homicides occurred in 2017.[7] Between 400,000 and 500,000 murders occur annually around the world each year.[8] Over 40 million abortions take place around the world each year.[9]

What is it that gives value to anything? A definition of "value" has been described as, "relative worth or importance ... a determined market value of a thing, intrinsically desirable".[10] Objects that are rare, such as diamonds and gold, or ancient artifacts, can be described as valuable. But a human being is not rare. What, then actually gives value to a human being?

It is interesting that it is how these chemical elements are put together that make us not only what we are, but who we are, and for some, gives us "infinite value". Yet so many people take life as not valuable as there are wars, murders, abortions and other human behavior that would seem to "devalue" the life of another human. Yet, it was a holy and infinitely all-knowing God who put this human form together. The Bible does not support the view that some human lives are worth less than others. All are made in the image of God and all are equally precious. "Do you not know that your bodies are the members of Christ? Shall I then take the members of Christ and make them members of a harlot? Certainly not! ... do you not know that your body is the temple of the Holy Spirit who is in you, whom you have from God ... For you were bought with a price: therefore glorify God in your body and in your spirit, which are God's" (1 Corinthians 6:15, 19–20).

The human body is fitly framed together, and there are many ways human anatomy can be studied. There is gross anatomy, where the various body structures are studied without regard to interaction or region of the body a structure may be located. There is regional anatomy, where there is regard to interaction of structures, but only within a specific part of the body. And there is functional anatomy, which seeks to establish relationships between structure and function. Within a certain region or area of the body, there are "anatomical parts" that have distinct shapes and forms which have distinct functions, and the location and placement, as well as interaction of these anatomical parts, can be viewed and studied. Each anatomical part is studied with respect to identification and function of the anatomy part, not only with respect to the region of the body where it is found, but also to the entire body.

The first study of anatomy begins as early as 400 BC with the Greek philosopher Hippocrates. He is considered the "Father of Medicine" and Medical School graduates give the "Hippocratic oath". During his life, it was believed that when the body became sick, diseased or died, it was because a god was mad and made you that way. Hippocrates began to look at the human body and our surroundings, as well as the religious beliefs, and began to speculate that these issues of the body may have a different etiology. It may not be related to the effects of some emotional or irrational god. He began to study the human body for the purpose of understanding how it works and how and why it becomes diseased and dies.

Aristotle continued this trend until about 350 BC. During this time, he developed specific methodologies of study, including terminology. He speculated that complexity of the human body was built from a variety of smaller and simpler components. Therefore, many of the medical terms used today have a Greek origin.

Later, around 150 BC, Claudius Galen advanced the theories of Hippocrates and Aristotle and became a major physician and surgeon in the Roman Empire. He even wrote an influential medical textbook that physicians followed for centuries. Therefore, there are medical terms of Latin derivation.

But proper treatment of injuries of war and of Gladiator battles became increasingly important and Galen became instrumental in the study and development of treatment of traumatic injuries. Although there was great envy among his peers as he became very popular, he demonstrated that through systematic techniques to study human anatomy, much could be learned about the body.

However, it was not until the invention of the microscope, as well as other science inventions and knowledge that advanced study of human anatomy was made possible. By the end of the 17th century the progression of the cell theory was well underway. This eventually led to the development of the organization of the anatomy into the body's structural hierarchy. This principle simply implies that atoms are the basic structure and function of all matter, and that atoms make molecules. More molecules can come together and make macromolecules (large molecules) which in turn can make cellular organelles, which make up cells, which make tissue (epithelial, connective, muscle, nerve), which make organs (stomach, liver, kidney, etc.), which collectively makes organ systems (digestive, urinary, nervous, etc.), which makes up the organism (the human body).

The design and organization of the human body may be fascinating and can be extensively studied through anatomy and physiology. Therefore, in studying the human body, we can compare the organizations and functions of the early tabernacle, the temple and the Church, and get a better understanding of not just what man is, but who God is, who we are, and our relationship with our creator. Even the mind of Isaac Newton stated, "How came the bodies of animals to be contrived with so much art, and for what ends were their several parts? Was the eye contrived without skill in opticks, and the ear without knowledge of sounds? … and these things being rightly dispatch'd, does it not appear from phænomena that there is a Being incorporeal, living, intelligent …?"[11]

Body

The word "body" is derived from the Greek word *soma*. A soma is a collection of "many things" into a "single thing". Though each individual part is important, the implication is that the whole is greater than the sum of the parts. Usage of the corporate term "body" include a "body" of water such as the Gulf of Mexico or the Atlantic Ocean. There is a "body" of a text. There are "body" shops for automobile "body" repair. There is a heavenly "body". There is a "body" of believers. There is a "body" of a church". Although a "body" can be described as being made up of many parts, the emphasis is on the body as a whole, not the parts that make it up.

However, the word *soma* is derived from another Greek word *saos* from which we get the word save, meaning to preserve the whole or total. Although a "body" (of anything) is considered a single entity, it is dependent upon the parts. Take away any of the parts, and the whole cannot exist. Thus, although the "body" is whole and considered as one, the parts of the whole become important.

> For as the body is one and has many members, but all the members of that one body, being many, are one body, so also is Christ .... For in fact the body is not one member but many. If the foot should say, "Because I am not the hand I am not of the body," is it therefore not of the body? And if the ear should say, "Because I am not an eye, I am not of the body," is it therefore not of the body? If the whole body were an eye, where would be the hearing? If the whole body were hearing, where would be the smelling? But now God has set members, each one of them, in the body just as He pleased. And if they were all one member, where would the body be? But now indeed there are many members, yet one body. And the eye cannot say to the hand, "I have no need of you"; nor again the head to the feet, "I have no need of you." No, much rather, those members of the body which seem to be weaker are necessary. And those members of the body which we think to be less honorable, on these we bestow greater honor; and our unpresentable parts have greater modesty. But our presentable parts have no need. But God composed the body, having given greater honor to that part which lacks it, that there should be no schism in the body, but that the members should have the same care for one another. And if one member suffers, all the members suffer with it, or it one member is honored, all the members rejoice with it. Now you are the body of Christ, and members individually. (1 Corinthians 12:12–27)

The various parts of the human body are there to serve the whole body. We can think of an automobile with all its "working parts".

There is a purpose for the automobile, but there are various purposes for each individual part of the automobile. And as they fulfill their individual purpose, they wind up serving the main purpose of the automobile. In similar fashion, there is a single purpose of a grocery store to deliver food to the public, or a school which serves the educational process. But there are many separate parts of these organizations which are important in fulfilling their purpose to serve the whole. And we understand the main purpose of existence of the whole organization in the first place. There can be no division in the body. There is a mutual concern for each part, even though there is one body.

Some body parts are uncomely such as the liver or bowels. Although they are hidden deep within the body, and may look gross if they could be seen, they are all very important and they make one body. The apostle Paul used this as an analogy to describe the make-up of the Church. In similar fashion, "body parts" of a church are important. The emphasis may be on the "Church", but there is the pastor, deacons, teachers, and other leaders that make up the Church.

It is the same with respect to the body (or soma) of man. The emphasis is the total man and its purpose, but all parts of it are important and are indeed necessary for the body to work to perfection toward its purpose. A lung is nice to take in life giving oxygen. But if there are no other body parts in which to give that oxygen, there is no need of a lung. The same can be said of a stomach. Taking in life giving food would be worthless without other body parts benefiting from the stomach taking in the food. Each individual body part is important in and of itself, yet collectively come together to edify the totality of man.

Man is a dynamic creature. That is, we are made to move about and function. As we examine the body, we see that the eyes are located on the front of the head and the ears are located on the side, but slanted toward the front. Our arms look to be on the side of our body but are actually "built" to work toward the front. However, this text is not just about the eyes, ears, and arms or other body features. It is about how these body parts are made and arranged in order to perform the role for which they were created. In addition, we can see, feel, touch, taste, smell and hear. It is not just a study about the senses we have. It is that we have all the necessary body parts or "tools" to interact not only with the environment, but with each other and with our God.

We can love, we can hate, and we can have compassion. In other words, we can have emotions that affect our lives and those around us. God has created us the way he has created us with a purpose in mind. "You … are built upon the foundation of the apostles and the prophets, Jesus Christ himself being the chief cornerstone; In whom all the building *fitly framed together* growing unto a holy temple in the Lord: on whom you also are built together for a habitation of God through the Spirit" (Ephesians 2:20–22).

Christians take on the name of Christ and implies that the very being of Jesus Christ lives within that Christian. "Then Barnabas departed for Tarsus to seek Saul. And when he had found him, he brought him to Antioch. So it was that for a whole year they assembled with the church and taught a great many people. And the disciples were first called Christians in Antioch" (Acts 11:25–26). Christians, in turn, are part of the Church that becomes a light that the world may see God and His glory.

> But even if our gospel is veiled, it is veiled to them who are perishing: whose minds the god of this age has blinded, who do not believe, lest the light of the glorious gospel of the glory of Christ, who is the image of God, should shine on them. For we do not preach ourselves, but Christ Jesus the Lord; and ourselves your bondservants for Jesus' sake. For it is God, who commanded light to shine out of darkness, who has shone in our hearts, to give the light of the knowledge of the glory of God in the face of Jesus Christ. But we have this treasure in earthen vessels, that the excellence of the power may be of God, and not of us. We are hard pressed on every side, yet not crushed; we are perplexed, but not in despair; persecuted but not forsaken; cast down but not destroyed; always carrying about in the body the dying of the Lord Jesus, that the

life of Jesus might be made manifested in our body. For we who live are always delivered to death for Jesus' sake, that the life of Jesus also may be manifested in our mortal flesh. So, then death is working in us, but life in you. (2 Corinthians 4:3–12)

Christians then, with differing talents, abilities and callings, perfect the Church for the glorifying of God. "… And He Himself gave some to be apostles, some prophets, some evangelists, and some pastors and teachers, for the equipping of the saints for the work of the ministry, for the edifying of the body of Christ, till we all come to the unity of the faith and of the knowledge of the Son of God, to a perfect man, unto the measure of the stature of the fulness Christ" (Ephesians 4:11–13).

God is glory. God is light. God is life. The creation of man makes this manifest.

With anatomy, there is structure. With structure, there is a purpose. The following chapters of this text will not only describe the physical anatomy of man but will show the divine design and purpose of these intriguing structures. Man was created by God, for God and in His image. We are a dynamic creation and God has a purpose and plan for man. Through the study of human anatomy in this manner we can develop a better understanding of its Creator and realize that the God of the universe is a God of love and a God of action.

… what you sow is not made alive, unless it dies. And what you sow, you do not sow that body that shall be, but mere gain, perhaps wheat or some other grain. But God gives it a body as He pleases, and to each seed its own body. All flesh is not the same, but there is one kind of flesh of men, another flesh of animals, another of fish, and another of birds. There are also celestial bodies and terrestrial bodies; but the glory of the celestial is one and the glory of the terrestrial is another. There is one glory of the sun, another glory of the moon, and another glory of the stars; for one star differs from another star in glory. So also, is the resurrection of the dead. The body is sown in corruption, it is raised in incorruption. It is sown in dishonor, it is raised in glory. It is sown in weakness, it is raised in power. It is sown a natural (physical) body, it is raised a spiritual body. There is a natural (physical) body and there is a spiritual body .... And as we have borne the image of the man of dust, we shall also bear the image of the heavenly Man. (1 Corinthians 15:36–49)

We really do have a glorious body. And in the study of this body we can gain a greater understanding of God, not just in the physical realm but in the spiritual realm as well. We can use multiple analogies and Biblical examples in explaining the form of the human body and its purpose, not just regarding man, but the whole of creation.

Anatomy

The word "anatomy" comes from the Greek word *anatome* which means to cut or dissect in such a way as to examine or study. The implication is that there is a difference between just cutting up compared to "dissecting" for the purpose of study. More specifically, it means to manually or artificially separate parts of an animal or plant for the purpose of studying structures and the relationships among these structures. By studying the anatomy of man, in a sense, we can study the anatomy of God. The human body is truly an engineering marvel. Areas of study such as anatomy, physiology, biomechanics and kinesiology are various disciplines that seek to gain a better understanding of how the body functions. Such understanding enables mankind to lead a better physical life through a variety of products and services available in today's modern world.

These include everything from medicines and other health related areas to shoes, clothing, bedding, and even the automobiles we drive. Though we may be aware that the human body is a uniquely formed creation, virtually limitless in its capabilities, it is often taken for granted and even abused. However, as we gain a deeper understanding as to what the body is made of and how it works, we also can become enlightencd in other areas as well.

The study of Anatomy can be accomplished in several ways. Regional Anatomy studies the body as parts of segments, such as studying the arm, leg or torso. Scripture uses these readily identified segments or parts of the body to explain a point. The arm, for example, is used as an illustration signifying strength, greatness and assumed security and safe haven. "Fear and dread shall fall upon them; by the greatness of your **arm** they shall be as still as stone till your people pass over, O Lord" (Exodus 15:16). "And he took them up in his **arms**, put his hands upon them, and blessed them" (Mark 10:16). Readers can identify with analogies using body parts. The following are but a few examples of other specific body parts that the Bible uses for life illustrations (There is a more complete concordance of anatomical body parts at the end of this text):

Ear – "The **ear** that hears the rebuke of life abides among the wise" (Proverbs 15:31). "Then reports of these things came unto the **ears** of the church which was in Jerusalem: and they sent forth Barnabas that he should go as far as Antioch" (Acts 11:22).

Eyelids – "Do not lust after her beauty in your heart; neither let her allure you with her **eyelids**" (Proverbs 6:25). "I will not give sleep to my eyes, or slumber to my **eyelids**" (Psalms 132:4).

Face – "In the sweat of your **face** shall you eat bread" (Genesis 3:19). "Afterwards I came into the regions of Syria and Cilicia; and was unknown by the **face** unto the churches of Judea which were in Christ ..." (Galatians 1:22–23).

Feet – "He brought me up also out of a horrible pit, out of the miry clay, and set my **feet** upon a rock, and established my goings" (Psalms 40:2). "The glory of Lebanon shall come unto you, the fir tree, the pine tree, and the box together, to beautify the place of my sanctuary; and I will make the place of my **feet** glorious" (Isaiah 60:13).

Hand – "And it came to pass at the seventh time, that he said, Behold, there arises a little cloud out of the sea, like a man's **hand** …" (1 Kings 18:44). "I indeed do baptize you with water unto repentance: but he that comes after me is mightier than me, whose shoes I am not worthy to bear: he shall baptize you with the Holy Ghost, and with fire: whose fan is in His **hand**, and he will thoroughly purge his floor, and gather his wheat into the barn; but he will burn up the chaff with unquenchable fire" (Matthew 3:11–12).

And there are many Scripture verses that use combinations of several body parts in order to "make a point".

> Ah sinful nation, a people of evildoers. Children that are corruptors: they have forsaken, the Lord, they have provoked the Holy One of Israel unto anger, they are fallen away. Why should you be stricken any more? You will revolt more and more: the whole **heart** is sick, and the whole **heart** faints. From the sole of the **foot** even unto the **head** there is no soundness in it; but wounds, and bruises, and putrefying sores: they have not been closed or bound up, or soothed with ointment. (Isaiah 1:4–6)

> They have all turned aside; they have together become unprofitable; there is none who does good, no, not one. Their **throat** is an open tomb; with their **tongues** they have practiced deceit; the poison of asps is under their **lips**: whose **mouth** is full of cursing and bitterness: their **feet** are swift to shed **blood**: destruction and misery are in their ways: and the way of peace they have not known: there is no fear of God before their **eyes**. (Romans 3:12–18)

> Strengthen the weak **hands**, and make firm the feeble **knees**. Say to them that are of a fearful **heart**, be strong, fear not: behold your God will come with

a vengeance, even God with a recompense; he will come and save you. Then the **eyes** of the blind shall be opened, and the **ears** of the deaf shall be unstopped. Then the lame shall leap as a deer, and the **tongue** of the dumb sing: for in a wilderness shall waters break out and streams in the desert. (Isaiah 35:3–6)

All living things may not have eyes, ears, hands and feet. But all living organisms, including man, do have four things in common. These include: 1) Use energy, 2) Grow, 3) Respond to the environment, and 4) Reproduce. Whether the organism is a bacterium, roach, slime mold, fish or human being, they all have these four characteristics. The design or anatomy is made to this end.

1. **Use Energy**: All living organisms need energy to survive. Televisions and home energy use *alternating current (AC)* energy of electricity, obtained from a power plant and carried to homes via power lines. Flashlights and automobiles use *direct current (DC)* energy, obtained from a battery. Living organisms, however, use a molecule called *adenosine triphosphate (ATP)*, energy that is generated from the respiration of glucose (sugar). (This chemical process of the respiration of glucose will be discussed later.) And this glucose comes from digested food that is consumed. Without food, there is no energy. And without energy there is no life. Jesus quoted Deuteronomy 8:3 when He said, "It is written, man shall not live by bread alone, but every word that proceeds out of the mouth of God" (Matthew 4:4). To be sure, a Christian may "feed on the Word of God" (the Bible) as the bread of life. But for a Christian, God can bless and we can grow in so many ways.

2. **Grow**: Living organisms have a "life span" or stages of development through which they must pass. A butterfly for example begins as a caterpillar and eats leaves or other green vegetation. But when they change into the butterfly their

source of food and energy comes from another source. As such with nature, they would not totally consume one source of energy (food). It is the responsibility of a Christian to grow and mature in order to live the life that God has given him.

3. **Respond to the environment**: In order to survive, organisms must be able to respond to the environment. They must know when it is too cold, too hot, if a predator is near. Having some knowledge of these things certainly can influence survival. A Christian certainly needs to be able to "sense" danger and respond in a positive and meaningful way to things life can bring.

4. **Reproduce**: If a species is to exist, they must be able to reproduce and "pass their genes" to the next generation or the species becomes extinct. Of course, as a Christian grows and matures, he will indeed influence others so that others can come to know Christ and be saved. Thus, Christians "reproduce". Imagine the world, if a generation of Christians does not reproduce. Christians would become extinct!

Like all other "living" things, man has also been planned and created to use energy, respond to the environment, grow and reproduce. The study of the design of man and the anatomy and physiology can be organized into five major areas. These include: organization, support and movement, control, maintenance, and reproduction. It is interesting that the number five in Scripture represents God's grace.[12] These and other numeric meanings have been described in my previous book *Fitly Framed Together: The Bible* (WestBow Press, 2013). God created the physical man but after the fall of man through sin, God's grace can redeem man from the eternal death and separation that follows the result of sin. There is nothing else in the realm of man that is able to do that.

In addition to meeting the four requirements of life, human anatomy is embedded within five major areas of the design or needs. These include Organization, Support and Movement, Control,

Maintenance, and Reproduction. And within these five areas of design and needs are the twelve systems of the human body. I believe that even these numbers are significant. The number four (4 common things of all life) represents the physical nature of creation (i.e., four seasons, four directions of north, east, south, west, etc.).

The number five (5 requirements of design and needs) represents God's grace. God's redemptive plan is required and needed by man and God did it. The number twelve (12 body systems) is actually a product of 3 x 4 (in Scripture, the number three represents the spiritual trinity of God, being the Father, Son, Holy Spirit). Of course, there were twelve "tribes of Israel" as well as twelve Disciples of Christ. Throughout Scripture it details the completeness and fullness of Almighty God. Thus, the creation of man with twelve body systems truly represents the union of the image of God (spiritual) and the nature of man (physical).

1. **Organization:** At conception, the human being consists of only one cell and then through cellular multiplication and differentiation, at birth that number has grown to over 200 billion. It was previously mentioned that by adulthood, the human body contains between 50 and 100 trillion cells, four tissue types, and nearly 200 different kinds of cells.[5] This description of one cell developing into 50 trillion cells and four tissue types is called differentiation. There is unity among the many body parts of the one body. Imagine a liver cell being "disappointed" for not being a brain cell. Or imagine a brain cell wanting to be a kidney cell because it did not want to be a "responsible" part of the brain. Or imagine a toe being ashamed for not being a finger. There is equal, but diverse. Diverse but the same. The same but not equal.

   Oftentimes, people like to imagine that people who are "different" are also "unequal", implying that the meaning of "equal" means "the same". To be sure, all are necessary and important, and cannot fall onto a rating scale of "good, better, best". All our various body parts are created equal for the purpose of glorifying the body, but they are different because they have different purposes. All people are created equal for the purpose of glorifying God, but they can be different because their purpose may be different.

However, as great or as small as these body parts may be, they are built with a specific purpose, and they are made from the basic unit of all physical structures ... atoms and molecules. And although these atoms and molecules are very small, they constitute the very foundation of anatomy. There is little doubt of the tremendous amount of organization that these atoms, molecules, cells, tissues and organ systems must have. The importance of even the smallest of these cannot be over emphasized when discussing the complexity and interactions that make up the human body. There are many examples of organization within the body.

2. **Support and Movement**: Even as Jesus Christ is the cornerstone and foundation of God's character and grace; man was created with a strong foundation for support and movement. God is not a passive God. Neither is man. Man is a dynamic being. Upon this basis, all other aspects of our lives hang. "... thus, the Lord God, Behold I lay in Zion for a foundation a stone, a tried stone, a corner stone, a sure **foundation** ...." (Isaiah 28:16). As God moves and inspires our lives we are to live and work for Christ. "And the spirit began to **move** him (Samson) at times in the camp of Dan ...." (Judges 13:25). "But be ye doers of the word and not hearers only ...." (James 1:22). The two body systems included here are the Skeletal System and the Muscular System.

    The number two can be referred to having a choice, one or the other. The skeletal system will focus on a choice between "stability and mobility", whereas the muscular system will focus on a choice between "strength and speed" of movement.

    Imagine a skeletal system with bones and joints that could not deliver stability or mobility for the body. Imagine a muscular system that could not deliver strength or speed of movement. At times we need stability. At other times we need mobility. At times we need strength. At other times we need speed. Making the correct choice at the right time for a specific need is important.

3. **Control**: As Christ dwells and rules in our lives we have the ability to sense our surroundings and see the needs of others. We, also, have the ability to respond, through Christ. "Put on therefore, as the elect of God, holy and beloved, put on tender mercies, kindness, humbleness of mind, meekness, long-suffering; bearing one another, and forgiving one another, if any man has a complaint against another: even Christ forgave you, so also do you. But above all these things put on love, which is the bond of perfection. And let the peace of God **rule** (control) in your hearts, to which you were called in one body..." (Colossians 3:12–15).

    Being able to perceive and respond correctly is important. The body uses two systems for sensory perception, response and control. They include the Nervous System and the Endocrine System.

4. **Maintenance**: Just as our physical body needs a continuous supply of food and oxygen and as our bodies continually fights off infections and diseases, our spiritual lives are the same. "As newborn babes desire the spiritual milk of the word that you may **grow** thereby ...." (1 Peter 2:2). "Study to show yourself approved unto God, a workman that needs not to be ashamed, rightly dividing the word of truth..." (2 Timothy 2:15). There are six body systems that maintain the body. These include the Integument System, the Cardiovascular System, the Respiratory (Pulmonary) System, the Digestive System, the Urinary System and the Immune System. In Scripture, the number six is an incomplete number and represents an incomplete or imperfect state. The number six is used nearly 300 times in the Bible and marks a secular incompleteness and indicates man's physical and sinful nature. The anatomy whose purpose it is to maintain the body include six systems.

However, the number seven represents the completeness and fullness of God. Thus, the human body, with its six "maintenance" systems, is incomplete without God.

Imagine God creating, but not able to support and maintain His creation. Imagine God not being able to control His creation. Imagine that there was no stability or control of your body ... nothing to support it, nothing to guide or control it. However, God in His infinite wisdom and power created a physical body that can support it and have a means of movement and control.

5. **Reproduction**: It is interesting that two make one, literally. As God made male and female (two), yet together they were to become one flesh (Genesis 2:24). And as this "one flesh" reproduced, they could make many. God's plan of sexual reproduction brings together genes from both genders to reproduce another individual who is like, but so very different from their parents. A person hears the "Word" and is "saved" and becomes a "child of God" (offspring equal reproduction). They also become part of "the Church" which is described in Scripture as the "Bride of Christ". Thus, an individual who becomes a Christian becomes "one with Christ". The Christian then becomes part of the "reproduction process" by sharing the gospel of Christ for others to hear and experience. Humans do not "save" other humans. Only Christ saves. But being "one with Christ" advances the gospel of Christ.

> Go ye therefore, and **teach** all nations, **baptizing** them in the name of the Father, and of the Son, and of the Holy Ghost, teaching them to observe all things whatsoever I have commanded you .... (Matthew 28:19–20)

> Then Philip opened his mouth and, and began at the same scripture, and **preached (taught)** unto him Jesus. And as they went on their way,

they came unto certain water: and the eunuch said, "See, here is water; what does hinder me from being baptized?" And Philip said, "If you believe with all your heart, you may." And he answered and said, "I believe that Jesus is the Son of God." And he commanded the chariot to stand still: and they went down both into the water, both Philip and the eunuch; and he **baptized** him. (Acts 8:35–38)

God used this process to introduce His son, Jesus, into the world. However, although Jesus' mother (Mary) was human, the father was the Holy Spirit.

Therefore, the Lord Himself will give you a sign; Behold the virgin shall conceive, and bear a son, and shall call his name Immanuel. (Isaiah 7:14)

And behold, you shall conceive in your womb, and bring forth a son, and shall call his name Jesus …. Then Mary said unto the angel, "How shall this be, seeing I know not a man?" And the angel answered and said unto her (Mary), "The Holy Ghost shall come upon you and the power of the Highest shall overshadow you: therefore also that holy thing which shall be born of you shall be called the Son of God." (Luke 1:31–35)

Physiology

Whereas the body or descriptions of parts of the body are described through anatomy, physiology is the operation or how things of the body work and function. The word "physiology" is derived from the Greek prefix "physi" to mean nature or referring to natural science, and "the suffix "ology" meaning study of. Nothing in nature or natural science can operate without energy. As previously stated, all living organisms need energy.

In the world of physics, we may be familiar with the equation $E = mc^2$, where E is energy, m is mass, and c is a constant (speed of light). If the mass of a 176-pound man (80Kg) is converted to pure energy, the amount of energy that can be derived is more than the largest atomic bomb on earth! But the human is not used AS energy. It must USE energy in order to be sustained and to continue in life. But in the physical world, abiding by the laws of physics, energy cannot be created nor destroyed. It can only be transferred. Which means there can only be a beginning energy source from which that energy is passed on to be used.

We have learned in school that the ultimate energy source for living organisms on earth is the sun, which gives off light energy. The sun gives off an incredible 1×10^{23} watts of energy every second! (that is a 1 with 23 zeros after it!) Using a chemical process, green plants (having chlorophyll) converts this light energy to the only energy source that organisms can use. These organisms take the light energy and add carbon dioxide (CO_2) and water (H_2O) and make oxygen (O_2) and glucose ($C_6H_{12}O_6$). It is this glucose molecule that is chemically able to collect and "bind up" the sun's energy. It is interesting that during this chemical process, life giving oxygen is also made. This chemical process of taking sunlight and converting it into oxygen and glucose is called **photosynthesis**. The following is the chemical equation that describes this process of photosynthesis.

$$\text{Sun's Light (energy)} + 6\ CO_2 + 6\ H_2O \Longrightarrow 6\ O_2 + C_6H_{12}O_6$$

The physiology of utilizing this energy contained in the glucose molecule is referred to as **aerobic metabolism or respiration.** This metabolic process is nothing more than the reverse of photosynthesis, except the resulting energy that is being transferred is eventually transferred to an ATP molecule, which is ultimately used by the organism.

Adenosine triphosphate (ATP) is an important organic molecule specifically designed to deliver energy to all the cells of the body. Whereas air conditioners and televisions require alternating current energy generated from electrical power plants, and cameras and flashlights use direct current energy provided by batteries, living organisms also require energy, provided by the ATP molecule.

The following is the chemical equation describing aerobic metabolism or respiration.

$$C_6H_{12}O_6 + 6\,O_2 \longrightarrow 6\,CO_2 + 6\,H_2O + ATP\ \textbf{(energy)}$$

Essentially this equation is the photosynthesis equation in reverse. In fact, it is the basic "combustion equation", where we can simply substitute the formula for things we "burn", such as gasoline and coal. After obtaining the heat energy from burning you will always get the products of carbon dioxide and water. The amount of carbon dioxide produced and emitted into the earth's atmosphere during the world's combustion activities such as driving automobiles, and burning coal and natural gas to make electricity, is the premise for the theory of "global warming" or "climate change".

Living organisms can only use ATP energy. And in the case of aerobic metabolism, living organisms convert the energy contained in the glucose molecule to ATP energy. In other words, the sun's light energy is eventually changed and converted into the ATP energy for use by the organism. Thus, we can say that we "burn" calories (the unit of the amount "food energy" we take in). And in this sense, without the original source of energy from the sun, there would be no living organisms.

To be sure in recent years there have been found heat vents at the bottom of deep ocean trenches where there is no sunlight. But there is still an original source of energy, and that comes from the heat vents that are products of plate tectonics, which give rise to volcanoes. Thus, there is this original source of energy that is needed for the existence of those organisms that live nearby. And in the life of a human, we could say that physically, there is an original source of energy where physiologically we have a "combustion equation" that takes place within us to provide us with the energy we need to survive.

This is similar in the life of a Christian. God is the ultimate source of energy and gives life to all things. Without him there would be no life. "Yet for us there is but one God, the Father, of whom are all things, and we for him; and one Lord Jesus Christ, through whom are all things, and through whom we live" (1 Corinthians 8:6). Thus, it was through God that everything was made (including man) and it is only through God that we can exist and continue living. Spiritually, there is a combustion within us, ignited by the Holy Spirit, God created life, giving us energy and power to do the will of God. God not only created a physical entity of living things (including man), but He also sustains it, literally.

Jesus – Incarnate of God

"In the beginning was the Word (Jesus), and the Word was with God, and the Word was God ... And the Word was made flesh, and dwelt among us..." (John 1:1,14). There are many "non-believers" who cannot fathom and understand the "concept of Jesus", and the idea that He was actually God in the flesh. Even for some believers, it may be difficult to grasp the meaning and purpose of an almighty, omnipotent, holy, righteous God taking on flesh and becoming a physical man.

"Let this mind be in you which was also in Christ Jesus, who being in the form of God, did not consider it robbery to be equal with God, but made Himself of no reputation, taking the form of a bondservant, and becoming in the likeness of men. And being found in appearance as a man, He humbled Himself, and became obedient to the point of death, even the death of the cross" (Philippians 2:5–8). It is easy for one to look at what "man" defines in life, and not see what God defines in life. God did not create man *AS* spirit, but created man as physical *WITH* a spirit.

There is a tremendous contrast between spirit and flesh. The flesh (body) is the sum of many parts. If any one of these parts is hurt or injured, the whole body is affected. The spirit, however, is a whole, without any parts. Without expounding in a Scriptural dissertation concerning the Spirit and Flesh, Galatians 5:16–26 gives us the following comparisons between the spirit and flesh.

Spirit	**Flesh**
Love	Sexual Immorality
Joy	Moral Impurity
Peace	Promiscuity
Patience	Idolatry
Kindness	Hatred
Goodness	Strife
Faithfulness	Jealousy
Gentleness	Anger
Self Control	Selfishness
Dissention	
Factions	
Envy	
Sorcery	
Drunkenness	

There are laws that seek to control and regulate those listed under the Flesh. It is interesting, however, that there are no laws that prevents or promotes those listed under the Spirit. Those that live in the Flesh, do fleshly things, and those that live in the Spirit, do spiritual things.

The Bible indicates that God is spirit and not confined to a physical body. "God is spirit; and those who worship Him must worship Him in spirit and truth" (John 4:24). As Solomon was preparing to dedicate the Temple, in his prayer he said, "But will God indeed dwell on earth? Behold, heaven and the heaven of heavens cannot contain You. How much less this temple which I have built!" (1 Kings 8:27). God is spirit and not physical. Scripture and reason affirm that the God of all creation cannot be limited to a physical body. However, this is the exact reason that the physical coming of Jesus was so important.

This link between physical and spiritual was obviously important enough to God, as He Himself took on flesh. And He did it without ceasing to be God! He was fully man, yet He was also fully God. When God created man, as told in the book of Genesis, it should be noted that man was created for eternity, not just the physical present. "Man" was created "perfect", without sin or any blemish, and prepared to spend eternity with God. When sin entered the world, not only did "physical" death of the body come with it, but a "spiritual" death came as well, meaning an eternal separation from God.

We find in Old Testament Scripture where God "revealed" Himself to various persons at various times and under various circumstances. "Then the Lord appeared to Abram ..." (Genesis 12:7). "And the LORD appeared to him ...." (Genesis 18:1). Some "appearances" may have been physical. As King Nebuchadnezzar was duped into throwing three of Daniel's friends (Shadrch, Meshach, and Abed-Nego) into a fiery furnace, he became anxious, not wanting the men to die but to be saved from the fire.

"Then King Nebuchadnezzar was astonished; and he rose in haste and spoke, saying to his counselors, 'Did we not cast three men bound into the midst of the fire.' They answered and said to the King, 'True O King.' 'Look,' he answered, 'I see four men loose, walking in the midst of the fire, and they are not hurt, and the form of the fourth is like the Son of God'" (Daniel 3:24–25).

Although God may have "revealed" Himself at various times and under specific circumstances, these "revealing's" cannot compare to the incarnate presence of Jesus, the Son of God. We can illustrate two main reasons for the incarnate presence of God through Jesus, and both have to do with "Death". God not only gives life but IS life. "And God formed man of the dust of the ground, and breathed into his nostrils the breath of life; and man became a living soul" (Genesis 2:7). "For with You is the fountain of life; In Your light we see light" (Psalms 36:9).

There can be no greater tragedy (of God or anything else in the universe for that matter) than for God to create a great, "perfect" world, only to have it destroyed and die (eternally) by the works of Satan. Satan delights in the death and destruction of God's creation of man. "... your adversary the devil walks about like a roaring lion, seeking whom he may devour" (1 Peter 5:8). Thus, even before the foundations of creation were laid, God had His "plan of salvation" ready. God was required to demonstrate His power over His creation, including life itself, that he and He alone had that power.

There are two reasons why Jesus Christ, the second person of the Triune of God (God the Father, God the Son, God the Holy Spirit), took on the limitations of a human body. A first understanding of the incarnate of God through Jesus, is that Jesus took on Flesh, but in the process, took on the works of the Flesh (as described above) and became sin, thereby deserving death. Christ died the fleshly death of a horrific crucifixion. He took on death, but overcame it, and continuing in this process, destroyed Satan, the author of sin and death.

On that first "Easter Sunday morning", as the women arrived at the tomb (of Jesus), they saw two angels. "Then as they were afraid and bowed their faces to the earth, they said to them, 'Why do you seek the living among the dead? He is not here. He is risen'" (Luke 24: 5–6).

Paul described Jesus this way. "Inasmuch then as the children have partaken of flesh and blood, He (God) Himself likewise shared the same (as Jesus); that through (physical) death (crucifixion and resurrection of Christ) he might destroy him who had the power of death, that is the devil; and release those who through fear of death were all their lifetime subject to bondage. For indeed He does not give aid to angels; but He does give aid to the seed of Abraham …. For in that He Himself has suffered, being tempted, He is able to aid those who are tempted" (Hebrews, 2:14–16, 18).

In other words, mankind sinned (succumbed to temptation) and that resulted not only in a physical death of the flesh, but an eternal death of the spirit as well. But through the incarnate of God in Jesus, God was able to redeem His creation (man). Had Jesus not been human (flesh), He could not have been in a position to conquer death.

A second understanding of the incarnate of God through Jesus is that, as Jesus was able to conquer death through His resurrection from the dead, He provided a means for sinful mankind (who do not have the power over death) to obtain eternal life.

"But now Christ is risen from the dead, and has become the first fruits of those who have fallen asleep (died). For since by man came death, by Man also came the resurrection of the dead. For in Adam all die, even so in Christ all shall be made alive" (1 Corinthians 15:20–22). "… and from Jesus Christ, the faithful witness, the first born from the dead …" (Revelation 1:5). "And He (Jesus) is the head of the body, the church, who is the beginning, the first born from the dead, that in all things He may have preeminence" (Colossians 1:18).

Because of the sin by Adam (man), death was ushered into the world and no one can escape. However, Jesus was the first "man" to die, but because of His power and authority, He was able to overcome it and rise again. To be sure, there are stories in the Bible where people were brought back to life (by someone), but in every single case, they all died (again). Through the resurrection of Jesus, there is life everlasting. There is no future death.

"Therefore, since Christ suffered for us in the flesh, arm yourselves also with the same mind, for he who has suffered in the flesh has ceased from sin" (1 Peter 4:1). Even as Jesus prayed in the garden of Gethsemane before his crucifixion, He prayed, "... and this is eternal life, that they may know You (God the Father), the only true God ..." (John 17:3). Jesus also said, "... I am the way, the truth, the life. No one comes to the Father except through me" (John 14:6). Jesus speaking, "My sheep hear my voice, and I know them and they follow me. And I give them eternal life, and they shall never perish; neither shall anyone snatch them out of My hand" (John 10:27–28).

Because of this, the Bible is actually a book of redemption. It not only illustrates the power (and ability) of God, but is also describes God's love and mercy and His willingness (and ability) to pay the cost and price for our salvation Himself.

Only Jesus (as flesh) could provide such a salvation. Had Jesus not been "Flesh" none of this could have been able to take place. Not even spiritual angels are qualified to do this.

> He has delivered us from the power of darkness and conveyed us into the Kingdom of the Son of His love, in whom we have redemption through His blood, the forgiveness of sins. He is the invisible God, the firstborn over all creation. For by Him all things were created that are in heaven and that are on the earth, visible and invisible, whether thrones or dominions or principalities or powers. All things were created through Him and for Him. And He is before all things, and in Him all things consist. (Colossians 1:13–17)

In other words, for God (God the Father) to be able to "save" man from death (from his sins), Jesus (God the son) had to become physical to be able to go through the "death process" and conquer death. "For the wages of sin is death ..." (Romans 6:23). Death was dominant because of sin. "Therefore, just as through one man (Adam) sin entered into the (physical) world, and death through sin; and thus death spread to all men, because all sinned ..." (Romans 5:12). So then, the physical Jesus took those sins upon Himself, becoming sin for us, and literally died the physical death for payment of our sins. "Not with the blood of goats and calves, but by His own (physical) blood he entered in the Most Holy Place once and for all, having obtained eternal redemption (for our sins)" (Hebrews 9:12).

Thus, the coming of Jesus in the "Flesh" is significant. His physical presence provided the best means for God to reveal Himself to humanity. The physical body of Jesus had its characteristically human limitations, yet His supernatural powers were also made known. And through His ministry on earth called on people to believe in Him as the Messiah and ultimately prove His claim since he had conquered death through his resurrection from the dead following His crucifixion. "By this you know the Spirit of God: Every spirit that confesses that Jesus Christ has come in the flesh is of God" (1 John 4:2).

Therefore, a purpose of God's salvation through grace is that we become new creatures in Christ. When we accept Jesus as our Savior, we are not the "original Flesh" that succumbs to death, but receive an everlasting life. It is through this transformative power that enables us to move toward those works of the Spirit as listed above. To be sure, we, still living on the earth in the flesh still sin. And left to our own power, we would not be able to overcome the death that comes with sin. But through the power of Jesus, who was able to overcome death, we have the assurance that we will have everlasting life.

There are many aspects of biblical study, and we can get bogged down in philosophies and theologies that turn our attention away from the real issue of redemption and salvation through Jesus. Yet each area of study ultimately settles on God, His people, and the relationship between God and His people through Jesus Christ. There are many aspects of human study, including anatomy. Although no one has ever physically seen God, He certainly is real and many people have experienced the joy of a personal relationship with Him.

The following chapters are a study regarding the physical anatomy of man, yet it is also a study into the anatomy of God as it deals with His relationship to man. *Fitly Framed Together: The Body* will illustrate some of these bodily or physical features of man and how in God's ultimate design of man and in His image, we can better understand the very nature of God. "Now the body is not for sexual immorality, but for the Lord: and the Lord for the body" (1 Corinthians 6:13). God has a plan, a purpose and a time table for man. Scripture provides a foundation for understanding life's meaning and finding abundant life. The more we know about the body, and the various, intricate anatomy of it, the more we can appreciate and understand the character of God, its creator.

It is interesting that biological science says that the body needs four things in order to survive. These include:

1. Air
2. Water
3. Food
4. Light

Scripture says that Jesus (God) is the

1. Breath of life – "The Spirit of God has made me, and the breath of the Almighty has given me life" (Job 33:4).
2. Living water – "Whosoever drinks of the water that I give him will never thirst. The water that I shall give him will become in him like a fountain of water springing up into everlasting life" (John 4:14).
3. Bread of life – "And Jesus said to them, I am the bread of life: He that comes to me shall never hunger ..." (John 6:35).
4. Light of the world – "Then Jesus spoke again to them saying, I am the light of the world. He who follows me shall not walk in darkness, but have light of life" (John 8:12).

REFERENCES

1. Cain, F. "Are There More Grains of Sand Than Stars." *Universe Today. Space and Astronomy News.* (November 25, 2013). https://www.universetoday.com/106725/are-there-more-grains-of-sand-than-stars/https://www.universetoday.com/106725/are-there-more-grains-of-sand-than-stars/ (accessed April 30, 2018)
2. "How Many Species on Earth?" *ScienceDaily.* (August 24, 2011). https://www.sciencedaily.com/releases/2011/08/110823180459.htm (accessed April 30, 2018)
3. Haub, C. "How Many People Have Ever Lived on the Earth." *Population Today* no. 2 (February 23, 1995): 4-5. https://www.ncbi.nlm.nih.gov/pubmed/12288594. (accessed April 30, 2018)
4. Binazir, A. "Are You A Miracle? On the Probability of Your Being Born." *The Huffington Post.* (August 16, 2011). https://www.huffpost.com/entry/probability-being-born_n_877853 (accessed April 30, 2018)
5. Wynsberghe, DV, Noback, CR, and Carola, R. *Human Anatomy and Physiology* (3rd ed.) McGraw-Hill, (1995).
6. Marieb, EN. and Hoehn, K, *Human Anatomy and Physiology* (10th ed.) Pearson Publishing, (2016).
7. "Total Number of Murders in the United States in 2017." Statisca.com (accessed January 24, 2019). https://www.statista.com/statistics/195331/number-of-murders-in-the-us-by-state/ (accessed April 30, 2018)

8. Press Release, United Nations Office on Drugs and Crime. (April 10, 2014). https://www.unodc.org/unodc/en/press/releases/2014/April/some-437000-people-murdered-worldwide-in-2012-according-to-new-unodc-study.html (accessed April 30, 2018)

9. Floyd, R. "Abortion is the Leading Cause of Death." *Washington Examiner.* (January, 22, 2019). https://www.washingtonexaminer.com/opinion/op-eds/abortion-is-the-worlds-leading-cause-of-death (accessed February 9, 2019)

10. *The Merrian Webster Dictionary*, Merriam-Webster (1994).

11. "Quotes from Isaac Newton". Goodreads.com. https://www.goodreads.com/quotes/523034-how-came-the-bodies-of-animals-to-be-contrived-withGoodreads.com. (accessed April 30, 2018)

12. Culpepper, MI. *Fitly Framed Together: The Bible*. WestBow Press. 2013.

[The author notes that there are many internet sites that cite quotations from others. And some of these quotations are questioned by current groups for various reasons and intents.]

CHAPTER 2

AN ORGANIZATION

Therefore thus says the Lord God, "Behold, I lay in Zion a stone for a foundation. A tried stone, a precious corner stone, a sure foundation: whoever believes will not act hastily. Also, I will make justice the measuring line, and righteousness the plummet. – Isaiah 28:16–17

A house or building is made of many parts. The foundation, walls roof all help to bring together a structure we call a house (or other building). However, even these parts have "parts". Bricks, concrete, wood, steel, plastics, as well as other material make up the basic parts of a structure. And the architect and construction team must put these materials together in a certain fashion for the house (building) to be complete.

Each room of the house is designed and built for a purpose. There is a kitchen, bathrooms, living room, bed rooms. And each of these rooms are not only designed and built for a purpose, but they are also designed and built in accordance to the occupant's desires and needs. The size, "style", color, décor and other factors of each room are constructed specifically with the occupant in mind. The house is not built just for occupancy, but for protection of the occupant against the weather elements, outside intruders, as well as for fun and enjoyment of family life. In other words, the house is not just a building or structure sitting on a piece of land. It literally becomes a home to the occupants.

Construction of the human body is very similar. It has many parts, stomach, brain, kidney. And each of these parts has a specific role in the body. But even these parts are made of "parts". Atoms and molecules are the basic unit of structure of all materials. Countless molecules are fashioned together to make a complete human body.

I have a neighbor who is a brick mason. He is a master craftsman and an expert at what he does. His work is impeccable. I can use the exact same materials and techniques that he does and mix and measure and set brick to the best of my ability and make a brick wall. In fact, I may step back and look at my creation and it may even look pretty good. But let an expert look and evaluate my work and it can easily be seen that it is not only not perfect, but in fact is actually bad. The mortar joints are not secure and the wall is not plumb.

But the human body is more than just a stationary, non-movable house. In addition to its "structure", there are countless chemical reactions and physiological processes occurring, and each of these must be monitored and controlled. Maintaining the balance of these required by the body is called homeostasis. With homeostasis, the body can function and perform its purposes in life, while at the same time it is able to maintain a balance in the mechanical and physiological processes that are occurring in the body all the time. Many times, as I have taught my Anatomy and Physiology classes and discuss a specific body part, I may use an expression of, "I would have forgotten about that," or say, "I would not have thought of making that little thing." As an anatomist, I am amazed at the fine, intricate details of human anatomy. Nothing is added that we do not need. Nothing is missing that we do need.

God in His infinite knowledge and wisdom created man, perfect. Nothing was left out. Nothing was put in that was not needed. There is nothing we can do to add or take away from the way the human body that has been so fashioned. In my previous book, *Fitly Framed Together: The Bible* (WestBow, 2013), the number seven, is presented throughout Scripture as representing perfection in God's creation. It is interesting that the human body can be considered conceptually at seven structural levels. These levels include; atomic/molecular, organelle, cellular, tissue, organ, organ system, and finally organism. In other words, atoms and molecules make up organelles (parts within a cell). The various organelles make up cells. Many cells make up tissue. Various tissues make up organs. Various organs make up organ systems. And the different organ systems make up the total organism (human).

Like the different structural components of a house which have specific functions, so it is with the parts that make up the body. There are certain "laws of physics" that components of the body must yield to and withstand. There certainly must be ways and means in which to get energy. And there must be some form of anatomy to withstand and even combat elements of nature (virus, bacteria) to prevent infection and even death. And the body has it all!

It has been said that the body is an engineering marvel. That is because like all else in the world, it must answer to the physical nature and properties of the universe and it is constructed using these principles. A major theme of the universe is force. Forces are responsible for movement. Characteristics of forces include magnitude, direction and point of application. A force with a greater magnitude will certainly have a greater result. But the direction and point of application of a force can determine the location of the effect (of the force).

Foundation – Constructional Engineering

Throughout His life, Jesus taught about His love, grace and mercy. As he met with His disciples for the last time, He instituted what we today call "the Lord's Supper". It is interesting that when Jesus was distributing the bread at the "Lord's Supper", He stated, "This is my body, that is broken for you" (Luke 22:19). Jesus was indeed fully human and had to answer to the physical "laws and principles" of nature. Yet at the crucifixion, the legs of the two malefactors being crucified with Him were broken, but "when they came to Jesus and saw that he was dead already, they break not his leg ... that the

Scripture might be fulfilled, a bone of him shall not be broken" (John 19:33–36). Jesus was not "killed" on the cross but "died" (of His own volition) on the cross.

This prophecy came from Numbers 9:12. Jesus also said, "No man takes (my life) from me, but I lay it down of myself. I have the power to lay it down, and I have the power to take it again." (John 10:18). God allowed the very essence of Himself to "be broken" for the redemption of our sins yet there is no natural or physical force or power that can "break" God.

Forces

A force can be simply defined as a "push or a pull". The physical human body not only generates forces but is also subject to outside forces acting upon it as well. Thus, the various components of the body must be able to withstand these forces or a break or tear of these human components will occur resulting in injury or even death. The design and construction of the human body must take natural forces such as gravity, acceleration, momentum and impulse, and others into consideration in order to ensure a long and prosperous life. To be sure, oftentimes the body does succumb to excessive forces and suffers bodily damage. However, there are aspects of human design and structure that are remarkable that reduces the possibility of tissue damage that could occur from force overloads.

It can be understood that if any force is applied to a material and the magnitude of that force is too great, that material can "break". But in addition to the characteristics of forces such as magnitude, direction and point of application, there are mechanisms or modes of force application. These include compression, tension and shear. **Figure 2-1** illustrates the mechanisms of compression, tension and shear and describes how they act. From an engineering point of view, a magnitude of force can be applied in a compression, tension or shear mode. This is a major principle that architects and construction companies use in building things such as homes, buildings and bridges.

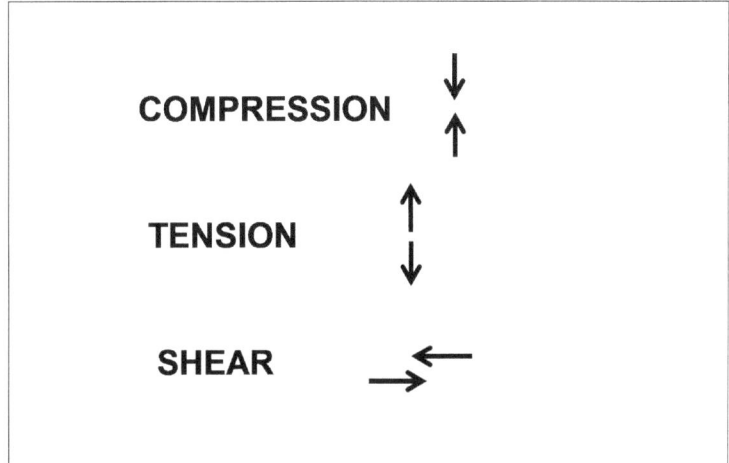

Figure 2-1. Illustration showing modes of force application. Mechanisms of Compression, Tension and Shear modes of forces.

A force can be applied to a material in a compression, tension or shear mode. **Figure 2-2** shows a comparison of modes of force applications to a material. Suppose it takes a force of 100 Newtons to break a material in a compressive mode. If this force is applied in tension, it will only take about 67 Newtons of force (or 67% of the maximum force application) for the material to "break". And, if the force is applied in a shear mode it will only take 33 Newtons or about 33% of the maximum force application to "break" the material.

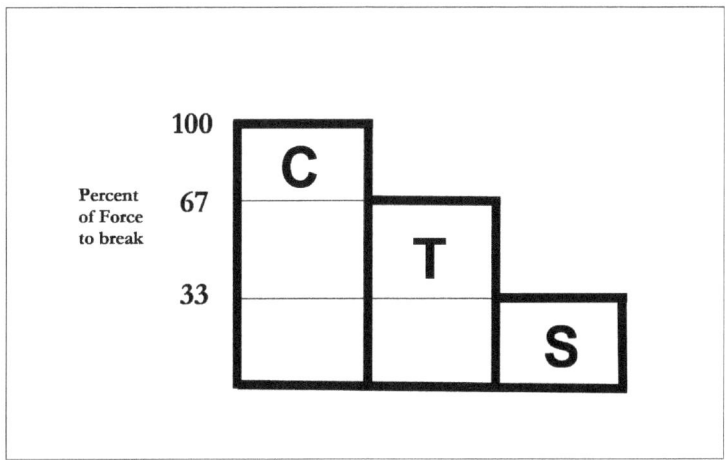

Figure 2-2. Illustration showing the relationship of material failure subjected to compression (C), tension (T) and shear (S) forces.

Thus, using this example, it is obvious that a material can withstand a force more efficiently if that force is applied in a compressive mode rather than in tension. And certainly, a shear mode of force application should be avoided. The body can do this in a variety of ways and some of these techniques will be discussed later in the text.

Special Molecules

Deoxyribose Nucleic Acid (DNA)

To be sure, the DNA molecule may be the most interesting molecule of living organisms. In 1953, Cambridge University scientists James D. Watson and Francis H.C. Crick announced their discovery of the make-up and shape of the DNA molecule. DNA stands for deoxyribonucleic acid, and is a molecule that contains instructions for developing, living and reproducing of living organisms. The structure of the DNA molecule looks like a twisted ladder. It has two long strands called nucleotides that are wound around each other, and in between are bases, which are the actual instructions for life. Much like the sequencing of letters of an alphabet to make words and sentences, these bases form "sequences" that ultimately become "genes", or the language of the cell.

These genes are the basis of life's instructions that are passed from generation to generation. It has been said that the Bible is **B**asic **I**nstructions **B**efore **L**eaving **E**arth, and no doubt it contains valuable information for living. Without appropriate instructions in the genes, subsequent generations would not know how to even come into existence and live. The Bible is not much different. "In the beginning was the Word, and the Word was with God, and the Word was God" (John 1:1). God is life and has given us the availability of true life through His word. "Jesus said, I am the way, the truth and the life. No one comes to the Father except through me" (John 14:6).

The DNA molecules are so long that they must be tightly coiled and packed in order to fit into a cell, or more specifically, into the nucleus of a cell. The tightly coiled DNA form structures we call chromosomes. Humans have twenty-three pair of chromosomes that make up the genes or instructions for life.

Adenosine Triphosphate (ATP)

Adenosine Triphosphate (ATP) is a molecule that is important to all living organisms. This molecule has the function of storing and delivering energy to the cell for its various activities and had been previously mentioned.

Collagen

In many engineering applications in construction, certain materials can be specially made or fabricated to withstand compression or tension or shear modes of force loading, depending on the use. The human body has similar capabilities. A major "foundation material" or molecule of the human body is collagen. The name collagen comes from the Greek word *kólla*, meaning "glue", and a suffix *-gen*, meaning "producing". Early techniques to make glue were to boil the skin and sinews of horses and other animals. It is the single most abundant protein in the body and can be considered "threaded glue" embedded throughout the body. Approximately one-third of all protein in the body is collagen. It can be found in fibrous tissues such as tendons, ligaments and connective tissue sheath found in muscle. It is abundant in corneas, cartilage, bones, and skin. Many commercial companies have tried to make and mimic the collagen molecule and incorporate it into cosmetics and skin creams to help reduce wrinkles in aging skin.

Figure 2-3 shows the design, shape and action of the collagen molecule. This molecule is the single most protein in the body and represents one-third of all proteins in the body. It is found most in the skin, ligaments, tendons, and bone.

This "foundation" molecule is ingeniously designed to literally convert a tension mode of force application into a compression mode, thus increasing the tolerance (before tissue failure) by 33%. It behaves like the old Chinese "finger trap" where you place your fingers into each end of the "trap" and pull. As you attempt to pull your fingers apart (in tension), the finger trap "compresses" more tightly around your finger. Thus, it literally changes the tension mode of the force, in which you are "pulling" your fingers apart, into a compression mode as it more tightly squeezes upon your finger. As various tensile forces are applied to the body, this small "foundation" molecule allows tissues such as ligaments, blood vessels and skin to withstand greater forces before they "break"!

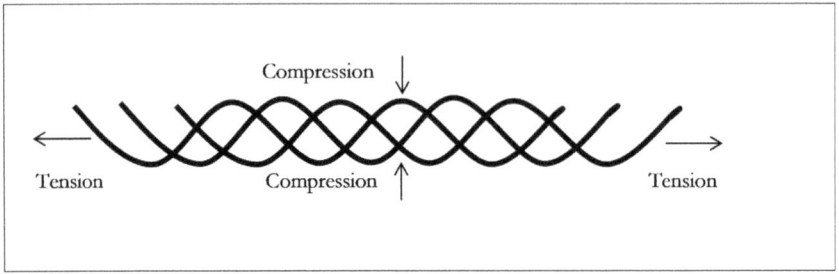

Figure 2-3. Illustration showing the shape and action of the Collagen molecule.

Laminin

Another "foundation" molecule important to the human body is Laminin. Laminin is a major protein that is found in the substrate or basement membrane of all internal organs such as the liver, kidney and spleen. It is also a major non-collagenous component of the basal lamina, upon which the epidermal layer of the skin sits. It acts like rebar of our body's "cementing" material and is vital in keeping the various structures of the body together. In other words, it is the responsibility of this molecule to basically hold the structures of the human body together and to keep the skin "stuck" onto the body.

Figure 2-4 shows the design and shape of Laminin. It is interesting to note the cross-shape of the molecule. To be sure, shapes and patterns of other molecules in the body can be perceived in their own right. And it can be alleged that physical structure of the body and thus physical life for humans cannot exist without the molecule Laminin. But it is certain that everlasting life apart from the cross of Christ is also not possible. "For the wages of sin is death. But the gift of God is eternal life through Jesus Christ our Lord" (Romans 6:23).

Figure 2-4. Illustration showing the shape of the Laminin molecule.

In Mathew 16:16, Peter affirms that Jesus is the Christ, the Son of the living God. But then Jesus said, "… you are Peter, and on this rock I will build My church, and the gates of hell shall not prevail against it" (Matthew 16:18). Jesus was not saying that He would build the church upon Peter. But rather the church would be built upon the faith in Him by believers who make up the Church.

Peter referred to Jesus as a "living stone" and believers as "living stones." "Coming to Him (Jesus) as a living stone, rejected indeed by men, but chosen by God as precious, you also, as living stones are being built up a spiritual house …" (1 Peter 2:4–5). Other Scriptural comparisons of Jesus (and the Church) to stones and foundation include: "Behold, I (God) lay in Zion a stone for a foundation, a tried stone, a precious cornerstone, a sure foundation" (Isaiah 28:16). "… and are built upon the foundation of the apostles and prophets, Jesus Christ himself being the chief cornerstone" (Ephesians 2:20). "For no other foundation can anyone lay than that which is laid, which is Jesus Christ" (1 Corinthians 3:11).

Thus, Jesus is the foundation (of the Church) and believers are building stones upon which the Church is built.

Other special molecules include:

Actin and Myosin

These molecules are major protein molecules that are in muscles. They are designed to make the muscle contract and shorten.

Chondroitin Sulfate and Calcium Hydroxyapatite

These molecules are designed to give cartilage and bone their unique properties.

Hemoglobin

This is a blood molecule designed to carry oxygen throughout the body. Whereas some oxygen can be dissolved in the liquid part of blood (plasma), a greater and more efficient mechanism of transporting oxygen throughout the body is because of the hemoglobin molecule.

Myoglobin

This molecule is like the design of hemoglobin. Myoglobin is found in muscle, helping to carry oxygen throughout the long muscle fiber. It is what makes the muscle look red.

Cells and Organelles

The cell is the basic unit of structure and function of the body. Most cells are too small to be seen without the use of a microscope. But if each cell of the body were the size of a standard brick used in construction of a house, we could build a human almost six miles high! Each cell has a specific function to do in the body, so each cell has specific organelles or "sub-cellular" components to help the cell perform its role in the body.

Nucleus

The most noticeable organelle of the cell is the nucleus. It is essentially a "filing cabinet" containing the DNA.

Mitochondria

The mitochondria an organelle that provides the ATP energy needed by the cell, for the cell to contribute to the cause of the body. The mitochondria are said to be the "powerhouse" of the cell. From a spiritual perspective, physical humans have power that comes from within. "And Jesus came and spake to them saying, 'All authority (power) is given to Me in heaven and on earth'" (Matthew 28:18). "Then they shall see the Son of Man (Jesus) coming in the clouds with great power and glory" (Mark 13:26). And Jesus can pass this power on to man. "And He (Jesus) said to them, 'I saw Satan fall like lightning from heaven. Behold I give you the authority (power) to trample on serpents and scorpions, and overall the power of the enemy, and nothing shall by any means hurt you'" (Luke 10:19).

Endoplasmic Reticulum

The endoplasmic reticulum is like a railroad track running throughout the cell. It provides some structural support inside the cell as well as providing an intracellular transportation system. It helps to deliver certain "raw materials" to specific parts of the cell and serves as a surface area for chemical reactions.

Ribosomes

The ribosomes are the center for protein synthesis and are like "workshops", essentially scattered along the endoplasmic reticulum, making specific products as determined by the instructions from the DNA.

Golgi

The principle function of the Golgi complex is to process, sort, package and deliver synthesized proteins and lipids (fats) to various parts of the cell, and even out of the cell. It can take "leftovers" from the ribosome "workshops" and modify or repackage proteins and fats. It ensures that most "raw products" entering the cell have been utilized and not "wasted", and thus the need to eliminate from the cell.

There are other organelles in the cell. These are the most important that are listed in this text.

Tissue

Although the body contain trillions of cells, there are only four tissue types. Each tissue has its own distinctive and distinguishing characteristic. The number four in Scripture represents the nature of physical creation. It implies the fullness and completeness of nature, including man. All distinctive and distinguishing characteristics of nature as created by God are represented. So it is with tissue types.

Epithelial Tissue

The cells of epithelial tissue are bound close together. The function of epithelial tissue is either protection, secretion or absorption. Some epithelial cells, such as those of the skin certainly help in protection. Some epithelial cells, such as those of the salivary glands or sweat glands produce or secretes something. And some epithelial cells that make up the intestines are designed to absorb the digested foods that are within the intestine. All these type cells must be numerous and close together.

Connective Tissue

Instead of the cells being close together, connective tissue cells are farther apart, with other material or a matrix between them. It is the matrix that is most important in connective tissue. Bone, cartilage, ligaments, tendons and even blood are connective tissue. The cells of these tissues make a particular matrix, specific to the function of the tissue. And it is the matrix that gives the particular strength or physical parameters utilized by the tissue for its purpose within the body.

Muscle Tissue

Muscle tissue is specifically designed to "contract" or shorten. There are three muscle types: skeletal, cardiac and smooth muscle. Each are specifically designed for their specific role in the body.

Nervous Tissue

Cells of the brain, spinal cords and nerves are designed to "transmit" messages throughout the body. These messages help the body to communicate the conditions and situations of the surrounding environment, as well as those within the body. Adequate knowledge and understanding of the surrounding environment, as well as the conditions within the body, is paramount for survival. The nervous tissue is responsible for this action.

Each of these four tissue types can be found throughout the body, some more concentrated in some body parts than others, but each designed and placed so that the body may prosper in health and even life itself. God uses these actions and body parts to best explain our designed nature and our communication with God through Scripture.

> My son, give attention to my words, incline your **ear** to my sayings, do not let them depart from your **eyes**, keep them in the mist of your **heart**; for they are life to those who find them, and health to all their flesh. Keep your **heart** with all diligence, for out of it springs the issues of life. Put away from you a deceitful **mouth** and put perverse **lips** far from you. Let your **eyes** look straight ahead, and your eyelids look right before you. Ponder the path of your **feet** and let all your ways be establish. Do not turn to the right or the left; remove your **foot** from evil. (Proverbs 4:20–27)

Organs and Organ Systems

Chapters three through six of this text will describe the twelve systems and corresponding organs that make up the human body. Of course, this is not an anatomy textbook, and exhaustive and intricate details of human anatomy cannot be detailed in such a short review. The major emphasis is to describe certain aspects of our anatomy that are interesting and are related to our Creator.

The Living Organism – Man

It is the collective organs and organ systems that make up the complete organism. The totality of physical man is made manifest through these 12 organ systems. Each system has a function, and each organ assigned a specific task within this system. These systems do not only combine to give life to man, but also are designed to protect the body from outside harm, either from outside physical forces or disease-causing bacteria that seek to destroy the body.

As a final addendum to the body's organizational make-up, within the body there are three separate body "cavities" or compartments. These body cavities include the cerebro-spinal cavity, the abdomino-pelvic cavity and the thoracic cavity. Naval ships and other sea worthy vessels are built with interior doors that can seal and lock tight, thus walling off and blocking the entrance of sea water if the outer hull of the ship has been breached. In other words, if the ship begins to sink, the area of damage causing the sinking can be separated from the rest of the ship. Though the ship is damaged, the entire ship would not sink.

The same can be said for these three body cavities. If there is a damage or bacterial invasion to one of these body cavities, it is the intent of the body cavity to contain the bacteria in this region, thus making it easier for the body to seek and destroy the bacteria ... and thus save the entire body. The body's ability to provide life-giving functions yet provide protection to ensure these functions can take place is incredible.

I have mentioned many times to my anatomy and physiology

students when I am informing and detailing certain body parts, that I am amazed at the construction of the human body. And oftentimes I would say, "If I had been the Designer and Creator of the human body, I probably would have left this 'thing' out, or I might have put something else (certainly not as good) in its place, or even someplace else in the body." It is good that the human body was not designed by a human "intellect", but by an infinite knowing God. The human body is indeed *Fitly Framed Together.*

CHAPTER 3

SUPPORT AND MOVEMENT

For in him we live, and move, and have our being. – Acts 17:28

The Skeletal System

Man was created to be dynamic, that is, move. Man must move in order to grow and gather food, and work to provide shelter. The muscular-skeletal systems are designed to provide every need of movement, body support and protection. The framework of our boney anatomy provides the body its structure and shape, as well as support and protect vital organs inside the body. The skeletal system provides levers for muscles to pull on for our movements through the joints and long bones. It also supplies the body with an infinite supply of calcium (which is vital for muscle contraction) as well as other essential minerals, and it is used as the site for red blood production.

> The hand of the LORD came upon me and brought me out in the Spirit of the LORD, and set me down in the midst of the valley, and it was full of bones. Then He caused me pass by them all around, and behold, there were very many in the open valley; and indeed they were very dry. And He said to me, "Son of man,

can these bones live?" So I answered, "O Lord GOD, you know." Again He said unto me, "Prophesy to these bones, and say to them, O dry bones, hear the word of the LORD! Thus says the Lord GOD to these bones: Surely I will cause breath to enter into you, and you shall live. I will put sinews on you, and bring flesh upon you, cover you with skin, and put breath in you; and you shall live. Then you shall know that I am the LORD." So I prophesied as I was commanded; and as I prophesied, there was a noise, and suddenly a rattling; and the bones came together, bone to bone. Indeed, as I looked, the sinews and the flesh came upon them, and the skin covered them over; but there was no breath in them. Also He said to me, "Prophesy to the breath, prophesy, son of man, and say to the breath, Thus says the Lord GOD: Come from the four winds, O breath, and breathe on these slain, that they may live." So I prophesied as He commanded me and breath came into them, and they lived, and stood upon their feet, an exceeding great army. (Ezekiel 37: 1–10)

Although the breath of life is still needed to make the body alive, this passage of Scripture illustrates the significance of the muscular-skeletal system as a structural foundation and beginning for the human body. It serves as a base of "flesh and bones".

Bone

Bone tissue may be the most interesting tissue in the body. Bone is connective tissue, in which the cells are not close together, but are separated and rather apart from each other and have other "stuff" between them called a matrix. This matrix of bone is calcium hydroxyapatite. It is a hard, cement like substance, which makes bone very hard. But, since it is a hard substance, diffusion of normal blood nutrients throughout bone tissue would be impossible. And if the bone were unable to get a blood supply and nutrients, it could not survive.

However, the bone cells, or osteocytes, are arranged in a circular fashion into what are called osteons. There is an expression, "Dry as a bone." However, living bone is anything but dry. In the center of each osteon is a Haversian canal, which contains a blood vessel. The osteocytes look like small spiders, having projections that resemble the legs of spider, coming out from the main body of the cell. These small projections finger outward into the osteon and wind up being close to the next osteocyte (small projections).

Although the osteocyte is surrounded by the hard cement-like matrix, when the blood nutrients begin to diffuse through the bone, the nutrients can pass through the osteocytes, moving from one osteocyte to another, without having to try to diffuse the hard, cement-like matrix of the calcium hydroxyapatite.

Figure 3-1 shows osteon and Haversian arrangement. The osteocytes are arranged in a circular pattern, making the osteon, with the Haversian canal in the center. Blood vessels traverse the Haversian canals. The nutrients from the blood vessels (within the Haversian canal) can diffuse outward from this central location, through the osteon, moving from one osteocyte to another until the outer edge of the osteon is reached. Then, there is another osteon which does the same. In this fashion, all the bone tissue can receive the life-giving nutrients supplied by the blood.

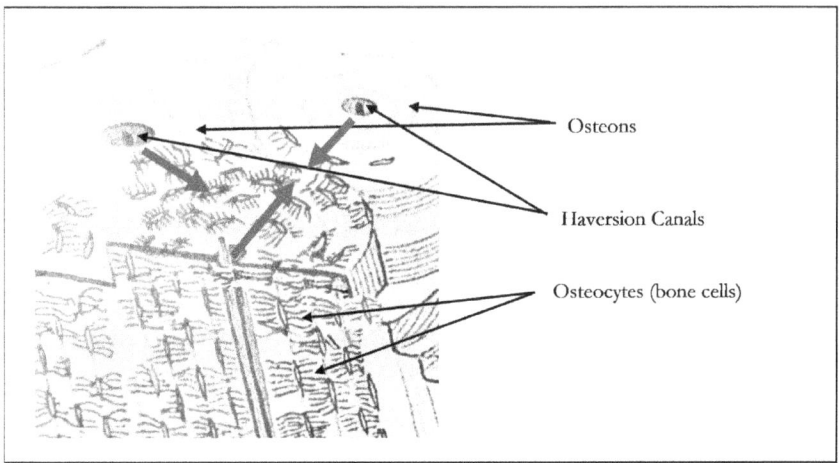

Osteons

Haversion Canals

Osteocytes (bone cells)

Figure 3-1. Illustration of bone at the microscopic level showing the arrangement of the osteons and how blood nutrients can diffuse from the Haversian Canals through the bone matrix and into the bone cells.

In addition to this matrix making the bone hard, it also has another amazing property. Calcium hydroxyapatite is a crystalline structure in which electrons which make up this molecule can "move around" when mechanical force is applied to it. As forces are applied to bone the electrons in the apatite molecule can shift.

Figure 3-2 is an illustration of the piezoelectric property of bone. When forces are applied to bone, the electrons of the apatite crystal molecules migrate. The illustration shows bone that is bent as a result of the force (exaggerated for illustration purposes). Along the concave side the region of bone becomes "electro-negative" whereas the convex side is "electro-positive". Bone will tend to grow in areas that are "electro-negative" and absorb in areas of "electro-positive". This property is referred to as the piezoelectric property of bone.

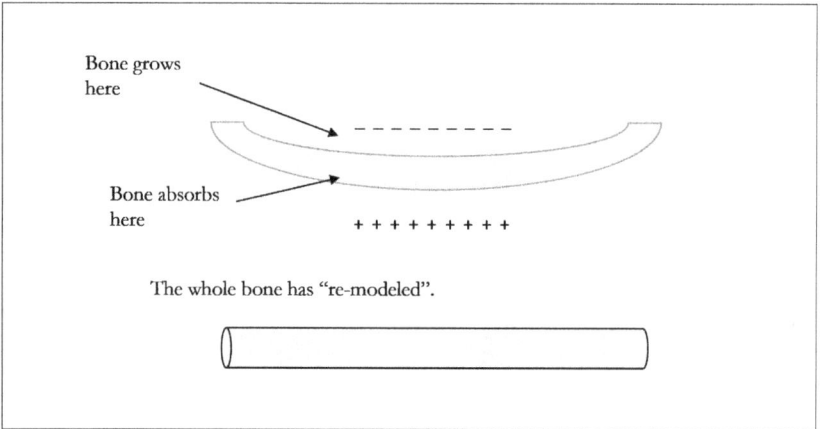

Figure 3-2. Illustration showing the piezoelectric property of bone. The upper picture shows a "bent" bone which demonstrates the negative electrons migrating toward the concave side, whereas the positive protons congregate around the convex side. The bottom picture shows the remodeled bone, where bone is absorbed in this electro-positive region, and is laid down or made in the electro-negative region, thus "straightening" the "bent" bone.

It is this piezoelectric property that gives bone an amazing ability to respond to stresses and forces that are applied to it. In fact, a bone that is broken, and even is "crooked", can heal and actually "re-straighten" as it heals. As we age and exercise and live our lives, and forces are applied to our bodies, the piezoelectric property of bone allows it to shape and form, and reform. It is this reason that when considering long space travel, astronauts under weightless conditions could have their bone be "absorbed" and disappear lack of gravity forces. Thus, there is the need for exercise.

Sometimes we may see an elderly person who has no teeth and see that their "jaw-bone" is very thin. As one chews on food the forces applied to the jaw bone stimulate it to grow more and thicker bone. But if there are no teeth, these forces are greatly reduced and the "jaw-bone" is gradually absorbed away. And it is this matrix that plays a key role in this action.

There are 206 separate bones in the skeletal system of the body, and each has a specific shape to serve a specific function. The key to the overall shape and arrangement of the bones that make up the skeletal system is based on an intricate relationship between stability and mobility. Considering the laws of physics, maximization of both stability and mobility is literally an impossibility. With 100% "stability" there is no mobility. With 100% "mobility", there is no stability. However, the skeletal system is designed to provide "stability" of the body when stability is needed, and the skeletal system also provides the body with "mobility" (when the muscular system is added) when mobility is needed. The shape of each bone is designed with the stability-mobility relationship in mind.

The body's skeletal system can be divided into two parts. The first is the axial system, which consists of the skull and spinal column, and some anatomist include the pelvis. The axial system is considered the "framework" or foundation of the skeletal system. It provides stability to the body as it offers a foundation base from which the rest of the body's anatomy can "hang". The appendicular system, or arms and legs, is attached to the axial system. The appendicular system is used for movement of the body.

However, although the appendicular system provides motion or mobility, there must be some stability, as there are forces generated both internally and externally upon the joints and bones of the body. And although the axial system provides stability, there also must be some mobility of the spinal column and torso. It would be difficult to discuss this aspect of the skeletal system of every joint, every bone, and every boney feature in a text such as this. However, here are a few examples.

Axial Skeletal System

Skull

Sitting at the top of the Axial Skeletal System is the skull. The skull has 29 bones that serves as a protective case for the brain, as well as for the eyes, ears and nasal passages. In addition to protection, the skull provides needed passageways to inside the body. Such passageways include the trachea, which provides an airway to the lungs, and the esophagus, which provides a passageway to the stomach.

Vertebral Column, Sacrum, Coccyx

The design and construction of the vertebral column is unique. It not only serves as a stabilizing anchor for the body, but it also must protect the delicate brain and spinal cord of the nervous system, as well as protect other vital organs.

If the design of the Axial Skeletal System was for stability and protection only, the vertebral column could have easily been a long, boney, hollow, tube. The brain and spinal cord could be safely tucked away inside the tube and the tube would provide the body with a core stability. However, as we tried to walk, we would be "stiff backed" and unable to bend over or turn around, because such a design would restrict any movement we might want.

Therefore, there are two design and construction features that make the vertebral column so unique. First, the vertebral is not a single, long hollow bone. There are thirty four vertebrae that make up the vertebral column, five fused bones that make up the sacrum, and four fused bones that make up the coccyx (or tail bone). These bones are arranged such that there is an overall shape to the Axial Skeletal System.

Figure 3-3 is a schematic illustration showing the vertebral column from a straight-on (anterior) view, and from the side (lateral view). The anterior view shows that the vertebral column is straight, or at least should be. Scoliosis is a condition of the spine that bends the vertebral into an S-shape. But it is interesting that the lateral view shows that there is an S-shape (in this direction).

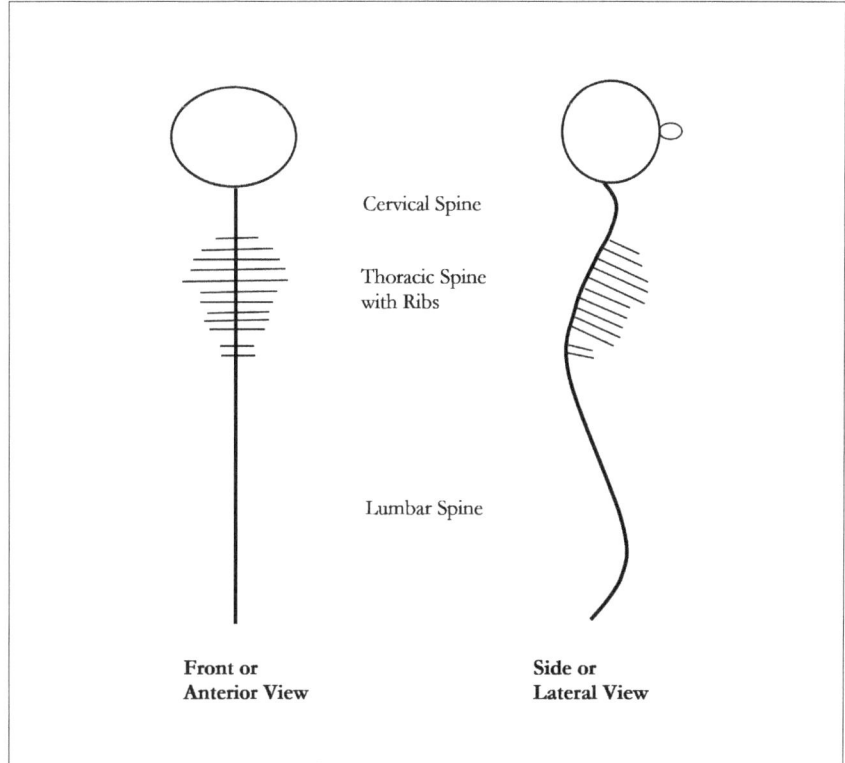

Cervical Spine

Thoracic Spine
with Ribs

Lumbar Spine

**Front or
Anterior View**

**Side or
Lateral View**

Figure 3-3. Illustration of an anterior and lateral view of the vertebral column. The anterior view shows that the vertebral column is straight whereas the lateral view shows that the vertebral column is a S-shape.

Although the overall function of the vertebral column is stability and protection, this S-shape gives it some "flexibility" and allows for additional movement. As one "flexes" or bends forward, this S-shape allows for rotation. If one twists or "rotates", there is also flexion. This is why a physician will ask a patient to bend forward in trying to assess scoliosis. If one has scoliosis (an S-curve in this plane), as the patient bends forward, the body (trunk) rotates, moving the ribs and making a "hump" on the back. The greater the degree of scoliosis, the greater the rotation and "hump". The S-curve or shape in the other plane (side or lateral view) allows the vertebral column to flex and rotate (at the same time), giving more mobility, even though it is mainly used for stability, and protection.

A second feature of the vertebral column is the design of individual vertebra. Each vertebra has a hole or foramen where the spinal cord can pass through. The boney surroundings provide a protective shield around the spinal cord, yet each vertebra can individually follow the S-curve shape of the vertebral column. The vertebrae articulate with each other, forming the S-shape. And each vertebra has a pair of joints on the top and bottom of the vertebra that accommodates this shape. These vertebral joints are called facets. It is the shape of these facets that give rise to any movement the spinal column may allow.

The shape of the facets of the vertebra of the neck allow the neck region of the spinal column (and head) to flex forward and backwards and rotate. It is nice that the head can turn and our eyes see what may be to the side of us, without us having to twist and turn the whole body in order to look in a particular direction. We can simple "turn" the head.

The facets of the lower back or lumbar region of the spinal column are arranged such that the body can "bend" forward, but cannot bend so much from side to side. Limited side to side movement of the lumbar region serves to help protect internal organs, and serves no other function. If the body needs to perform some task to the side of the body, it is more efficient to turn the body, and then the eyes, ears, arms and legs are more in alignment to perform the task at hand

The vertebrae of the chest or thoracic region of the spinal column are arranged, in conjunction with the ribs, to give zero movement of the chest or thoracic cavity. The lungs and heart are housed inside the thoracic cavity, and any movement within this space or shifting of these organs would be detrimental to these organs. Thus, although there can be movement of the overall spinal column and torso, the space within the thoracic cavity is extremely immobile, providing safety to the heart and lungs.

The sacrum is located at the bottom of the vertebral column and connecting to the pelvis. It provides strength and stability to the pelvis. The coccyx, or tailbone, is actually a vestige of an embryonic tail, that is probably used as a balance as the fetal development progresses. By the eighth week (obviously very early in development) much of it has disappeared. One might consider the development of our young Christian life. Maybe there was something we had early in our life that was needed. But as our Christian life matured, these things are not needed anymore. "When I was a child, I spoke as a child, I understood as a child, I thought as a child; but when I became a man, I put away childish things" (1 Corinthians 13:11).

Ribs

The arrangement and connection of the ribs to the vertebral column is interesting. There are twelve total ribs (and yes, males and females have the same number of ribs). The arrangement of the ribs can be described as five, five, two (5, 5, 2). **Figure 3-4** illustrates the arrangement of the ribs from the vertebral column.

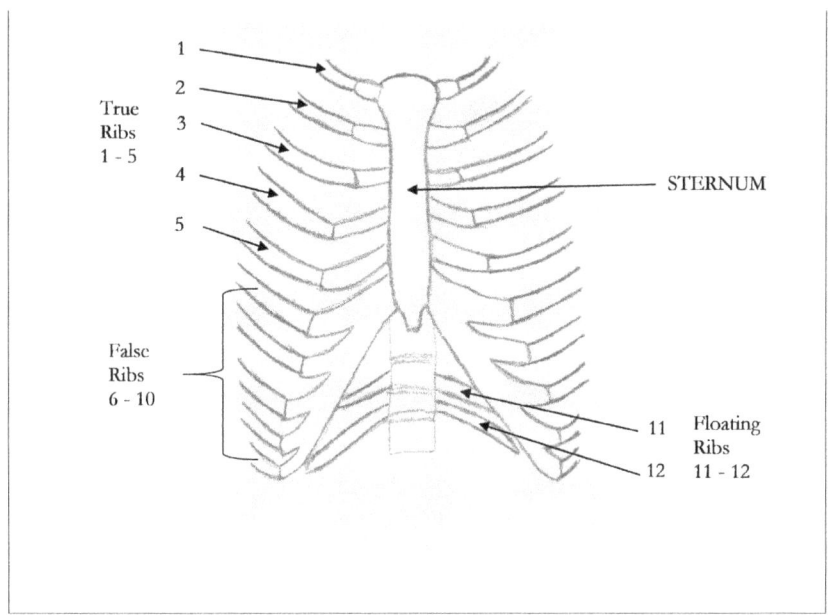

Figure 3-4. Illustration showing the arrangement of the bones of ribs. There are five pairs of ribs that are independent of one another, attached individually to the sternum. There are five pairs of ribs that are connected with each other and collectively connected to the sternum. There are two pairs of ribs that do not extend around and connect to the sternum in any fashion.

The first five pair of ribs come from the vertebral column are referred to as "true ribs". They begin in the back and circle to the front, individually connecting to a flat chest bone called the sternum. The attachment of the boney ribs to the boney sternum is made through a cartilage connection called costal cartilage. This costal cartilage is less brittle than bone and can absorb more force than bone before it breaks. Certainly, ribs can break. But the costal cartilage helps reduce the probability of this type of rib injury from occurring.

The second five pair of ribs are referred to as "false ribs". They circle toward the front, but stop short of the midline of the front of the torso and collectively connect to the costal cartilage. Some anatomists extend the true ribs through seven, although ribs six and seven are also attached to ribs eight to ten via the costal cartilage. It is at this point that the costal cartilage angles outward, leaving some "open space" in the front of the torso below the sternum. Imagine if these ribs did come all around to the front and connect to an extended sternum. There would be boney ribs extending downward almost to the belly button or umbilicus, severely restricting expansion of the upper abdomen. This would be very "unpleasant". The combination of these ten ribs create a cage that gives complete protection to the heart and lungs.

Note that in **Figure 3-3**, the lateral view of the vertebral column shows that the ribs angle downward, thus creating a minimal amount of chest space. However, when deep breathing and inhalation of air is needed, the ribs extent outward, expanding the space in the chest, allowing for the lung to fill more completely with air. Most of the time, the chest cavity is smaller in size for normal physical activity. But when more intense activity occurs and heavy breathing and inhalation is needed, the ribs extent outward and the chest cavity can expand, providing the additional space for the inflating lungs.

The final two ribs are called "floating" ribs, but they do not "float". They simply do not attach to the front of the torso as the other ten ribs do. By the time we get down in this region of the body, the heart and lungs have been protected. These two ribs offer additional protection for the kidneys.

Appendicular Skeletal System

The Appendicular System gets its name from "appendix". Many textbooks have an "appendix". It is simply something that is "added on". Back in the day when there were those individuals naming our anatomy, our "appendix" was discovered. But the function of it was not known and it was observed to be just stuck on or "added on". Thus, the name "appendix". Of course, we now know the importance of the appendix, but it has retained that name.

The Appendicular System include the arms and legs of our anatomy, which are stuck on or "added onto" the Axial System. The Axial System gives structure and support to the Appendicular System. Thus, whereas the Axial System was mainly designed for stability (with some mobility components included), the Appendicular System is mainly designed for mobility (with some stability components included). Description of the Appendicular System does not only include the design and shape of the bones, but joints that are created and used for this mobility.

Shoulder/Hip

The design features and anatomy of the shoulder joint and hip joint are uniquely different. Although the shoulder joint and arms must be anatomically constructed to be very mobile as we engage in our everyday life, it must also have some stability. Greater forces pass through the hip joint than shoulder joint. As such, the hip joint must have greater stability than the shoulder, yet we obviously use the hip joint for mobility. How are the shoulder and hip designed to perform their needed tasks?

The shoulders and arms are not just stuck on the sides of the body. In fact, both arms angle outward toward the front of the body. **Figure 3-5** is a superior or top view of a person. The clavicle or "collar bone" is S-shaped. We have previously discussed the advantage a S-shaped anatomy and how it gives additional movement. In addition, the general line of the clavicle angles back toward the shoulder, whereas the spine of the scapula or "wing bone" angles forward. This angling of the scapula forward actually makes the shoulder point more toward the front of the body, which, of course, is where we utilize the arm and hands, and makes it more functional than if the arms went straight out to the side.

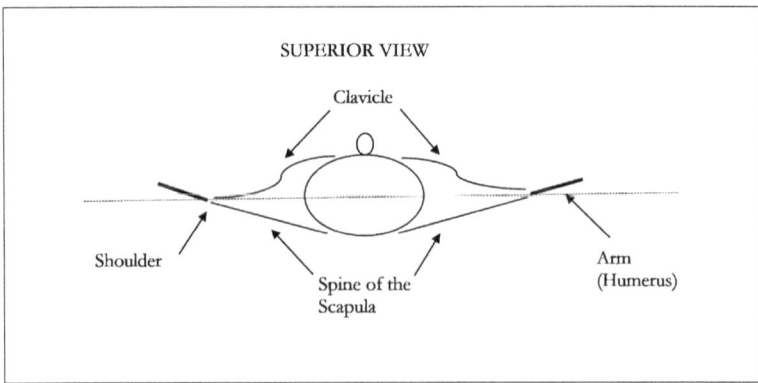

Figure 3-5. Illustration of a superior or top view of a person, showing the S-shape of the clavicle articulating with the spine of the scapula in the shoulder. The humerus of the upper arm does not just go straight out from the side the body but are actually slanted or "angled" toward the front of the body.

Figure 3-6 shows the scapula, and the humerus, the bone of the upper arm. The actual shoulder joint (gleno-humeral joint) is where the humeral head and glenoid come in contact or articulates. In the normal anatomy where the arm is hanging down to our side, the scapula is in its normal anatomical position and the humerus and arm hang downward. In this position there is no great force being applied to the shoulder joint, thus mobility and movement in any direction can easily be accomplished.

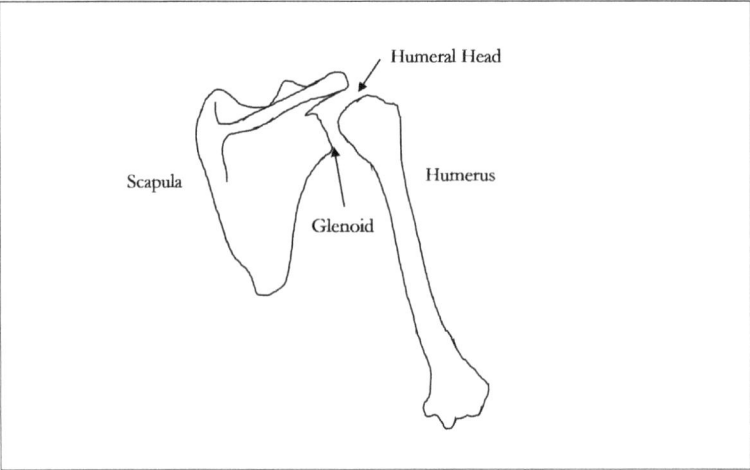

Figure 3-6. Illustration of the normal anatomy and boney arrangement of the scapula and humerus in the shoulder.

However, if the arm is lifted upward over our head, there would be a force that is generated and acts downward upon the shoulder joint. If the scapula were to remain in its "normal" position, this force would consist of a shear mode and cause the humeral head to slide downward and off the glenoid. This would lead to a dislocation of the shoulder joint. In a more extreme, but accurate scenario, the whole arm could literally slide downward and into the torso (chest and abdominal region). Fortunately, this does not happen. Thus, when we lift something up over our head, we are not as interested in mobility as we are stability. The anatomy of the shoulder joint can do just that.

Figure 3-7 shows the anatomical position of the scapula as the arm is lifted upward above the head. The scapula rotates upward to accommodate this raising of the arm. By doing so, the glenoid, or flatter portion of the scapula in this area that is in contact with the humeral head, creates a surface that is approximately 90° to the force. This creates a perpendicular angle where the force of the arm (humerus) acting downward is in a compressive mode, instead of a shear mode. This reduces the chance of the humeral head sliding off, thus eliminating possible injury and dislocation. Thus, the very shape of the scapula and positioning of the glenoid, as well as the shape and humerus, especially the humeral head, as well as the arrangement and function of the muscles in this region of the shoulder, all contribute to the safe yet effective movement of the shoulder.

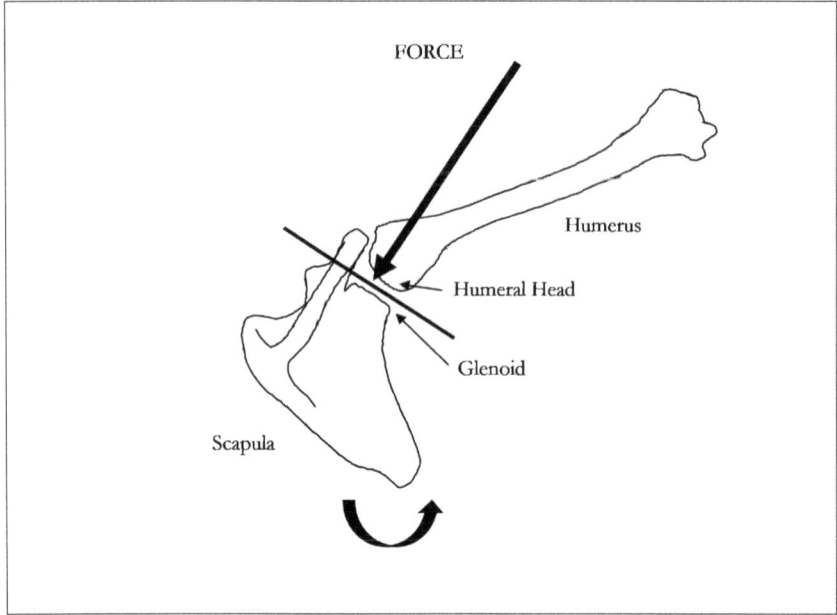

Figure 3-7. Illustration of the anatomy and boney arrangement of the scapula and humerus of the shoulder when the arm is raised. This shows that the scapula upwardly rotates when the arm is raised. The force that would travel down the arm and into the shoulder will meet perpendicular with the glenoid of the scapula in a compressive mode. If the scapula did not rotate upward to achieve this orientation, the force would enter the shoulder downward in a shear mode and dislocate the shoulder.

Figure 3-8 compares differences between the shoulder joint and hip joint. The anatomy of the hip is different from the shoulder. In the shoulder, the humeral head is not a complete sphere. However, it is larger than the glenoid. And because of the size difference between the humeral head and glenoid, the shoulder cannot act like a "ball-in-socket" joint. For the humerus (arm) to move, the humeral head literally must slide across the glenoid. This sliding mechanism gives rise to greater motion than does a "ball-in-socket" joint. Thus, the shoulder is designed mainly for movement, and the upward rotation of the scapula helps accommodate forces and helps with stability.

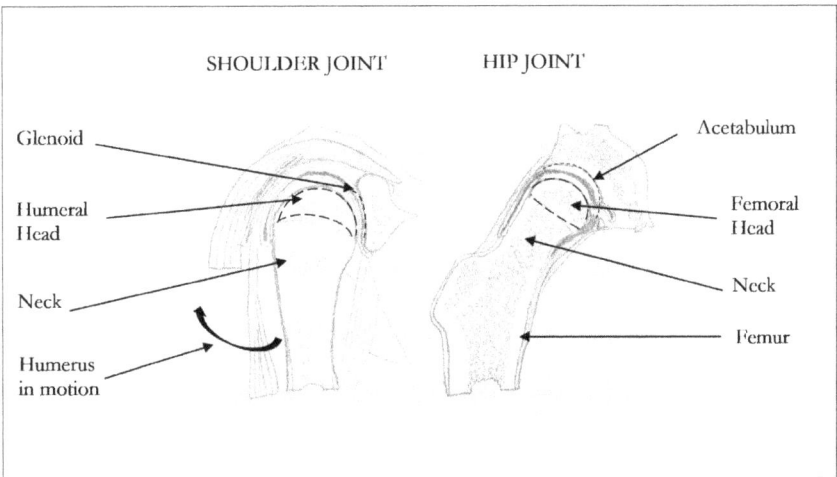

Figure 3-8. Illustration showing differences between the Shoulder Joint and Hip Joint. The shoulder joint is not a ball-in-socket joint. The humeral head less than half a sphere, but the surface area is still larger than the glenoid. Thus, a sliding motion takes place within the shoulder. The femoral head is larger than a sphere, but the acetabulum is large enough to accommodate it in a tight "socket". While there is not much of a neck on the humerus, the neck of the femur is much larger.

However, in the hip, the head of the femur, or thigh bone, is a larger sphere than that of the humeral head. And, it is similar in size to the acetabulum or hip "socket". Thus, the hip joint is a true "ball-in-socket" joint. This articulation literally "locks" the femoral head within the acetabulum and allows the joint to accommodate greater forces than the gleno-humeral joint of the shoulder. The scapula of the shoulder literally moves, making the shoulder more mobile but less stable than the hip. The pelvis does not move and the hip joint itself forms a "ball-in-socket", making it more stable, but with limited mobility.

One way the hip makes up this for the loss of movement is through a special capsule or ligament. **Figure 3-9** shows this special tissue structure called the Y-Ligament. As shown in this illustration, when the hip is downward, as if standing, or extended backward, as in running and "pushing off", this ligament becomes tight, thus adding support and stability to the hip. And, of course, it is when we are standing or "pushing off" when we need the greatest amount of stability.

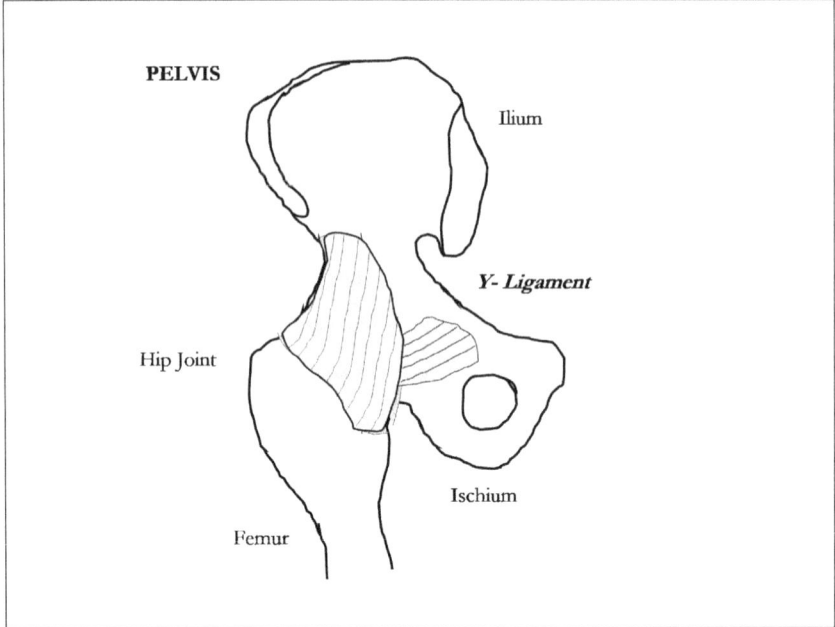

Figure 3-9. Illustration showing the Y- Ligament of the hip. As the hip flexes the femur moves forward, unwinding the Y- Ligament, making the hip joint loose. When the hip extends the femur moves backward, thus tightening the Y – Ligament, making the hip joint tighter.

When the hip is flexed and the knee and leg are moved forward, this Y-Ligament becomes loose, decreasing the stability, but increasing the mobility. But it is generally in this anatomical position when the foot is lifted off the ground, as if walking or running. And when the foot is off the ground there is little need for added stability. When the foot is off the ground, we are more able to move the foot around in space and place it in a location on the ground that we desire. And then, when the foot is planted on the ground and the leg extended downward and we want to "push off", the Y-Ligament has tightened back up again, giving us stability, when we need it most.

Wrist/Ankle

There are two bones in the lower arm or forearm. They are the radius and ulna. There are also two bones of the lower leg. The larger bone of the lower leg is the tibia and the smaller bone the fibula. In the forearm, the radius is the bone that allows for the "twisting" or pronation-supination of the lower arm. The ulna forms a hinge joint with the humerus at the elbow so the elbow can extent and flex. In the lower leg, the tibia articulates with the thigh bone or femur and forms the knee joint. But the fibula does not "connect" at the knee, nor does it move. The tibia carries all the weight or force of the lower leg and transfers it to the upper leg and body, while the fibula is for muscle attachments and movement.

But as we move down the forearm and lower leg and get closer to the wrist and ankle, the length and shape of the radius and ulna, as well as the tibia and fibula, become important. The farther most or distal ends of the radius and ulna are called styloids. These are the hard "bumps" that you can feel at the wrists. The farther most or distal ends of the tibia and fibula are called the malleolus. These are the "bumps" that you can feel at the ankles.

The radial styloid is more distal than the ulna and is closest to the thumb. The ulnar styloid is closest to the little finger. This boney difference allows for less movement of the hand/wrist in the thumb direction, called radial deviation, and more movement of the hand/ wrist toward the little finger, called ulnar deviation.

The natural function of the arms and hands are to "gather" toward the midline of the body. This gathering function is to bring objects not only toward the body, but toward the middle of the body. As the body stands in the "anatomical position" the arms are out to our side and the palms of the hands facing forward. The greater ulnar deviation allows the hands to move (gather) toward the midline. (Movement in the thumb direction is away from the body.) **Figure 3-10** shows the bones of the lower arm and lower leg and illustrate the length and shapes of the radius and ulna, and that of the tibia and fibula.

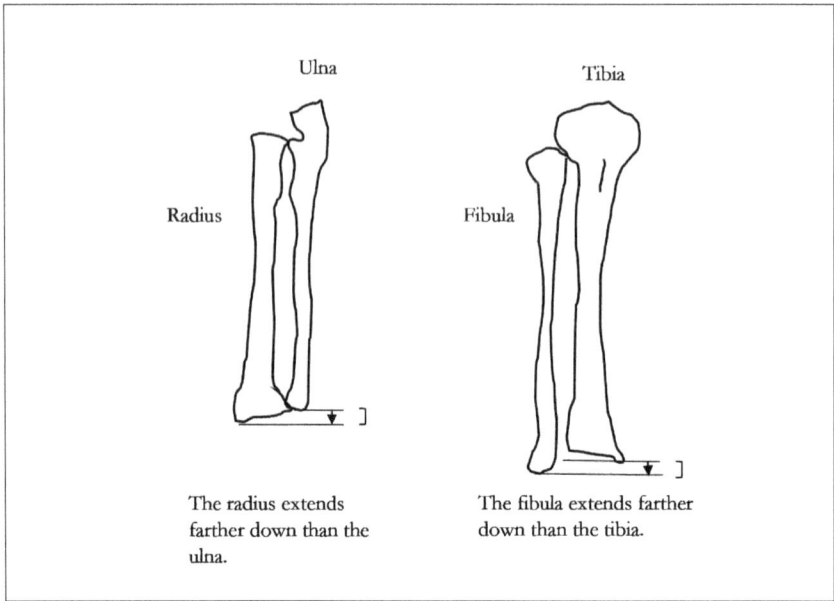

The radius extends farther down than the ulna.

The fibula extends farther down than the tibia.

Figure 3-10. Illustration of the bones of the lower arm and leg. It shows that the radius of the arm and the fibula of the leg extending farther downward than the ulna and the tibia.

Within the wrist, articulating with the ulna (on the little finger side of the hand), there is a wrist bone called the hamate. It has a "hook" or boney process that extends out from the body of the hamate, allowing for the attachment of a stronger muscle than would traverse and attach to the thumb side of the wrist. There is no such hamate type bone near the thumb with a boney process. In fact, sitting over this "hook" of the hamate is another wrist bone called the pisiform. The pisiform is a "pea" shaped bone that acts like the knee cap. Before the muscle can attach to the "hook" of the hamate, it passes over the pisiform, giving it a better angle of pull upon the wrist, giving the muscle even stronger characteristics. The details of muscle anatomy will be discussed later. The combined effects of the differences in radial and ulnar styloids, and resulting greater ulnar deviation, and the effects of the hook of the hamate and pisiform bones, resulting in greater muscular strength, gives the wrist and hand great advantages in moving objects.

In the lower leg, the end of fibular malleolus is more distal than the tibial malleolus. The fibula is on the side or sits lateral in the lower leg. The more distal position the fibular malleolus gives extra stability to movement, if the person wanted to move laterally or plant the foot and change direction (such as an athlete running and wanting to change directions). It gives a strong, boney background from which the foot and ankle can "push" against laterally, so we can move from side to side.

When walking, the reaction force exerted upon the foot will be equal to the body weight. However, when running, this force can exceed three times the body weight. Therefore, the foot and ankle must provide a stable foundation. But the foot is also needed in propelling the body forward. Thus, in addition to stability, it also needs motion. How can it do this? It has to do with the shape of the talus, or ankle bone that forms most of the ankle joint.

Figure 3-11a shows the shape of the talus. The front part, or anterior portion of the talus, is wider than the back or posterior portion. When the ankle is in dorsi flexion, that is, when the toes go up, the wide portion of the talus moves up into the ankle joint. This wider portion of the talus fills the inside of the ankle joint and does not allow for any movement, only stability. However, when the toes go down in plantar flexion, the narrow part of the talus moves up into the ankle joint. This creates a little space within the joint, allowing for increased movement, and less stability. **Figure 3-11b** illustrates this process.

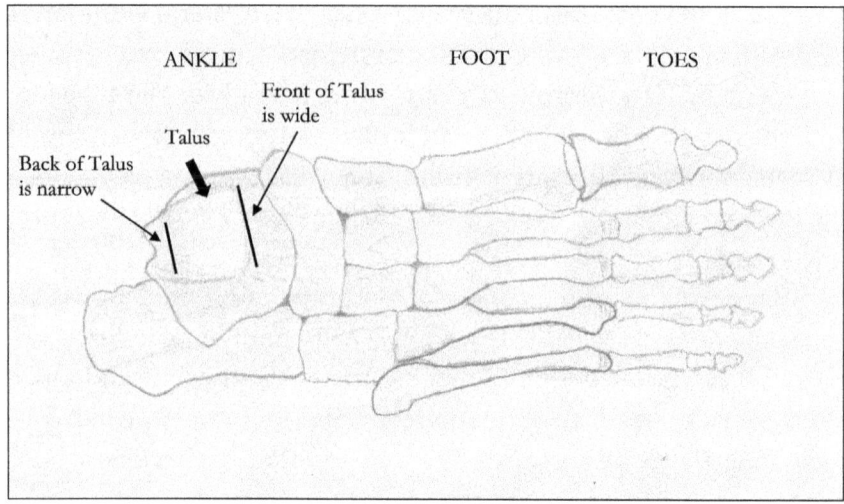

Figure 3-11a. Illustration showing the shape of the Talus in the ankle. It is wide in the front (anteriorly) and narrow in the back (posteriorly).

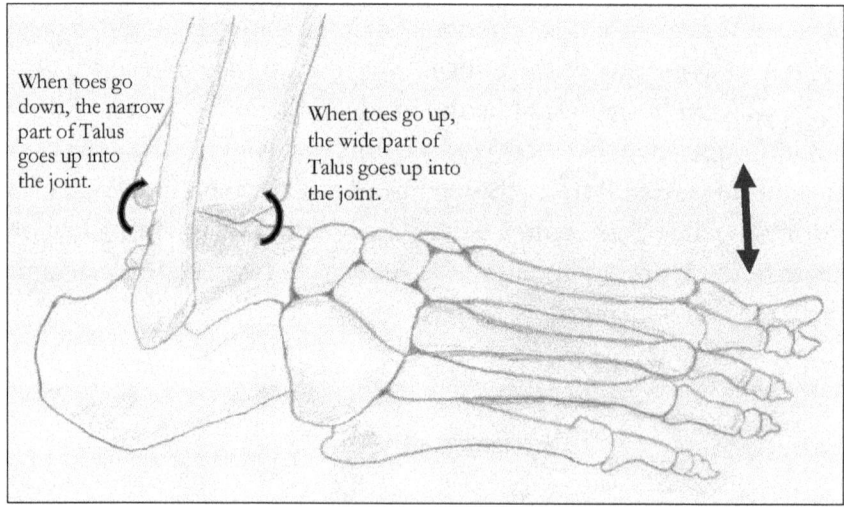

Figure 3-11b. Illustration of the foot and ankle. When the toes go up (dorsi flexion), the wide part of the Talus moves up into the ankle joint. This gives stability. When the toes go down (plantar flexion), the narrow part of the Talus moves up into the ankle joint, creating room in the joint for mobility.

During walking or running, when the foot is forward of the body, the heel is the first part of the foot to strike the ground. Therefore, when the foot is in this weight-bearing position, stability is needed most. During this support phase of walking, the ankle is in dorsi flexion. The toes are pointing upward and the heel is contact with the ground. Thus, the wide part of the talus is up in the space of the ankle joint, providing stability just when this part of the walk-run phase needs stability.

As the walking or running phase continues, the body "swings" across the leg and the ankle. The body is now in front of the foot and the foot is still in dorsi flexion, ready to "push off. And of course, this pushing off will require force, which will require continued stability of the foot/ankle.

But immediately after "push off" the foot is off the ground. The foot is now in plantar flexion, toes pointing downward. The narrow part of the talus is now up into the ankle joint, creating space and availability of movement. Very little force is passing through the foot/ankle at this point. The foot, now, can move and be positioned wherever the body wants to plant the foot for the next step or phase of running.

In other words, greater forces pass through the foot/ankle when the ankle is in dorsi flexion, and it is during this dorsi flexion that the wide part of the talus fills the space of the ankle joint, providing stability. Then, when the ankle is in plantar flexion, the narrow part of the talus is in the space of the ankle joint, leaving space for movement, providing mobility.

Pelvis

The design and structure of the pelvis may be the most interesting of all skeletal features. This is because the shape of the pelvis determines the overall anatomy of the axial system, which of course are the arms and legs. The "default", of the pelvis is to satisfy and meet the needs of the female for childbearing.

Figure 3-12 shows the male and female pelvis, comparing the size of the pelvic brim and subpubic angle. Looking at the male pelvis, if this were the female pelvis, the pelvic brim would not be large enough to allow a developing baby within the womb to drop down for birth, and the subpubic angle of a male pelvis would not be big enough to allow passage of a baby from the womb to the outside world through the birth canal. In other words, if this were a female pelvis, the baby would have no way out of the womb and birth could not take place.

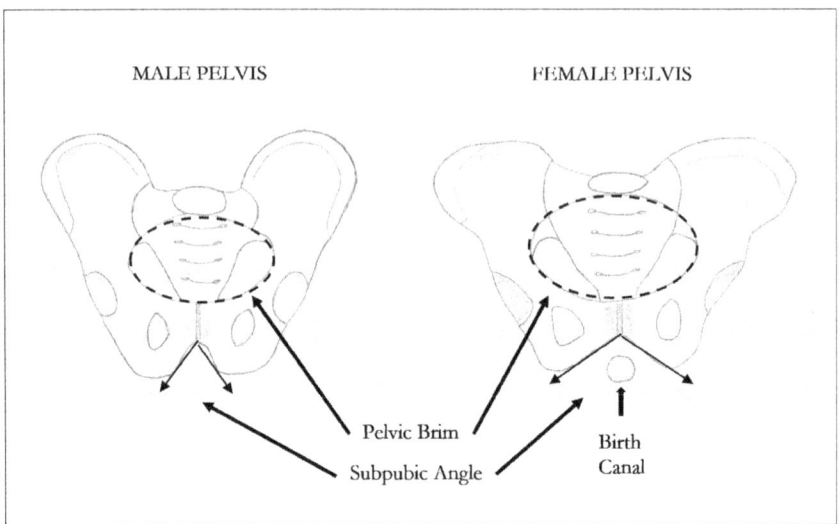

Figure 3-12. Illustration showing the differences between the anatomy of the male and female pelvis. There is a larger pelvic brim and a wider subpubic angle in the female pelvis, allowing for easier passage of the baby through the pelvis and out the birth canal (vagina). This difference is what makes the female "hips" wider than that of males.

However, the pelvic brim and subpubic angle of the female pelvis are greater, creating more room for the development of the baby, and for the expansion of the birth canal and passage for the baby from the womb to the outside world during birth. But, for these vital changes to happen, the entire boney, pelvic anatomy must "widen out" or "spread out". This adjustment makes for the "wider" hips that females have, and gives females the classic female "curvature" transitioning from the waist to the hips.

Although the wider hips are necessary for child birth, this anatomy creates some interesting consequences as it relates to the appendicular skeletal system, or arms and legs. **Figure 3-13** illustrates how the wider pelvic anatomy affects the joint angles of the arms and legs. As one walks in a normal gait, the arms swing back and forth. For a female, because of the wider hips, if there was not a corresponding change in the *carrying angle* of the elbow, the lower arm and hand would strike the hip with each step. Therefore, the *carrying angle* is greater in females than for males. The greater carrying angle allows the lower arm and hands of females bend slightly or point away from the hip, allowing for nonrestrictive swinging and movement of the arms.

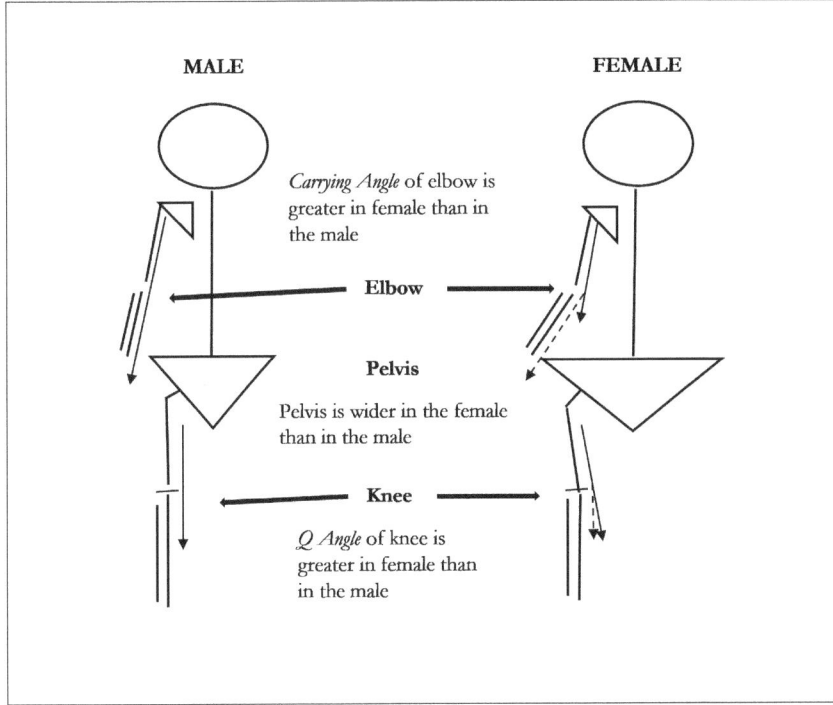

Figure 3-13. Illustration showing the differences in the angulation of the elbow and knee joints of the male and female.

However, the greater carrying angle for the female puts the female at a disadvantage when trying to do activities with the arms like throwing and lifting. The greater Q angle puts the female at a disadvantage doing activities like running and jumping. In addition, the female is more vulnerable to knee injuries such as patella (knee cap) dislocation and overuse problems (patella femoral syndrome), where the lateral aspect of the knee will sustain more force and thus become more susceptible force overload issues.

The widening of the female pelvis (and other gender factors such as quantity and location of fat deposits) lowers a female's center of gravity. This, as well as the increased Q angle, are the reasons why females cannot run as fast or jump as high as males. To be sure there are those that tout that females are "equal" with males, especially where physical workloads are concerned. But, the fact of the matter is that there are indeed specific anatomical (skeletal) differences between males and females, which correspond to different outcomes of physical workloads.

Knee

The knee is probably the most complex joint of the body. Being between the foot and the hip, this special joint must be able to provide stability, yet mobility and seemingly at the same time. The knee does have collateral ligaments on either side of the knee to provide "side-to-side" stability during movement, and has cruciate ligaments in the center of the knee to provide "front-to-back" stability. However, greater stability is needed, and needs to be accomplished without compromising mobility. How can this happen?

Figure 3-14 shows the anatomical features of the knee. The top part of the tibia is rather flat while the bottom part of the femur is rounded. The knee is not a hinge joint, but acts similar to the shoulder joint, in that the rounded part of the femur "slides" across the top of the tibia. This sliding motion gives the knee considerable mobility, like a rocking chair on the floor. During flexion, the tibia slides all the way to the back of the femur, giving the knee its generous mobility.

The ends of the femur are called condyles. There is a lateral and medial condyle. However, these two condyles are not alike. The lateral condyle is longer and narrower, while the medial condyle is shorter and wider. When the knee is bent, the leg is off the ground and not weight bearing. It is when the knee is in extension and the leg in contact with the ground that weightbearing occurs and greater stability is needed. As the knee moves toward full extension, the medial condyle runs out and straight extension stops. However, the lateral condyle still has a way to go before it runs out. At this point (usually within the last 10 degrees of extension) with continued extension, there is internal rotation of the femur upon the tibia. This internal rotation "twists" and tightens the surrounding tissue and ligaments, increasing stability.

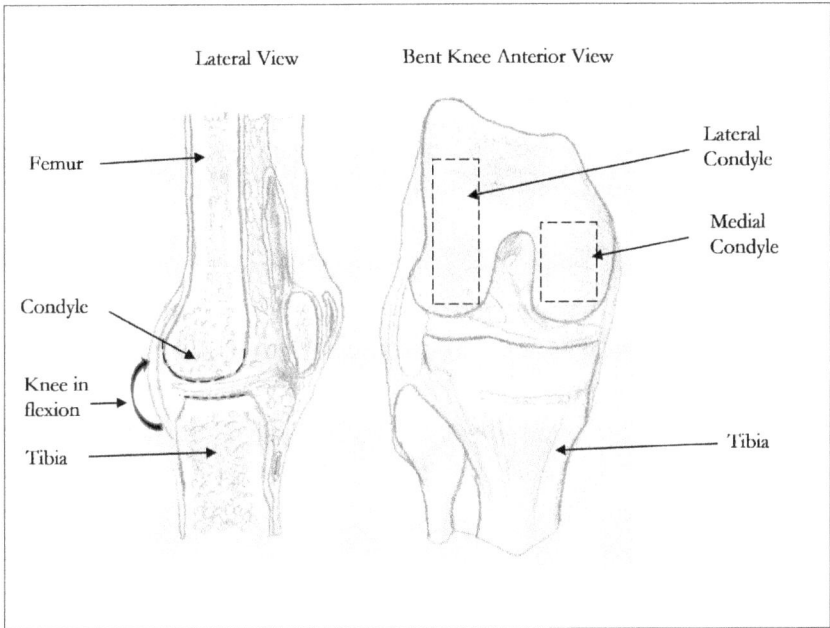

Figure 3-14. Illustration showing the knee joint. The lateral view shows how the tibia slides around and up the femoral condyle in flexion. The anterior view shows the medial condyle is wider and not as long as the lateral condyle. This allows the femur to internally rotate upon full extension, thus tightening the capsule and ligaments of the knee, making it more stable in extension.

These are but a few examples of the design of the Skeletal System and shape of bones, as they provide stability when the body needs it most, and provide mobility when the body needs it most. God is always able to provide us our best needs, when we need them the most.

The Muscular System

Bones may operate as a system of levers that involve long bones and joints. But it is the muscles that provide the power to make them move. Whereas the design of the skeletal system is based on a relationship between "stability" and "mobility", the design of the muscular system is based on a relationship between "strength" and "speed" of motion. There are five major factors that affect this relationship between strength and speed of motion. The first factor affecting strength of a muscle is length. Very simply, "the longer, the stronger". The longer a muscle is, the more strength it can generate. This is one reason why when we throw a ball, we bring the arm back, in order to throw the ball forward. In bringing the ball back we "stretch" the muscle, making it temporarily longer, thus making it stronger.

We have muscle that traverse our arms and legs. Of course, these muscles cross a joint, creating movement. However, we also have muscles that cross two joints. These two joint muscles are obviously longer, and thus, stronger.

A second factor is cross-section diameter. Other factors being equal, the thicker or greater the cross-section diameter a muscle is, the stronger the muscle. Thus, it is structured more for strength of movement, compared to speed of movement. **Figure 3-15** gives an example of two muscles with different cross-section diameters. The greater the cross-section, the greater the strength.

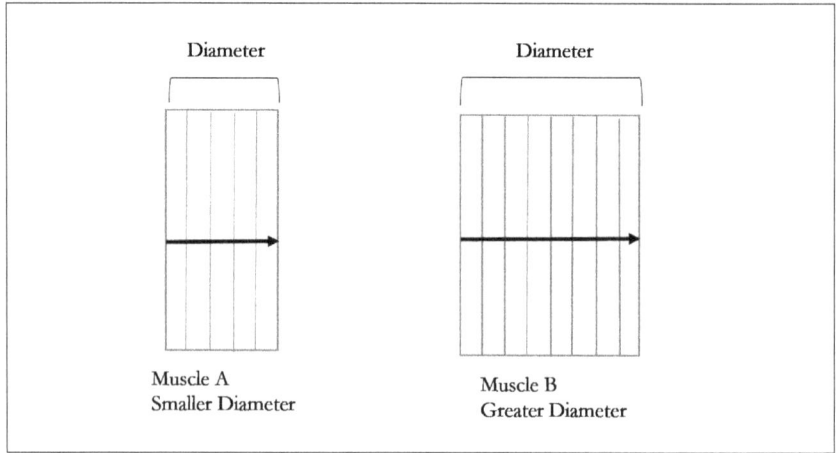

Figure 3-15. Illustrating differences in muscle diameter. Muscle B, having a greater diameter would be the stronger of the two muscles.

As an individual "works-out" with weights in a weight training program, the exercised muscles become "bigger". This process of muscles becoming bigger is called hypertrophy and occurs because of the "Force Overload Principle". The continual pounding of waves upon the shore is what shapes and determines the making of sand and the shoreline. So it is with muscles. With continual use and strength training using the "Force Overload Principle", muscles can get increasingly stronger. As forces upon the muscles increase, the muscles respond by increasing in size, thickening and gaining an increase in cross-section diameter. This is called hypertrophy. With hypertrophy there is a corresponding increase in muscle strength.

However, if these forces are diminished, over time, muscles will correspondingly diminish in size and become weaker. This is called atrophy. In other words, the more we use our muscles the stronger and more stable they become. The less we use them, the weaker they become. The physical body responds to the environment, diet and exercise. If we eat healthy food and exercise, our body becomes stronger. If we do not eat healthy food or exercise, the body becomes weaker.

So, too, our spiritual body responds. Our "diet" is the word of God. It is spiritual food that needs to be "eaten" regularly. "Exercise" is our action and behavior in response to the Word. The more we study and "use" God's word, the stronger our spiritual life can become. However, if we fail to study and maintain God's Word in us, the weaker we can become.

To be sure, believers still sin. But a pattern of Godly behavior should be seen and manifested in the life of a Christian. The life of a Christian should be that of "participation", not just "imitation" (of Christ). I may be able to watch people exercise, and understand its benefits, but unless I literally do it myself, I receive no benefits of exercise. Man is a dynamic creature. That is, the physical attributes of man were created to move, be energetic. And using the "Force Overload Principle", exercise can enhance one's physical abilities. So it is with a Christian. Exercising "spiritually" can strengthen and develop our muscle of faith. As parents we desire that our children grow up to be "big and strong". It is the desire of our Heavenly Father that we become spiritually "big and strong".

It is interesting that many non-Christians in the secular world say that Christians are weak. But there are nearly 200 Bible verses in the Old Testament alone that mention "strength". It is not God's intention that believers should be weak. The Psalmist said, "The Lord is my rock and my fortress and my deliverer; my God, my strength, in whom I will trust" (Psalm 18:2). "The glory of young men is their strength" (Proverbs 20:29).

Paul told Timothy in the New Testament, "But the Lord stood with me and strengthened me, so that the message might be preached fully through me ..." (2 Timothy 4:17). He also said, "I can do all things through Christ who strengthens me" (Philippians 4:13). Being strong in Christ is important. Astronaut James Irwin stated that, "Jesus walking on the earth is more important than man walking on the moon".[1]

Many muscles are what is considered a "one-belly" muscle. That is, the mass of a specific muscle is a single unit of muscle tissue. There is a single "bulge" of muscle mass in a "one-belly" muscle. However, some muscles are a "two-belly" muscle, some are even a "three-belly" muscle. The mass of a specific muscle may act as one muscle unit, but a "two-belly" muscle has two distinct muscle masses that make up the muscle. This muscle is obviously thicker, and therefore stronger.

However, there are some muscles of the body that have an advantage of increased cross-section diameter without having to be larger, thicker muscles. **Figure 3-16** shows a comparison of Fusiform and Pennate muscles. Most muscles of the body are Fusiform. That is, the direction of the muscle fibers is in the same direction of the intended movement. To be sure, these muscles can increase in muscle diameter, and thus, increase in strength characteristics with strength or weight training.

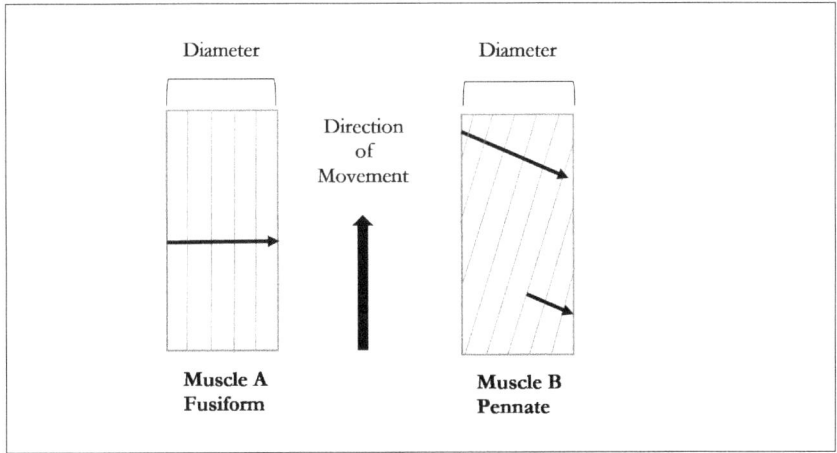

Figure 3-16. Illustration showing Fusiform and Pennate muscle types. Muscle A is a Fusiform and muscle B is a Pennate. The Pennate muscle has a greater cross section diameter and therefore would be the stronger of the two types of muscle.

But Pennate muscles are comparatively stronger than Fusiform muscles, because their muscle fibers run obliquely to the direction of the movement. The cross-section diameter is defined as a cross section that is perpendicular or 90° to the line of the muscle fibers. One can simply measure the cross-section diameter straight across the "thickness" of a Fusiform muscle.

However, as one measures the cross-section diameter of a Pennate muscle that is the same "thickness" of a Fusiform muscle, and measurement is perpendicular or 90° to these fibers, there will be multiple areas in the muscle in which the cross-section diameter measurements can be made, and these will need to be added together to get the total cross-section diameter. Therefore, the sum of these multiple measurements of perpendicular diameter is greater than that of the Fusiform muscle, and the Pennate muscle will have a greater strength.

Since the direction of the muscle fibers is oblique to the direction of movement in the Pennate muscle, the direction of muscle contraction is not in the same direction of the motion. Thus, the speed of motion in the direction of intended motion is less, but strength of motion is gained. Placement of muscle inside the body is limited by space and direction of intended motion. In strategic places, the body uses

Pennate muscles when strength is more important than speed of motion.

A third factor affecting muscle strength is point of insertion. **Figure 3-17** compares a muscle that inserts close to the joint to one that inserts farther away from the joint. The farther away the muscle insertion is from the joint, the greater the strength capability of that muscle. It is similar to the action one would have lifting a wheel barrow. The farther away from the wheel (closer to the end of the handle) one can grasp and lift the wheelbarrow, the easier it is to lift the wheelbarrow.

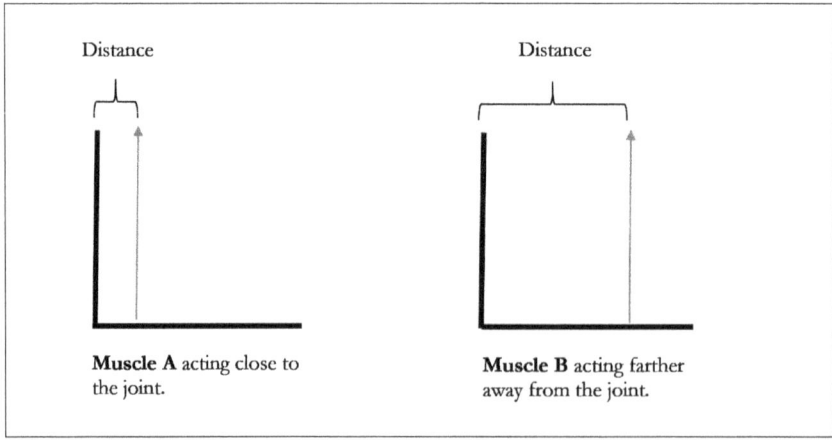

Figure 3-17. Illustration comparing of Points of Insertion of muscles. Because Muscle B inserts farther away from the joint than Muscle A, Muscle B would exhibit a stronger strength capability.

A fourth factor is angle of pull. A muscle inserting onto a bone and pulling closer to 90° or perpendicular to the bone can generate a greater force than a muscle that slants into the bone and pulls at an angle. **Figure 3-18** compare muscles that pull at angles of 90° and 60°. If all other factors are equal, the muscle pulling at 90° will be able to pull with a greater force, and thus be the stronger of the two muscles. Anatomically, some muscles insert close to the joint while others insert farther away from the joint, and thus create different angles of pull by the various muscle within the body.

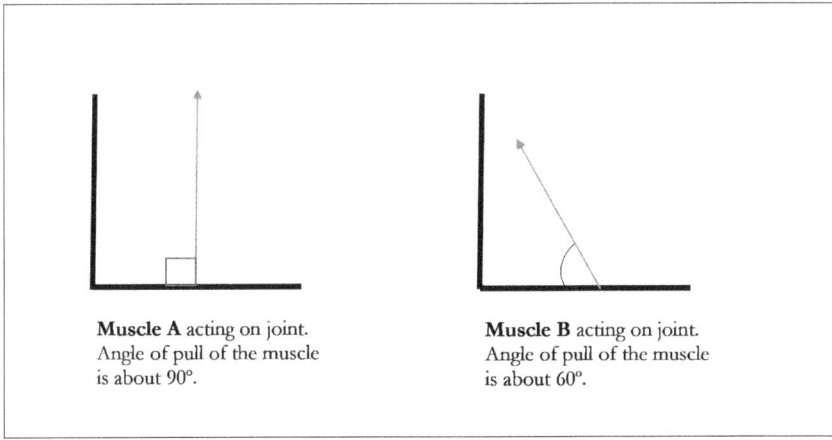

Muscle A acting on joint. Angle of pull of the muscle is about 90°.

Muscle B acting on joint. Angle of pull of the muscle is about 60°.

Figure 3-18. Illustration of differences of angle of pull by a muscle. Muscle A, pulling at an angle of 90° would exert a greater force of pull than Muscle B.

As we move and our muscles contract and work to make that movement, the different muscles work together in what is referred to a concert. As various musical instruments playing in harmony can make beautiful music, so to, muscles work "in concert" to make smooth, purposeful movement. The factors of length, diameter and angle of pull work continuously throughout the range of movement.

Figure 3-19 Shows the arrangement of three muscles found in the forearm. The Biceps Brachii is a "two-belly", two joint (longer muscle) and inserts close to the elbow joint. The fact that it inserts close to the joint would make it a "weaker" muscle. However, its angle of pull is close to 90°, and it is a longer (it crosses the elbow and shoulder joints), "thicker" muscle (two belly), having a large cross-section diameter. Thus, the latter three characteristics would give it major strength characteristics, making it a very strong muscle. The angle of pull of the Brachioradialis gives it a weak, strength characteristic, but it is a long muscle, and it inserts farther down the forearm, giving it a couple of strength characteristics. The structure and arrangement of the Brachialis is somewhere in between these two muscles, being average length and about 45° angle of pull.

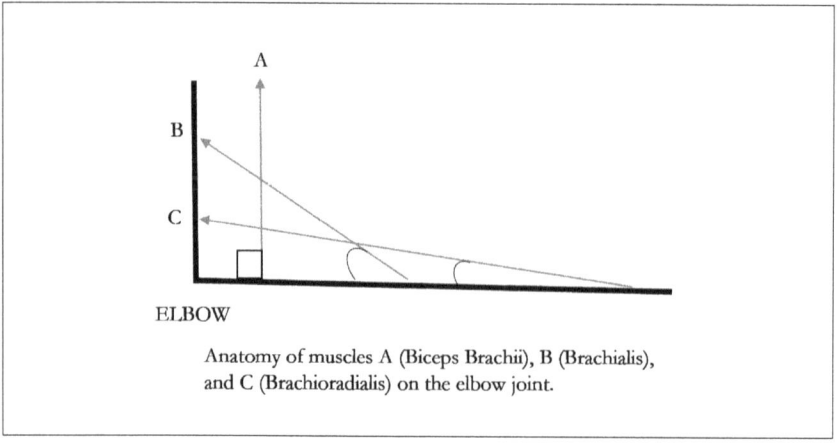

Anatomy of muscles A (Biceps Brachii), B (Brachialis),
and C (Brachioradialis) on the elbow joint.

Figure 3-19. Illustration of the arrangement of forearm muscles showing muscle angles before flexion.

Have you ever tried to do a pull up? It seems to be easy to begin with, but as you continue to pull yourself up and you get closer to the bar that is over your head, it becomes increasingly more difficult to pull yourself up. This is because as you move and the joints flex, the muscles you are using become shorter and their angles of pull changes. **Figure 3-20** illustrates what happens to the strength characteristic of the muscles in the forearm as the elbow flexes.

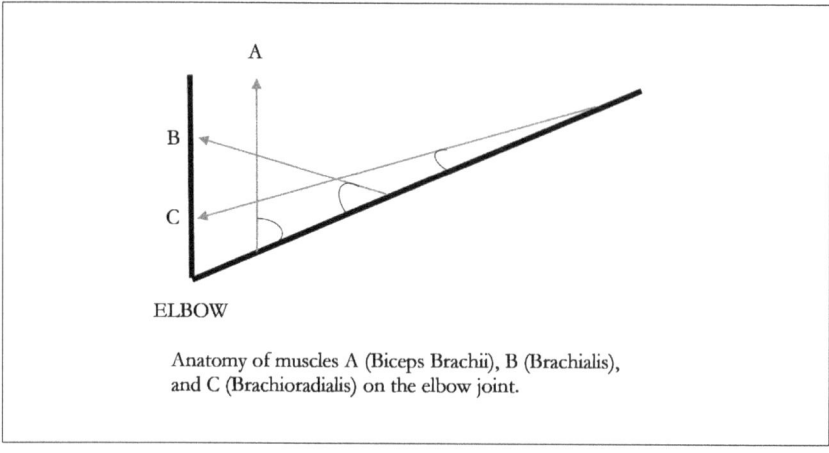

Anatomy of muscles A (Biceps Brachii), B (Brachialis),
and C (Brachioradialis) on the elbow joint.

Figure 3-20. Illustration of the arrangement of forearm muscles showing muscle angles after flexion.

When a movement occurs, all muscles involved with the movement will shorten in length, thus losing this aspect of their strength capabilities. In addition, angles of pull by these muscles will change as the movement goes through its range of motion. In this example, the decrease in the angle of pull by the stronger Biceps Brachii also weakens the strength characteristic of this muscle. However, the angle of pull improves for the Brachialis and Brachioradialis, essentially increasing this aspect of strength characteristics for these muscles at this point in the range of motion. In other words, each of the forearm muscles have inherent, built in strength capabilities before movement begins, and these characteristics will change during movement. However, during movement some strength characteristics of some muscles may improve during the range of motion. Thus, the muscles working together or "in concert", to produce a smooth, efficient, and purposeful movement throughout the entire range of motion.

This is like the talents and characteristics of believers and church members. Each person has specific characteristics and talents. And as the local church works in the resident community, one person does this, another person can do that, and another does something else. Some may consider one person stronger and doing more of the work while others think another person is weaker and will do less. However, in the big scheme of things, they all work together, in concert, "for the glory of God!"

A fifth factor that affects the strength of a muscle is number of motor units the brain can activate in order to stimulate muscles. It should be apparent that the more muscles (or muscle fibers) that are used for a movement, the greater the strength capabilities of that movement. A motor unit is defined as a single neuron and the number of muscle fibers it innervates. A single motor unit stimulating muscles that give eye movement may innervate only three muscle fibers, giving great control and finesse to the movement of the eye. However, a single motor unit of the Gluteus Maximus may innervate as many as 3,000 muscle fibers, giving not so much control and finesse, but greater strength of movement. Imagine how much stronger 3,000 muscle fibers are compared to three. But then, what if one hundred motor units of the Gluteus Maximus is activated and innervates

300,000 muscle fibers? Three hundred thousand muscle fibers can generate more strength than 3,000.

This motor unit control is routinely governed by the brain. The brain generally has an idea as to how much strength is needed for a movement and thus stimulate a correspondingly number of motor units to initiate that movement. But additional factors can be included. Have you ever heard of a "little old lady" picking up the side of a car in an emergency to rescue a family member, or something like this story? With extra "mental concentration", or mental focus, additional motor units may be summoned and therefore more muscle fibers innervated for extra strength. In other words, with additional mental focus and application, greater strength can sometimes be summoned.

Sometimes, lack of focus can create negative issues in the life of man. We may take things for granted and relax and lose focus. When we lose our focus on God, we can fail to have the strength we need to get through or perform a specific task. Peter found this out the hard way.

> But immediately Jesus spoke to them, saying, "Be of good cheer! It is I; do not be afraid." And Peter answered Him and said, "Lord if it is You, command me to come to You on the water." So He said, "Come." And when Peter had come down out of the boat, he walked on the water to go to Jesus. But when he saw that the wind was boisterous, he was afraid and beginning to sink he cried out saying, "Lord save me!" (Matthew 14:27–30)

Peter took his eyes off Jesus and lost his spiritual focus. Peter did not "innervate" enough "spiritual" muscles to give him the strength he needed to believe Jesus. He lost his sight and focus of Jesus and began to sink.

Figures 3-21 and **3-22**, are a couple of examples of other muscle of the body that demonstrate particular strength factors. **Figure 3-21** is a graphic illustration of the Latissimus Dorsi and Pectoralis Major. The Latissimus Dorsi is a large muscle of the back. It sits in the back of the body, but operates the arms (shoulder joint), as it attaches to the humerus. The Latissimus Dorsi "twists" or folds as it passes under the arm, creating a portion of muscle that actually forms the posterior aspect of the "arm pit". Thus, the most distal muscle fiber emerging from the back attaches most proximally onto the humerus. By having this arrangement, the muscle fibers of the Latissimus Dorsi are longer. Remember, the longer muscle fibers are, the stronger they are. If the muscle fibers emerging from the upper part of the back just went straight under the arm and attached to the upper part of the humerus, these muscle fibers would be shorter and the overall strength capability of the Latissimus would be weaker.

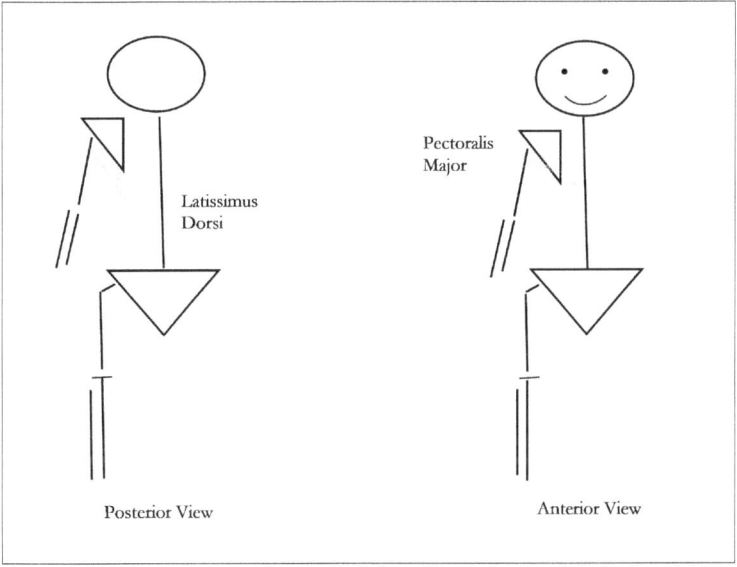

Figure 3-21. Illustration showing the Latissimus Dorsi muscle of the back and the Pectoralis Major muscle of the chest. The muscle fibers of the Latissimus Dorsi cross and form the posterior fold of the arm pit. The muscle fibers of the Pectoralis Major cross to form the anterior fold of the arm pit

The Pectoralis Major, or "Pecs" as many people call it, is a major muscle in the chest region. The muscle fibers of the Pectoralis Major are like the Latissimus Dorsi. They emerge from farther down the chest but attach proximally, or farther up, onto the humerus. Thus, it also "twists" or folds as it passes under the arm and creates a portion of muscle that forms the anterior aspect of the "arm pit". And like the Latissimus Dorsi, this arrangement of muscle fibers makes these fibers longer, and thus, stronger. So, we have the Latissimus Dorsi in the back, and the Pectoralis Major in the front, and they work together, or in concert, to create enhanced strength capabilities of arm movement. They complement each other very well.

Figure 3-22 is a graphic illustration of the Deltoid and the Adductor muscle group. This illustration exhibits several strength factors. The Adductor muscles are a group of muscles on the inner thigh that are often referred to as "groin" muscles. These muscles travel from the lower part of the pelvis to the femur and tibia. Muscles of the adductor group include the Adductor Brevis, Adductor Longus, the Adductor Magnus, and the Gracilis.

The Adductor Brevis is a short muscle (thus minimal strength), but has a good angle of pull. The Adductor Longus is a "long" muscle, and the Gracilis also crosses the knee joint in order to attach to the tibia, and thus is a long muscle as well. Therefore, these two muscles can exhibit greater strength, although their angle of pull would not be good. And the Adductor Magnus is a big muscle. And because there is so much muscle mass, it has good strength capabilities.

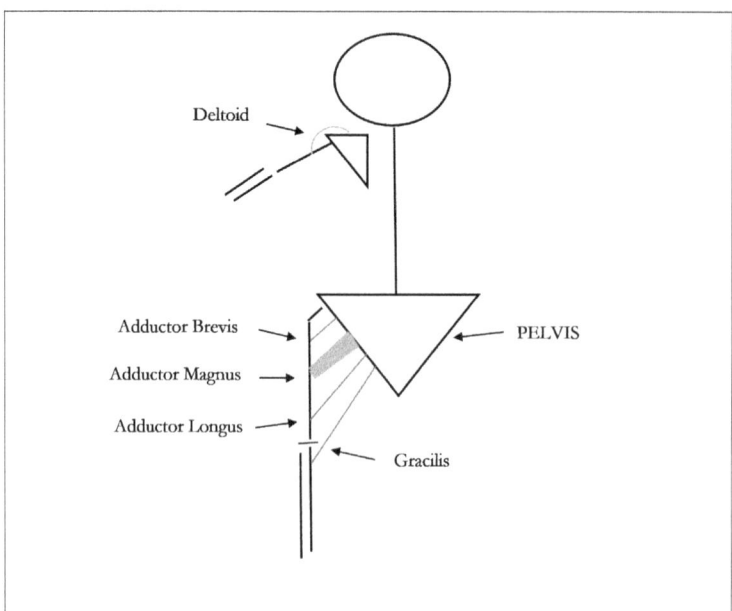

Figure 3-22. Illustration showing the Deltoid, and the Adductor muscle group (Adductor Brevis, Magnus, Longus and Gracilis).

The arm is a fairly long "lever", and thus needs considerable force and strength to lift it. The Deltoid muscle of the shoulder is a main muscle used by the shoulder (arm) to lift and elevate the arm. But the Deltoid is a fairly short muscle. And its attachment onto the humerus of the arm occurs very close to the shoulder joint and creates a poor angle of pull. These factors would not exhibit good strength characteristics.

However, the Deltoid makes up for these diminished strength capabilities by being a pennate muscle. Though it is anatomically restricted in its size and position in the body to perform its task, it can generate enough force to lift and raise the arm because it is a pennate muscle.

Remember, when raising the arm above the head, how the scapula needed to upward rotate in order to present a much-needed compression mode of force in the shoulder? Well, there must be muscle to upward rotate the scapula and there must be muscle to downward rotate the scapula. **Figure 3-23** show the Trapezius and Rhomboid muscles. The Trapezius is used by the body to rotate the scapula upward, while the Rhomboid rotates the scapula downward. Note how the muscle fibers of the Trapezius traverse the back and attach to the spine of the scapula, creating maximum efficiency for effectively moving or rotating the scapula in the desired direction.

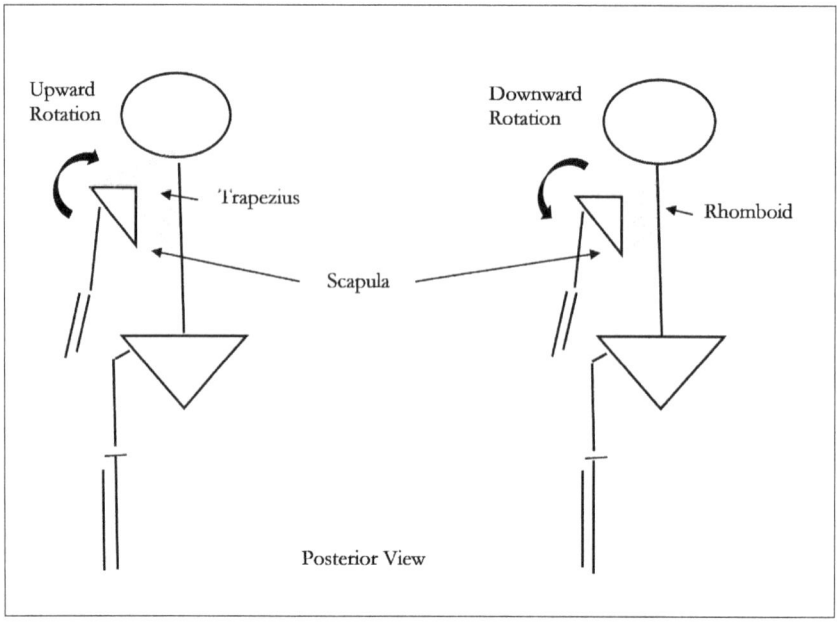

Figure 3-23. Illustration showing the relationship between the Trapezius and Rhomboid muscles. The Trapezius moves the scapula upward and the Rhomboid moves the scapula downward.

The muscle fibers of the Rhomboid slant upward from the medial border of the scapula, to effectively pull this portion of the scapula and downwardly rotate the scapula. Thus, the Trapezius and Rhomboid work opposite of each other to move the scapula up and down as we use the arm. However, when used together, the shoulder(s) can be drawn backward or "shrugged" upward. In other words, they can be used together for entirely different movements of the shoulder. Other muscles would not be needed for these functions.

We may think that our actions and behavior are exactly "opposite" from someone else. And that may be true and God uses both. However, even people with the most opposite behaviors and talents can be used together for the glory of God. This is a big world with many needs. God uses many different people with many different talents for His good will.

Throughout the body and at most joints, we will find "pairs" of muscle that work together for flexion or extension of a joint. This is to ensure an even pull of forces by the muscles on either side of the joint and enable a more efficient movement in the desired direction that is needed.

Figure 3-24 shows two muscles that flex the wrist and two muscles that extend the wrist. The Flexor Carpi Radialis and Flexor Carpi Ulnaris attach on the palm side of the wrist and on either side of the wrist in order to "flex" the wrist. (Wrist bones are referred to as "carpal" bones.) The Flexor "Carpi" Radialis attaches to the radial (bone) side of the wrist and the Flexor "Carpi" Ulnaris attaches to the ulnar (bone) side of the wrist.) The position of these attachments gives an "even pull" in flexion. That is, like two ropes attached on either side of a box, it can give an even movement in the direction of the pull. If there was only one rope attached to the side of a box, as the box was being pulled in the direction of the pull, there would be a twisting or turning of the box as it was being pulled. And, of course, two muscles pulling on either side (of the joint) can exhibit greater strength than only one muscle that is pulling from the center (of the joint).

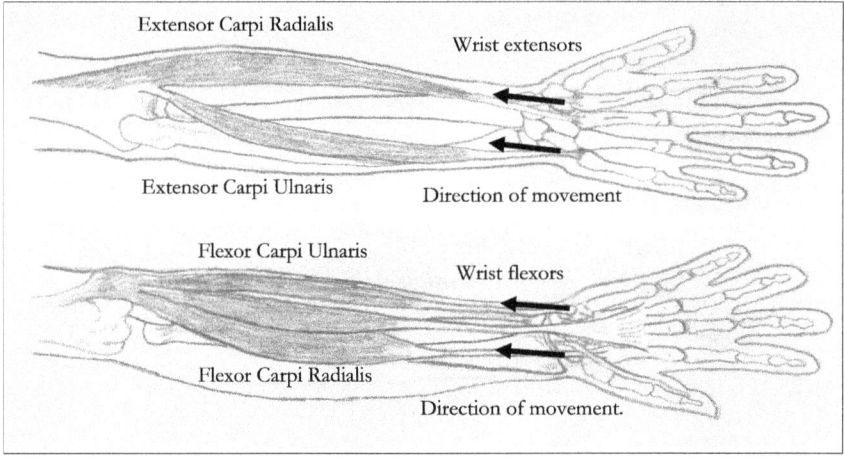

Figure 3-24. Illustration showing the wrist extensors and wrist flexors. The Extensor Carpi Radialis and Ulnaris attach to the back of the wrist. The Flexor Carpi Ulnaris and Radialis attach to the palm side of the wrist. They all attach to either side of the wrist to give an even pull in the direction of movement.

Likewise, the Extensor Carpi Radialis and Extensor Carpi Ulnaris exhibit the same feature. The Extensor Carpi Radialis and Extensor Carpi Ulnaris attach to top or back of the wrist and on the radial and ulnar side of the wrist, creating a mechanism for a smooth, efficient extension movement.

However, these extensor and flexor muscles do not necessarily need to be used solely for "flexion" and "extension". **Figure 3-25** is a graphic illustration showing how these four muscles can be used for other purposes. If one looks straight onto a fist or looks up the arm (toward the shoulder), the extensor muscles are on the top of the wrist and the flexors are on the bottom. Radial and ulnar deviation were discussed earlier. If both the Extensor Carpi Radialis and the Flexor Carpi Radialis are used together, then there is movement in the radial direction (radial deviation). And, if the Extensor Carpi Ulnaris and Flexor Carpi Ulnaris are used together, then there is movement in the ulnar direction (ulnar deviation).

In addition, for the hand and fingers to be effectively used, the wrist must be independently stabilized. By utilizing these four muscles at the same time the hand and fingers are being used, they provide stability on top and bottom, as well as to the sides of the wrist, immobilizing the wrist for hand and finger use. Thus, these muscles can have multiple functions.

Therefore, although we may name a muscle and ascribe a specific movement for it, many muscles have multiple functions, and in combination with other muscles can create an entirely different movement.

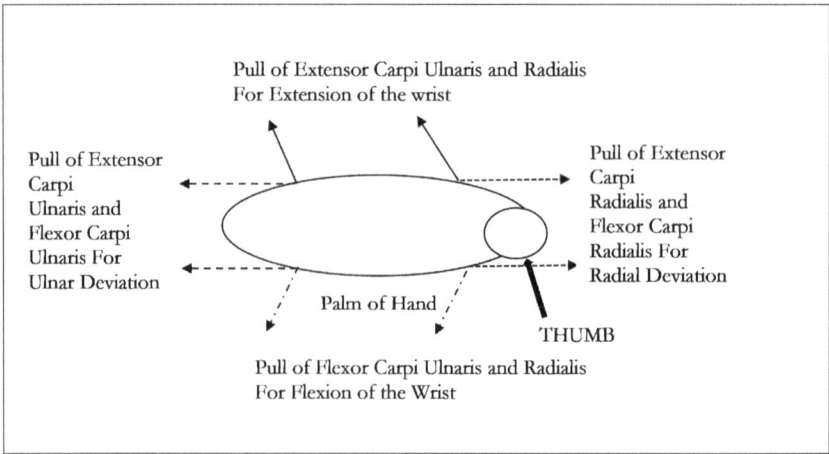

Figure 3-25. Illustration of a right hand, viewing the hand straight on, showing how the wrist flexors and extensors can also be used for radial and ulnar deviation.

The hand is an intriguing piece of anatomy. Consider all that it does. The hand and fingers can delicately work the strings of a violin, guitar or harp, move along the valves and pads of other musical instruments, glide across the keys of a piano, use a needle and thread for sewing, yet we can use the hand for heavy grasping, lifting and pounding. Isaac Newton described it this way, "In the absence of any other proof, the thumb alone would convince me of God's existence."[2] In consideration to the importance of its use, the Bible gives nearly 400 references to the hand/fingers.

Figure 3-26 is an illustration showing the muscles that operate the hand and fingers. The Flexor Digitorum Profundus and Superficialis muscles are located outside of the hand, in the lower arm (forearm). Therefore, these muscles are long muscles and thus, strong. These muscles can provide great strength for grasping and holding. There is a Profundus and Superficialis for each finger, giving great control for using any individual finger, or combining several for a specific task.

The Extensor Digitorum muscle is also located outside the hand in the lower arm. But it acts "collectively" on the fingers and joints, giving extension capabilities for all fingers at once. Then there are the Lumbricals. The muscle of the Lumbrical is in the hand. But the tendon moves up and onto the top of the fingers, merging with the Extensor muscle and another structure.

This other structure is the Dorsal Hood. The Dorsal Hood acts like a weaved basket, sitting on top of the finger. As the joints are flexed and fingers curl, as if to grasp or hold a suitcase handle, tremendous force passes through these finger structures. The Dorsal Hood acts like an auxiliary support. The Extensor muscle is also attached to the Dorsal Hood, and in this finger "configuration", it is stretched (becoming longer), giving it extra strength, while the Lumbricals are also pulling and have tension on the Dorsal Hood. The position of the Dorsal Hood on the top of the fingers, as well as the combined tension and strength given it by the Lumbricals and Extensor and muscle, make for a rather unique anatomy, giving the fingers the structural integrity, it needs when holding and supporting such loads.

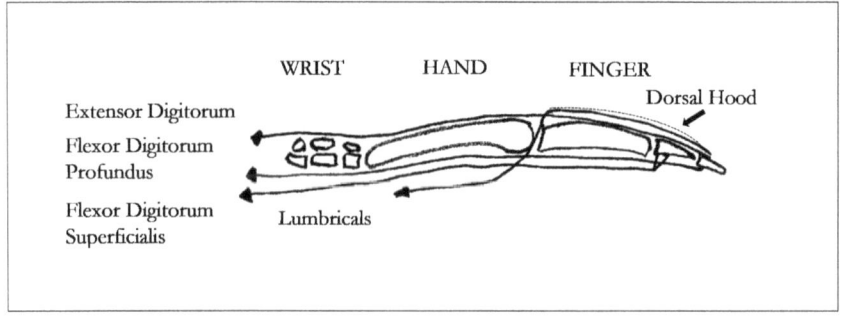

Figure 3-26. Illustration showing the muscles that operate the hand and fingers as wel as the Dorsal Hood.

In the 15th century village near Nuremberg, there lived a family with 18 children. Of the 18 children, there were two sons, Albert and his younger brother Albrecht. They both wanted to pursue their talent for art, but they both knew they would not be able to finance their studies. But they both worked out an agreement. They would flip a coin, and the winner would go off to school and study art, and the loser would work to finance it.

Albrecht, the younger won the coin toss and went off to Nuremberg to study. Albert, meanwhile went down into the mines and worked, financing his brother's studies. Albrecht was a success in his arts and crafts, often surpassing even those of his professors.

After four years, Albrecht returned to his village and a festive dinner to celebrate his return was held in his honor. During the cheerful occasion, Albrecht proposed a toast and indicated that it was Albert's turn to go and study and he would enter the mines to support him. However, Albert refused, citing his gnarled and arthritic hands. Working in the mines had taken its toll on Alberts hands, and he would be unable to pursue his passion for the arts. It was too late for him.

More than 450 years later, Albrecht Durer's works of masterful portraits, sketchings, woodcuts, and engravings can be seen around the world in private collections and in museums. But there is one etching that is especially significant. We know it as "The Praying Hands". It is believed that, in honor of his brother's sacrifice for him to be able to study art, Albercht painstakingly drew his brother's abused hands with palms together and gnarled fingers stretched upward. Since then, many figures and sculptures have been made, using this etching as a model, and have been the inspiration of many. The hand indeed, is a powerful tool!

In addition to the description and shapes of the 206 bones, practically every muscle of the 706 muscle groups in the body can be described in some form or fashion, labeled and defined, by the strength factors of muscle length, muscle diameter, point of insertion and angle of pull. Most have a defined function, yet in combination with other muscles can create movement in other directions. The design of the skeletal system, with its boney shapes and anatomical positioning, and the strength characteristics of muscles, derived from their lengths, angles of pull and points of insertion, all work together to provide maximum strength then we need it most, and yet provide maximum mobility and stability when we need it most. Truly, for support and movement, the Skeletal System and the Muscular System are *fitly framed together.*

REFERENCES

1. James B. Irwin. *High Flight Foundation*. https://www.highflightfoundation.org/ (accessed April 23, 2015).
2. "Quotes from Isaac Newton". Biography Online. https://www.biographyonline.net/scientists/quotes-newton.html (accessed April 30, 2018).

[The author notes that there are many internet sites that cite quotations from others. And some of these quotations are questioned by current groups for various reasons and intents.]

CHAPTER 4

CONTROL

Did you not hear long ago how I made it? From ancient times that I formed it? Now I have brought it to pass, that you should be for crushing fortified cities into heaps of ruins. Therefore, their inhabitants had little power. – Isaiah 37: 26-27

It is evident that for the Christian, there is little doubt that God not only created the world, but that He is still in control. While we ponder world events of today, with its anarchy and evil actions that take place, and though it seems that the world is spinning out of control, Christians can take comfort that God is still in charge. He is still in control! And though we may understand that God certainly has more power and control of the universe than man does, as part of our creation, God included anatomy to give us control of our physical bodies and our own sense of "power".

And as God created man, part of that anatomy not only included Organization, Maintenance, Support and Movement, but also of Control. There must be some aspect of our anatomy that controls body functions. After all, we do not tell our bones when to grow, or keep reminding our heart to beat. And females did not wake up one morning and decide to grow their breasts that day. All the anatomical and physiological processes are deliberately and specifically controlled. Some control must be done in immediate response to some stimulus, while other actions take place over a longer period of time. But they all must be coordinated.

The body is constantly reacting and adjusting to internal, as well as external, changes. Messages are conveyed throughout the body for interpretation, integration and ultimate regulation and control. Nervous System and the Endocrine System are the two regulatory and control systems of the body. The Nervous System uses neurons for quick messaging and reaction, while the Endocrine System uses endocrine glands and hormones for a slower response. Both systems can regulate body functions and give the body complete control of its twelve organ systems.

The Nervous System

The Nervous System is the body's principle immediate control and integrating center. It can be divided in various components for study. These include the Central Nervous System and the Peripheral Nervous System. The Peripheral Nervous System can be further divided into the Somatic and the Autonomic Nervous system. **Figure 4-1** illustrates the organization of the Nervous System.

The Central Nervous System is made up of the brain and spinal cord, whereas the Peripheral Nervous System consists of the nerves that go out of the Central System and into the rest of the body. These nerves serve the body for sensory and movement functions. The Somatic Nervous System include all the nerves that are outside of the Central Nervous system and out in the body. Nerve cells, or neurons of the Central Nervous System, cannot regenerate or reproduce if they are damaged. They do not have the ability to repair or restore the damaged area to its original good state. This is why injuries to the brain or spinal cord are so serious. Paralysis and death can result from damage to neurons of the Central Nervous System.

Neurons of the Peripheral Nervous System have the same genetic material as neurons of the Central Nervous System. However, neurons of the Somatic Nervous System can regenerate and survive injury.

They can repair and restore the injured area back to the original, good state. There are examples of fingers and limbs being amputated and re-attached. Like broken telephone wires, neurons of the Somatic Nervous System can be "sewn together" and repaired.

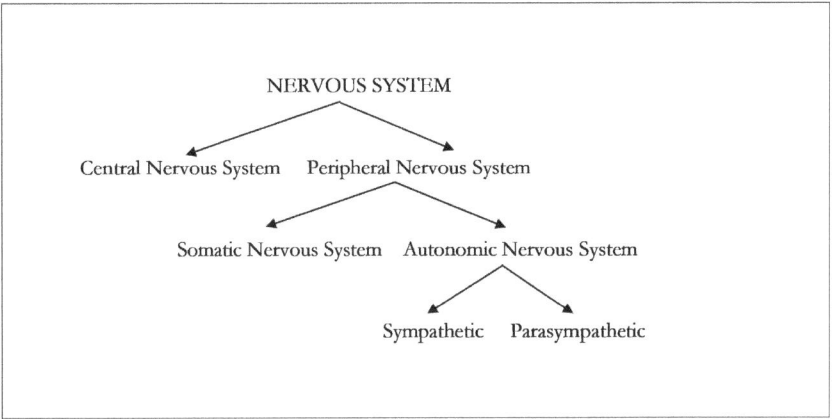

Figure 4-1. Organization of the Nervous System. It can be broken down into the Central Nervous System and the Peripheral Nervous System, and the Somatic and Autonomic Nervous Systems.

Within the Somatic System we find the Autonomic Nervous System. The Autonomic Nervous System regulates activities "automatically". Examples of this would be changes of pupil size, dilation/constriction of blood vessels, adjustments in heart rate and blood pressure, as well as movements of the gastrointestinal track. There are two parts of the Autonomic Nervous System. Increased "excitement", resulting in an increased heart rate and blood pressure, pupil dilation and decreased gastrointestinal movement is controlled by the Sympathetic System. A "calming effect" of the body, or a back to "normal" state, is controlled by the Parasympathetic System.

The Parasympathetic Nervous System can be called "rest and digest" (R & D), whereas the Sympathetic Nervous System can be called "fright, flight or fight" (F, F, F). Even in the "rest and digest" part, the body is still active, as he body "rests" to digest and absorb food. When the body is in "fright, fight or flight" mode, the body's primary responsibility is to provide the energy needed to either "flight or "fight", in response to the "fright". And in doing so it, then, shuts down things like digestion, and increases metabolism, as well as increases respiration, heart rate and blood pressure in order to provide more glucose and energy in the blood, and then sends more blood to the muscles where they can be quickly used.

For example, in a possible "emergency" situation where you may be "frightened", you may have to flee or "flight", or stay and "fight". In either case, it will require additionally more energy than what your body is producing at that moment. In that response, your metabolism increases, providing more energy. In other words, without having to "think" about it, your body takes a "preemptive" approach and is "automatically" prepared for the response to that emergency. And after the "emergency" is over, the Parasympathetic System can get the body back to "normal".

"The Lord is my rock and my fortress and my deliverer; my God, my strength in whom I will trust" (Psalm 18:2). It is comforting to know we have an "automatic" nervous system that can "pre-prepare", so that in times of need, we are already "ready", for what is about to confront us.

Neuron

The essential functional part of the nervous system is the nerve cell or neuron. The neuron can propagate an impulse or signal message from one end of it to the other. Most of the length of a neuron is made up of structures called axons and dendrites. The length of these neurons can range from a few micrometers to almost three feet.

The speed at which an impulse or signal can travel can also vary. "Normal" impulse speeds are generally 1.5 to 30 feet per second. These speeds are routine within the brain and spinal cord. The distances that these impulses need to travel are very short. But greater speeds are needed outside the Central Nervous System. The arms and legs are long extremities, and the distances the neural impulses need to travel are greater. Sensory and motor neurons that serve these parts of the body must be able to travel faster. These neurons indeed have a special way they can accomplish a greater speed of impulse that is needed.

Surrounding the long axons and dendrites of neurons are special cells called Schwann's cells. These cells encircle the axons and dendrites and collectively form a covering called myelin. In between these Schwann's cells are small gaps or nodes that allow for the propagation of the impulse down the axon or dendrite. But since these gaps or nodes are farther apart, it helps the propagation of the impulse to travel faster. Impulse speed of myelinated neurons can reach speeds of 360 feet per second, or from 12 to 250 times faster than nonmyelinated neurons. Neurons that interact with other neurons within the spinal cord and brain are not myelinated. Therefore, they are not white, but gray. Therefore, we sometimes speak of the brain and neurons of the brain as "gray matter".

Neurotransmitters

But neurons that can propagate an impulse or signal down its length is only part of the story. At the end of the neuron, when the impulse has reached the "end of the line", it stimulates the release of neurotransmitters, or chemicals, that can affect another neuron, or organ, or other body tissue that can respond to the neurotransmitter. And for these receiving neurons, or cells of organs of other body tissue, to receive the impulse or message, they must have special receptors. The space between the end of a neuron (that is releasing the neurotransmitter) and the neuron, cell of an organ, or other body tissue that is receiving the neurotransmitter, is called the synapse.

Neurotransmitters have a specific molecular shape and the receptor sites must have a complimentary molecular shape for the neurotransmitter to bind to, and work. A particular neurotransmitter will not work if trying to bind to a different receptor site (that does not match its shape). Thus, there are specific transmitters and specific receivers for specific purposes. Thus far, about fifty different neurotransmitters have been identified in the body.

An example of one of these neurotransmitters is acetyl choline. For a muscle to contract and a movement to occur, a neuron would traverse the body and end on a muscle fiber (cell). The neuron would release acetyl choline. The acetyl choline would then bind to a receptor site on the muscle fiber (cell), initiating the contraction process of the muscle. Only the muscle would have the receptor sites that are complimentary to the acetyl choline, and thus, only the muscle would respond to acetyl choline in this region of the body. Acetyl choline is also used by the autonomic nervous system to bring the body back to "calm" after an excited state has taken place.

Other examples of neurotransmitters include: dopamine, where too little results in Parkinson's disease and too much leads to schizophrenia; serotonin, which affects sleep, appetite and mood; norepinephrine, considered a stimulant which is used by the autonomic nervous system to increase heart rate and respiration and reduce blood flow to the gastrointestinal area.

We are like neurotransmitters. Each of us have differing speech and mannerisms. Talents that may appeal to some, but not others. But God uses each of us to match and compliment those He chooses for us to interact with. "For as we have many members in one body, but all the members do not have the same function, so we, being many, are one body in Christ, and individually members of one another. Having then gifts differing according to the grace that is given to us, let us use them ..." (Romans 12:4–6).

In this modern day of medicines and drugs, we now have the capability of making chemicals (drugs) that can "mimic" neurotransmitters. For example, pain relievers such as aspirin act like a neurotransmitter that a sensory neuron would emit and transmit a "message" that there is pain. The aspirin molecule binds to the receptor site, in effect blocking the real neurotransmitter that would ordinarily do this. With the aspirin molecule bound to the receptor site, the propagation of the impulse or message to the brain is stopped. Thus, the brain does not receive a "message" that there is pain in the area. To be sure, not all aspirin molecules bind to all receptor sites, and therefore there may still be some pain. But it has decreased the "messaging" to the brain and the pain has lessened. Other "pain relievers" may be more effective in using this mechanism to decrease messaging to the brain and therefore reduce pain.

There are other "chemicals" that can bind to other specific receptor sites of organs that can affect that organ as well. Depending on the need, specific receptor sites of specific organs and tissues can be targeted for binding, or stimulation. There are some "chemicals" (drugs) that can bind to specific receptor sites that instead of blocking the further transmission of an impulse, it propagates an impulse or message that the brain will interpret as a real sensation, but in fact is not real. Some of these chemicals are hallucinative drugs that can do severe damage to the brain and body.

Brain

The human brain weighs less than 3 pounds, yet consumes 20% of the oxygen we take in. It contains over 100 billion neurons. Each neuron may have between 1000 and 10,000 synaptic connections with other neurons in the brain. Thus, there could be as many as 100 trillion synapses in the brain.[1] To get an idea of how many "100 billion" is, if you spent $5.5 million a day, it would take you 50 years to spend $100 billion. If you wanted to spend the $100 billion in one year, you would have to spend $274 million a day! One hundred billion neurons are a lot of neurons.

The brain is the main administrative portion of body control. All integrative messages, thoughts and process take place in the brain. Even while we sleep, the brain is working to regulate and coordinate the body's many functions and their relationship to outside environment.

In a text such as this, it would be impossible to discuss the intricate details of the brain. Specifically designed, the brain not only controls and coordinates body systems and functions, it also has the capacity for thinking and reasoning. Because of the incredible thinking power and thought ability of the human brain, mankind has invented methodologies to travel on land and in space, developed the computer with all its capabilities, and developed modern medicines as well as medical and surgical techniques. Wisdom is important and good use of the thinking capabilities of the brain can benefit man.

"The fear of the Lord is the beginning of knowledge; Fools despise wisdom and instruction" (Proverbs 1:7). "My son, pay attention to my wisdom; Lend your ears to my understanding, that you may preserve discretion, and your lips may keep knowledge" (Proverbs 5:1–2). "How much better to get wisdom than gold! And get understanding is to be chosen rather than silver" (Proverbs 16:16). "Wisdom is good with an inheritance, and profitable to those who see the sun. For wisdom is a defense as money is a defense, but the excellence of knowledge is that wisdom gives life to those who have it" (Ecclesiastes 7:11–12). "Happiness is the man who finds wisdom, and the man who gains understanding" (Proverbs 3:13). "Get wisdom! Get understanding! Do not forget, nor turn away from the words of my mouth. Do not forsake her, and she will preserve you; love her, and she will keep you. Wisdom is the principle thing; therefore get wisdom. And with all your getting, get understanding" (Proverbs 4:5–7).

Sometimes it seems that mankind thinks it knows more than it actually does. We may live in an age of increasing knowledge, but our ability to think and reason is limited. "But the natural man does not receive the things of the Spirit of God, for they are foolishness to him; nor can he know them because they are spiritually discerned. But he who is spiritual judges all things, yet he himself is rightly judged by no one. For who has known the mind of the Lord that he may instruct Him? But we have the mind of Christ" (1 Corinthians 2:14–16).

In using the brain for wisdom and thinking abilities, we often refer to the brain as the "mind". "And Jesus said to him, you shall love the Lord with all your heart, with all your soul and with all you mind. This is the first and great commandment" (Matthew 22:37–38). Therefore, the mind is very important. Our minds eventually dictate a priority of what is important to us. Sometimes we may say, "I've made up my mind, so don't confuse me with facts." We certainly can be swayed in directions that are not good, simply because we let emotions control the mind rather than facts. Our minds can be perverted and corrupt, and cause self-glory, and certainly cannot compare to the mind and "thinking" of God."

> Where were you when I (God) laid the foundations of the world? Tell me if you have understanding. Who determined its measurements? Surely you know! Do you know the ordinances of the heavens? Can you set their dominion over the earth? Can you lift up your

voice to the clouds, that an abundance of water may cover you? Can you send out lightnings, that they may go and say to you, 'Here we are!' Who has put wisdom in the mind or who has put understanding in their heart? Who can number the clouds by wisdom? Or who can pour out the bottles of heaven, when the dust hardens in clumps and the clods cling together? Shall the one who contends with the Almighty correct Him? He who rebukes God, let him answer it. (Job 38:4–5, 33-38; 40:2)

Though I were righteous, my own mouth would condemn me; Though I were blameless, it would prove me perverse. (Job 9:20).

And you do not know the way of the wind, or how the bones grow in the womb of her that is with child, so you do not know the works of God who makes everything. (Ecclesiastes 11:5)

God has given us a description of our minds. He says it is alienated (Colossians 1:21), blinded (2 Corinthians 3:14), corrupted (1 Timothy 6:5), darkened (Ephesians 4:18), debased (Romans 1:28), deceived (Colossians 2:8), defiled (Titus 1:15), deluded (Colossians 2:4), futile (Ephesians 4:17). These descriptions do not paint a pretty picture of the mind of mankind. However, God also says that our minds can be obedient (Hebrews 8:10), willing (1 Chronicles 28:9), and have the mind of Christ (1 Corinthians 2:16).

The fact of the matter is that without proper understanding of God's Word, non-believers as well as believers, can make up their own ideas and thoughts, which of course can be wrong. In their attempt to "spread the Gospel", good intending Christians can be significant stumbling blocks to the world. "Wisdom is better than weapons of war; but one sinner destroys much good" (Ecclesiastes 9:18). "But beware lest somehow this liberty of yours become a stumbling block to those who are weak … And because of your knowledge shall the weak brother perish, for whom Christ died?" (1 Corinthians 8:9, 11).

Although the human brain is used for thought, it also a vessel of pleasure. Pleasure appeals to the flesh and generates "physical highs" of specific body parts. Whereas the spirit is a whole and not the sum of many parts like the human body, the whole body can be influenced if any one of the many "pleasures" it enjoys. The body may have its five senses: hearing, sight, smell, taste, touch. But there are other "pleasures' the mind can enjoy. Such pleasures may be listening to a beautiful song, watching a colorful sunset, the sensation of a soft kiss upon the cheek by a young grandchild.

The part of the brain that controls basic emotions such as pleasure, fear, anger, hunger, sex and other feelings is called the Limbic System. It is a complex system of nerves and other structures that are found deep in the center of the brain. This system is important. Through its involvement with our emotions, it controls much of our behavior. Much of the development of this system takes place as we grow and develop in our childhood. There is much that can influence it. What may please one person may not please another.

Many believe this is where the human "conscience" resides. Many would have us to "follow our conscience". But this philosophy is flawed. The conscience can be trained. It is trained by the flesh, and we have previously seen other works of the flesh. A light bulb (with electricity) will generate its own light. However, a skylight needs "another" light (like the sun) in order to work. The conscience is like the skylight. We often think that the conscience is (or should be) our guiding light, shining and directing us in our life and behaviors. But this is not true. It is the conscious that needs the light, the guiding and direction. Thus, it is not the conscious that truly leads, but rather, what has "enlightened", trained and directed the conscious that really leads us.

Pleasure in the spiritual sense, is derived differently. The spirit is one and not like the physical, a sum of the parts. The physical has a beginning and an end. As such, there must be a continual addition of "pleasure" that appeals to the fleshly body. However, the spirit has no beginning or end. There is no limbic system or conscience in the spirit to control its behavior.

Much can be said and studied about human behavior. Although there are many acts of kind and decent human behavior, one does not have to look to far to see its depravity. Medical psychiatry and psychology are growing sciences. Isaac Newton once said, "I can calculate the motion of the heavenly bodies, but not the madness of people."[2] It has been said that, "Sometimes we need a check-up from the neck up."

Spinal Cord

The spinal cord is the main "conduit" from the brain to the nerves, which go out into the body tissues. It is only about eighteen inches long and does not even travel the entire length of the spine, ending at about the L_2 level in the lower back. Neural impulses enter the spinal cord from the outer portion of the body via the Peripheral (Somatic) Nervous System, where incoming "sensory nerves" bring information from the body (arms and legs) and pass it on to the spinal cord (and brain). Outgoing "motor nerves" supply conscious, voluntary control of skeletal muscles, which provide movement for the body. In cases of a reflex arc, a signal can be immediately and spontaneously sent back out to the body at the same time as the signal is traveling up the spinal cord.

Man has the twelve different "body systems" and various body "organs". And we have five senses of touch, smell, taste, sight and hearing that are manifest from our nervous system. But that which we feel or sense as "pleasure" that appeals to the flesh (physical "highs"), originates in the limbic system of the brain, deep within the hypothalamus. But the limbic system receives input from sense organs such as eyes, ear, nose, etc. And as such, since our "flesh" is simply the sum of the parts, "pleasure" can begin from any of these parts.

Special Senses

Man has five senses that are considered essential to life. These include, sight, hearing, taste, smell and touch (feeling). It is certainly essential to touch or feel, especially heat and cold. Man must be able to "sense" the environment in order to respond appropriately.

Touch, Pain, Heat, Cold

The skin is richly supplied with cutaneous skin receptors. Located near the surface of the skin are small encapsulated nerve endings called Meissner's corpuscles. These small disc-looking sensors are receptors for discriminative touch, allowing us to become aware of light touch, such as a fly on the skin or even the touch of our clothing. In addition to sensing light touch it can give us a pattern of feeling, helping us distinguish between a smooth piece of plastic and sand paper.

Embedded deeper into the skin there are Pacinian corpuscles, which help us discern deeper touch or pressure, alerting us to bumps and possible excessive force on the skin. There are also Thermoreceptors that sense heat and cold, and Nociceptors (the prefix "noci" meaning to harm) or pain receptors, that can sense tissue damage and pain. These are scattered throughout the dermis of the skin.

Found in various regions of the cardiovascular "tubing" such as arteries, veins and capillaries are Chemoreceptors, which respond to "chemical" changes such as increases or decreases in oxygen, carbon dioxide or pH of cellular environments. And found within the joints there are Mechanoreceptors, which can discern joint (limb) movement through acceleration and mechanical forces. Such sensory structures help the body perceive and recognize its position in space, and its movement. Such sensory perception is not easily artificially reproduced.

The body goes to great lengths to monitor its many chemical and mechanical activities and recognize the status of the surrounding environment. Such careful attention and focus help to guard against potential hazards and dangers. Such is the same for our spiritual lives. "Be sober and vigilant; because your adversary the devil walks about like a roaring lion, seeking whom he may destroy" (1 Peter 5:8).

Smell, Taste

Located in the roof of the nasal cavity is olfactory epithelium, the organ of smell. Olfactory sensory neurons are surrounded by supporting cells. On one end of each olfactory sensory neuron are olfactory cilia, or small hair like structures, covered in mucous. This mucous helps capture and dissolve airborne odorants that the nose "sniffs" in. The olfactory cilia are then stimulated by the captured odorants, and the sensory impulse is transferred to the other end of the sensory neuron. The opposite end of the sensory neuron collectively makes up the olfactory nerve, which then sends the "smell" message to the brain for interpretation.

There are essentially three types of taste "buds" on the tongue. These are the Vallate papillae, larger rough structures located on the back of the tongue, Foliate papillae, located in the back sides of the tongue, and Fungiform papillae, smaller taste "buds" that are located over most of the surface of the tongue. All of these "taste buds" are surrounded by epithelial cells, designed to support and protect the taste "buds". Often a food or drink placed in to the mouth can be too hot or cold and these sensitive sensory receptors need protecting.

In addition, taste is 80% smell.[2] Undoubtedly certain foods have certain, specific smells. When nasal congestion blocks access of these food odorants to the olfactory receptors, food tastes bland. Temperature and texture of foods can also enhance or detract from their taste. Therefore, the mouth also contains thermoreceptors, mechanoreceptors and nociceptors. Thus, taste and smell work together for the total enhancement of eating and tasting experience. And, of course, the epithelial cells of the tongue, and the supporting cells of the olfactory epithelium, help to support and protect these important special sensory anatomies. It is a very clever design.

Being able to recognize these smells and tastes are paramount in the ability to distinguish the good and the bad of foods and smells.

We certainly want to avoid those things that may harm us. On the other hand, we want to appreciate and enjoy the pleasures of eating. In the life of a Christian, we certainly need to able to distinguish and recognize those things that are harmful so we can avoid the bad, but we should also relish and enjoy the goodness of the good that God can give us.

Sight

In California there is a powerful telescope located high in the mountains. It is said to be so powerful that if someone climbed up the Empire State Building in New Your City and struck a match, the telescope could detect the glow of it. Also, the Hubble Telescope circling the earth has been responsible for seeing countless stars and galaxies of our vast universe. Thus, imagine the value of sight.

Anatomically, we can receive sight only one way, and that is through the eye. It is obvious that sight can only occur if there is light. Light is not like sound. Sound, is a literal movement or vibration of physical "air". And this vibration of physical air can be "picked up" by the ear to discern sounds. Hearing will be discussed later.

However, visible light is small part of the electromagnetic spectrum, which includes wavelengths of radio and television, telephone, ultraviolet, X-Ray and gamma radiation. The eye must have specific anatomy to convert these wavelengths of visible light to signals or neural inputs so the brain can recognize what is being seen. This process is very delicate. Light must pass through the eyes unobstructed and interpreted without any interference. If there is a blindfold or obstruction covering the eye, the eye cannot see. If any aspect of the anatomy is flawed, there can be no perfect vision.

Our eyes are like a "stereo" camera. We have two eyes, strategically spaced apart, to give us "stereo vision or depth perception … The eye itself is shaped like a round golf ball. The outer white portion is called the sclera. Eye movement is finely controlled to not only move the eye to "look around" and see, but also to track and smoothly follow a moving object.

The front of the eye, instead of being white, is clear (obviously to let the light shine through). This portion of the sclera is called the cornea. The light initially passes through the cornea in its way toward the back of the eye, which contains the functional unit of a seeing eye, called the retina. But before that, the amount or intensity of the light entering the eye must be controlled.

The iris, or that part of the eye that gives it its color, is a diaphragm that responds to the intensity of the light. The greater the intensity of the light, it creates a smaller aperture to allow less light to enter. The less the intensity of the light, it creates a larger aperture, to allow more light to enter.

After the amount of light is controlled, the focusing mechanism must take place. The intensity-controlled light now passes through a lens, which then focuses the light onto the back of the eye containing the retina. The focusing by the lens takes place by muscles that can change the shape of the lens, thereby adjusting the focusing of the light. As the aging process continues, these muscles can weaken and the lens can become more brittle, making focusing more difficult. This may lead to the need for glasses.

Since focusing is so important, the overall shape of the eye is important, in that the shape of the eye should remain constant. If the shape of the eye changes, then the focusing process cannot take place. Thus, inside the front of the eye there is a water fluid called aqueous humor, and inside the back of the eye is a thicker, gel-like substance called vitreous humor. The function of these liquids is to keep pressure on the inside of the eye and help maintain the shape of the eye.

After the light has entered the eye, intensity controlled and focus obtained, it is now ready to be "captured and interpreted" in the retina. The retina contains a dark layer of tissue called dark pigment layer. It is black, of course, to not reflect any light. It would be detrimental to sight if once inside the eye light were to be able to "bounce" around and be reflected into other regions of the eye. The light then passes through three important cells. These are the ganglionic cell, the bipolar cell, and finally the rod (for black or white vision) or cone (for color vision).

Figure 4-2 illustrates the arrangement of the ganglion cell, the bipolar cell and the rod or cone. These components make up the internal anatomy of the retina, the functional part of the eye that allows us to see. The light literally passes through the ganglion cell, then through the bipolar cell, before reaching and stimulating the rod or cone. Only then can the rod or cone cell be properly stimulated to pass that light message on to the brain via the optic nerve for interpretation. The rod or cone then stimulates the bipolar cell and then the bipolar cell stimulates the ganglion cell. It is the ganglion cells which collectively makeup the optic nerve, which leaves the eye and goes to the brain for interpretation. It is with this sensitive process whereby we not only see "light", but also interpret what it is that we "see". If any one part of this system fails, we cannot see.

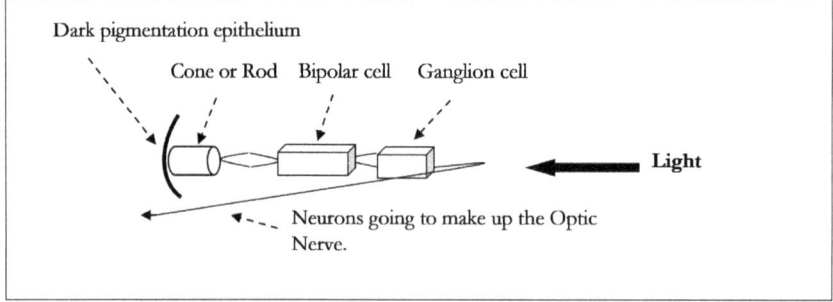

Figure 4-2. Illustration showing the internal anatomy of the retina of the eye. The dark pigment epithelium helps to absorb light and not scatter light. Light passes through the Ganglion cell, Bipolar cell, and Rod or Cone. The light stimulates the Rod or Cone. The Rod or Cone stimulates the Bipolar cell. The Bipolar cell stimulates the Ganglion cell, which sends the message to the brain via the optic nerve.

There is a story told in Mark 10:46–52.

> And they came to Jericho: and as he went out of Jericho with his disciples and a great number of people, blind Bartimeus, son of Timeus sat by the highway begging. And when he heard that it was Jesus of Nazareth, he began to cry out and say, "Jesus, Son of David, have mercy on me." And many charged him that he should keep quiet; but he cried the more a great deal, "Son of David, have mercy on me." So Jesus stood still,

and commanded him to be called. Then they called the blind man, saying to him, "Be of good cheer, He is calling you." And throwing aside his garment, he rose and came to Jesus. So Jesus answered and said to him, "What do you want me to do for you?" The blind man said unto him, "Rabboni, that I might receive my sight." And Jesus said to him, "Go your way; your faith has made you well." And immediately he received his sight, and followed Jesus on the road.

Scripture uses this story as analogous to our spiritual blindness. The Hubble Telescope can see far into the universe, but it was not always like that. From the beginning, there was a "flaw" that prevented the great telescope from "seeing" into the universe. The problem was located and fixed. Soon, it began to send countless images that have captured the awe and amazement of scientist and lay persons alike.

Light reveals what is on the floor in front of us to be seen. God's light allows us to see life in its length, width and height. In all its goodness and fulness. We may not be able "to see" our sins because our "spiritual eyes" are covered. The functional unit of our eyes, the retina, consists of a dark pigment layer and three cells. We cannot interpret light that is simply bouncing around and reflected everywhere, thus the dark pigment layer is needed. And all three cells must be functioning correctly. After that, there is "interpretation". If any one thing is not properly working, then our sight is limited.

We may see ourselves as a righteous, upright, "good" person. But the Bible says otherwise. "But we are all as an unclean thing, and all our righteousness are as filthy rags …." (Isaiah 64:6). If you notice in the story in Mark, the man was physically blind and poor. Man, in general, as a sinner, is blind, and poor spiritually. However, Jesus had compassion on him and healed him. Essentially all we can do is plea for mercy (from God). We have clothing that in our opinion is righteousness, but in the sight of God it is filthy rags. Notice that the blind man cast his garments away (as filthy rags) before he came to Jesus.

As the eyes are to the body, so is faith to the soul. The eyes can give direction and alert the body to dangers. It not only sees the bad things that can destroy the body, it can also see the good things in which to rejoice. But in either case, the eye must be protected and be made sensitive to the things that can harm it.

Eyelashes protrude from the eyelids. Even as a spec of dusts approaches the eye, the eyelash is made aware of it and automatically closes the eyelid in order to protect the eye. In other words, the eye becomes sensitive immediately for its protection. Even if a small speck of dust does manage to get into the eye, not only the eye, but the whole body reacts immediately and focuses its attention to the irritation of the eye. Other body areas may be sensitive, but may not react fast enough or not at all which can cause great harm or even death to the body.

Today's world has become insensitive to sin. The spiritual eye of faith has been compromised and does not see the dangers that are before it. What use to be considered sin is no longer considered sin. It is interesting that to get rid of light you need total darkness. But to get rid of darkness you only need a little light. How we view the light with our spiritual eyes are important.

Certain physical issues such as cataracts can affect vision. A cataract is a clouding of the lens in the eye, which affects the light passing through the lens. This can lead to a decrease in vision. Cataracts often develop slowly and can affect one or both eyes. Oftentimes, the cataracts develop so slowly we do not notice until after a period of time, we simply cannot see so well. This development is like the atherosclerosis is of the heart discussed previously. The sense of sight can give us a full, more complete life, safe life. However, if anything hinders our sight, we cannot see dangers that lay before us, nor will we be able to see the good things of life, and thus, not fully experience the life God has given us.

It is the desire of God that we fully experience what He has placed before us. "That the God of our Lord Jesus Christ, the Father of glory, may give you the spirit of wisdom and the revelation in the knowledge of him: The eyes of your understanding being enlightened; that you may know what is the hope of his calling, and what are the riches of his glory of his inheritance in the saint's" (Ephesians 1:17–18).

The tear glands are located above and to the outer edge of the eye. When we "blink" and shut the eyelids, the eyelids act like a "squeegee" and wipe or sponge the tear toward the corner of the eye near the nose. There is a "funnel-like" structure and small hole located there called the lacrimal caruncle and lacrimal punctum. These structures collect and drains away the tear into the sinuses.

Besides the normal moisturizing that tears give the eye, the shedding tears in crying are acts of deep emotion. It is a healing process. "Weeping may endure for a night, but Joy comes in the morning" (Psalm 30:5). It is interesting that the death and burial of Jesus occurred late in the day and toward the darkness of night. But it was in the morning as light began to fill the sky that He arose from the grave!

However, it often seems that there are more people who weep over dead animals than over a sermon preached on the cross and knowing that souls will die and go to hell. In many cases, our tears are somehow paralyzed when we need them the most!

Ear

We have two ears and only one mouth. Therefore, it has been stated that we should listen twice as much as we speak. "So then my beloved, let every man be swift to hear, and slow to speak ...." (James 1:19).

Unlike visible light, that is a small portion of the electromagnetic spectrum, sound is simply the movement or vibration of the air. Light may travel through the vacuum expanse of outer space, but sound cannot. The hearing portion of our ear acts much like a transducer. It takes mechanical movement of the air and converts it to electrical signals.

Sound waves are literally "funneled" into our ears with the outer portion of the ear called the pinna. Its shape and size help direct the vibrating air into our ear via a tube called the auditory canal. The collection of vibrating sound waves then strikes the fabric of a skin like structure called the tympanic membrane (we may call it the "ear drum"). This tympanic membrane will then vibrate against a bone called the malleus, which in turn will strike and vibrate a second bone called the incus, which in turn will strike and vibrate a third bone called the stape.

This final bone lies up against the functional unit of the ear called the cochlea. The cochlea is a coiled, snail looking structure that contain a fluid and a "floating" membrane. Below this membrane are cells called "hair cells". As the stape vibrates it transfers this vibration to the fluid which moves the membrane. As this membrane vibrates and moves, it will touch the hairs of the hair cells. The combination and simultaneous arrangement of this stimulation is what will determine the nature of the sound. Just like the summation of all the ganglion cells made the optic nerve, these hairs cells make up the cochlea nerve, or hearing nerve, that goes to the brain for interpretation.

Since sound it the result of vibrating air, the relative pressure of the air is important. The separation and distance between air molecules must be the same on both sides of the tympanic membrane. The sense of hearing can change dramatically if this pressure is not regulated and "balanced". A tube runs from inside the ear to the pharynx in the nasal cavity. This tube is called the Eustachian tube. It serves to neutralize the pressure in the auditory canal which is on the other side of the tympanic membrane. Sometimes, chewing gum, opening the mouth or holding the nose while gently blowing can help speed up this process when flying or going up or downhills fast.

Oftentimes young children and babies get inner ear infections. A general mechanism of this problem occurs when the child drinks milk or consumes other non-solid foods. The angle of the Eustachian tube is not as great in a child as in an adult. This angle can be made worse if the baby or child is laying down. The milk or non-solid food can then migrate up this Eustachian tube and remain there and harbor bacteria that can lead to an infection. A physician may have to place a small tube through the tympanic membrane to allow for drainage and pain relief.

Just like sight, if anything is wrong with any part of this hearing anatomy, hearing can become impaired. Childhood issues and "tubes" can affect the tympanic membrane later in life, making the tympanic membrane not vibrate as effectively. In addition, the aging process can make the bones of the ear more brittle and less effective, reducing hearing.

There is an old Hymn, "Open mine Eyes That I may See".

Verse: I.	"Open my eyes, that I may see Glimpses of truth Thou hast for me;
	Place in my hands the wonderful key That shall unclasp, and set me free."
Chorus:	"Silently now I wait for Thee, Ready, my God, Thy will to see:
	Open my eyes, illumine me, Savior divine!"
Verse 2.	Open my ears, that I may hear Voices of truth Thou sendest clear;
	And while the wave-notes fall on my ear, Everything false will disappear."
Verse 3.	"Open my mouth, and let me bear Gladly the warm truth everywhere;
	Open my heart, and let me prepare Love with Thy children thus to share."
Verse 4	"Open my mind, that I may read More of Thy love in word and deed;
	What shall I fear while yet Thou dost lead? Only for light from Thee I plead."

There is a story of a job posting of a telegraph operator during the time of the Great Depression. Applicants crowded into a small room. A man entered the room and took his seat with the others. Across the room was a door marked, "Private". There was the usual noise and conversations taking place among the applicant. But after only a few minutes, the man jumped up and ran to the door, opened it and went in. While the other prospective candidates were talking and waiting, the man heard the tapping on the door, in Morse code saying, "If you can hear this, come on in and you can have the job." So, the man did! He listened and heard.

The anatomy of our ears not only help us to hear, but they are also responsible for giving us our balance. There are three tubes or semicircular canals sitting above the cochlea in the inner ear. Each semicircular canal is oriented in the three different planes or directions of our world, or the X, Y, Z planes. Inside each tube is a fluid that contains small sand-like particles of calcium called otoliths. These otoliths are subject to gravity and centrifugal forces. When the body moves or is oriented a certain way with respect to the downward pull of gravity, these otoliths move. Like the hair cells of the cochlea, these hair cells will send a message to the brain as they are touched by these otoliths. Our brain can then "figure out" what is going on with the body with respect to movement and gravity.

It is interesting that as the eye utilizes three specific cells for sight to occur, the ear needs three specific bones for hearing to occur, and three semicircular canals are needed for balance to occur. In each case, seeing, hearing, and balance are important senses to the body. In seeing, hearing, and balancing in the surrounding environment, we get a greater understanding and appreciation of our body's orientation, noting a sense of gratitude and potential dangers. However, if any of these senses are adversely affected, this appreciation and understanding can be greatly diminished and our body will not know up from down!

Our nervous system is remarkable. The human brain is unmatched in the universe. Its thinking and mental abilities are limited by only ourselves … but here is the point. "For my thoughts are not your thoughts, nor are your ways My ways, says the Lord. For as the heavens are higher than the earth, so are My ways higher than your ways, and my thoughts are higher than your thoughts" (Isaiah 55:8–9).

Though we can look around us and see the technology and wonderful things that have been accomplished in this world by man, they pale in comparison to the thoughts and accomplishments of God. Although man can materially think and reason in this physical world, there are still many mistakes that are made. And if man can make mistakes in this physical world, imagine his thoughts regarding God and the spiritual world.

The Endocrine System

The Endocrine System is a control system that operates differently from the Nervous System. It is responsible for maintaining homeostasis, working with the Nervous System to help the body react to stress, and is a major regulator of growth and development, including sexual development and reproduction.

Whereas the Nervous System uses nerves for immediate feedback and response, the Endocrine System is made up of specialized tissue called endocrine glands, which secrete specialized chemical substances, called hormones, into the surrounding tissue. (That is where the name endocrine comes from. "Endo" means inside. "Exo" means outside. Exocrine glands secrete their products to outside the body. An example of an exocrine gland would be a sweat gland, where the sweat is secreted to outside the body.)

Hormones secreted by the endocrine glands are picked up by the blood and transported all over the body. However, hormones affect only specific "target cells". These target cells have compatible receptor sites that will respond only to the hormone for which it is designed, like the action of neurotransmitters in the Nervous System on their respective receptor sites.

The involvement of endocrine glands and use of hormones is a slower process than the reaction and response of the Nervous System. For example, I would doubt if any female woke up one morning, yawned, looked at herself in the mirror and said, "I think I will grow some breasts today." It does not work that way. Only in due time and as a result of other controlling events that certain endocrine glands and hormones act.

Often, Christians get impatient and want God to do something now. It took 1,500 years and forty plus different writers for God to complete the Bible, His word to us.

"Rest in the LORD, and wait patiently for Him" (Psalm 37:7). Wait on the Lord; Be of good courage, and He shall strengthen your heart; Wait, I say, on the Lord" (Psalm 27:14). "But those that wait on the Lord shall renew their strength; They shall mount up with wings like eagles, they shall run and not be weary, they shall walk and not faint" (Isaiah 40:31).

The following is a list of endocrine glands, the hormones they secrete and the actions of the hormones. As one can see from the list, there are many endocrine glands and many hormones. The actions of the hormones are very important and necessary for the development and life of an individual. The effects of the Endocrine System cannot be taken lightly.

- **Hypothalamus** – Located at the base of the brain. Releases no fewer than seven hormones which helps control the Pituitary Gland.
- **Pituitary Gland** – Located beneath the hypothalamus. Considered the master gland" of the endocrine system. Secretes *Antidiuretic Hormone (ADH)* and *Vasopressin*, which controls water retention and blood pressure; *Oxytocin*, which stimulates contraction of the uterus during childbirth and ejection of milk from the breasts; *Growth Hormone (GH)* and *Somatotropic hormone (STH)*, which controls the growth of bones and muscle and regulates protein, fat and carbohydrate synthesis and metabolism; *Prolactin*, which promotes breasts development and milk production after childbirth; *Thyroid Stimulating Hormone (TSH)*, stimulates the thyroid gland and the secretion of its hormones; *Adrenocorticotropic Hormone (ACTH)*, stimulates the Adrenal Cortex and the secretion of its hormones; *Luteinizing Hormone (LH)*, Female: stimulates production of the egg and production of progesterone and estrogen, Male: stimulates development of testes and production of testosterone; Follicle Stimulating Hormone (FSH), Female: stimulates ovarian (monthly) cycle and ovulation, Male: stimulates sperm production, Melanocyte Stimulating Hormone (MSH), controls production of the skin pigment melanin.
- **Thyroid Gland** – Located in the throat. *Thyroxine and Triiodohyroxine*, increases metabolic rate, sensitivity of cardiovascular system to sympathetic nervous system, affects

maturation and homeostasis of skeletal muscle; *Calcitonin*, lowers blood levels of calcium and phosphates.

- **Parathyroid Gland** – Located in the throat. *Parathyroid Hormone (PTH)*, Increases blood levels of calcium and phosphates.
- **Adrenal Medulla** – Located on top of the kidneys. *Epinephrine (adrenaline)*, increases heart rate, blood pressure and blood glucose level, regulates capillary blood flow to skeletal muscles and gastrointestinal area; *Norepinephrine*, regulates capillary blood flow to skeletal muscles and gastrointestinal area, increases metabolic rate.
- **Adrenal Cortex** – Located on top of the kidneys. *Cortisol, Corticosterone, 11-deoxycorticosterone*, regulates metabolism and body growth, promotes secretion of ACTH and anti-inflammatories; *Aldosterone*, increases sodium retention and potassium loss in the kidney; *Gonadocorticoids*, affects ovaries and testes.
- **Pancreas** – Located behind the stomach. *Insulin*, decreases blood sugar; *Glucagon*, increases blood sugar; *Gastrin*, stimulates acid secretion and gastric motility of the stomach.
- **Ovaries** – Located above the urinary bladder and to either side of the uterus. *Estradiol, Progesterone* affects development of female sex organs and female characteristics, influences the menstrual cycle and maintains pregnancy; *Inhibin*, inhibits FSH secretion by the pituitary gland.
- **Placenta** – Located within the uterus during pregnancy. *Estrogens, Progesterone* and *Chorionic Gonadotropin* (hCG), maintains pregnancy.
- **Testes** – Located at the base and outside of the torso. *Androgens (Testosterone)*, affects development of male sex organs, sperm, and male characteristics.
- **Thymus** – Located in the upper portion of the chest. *Thymosin alpha, Thymosin B_1 – B_5, Thymopoietin I and II, Thymic Humoral Factor (THF), Thymostimulin, Factor Thymic Serum (FTS)*, Develops T cells and some B cells into antibody-producing plasma cells.

- **Digestive System** – (Throughout the digestive tract.) *Secretin, Gastrin, Cholocystokinin (CCK)*, controls acid concentration in the stomach, controls the release of digestive additives and enzymes.
- **Heart** – Located in the chest. *Atrial Natriuretic Peptide (ANP)*, maintains a balance of body fluids, helps maintain blood pressure.
- **Pineal Gland** – Located toward the center of the brain. *Melatonin*, controls the body's reactions to light and dark.

Much can be said for the endocrine glands, the hormones they secrete, and the actions of the hormones. Some hormones act quickly, while others take a very long time before their actions become manifest. But the coordination and administration of these powerful hormones cannot be taken lightly, and the body does a good job in regulating and managing these influential chemicals. Each anatomical and physiological process that the body does is controlled by some hormone.

To be sure, the human body and the life of an individual is very complex and each intricate detail is not only important, but is carefully controlled. "But the very hairs of your head are numbered. "Do not fear therefore; you are of more value than many sparrows" (Luke 12:7). God is aware of your physical development and living needs. He created you and your physiological processes. We take these hormones and their actions for granted, and it is good that we do have to worry about them. But God created them and He is in control of all things.

REFERENCES

1. "Quotes from Isaac Newton". Goodreads.com https://www.goodreads.com/quotes/7269137-i-can-calculate-the-motion-of-heavenly-bodies-but-not (accessed April 30, 2018).
2. Wynsberghe, DV, Noback, CR, and Carola, R. *Human Anatomy and Physiology* (3rd ed.) McGraw-Hill, (1995).

[The author notes that there are many internet sites that cite quotations from others. And some of these quotations are questioned by current groups for various reasons and intents.]

CHAPTER 5

MAINTENANCE

I lay down and slept; I awoke; for the Lord
sustained me. – Psalms 3:5

It is a good feeling to go to sleep at night and not have to worry or be concerned about trying to maintain life in your body. It is good to know that you do not have to remind your heart to beat. It is nice to not have to figure out how to digest your food. The body has six organ systems that help to regulate and maintain the body. These include the Integument, Cardiovascular, Respiratory, Digestive, Urinary and Immune systems. Without these systems, the body could not survive.

The Integument System

If the Integument System of the body is made up of the skin, hair and nails. The main function of the Integument System is to protect the underlying tissue from the surrounding environment. It certainly serves as a protective covering, but it also protects the body from the "elements" of the environment as it houses "gauges" or sensory devices that detects heat, cold, wet, dry, etc. which also gives us protection.

Skin

The skin can be considered an "organ", and is the largest organ of the body. It makes up about 15% of the total body weight. The most outer part of the skin is called the epidermis. It is made up of squamous epithelial cells, or flat cells that are stacked on top of each other like pancakes. Another type of cell that is found elsewhere in the body is the columnar cell. As the name implies, a columnar cell is "taller" and is a larger cell. It can be found in the intestines. Its function would be absorption, absorbing food and transferring it to the blood supply. The columnar cell, and the squamous cell look different because they have different functions.

The design and use of the squamous or flat cell which makes up the tissue layer epidermis of skin is interesting. **Figure 5 -1** illustrates the two types of cells, and explains how stratified squamous epithelium, or smaller flatter cells that are layered, offer greater protection than the single columnar cell. If trauma or damage is unavoidable, then loosing several squamous cells is better than losing a single columnar cell. Unaffected squamous cells that are deeper into this cellular layer can then regenerate cells and replace the damaged or lost cells above them. However, if the columnar cell is lost, there is no additional protection for the tissue that remains below it.

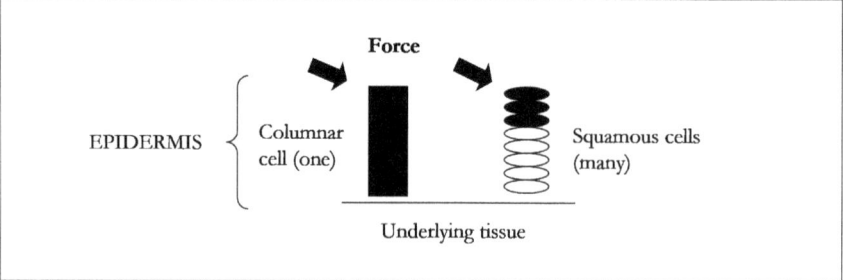

Figure 5-1. Illustration showing a comparison of columnar and squamous cells of the epidermis of the skin if damaged. If a force trauma were to damage the columnar cell, all of the epidermis would be destroyed. Whereas if the force trauma were applied to the squamous cells, all of the squamous cells would not be destroyed and thus could regenerate.

The construction of the skin also utilizes the compression, tension shear concept of force application as it relates to possible injury. Instead of the top or surface of the skin being flat, there is a microscopic formation at the top of the skin called the dermal papilla. It is a series of curves, bumps and wavy ridges. Instead of "feeling" a shear mode as a force "scrapes" across, the dermal papilla senses a compressive mode, which means it can withstand 67% more force before it breaks or "tears".

Figure 5-2 illustrates what underlying layer of the skin would look like if this underlying layer were flat and straight. If a force came on a slant or at a sideways angle, it would be easy for the skin to peel away from the rest of the skin and to literally "slough off". **Figure 5-3** illustrates what the underlying layer of skin actually looks like. On top of cellular layer of skin is the corneum. The corneum, is a layer of dead cellular debris and other material that offers some protection to the cellular layer below.

Below the corneum is the curved, wavy layer of the dermal papilla. Within the dermal papilla is the cellular layer of the skin which are stratified, squamous epithelial cells (flat cells that are stacked on top of each other). The squamous, epithelial cells are close together and tightly arranged. The closeness of these cells helps them protect and perform their functions more effectively.

But the main feature of this cellular layer is the curved, "wavy" layer called the dermal papilla. If a force were applied at any angle, the mode of force application would be a compressive mode (and not shear, as shown in Figure 5-2). Thus, the skin would not tear and "slough off". This entire upper region of the skin is referred to as the epidermis.

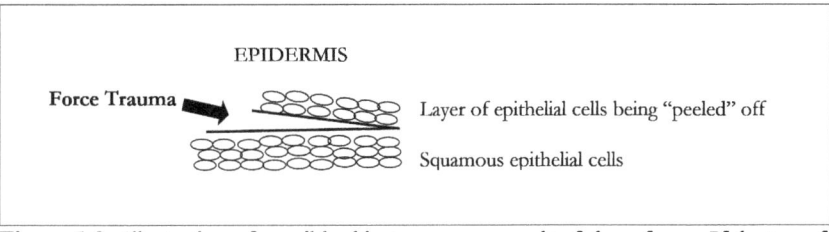

Figure 5-2. Illustration of possible skin trauma as a result of shear force. If the top of the skin were "flat", then force trauma from the side or in shear mode would cause the top layers of skin to "slough off" and tear away from of the epidermis.

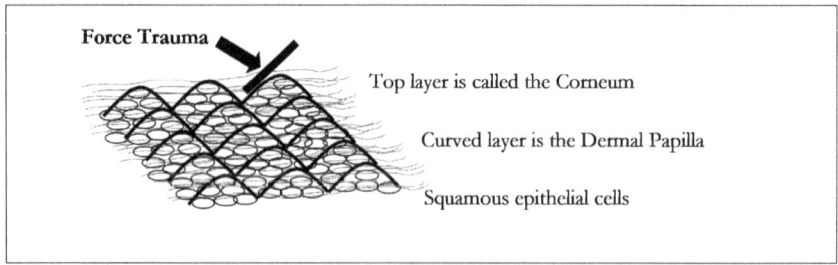

Figure 5-3. Illustration showing the effects of the Dermal Papillae. The curved layer of the Dermal Papilla allows for a force trauma in any direction upon the skin to be received in a compressive mode (not shear) and thus not be "sloughed off" or tear away from the epidermis.

The most bottom layer of the skin is called the hypodermis ("hypo" meaning "below"). Within the hypodermis we find a layer of fat, and within this protective layer of fat we find a "neurovascular bundle". The neurovascular bundle is simply a pipeline of small arteries and veins, as well as a "wiring" network of nerves, traversing in this lower layer of the skin, together. The function of the neurovascular bundle is important and the added fat surrounding them give this added protection. In between the epidermis and the hypodermis is the thickest part of the skin called the dermis.

Scattered throughout the dermis are different exocrine glands and special sensory receptors. The function of exocrine glands is to secrete substances to the outside of the the skin. These exocrine glands can be separated into three major groups. The first are the Merocrine glands, which are glands that can secrete its contents without damaging the cells that make it. Hence, they are "merry" and happy that they are still alive after producing its content. Such a gland includes the sudoriferous or sweat gland.

At times when the body is hot and needs cooling, the cells of the sudoriferous, or sweat gland, produces a watery solution. This watery solution is called sweat and is spread onto the surface of the skin and evaporates, cooling the skin. The primary products found sweat are water and a few simple salts. The water and salt molecules are rather small and can easily pass from inside the cells that make up the sweat gland, through the cell membrane to the outside, without damaging the cells or cell membrane. This is a reason why your body can produce so much sweat in hot weather or in heavy exercising, as it does not harm the cells of the sweat gland in producing so much sweat.

A second type of exocrine gland is the Holocrine gland. The Holocrine glands derive their name from the term "holocaust" (death). These cells are the opposite of the Merocrine glands. Instead of being happy and "merry", cells of the Holocrine gland must literally die in order to release its products to the surface of the skin. An example of a Holocrine gland is the sebaceous gland or oil gland. The oil molecules that are made by the cells of the sebaceous or oil gland are large. These large oil molecules are too big to pass through the cell membrane without rupturing the membrane. The cell breaks open and the cellular content spills out and the cell dies. Thus, cells of sebaceous or oil gland make the oil, then die releasing the oil. Therefore, utilization of these glands must be prudent and not overly needed.

A major purpose of oil on the skin is to trap and capture microscopic bacteria, which are simply waiting to enter the body through the skin and infect and destroy the body. As these bacteria are trapped, one can simply bathe and wash away the bacteria. But the cells that produce the oil perish as the oil is released from the cell. The oil molecules are larger than water or salts, making it impossible to easily pass through the cell membrane and make its way to the surface of the skin. The cell membrane must rupture for the oil to be released. The cell dies and thus the name "holocrine".

This "sacrifice" sounds like the sacrifice Jesus gave, of Himself for the redemption of His people from the wages of sin. "...Jesus Christ, who gave Himself for our sins, that He might deliver us from the present evil age, according to the will of God and Father" (Galatians 1:3–4). The sebaceous gland must die in order to protect the body from the perils that bacteria can bring. Jesus gave Himself and died in order to save man from the perils of Satan and sin.

Physically however, the body has a neat "trick" in order to minimize the amount of oil needed, and thus minimize the number of cells that must be sacrificed. The sebaceous glands are "attached" to hair follicles. The sebaceous glands use the hair like a mop. They secrete only a minimal amount of oil where the hair can spread out a thin layer of oil over the surface of the skin, enough to still be able to capture lurking bacteria. It is an ingenious mechanism to help guard the skin against bacteria that would want to enter the body through the skin and do harm to the body.

A third type of exocrine gland found in the skin are Apocrine glands. The products that are made by Apocrine glands are somewhat larger than the water and salts that are made by the Merocrine glands, but smaller than molecules made by Holocrine glands. But these molecules are large enough to cause damage to the cells of the mammary gland as it leaves the cell and passes through the cell membrane. The cell does not die, but it is damaged. An example of an Apocrine gland is the mammary gland. Mammary glands produce milk. Milk is essentially water and a few salts, similar to sweat, but it also contains larger fat and sugar molecules. Thus, the mammary gland is basically a modified sweat gland, which has been designed to make some fat and sugar molecules, but are damaged in doing so.

Scattered throughout the dermis of the skin are special sensory receptors. These special sensory receptors help detect touch, heat, cold and pain. These senses are necessary protectors to keep us aware of our surroundings and help guard against harm to the body. These special receptors will be discussed in greater detail later with the Nervous System.

There are a great many collagen molecules "filling the gaps" within the dermis of the skin, providing structural integrity to the skin. The structure of the collagen protein molecule has been previously described. Its structure alone helps provide the strength support to the skin. However, as we age, the amount of collagen found in the skin decreases. Thus, the skin becomes thinner and becomes more susceptible to bruising and damage.

Hair

The human body has as many as 125,000 hairs on their skin, but all other land mammals have "fur". The thick matting of hair, or fur, of animals is their clothing, protecting them from the elements of the earth and other dangers. It has been shown that human hair helps to spread and "mop" the oil around on the surface of the skin in order to trap and collect harmful bacteria. And, though it seems to be too scarce in order to keep in body heat, it can trap the air that is closest to the skin to help keep much of the body heat from escaping rapidly. Since the introduction of sin into the world, man has had to use clothing for protection against the elements of the earth and to hide their guilt and shame from sin. As many as 50–100 hairs can be lost per day.

Like all other parts of the body, hair development and growth are dependent upon an adequate blood supply. This intimate relationship between blood and hair has been recognized for quite some time. In addition to receiving the nutrients that the blood brings; it was found that the hair picks up practically all other elements and compounds that are in the blood. Forensic science can now examine the physical content of hair and determine what and even when certain chemicals or compounds were ingested. Previous "mysterious" causes of death have now been studied and found that many were cases of homicide. Present day examination of a hair of an individual can show what and when certain drugs have entered the body. Such results can convict a person to prison or keep an individual from getting a job.

Oftentimes, things we have done in our past are still with us. And whether we can still see it or detect it, it remains, oftentimes for others to see. However, we have a God that can remove these things that can be a further deterrent in our lives. "As far as the east is from west, so far has He (God) removed our transgressions from us" (Psalm 103:12).

There are many dangers that can harm the body. Many are obvious, but many are not. God can be thought of as analogous to this epithelial lining. Anything that reaches us must first go through Him. This is very similar to the skin. Much of the protection that the skin provides is obvious. But there are other dangers we cannot see such as bacteria. And there are hidden dangers lurking in the environment such as subtle effects of touch, heat and cold. From the dermal papilla and stratified squamous epithelium, to the special glands and sensory receptors, the skin has a unique anatomy and means to provide the body with protection from unseen dangers.

> Put on the whole armor of God, that you may be able to stand against the wiles of the devil. For we do not wrestle against flesh and blood, but against principalities, against powers, against the rulers of darkness of this age, against the spiritual hosts of wickedness in the heavenly places. Therefore take up the whole armor of God that you may be able to withstand in the evil day, and having done all, to stand ... taking the shield of faith with which you will be able to quench all the fiery darts of the wicked one. And take the helmet of salvation, and the sword of the Spirit, which is the word of God. (Ephesians 6:11–17)

In the above passage of Scripture, we "wrestle" against evil things we cannot see. And though we may not see them, they still exist and are dangerous none the less. God provides the protection we need from the spiritual dangers that we cannot see. We may understand the need for armor in the act of battle. It is essential for protection and survival. But armor is not effective useless unless it is worn.

"And I give them eternal life, and they shall never perish; neither shall anyone snatch them out of My hand" (John 10:28). It seems however, man seeks to provide for his own needs and protection. Even in the first sin, man tried to hide his nakedness with "fig leaves" (Genesis 3:7). Such a covering was not sufficient. God had to slay an innocent animal in order to provide an adequate covering. The covering of sin cannot be woven by human hands. Only God can provide for such a sacrifice. Only God can provide such a covering.

The Digestive System

> And the king appointed for them a daily provision of the king's delicacies and of the wine which he drank, and three years of training for them, so that at the end

of the time they might serve before the king ... But Daniel purposed it in his heart that he would not defile himself with the portion of the king's delicacies, nor with the wine which he drank; therefore he requested of the eunuchs that he not defile himself ... So Daniel said to the steward ... Please test your servants for ten days and let them give us vegetables to eat and water to drink. Then let our appearance be examined before you, and the appearance of the men who eat the portion of the king's delicacies; and as you see fit, so deal with your servants. So he consented with them in this matter, and tested them for ten days. And at the end of the ten days their features appeared better and fatter in flesh than all the young men who ate the portion of the king's delicacies. (Daniel 1:5–14)

This is a story in the Bible discussing the importance of a good, healthy diet. Of course, in today's world, food and food preparation are different that than in past times of Biblical history. It is understood that our diet should be "well rounded". But understanding the type and amount of food consumed can be confusing.

Food

It has been said you are what you eat. To a great extent, this is true. We may understand that the purpose of digestive system is to "digest" the "food" we eat, and then prepare it to be utilized by the body, for energy production and construction and maintenance of the body. But an individual cannot "eat" just anything and expect just anything to be beneficial to the nutritious growth and development of the body. There are many things that we can eat and ingest that are poisonous and will kill. And there are things we can eat and ingest that are not poisonous but have no nutritious value either. These things may not specifically harm, but they will not help, either. In addition, there are things that we may eat that, although may not be immediately poisonous, if continually ingested over many years, may lead to serious, harmful health issues, and as such, we may not live a rich, rewarding, and long life. Thus, the foods we chose to eat do indeed matter.

To be sure, there are things such as arsenic and potassium cyanide that are poisonous and cannot be changed or altered to make it not poisonous. However, there are some things that, without proper "processing", can be detrimental to our health. But many of these can be altered to not only be non-poisonous but can be made to be enjoyable to eat. We remember stories of the Pilgrims and the first Thanksgiving celebration. Today we enjoy the turkey and dressing dinner with "all the fixin's". One of the food items we may enjoy is cranberry sauce. The cranberry itself looks like the beak of a crane, thus its namesake.

But the cranberry itself is very sour, and if eaten raw, can make you sick. In the natural setting, the plant thrives in bad soil and keeps company with Poison Ivey and the like. It takes a special processing to make the cranberry a sweet and delectable food. In other words, we do not want to take something and make it poisonous, but rather we want to take something and make it most enjoyable and beneficial for consumption.

God's Word, the Bible, can be considered bread (food) to be "eaten". Scripture can be "taken in" to help us "grow" spiritually. "Behold, I (God) have put My words in your mouth" (Jeremiah 1:9). "But He (Jesus) answered and said, 'Man shall not live by bread alone, but by every word that proceeds from the mouth of God'" (Matthew 4:4). "... as newborn babes, desire the pure milk of the word, that you may grow thereby" (1 Peter 2:2). "If you instruct the brethren in these things, you will be a good minister of Jesus Christ, nourished in the words of faith and of the good doctrine which you have carefully followed" (1 Timothy 4:6).

God's Word certainly is not poisonous. It is perfect the way it is. However, some have tried to "alter" Scripture and have perverted and distorted Scripture in such a way as to make it to be like "a poison". Similar to taking the cranberry and willfully and deliberately cooking and making it presentable to the body for consumption, so too, in many cases, God's Word has been willfully and deliberately "changed" to make it seem as though it would "taste" better and be healthier to be "eaten" or "taken in", after the change.

Oftentimes, people misquote the Bible, thinking it is saying one thing but in fact it does not say that at all. Many people love to quote Scripture "out of context", insisting that the Bible is expressing a certain thought when it really is not. However, the Bible must be willfully and deliberately studied in such a way that it gives growth and can actually be enjoyable to read and study.

Biblical illiteracy has been an issue that has recently emerged. Recent surveys have indicated that as many as 90% Americans believe in God, 76% of Americans profess to be Christian, yet, only 70% believe in hell, and as few as 20% regularly attend a church, and less than 5% even tithe [1,2,3,4]. These numbers certainly do not match up in understanding of what the Bible says regarding Jesus and the doctrine of salvation. Thus, it seems that many individuals have not willfully and deliberately studied the Bible but have simply ingested bits and pieces that have come from areas that are like Poison Ivey (where the cranberry like to reside).

From the beginning, man has had to eat. In fact, we need to eat "daily" or fairly often if we are to receive the benefit derived from "food". The food that we eat sustains us for only a short period of time, and then we must eat again, and again ... and again. It is interesting that the "spiritual food" we eat can sustain us indefinitely.

"And the Lord God commanded the man saying, Of every tree of the garden you may eat freely, But of the tree of the knowledge of good and evil, you shall not eat of it: for in the day that you eat from it you shall surely die" (Genesis 2:16–17). Surely, ingesting the wrong things can be detrimental to the health of man. Ingesting the "right" things, however, is good.

God provided the children of Israel with food as they left Egypt and "wandered" in the wilderness. For forty years, God specifically provided them with meat, bread, and water.

> And the Lord spoke to Moses saying, "I have heard the complaints of the children of Israel, speak to them saying at twilight you shall eat meat, and in

the morning, you shall be filled with bread" … So it was that quails came up at evening and covered the camp, and in the morning the dew lay all around the camp. And when the layer of dew lifted, there on the surface of the wilderness was a small round substance as fine as frost on the ground. And when the children of Israel saw it they said one to another, "it is manna:" for they did not know what it was. And Moses said unto them, "this is the bread which the Lord has given you to eat." … So they gathered it every morning, every man according to his need. (Exodus 16:12–15, 21)

Strike the rock and water will come out of it, that the people may drink. (Exodus 17:6)

Oftentimes we use eating as a social even and the enjoyment of company and fellowship. In the story which we refer to as the Prodigal Son, we see that the father made a feast, not just for eating to obtain nutrition, but for celebration and fellowship. "But the father said to his servants, bring forth the best robe and put it on him; and put a ring on his hand, and shoes on his feet: And bring the fatted calf, and kill it; and let us eat, drink and be merry; For this my son was dead, and is alive again; he was lost, and is found. And they began to be merry" (Luke 15:22–24).

Jesus was criticized for eating (socializing) with "sinners". "And when the scribes and Pharisees saw him (Jesus) eat with the tax collectors and sinners, they said to his disciples, how is it that he can eat and drink with the tax collectors and sinners?" (Mark 2:16). Even after He was resurrected, Jesus ate. "And he (Jesus) said to them, 'why are you troubled? And why do doubts arise in your hearts. Behold my hand and my feet, that it is I myself: handle me, and see; for a ghost does not have flesh and bones, as you see I have.' And when he had spoken, he showed them his hands and his feet. And while they still did not believe for joy and wondered, he said to them, 'do you have anything to eat?' And they gave him a piece of broiled fish and a honeycomb. And he took it and did eat before them" (Luke 24:38–43).

In addition, Jesus even used an eating occasion, a "wedding supper" to describe a social "togetherness" in affection and love. Of course, the grand finale of Scripture, so to speak, is the marriage supper of Christ upon His second return to "gather His bride". "Alleluia! For the Lord God Omnipotent reigns! Let us be glad and rejoice and give Him glory, for the marriage of the Lamb has come, and his wife (church) has made herself ready ... Blessed are those who are called to the marriage supper of the Lamb!" (Revelation 19:6–9).

It seems clear that the Bible puts a major emphasis on eating and uses eating analogies in helping to describe man's purpose and God's ultimate plan of salvation and redemption. We certainly grow in those things that we feed on. It is important to "feed" our "spiritual life", and we can do this by reading and studying the Bible, going to church, and associating with other believers.

It is one thing to recognize that the Bible is God's Word, or "spiritual food" for our benefit. It is quite another to not "eat" the Word of God for our spiritual growth. As children, we oftentimes "played" with our food. We would "play" and pretend that we were eating and partaking, but in fact we were simply mocking what has been set before us. As we grew older, we would not necessarily "play" with our food, so much as picking and choosing what we eat. Such is the case with God's word. As "newborn children" we might "play" in the Word of God, and never grow and mature as we should, for lack of "spiritual food." But then as we get older, we still lack the proper "spiritual food" as we simply pick and choose what we like, and never engage with things which we do not like.

Food is called "food" for a reason. It nourishes us and sustains us, giving us the carbohydrates, fats, proteins, vitamins and minerals that we need in order to live. We should consume God's "food" in a similar manner. Just like our physical body has means to digest and absorb physical food, even so, our spiritual "body" must be fed God's Word and digested.

Therefore, we must know the foods that are good for us and consume those things that can help us grow and flourish. And we must "starve" ourselves of those things that do not help us grow and may bring us harm or death. Over time we are taught and learn many things. What we "ate" and learned as a child can still nourish and sustain us today. In like manner, the "spiritual man" must be starved of the earthly things that can harm and kill us. We must feed on God's Word so that as Christians, or children of God, we can grow and flourish. God's Word provides all that we need. God's Word fulfills.

But like some foods that cannot be eaten and digested easily, some of God's Word may be difficult to read and comprehend. Wells that are dug and may not have a modern-day pump that can pump the water to the surface. Instead, a bucket with a rope attached to it may be used. The bucket is lowered down into the well to retrieve the water. The bucket fills up with water and it can be drawn back up with the rope. Sometimes, however, as the bucket of water is being lifted, the rope may break, leaving the bucket down into the well. A "grappling hook" is then needed to drop into the well and "fish out" the bucket and bring it back to the top for use again. And doing this requires time and effort.

Cows have multiple stomachs. Grass contains a lot of cellulose and other difficult parts to digest. In the process of eating and digesting grass, cows must "regurgitate" the digesting grass back into their mouths for further chewing and processing ("chewing the cud"). Only in this fashion can the cow completely digest the grass.

So it is with Scripture and our spiritual lives. Sometimes certain Scripture is hard to read and difficult to comprehend. We need to spend time in God's Word and "grapple" with it and regurgitate its contents over and over before we can truly apply it to our life.

To be sure, the Scripture says that "man shall not live by bread alone but by every word that proceeds out of the mouth of God" (Deuteronomy 8:3). However, Scripture also notes that bread was so important for life that God accepted it as an offering (Leviticus 2:4–10). And on two occasions Jesus fed the multitude with bread and fish (Jesus feeds 5,000; Matthew 14:15–21 and Mark 6:30–44. Jesus feeds 4,000; Matthew 15:32–38 and Mark 8:1–9).

We may be familiar with the terms, carbohydrates, fats and proteins. But these molecules are only parts of larger "chunks" of matter and larger molecules that we call "food". Digestion is the breaking down of these large "chunks" and molecules into the smaller molecules of carbohydrates, fats, and proteins for use by the body. This is kind of like a house that is being demolished and the various parts of the house are now being salvaged and broken up into smaller parts, not to be discarded, but to be used in building another house.

The house would be broken down, and each nail, board, brick and other material would be removed and separated for use again. To do this properly, there must be appropriate demolishing equipment and a logical, systematic processing schedule in which this is most effectively accomplished. And regardless of efficiency, there will always be some waste that must be removed. Food, then, would be like the house and the demolition process is digestion. Thus, our digestive system must have an entryway, then a series of ways and means to break down these larger "chunks" and molecules, and organize, process and absorb the smaller molecules, and then have a passageway of exit for the waste.

Although "food" is eaten for its raw products and materials that the body uses for building, it certainly is used for energy. To accomplish physical labor, the body uses physical power, thus needing physical energy. The physical energy required by the body comes from the fuel provided by the food we eat and the oxygen we breathe in. The ATP energy molecule, and metabolism had been previously discussed. The point, here, is that in order to accomplish physical works and labors of the body, a source of energy is needed. To accomplish spiritual works and labors, spiritual power is needed. The source of spiritual power cannot come from physical sources such as food. It can only come from God. Starvation is the result of being physically removed from food. It can result in physical death. To be removed from God is the definition of death. Spiritual starvation can lead to spiritual death and eternal separation from God.

The human digestive system is well designed bring in food, break it down, and prepare it for use by the body. The average length of the digestive tract is about twenty-eight feet. At the entrance of this tract or tube is the oral cavity, consisting of the lips, mouth and tongue. It is used for the "entrance way" and mechanical breakdown of the "food". It makes portions of this food small enough to pass down the next part of the tube, the esophagus and into the stomach, and eventually into the intestines for absorption into the body.

Oral Cavity

Most of the nutrients that we eat cannot be used in their existing form. They must be broken down into smaller components. The oral cavity is the entrance of the digestive tract, also known as the alimentary canal. It is in the oral cavity that the foods we eat are initially broken down and begin their journey into the body. The oral cavity consists of the mouth, lips, tongue and salivary glands.

Mouth

The mouth is an amazing body part. Man does not have a "pouch" or area in which to "shovel in" food like a funnel, to be stored until later needed. However, man does have such a similar structure. This structure is the oral cavity and includes the lips, mouth and tongue. But in addition to being used for eating, the oral cavity is also used for communication. There are nearly 450 references of the mouth, lips and tongue found in the Bible. And most of these references are related to speaking. It is this ability to speak and communicate that separates humans from other animals.

> In the multitude of words sin is not lacking, but he who restrains his lips is wise. The tongue of the righteous is choice silver. (Proverbs 10:19–20)

> A worthless person, a wicked man, walks with a perverse mouth. (Proverbs 6:12)

> Indeed, we put bits in horses' mouths that they may obey us, and we turn their whole body ... Even so the tongue is a little member and boasts great things. See how great a forest a little fire can kindle. And the tongue is a fire, a world of iniquity. The tongue is set among our members that it defiles the whole body ... But no man can tame the tongue. It is an unruly evil, full of deadly poison. With it we bless our

God and Father, and with it we curse men, who have
been made in the similitude of God. Out of the same
mouth proceeds blessings and cursing. My brethren,
these things ought not to be. (James 3:3–10)

Yes, man certainly uses the lips, mouth and tongue for foul
communications. Yet, in order to use them for eating, all speaking
must cease. In order to bring nourishment *in*, the body must cease
its *outward* communications.

Lips

During the food consuming process, the mouth receives "chunks"
of food. The lips are basically two fleshly, muscular folds that surround
the opening of the mouth. It is covered by transparent epithelium.
This transparent epithelium allows for the underlying blood vessels
to be seen, giving the lips the reddish-pink appearance (and the bluish
appearance when the body is cold). The purpose of the lips is to hold
the food in place while it is being chewed. The lips are extremely
sensitive and are abundantly supplied with blood and lymphatic
vessels and sensory nerve endings.

It is because of this sensitivity that the lips are also used for
kissing. Kissing is a cultural expression of love, passion, friendship
and peace, as well as other feelings and affections. The act of kissing
has been going on for thousands of years. "So she caught him and
kissed him" (Proverbs 7:13). "Your lips, O my spouse, drip as the
honeycomb; honey and milk are under your tongue, and the fragrance
of your garments is like the fragrance of Lebanon" (Song of Solomon
4:11). And sometimes this passion can get us in trouble. "My son, pay
attention to my wisdom; lend your ear to my understanding, that you
may preserve discretion, and your lips may keep knowledge. For the
lips of an immoral woman drip honey, and her mouth is smoother
than oil; but in the end she is as bitter as wormwood" (Proverbs 5:1–4).
Judas Iscariot identified Jesus with a kiss in his betrayal of Jesus in
the Garden of Gethsemane (Matthew 26:47–49). There are nearly 150
references to kissing in the Bible.

Tongue

The tongue is composed of an interlacing of muscles, covered by epithelial tissue and "taste buds". The function of the tongue in the digestion process is to help move the food around in the mouth for effective chewing by the teeth, swallowing, and tasting and feeling the consistency of the food that is being eaten.

There are three types of taste buds in the tongue. Located along the back sides of the tongue are foliate papillae. The term "papillae" means a nipple-like projection. The term foliate comes from the word meaning foliage or plant-like. Thus, foliate papillae are "taste buds" that have a foliage type or rough, nipple-like texture located on the back sides of the tongue. Vallate papillae are in a V-shaped row at the back of the tongue. Most of the tongue, however, is covered with fungiform papillae, or mushroom shaped taste buds.

The functional cells of the taste buds are called "gustatory cells". These nerve cells can distinguish the various flavors and tastes of food and send the message to the brain for interpretation and identification. The gustatory cells are covered by a layer of epithelial tissue. In case the food or liquid is too hot or too cold, the sensitive gustatory cells are protected from damage. It is interesting that the taste buds are protected from foods or liquids that come into the mouth that are too hot or too cold and can cause damage. Thus, it is the epithelial tissue that is generally damaged, and not the gustatory cells. It would be nice if the mouth had a similar protection mechanism to protect it from vile words that may come out.

At the roof or top of the mouth is the palate. The palate is a hard plate that provides a rigid surface against which the tongue forces food during chewing. In addition, the palate is slightly corrugated which helps create friction and aids in the process of moving the food around and effective chewing.

Salivary Glands

There are three salivary glands associated with the oral cavity which secretes saliva. These include the submandibular gland, located under the tongue at the floor of the mouth; the sublingual gland, located just in front of the submandibular gland; and the parotid gland, located in front of the ear in the cheek. Saliva is mostly water (97– 99.5%). It is not uncommon to produce over a quart and a half of saliva a day.

In addition to keeping the sensitive tissue of the oral cavity moist, saliva also protects the oral cavity against microorganisms and harmful pathogens. It contains an antibacterial enzyme *Lysozyme*, that helps prevent bacterial growth in the mouth. Saliva also contains *Defensins*, a local antibiotic which also inhibits growth of certain bacteria. And saliva contains an agent known as IgA antibody. Collectively, these products inhibit growth of certain bacteria and fungus within the mouth and helps keep a healthy oral environment.

There are also small amounts of *bicarbonates* and *phosphates*, which helps to maintain a slightly acidic pH, as well as the digestive enzyme *amylase*. Amylase is an enzyme that helps to break down larger carbohydrate molecules into smaller sugar molecules. If you could keep a piece of bread or unsalted cracker in your mouth long enough, it would begin to taste sweet, as more and more sugar molecules are made from the larger carbohydrate molecules. However, it generally is unable to complete this process before the food is swallowed but will continue its action as the food moves to the stomach.

Teeth

This mechanical breakdown is accomplished by our teeth. The arrangement of the teeth is well suited for physically breaking down the food we chew into the smaller pieces. The number of teeth may vary depending of age and size of mouth. In an adult, there are generally a total of 16 teeth on the bottom of the mouth, 8 on either side of the mouth or jaw, as well as a total of 16 on the top, 8 on either side of the mouth or jaw, for a total of 32 teeth. In the center of the mouth, there are 4 upper front and lower front teeth which are called incisors. They are chisel-shaped and are best used in cutting or shredding food. On either side of these are 2 upper and lower "canine" teeth. The "canine" teeth have a pointed end which can tear food.

Toward the back of the mouth and on either side of the jaw, there are 2 premolar teeth and 3 molars. These teeth are used for grinding he food into smaller bits for easier digestion. Proper chewing of food is very important. We may choke or have difficulty or delayed digestion with insufficient chewing.

Newborns and younger children do not have as many teeth as adults. They must rely on milk and soft foods for survival. However, it is a natural process to lose our "baby teeth" and gain the adult teeth in order to move from milk, exclusively, to a greater variety of solid food. And this greater variety of food will help us to grow stronger and healthier.

So it is with God's word. Many may say that they are "born again" Christians. And as "new-born" Christians, we should desire to feed on God's word, just like a new-born desires and needs milk. "As newborn babies desire the pure milk of the word, that you may grow thereby, if indeed you have tasted that the Lord is gracious" (1 Peter 2:2–3). And, over time, as we read God's Word more and more, we will learn more and more about God and "grow" spiritually.

But a major problem is that many believers do not continue to read and study the Bible. And as such, they remain "babes" and never mature, spiritually. "For though by this time you ought to be teachers, you need someone to teach you again the first principles of the oracles of God; and you have come to need milk and not solid food. For everyone who partakes only of milk is unskilled in the word of righteousness, for he is a babe. But solid food belongs to those who are of full age, that is, those why by reason of use have their senses exercised to discern both good and evil" (Hebrews 5:12–14). Thus, as we pass from infancy to child to adulthood, and our teeth respond and prepare us for more solid food and move away from milk, exclusively, so we should be able to grow and handle God's word as we develop spiritually.

Our bodies cannot use the larger molecules of the carbohydrates, fats and proteins of "food". Whether by teeth or enzymes, these molecules must be broken down in order to be utilized by the body. Only when these larger pieces of meat and vegetables are reduced to their individual molecules can they be rearranged and formulated for our better use. God does the same thing. God uses broken things.

> The word which came to Jeremiah from the Lord saying, "Arise and go down to the potter's house, and there I will cause you to hear my words." Then I went down to the potter's house, and there he was, making something at the wheel. And the vessel he made was marred in the hand of the potter, so he made it again into another vessel, as it seemed good to the potter to make. Then the word of the Lord came to me saying, "O house of Israel, can I not do with you as potter," says the LORD. "Look, as the clay is to the potter's hand, so are you in my hand ...." (Jeremiah 18:1–6)

Only things that are fit for a specific purpose are used for a special purpose. Our ATP (energy) comes from a 6-carbon sugar called glucose. A carbohydrate molecule may contain hundreds of these carbon molecules, and as such, must be broken down into the simple glucose molecule in order to be used.

There is little argument as to the importance of the teeth. Oftentimes, disease or injury can reduce the number of teeth we have in our mouth, thus limiting how we can break down our food into the small portions needed for further digestion. We generally take our teeth for granted until we need to go to the dentist for tooth repair, fillings or dentures. But it is better if we do routine "maintenance" of our teeth by regularly scheduling dental "check-ups" with our dentist. And this is good ... for our teeth. But sometimes we treat God like we do a dentist. We only go to Him only during the times we are in pain or are in need to do so. We certainly need to take care of our teeth when we are young and while we can. So it is with our relationship with God. We must cherish our relationship with God and maintain our attention and care of our Bible study so that as we "feed" on God's Word, we can become spiritually fed, strengthened and maintained.

Stomach

After the chewed food is tightly packaged into a small "bolus" of food, the food is sent to the stomach through a tube called the esophagus. This 10-inch tube connects the mouth with the stomach. The stomach is a J-shaped, muscular structure that serves as a "holding tank" for eaten food. It is not just a bowl of "acid" that is ready to further breakdown the food that enters. If it were a bowl of acid, the acid would "eat" away and destroy the stomach itself. The stomach is designed to secrete acid only when the larger fat and protein molecules are present.

The lining of the stomach contains three kinds of cells: (1) chief cells which secrete pepsinogen, an inactive form of the enzyme pepsin; (2) parietal cells, which produce hydrochloric acid; and (3) mucous cells that secrete a watery mixture with mucin in it. As the food enters the stomach, these cells are stimulated to begin their role in the digestive process. Large protein and fat molecules in the food need time and chemistry to help break them into smaller molecules. The pepsinogen is converted to pepsin to help breakdown the larger protein molecules and is aided by the hydrochloric acid. But the products of the chief and parietal cells are not secreted when not needed, as when the food is mainly carbohydrates. Sometimes, however, these cells may produce too much acid, causing "acid indigestion". Taking an "antacid" can neutralize excess acid. As a pro-active approach, some medications prevent the parietal cells from producing the acid in the first place. The mucous cells produce mucin, which helps the food "slide" easily through the rest of the digestive tube or tract.

The surrounding tissue of the stomach is muscle, which periodically contracts and relaxes and contracts again, essentially stirring and mixing the enzymes and acid into the food "mixture" that is in the stomach. After mixing, the food is now ready to enter the small intestine, where continued breakdown of food molecules and absorption can take place.

"Foods for the stomach and the stomach for foods, but God will destroy both it and them" (1 Corinthians 6:13). The physical needs of the body can be provided by food. And one can discuss the merits of the various types of foods and nutrients, as well as the actions of the digestive system to breakdown and absorb and utilize the food. Though it is helpful to understand food and the nature of the body in which to eat, breakdown and absorb the life-giving nutrients, the physical body will eventually die and in the end, all will pass away. There will be no further need for physical food.

"The life is more than food, and the body is more than clothes" (Luke 12:23). To be sure we do live in a physical world and, as such, emphasize things of this physical world. However, all things physical are temporary and will eventually end. Spiritual things are forever. Man should not fail to place importance on spiritual things.

Small Intestine

The small intestine is a tube-like structure that is about twenty feet long and one inch in diameter. The first part of the small intestine is called the duodenum which is only ten inches long. It is at this point where small amounts of food that has been in the stomach is released into the small intestine. This portion of the small intestine is unique in that it is at this section of the small intestine that bile, which has been stored in the gall bladder, is added to the food that is being digested. Bile is a substance that is similar to detergent and is used to help break down the larger fat molecules. Like soap dissolving and washing off grease and oil from the skin, so does bile in breaking down and emulsifying fats. In addition, the pancreas adds more of the carbohydrate enzyme amylase to the bolus of food at the duodenum. Thus, the duodenum serves as an entrance point for important digestive substances to help breakdown and digest food.

However, the duodenum also has another function. It is at this entrance to the digestive tract that bacteria can gain entrance to the body. As food is absorbed into the body, bacteria can also gain access to the inside of the body. The duodenum also serves a lymphatic or immune system function, searching out and destroying bacteria that would enter the body at the beginning of the intestines. This function will be discussed further as part of the lymphatic or immune system.

"For as we have many members in one body, but the members do not have the same function, so we, being many, are one body in Christ, and individually members of one another. Having then gifts differing according to the grace that is given to us ..." (Romans 12: 4–6). Like the various parts of the body have a function and serve the body, so it is with us as each of us have been given talents and abilities to serve the Lord. In the case of the duodenum, it has a main function of being the receiving area for important digestives agents to aid and support digestion. But being placed in this position, it also has been given another task, and that is to guard and protect the body against potential dangerous bacterial agents, if needed. There may not always be harmful bacteria in the area. But when there are, the duodenum is ready!

God has given us talents and abilities and has placed up in our homes and jobs. But in doing so, He has also given us specific skills to do specific things when called upon and needed. At various times in the life of humans, there are moments of need. Weather or "natural" disasters, sickness, death, financial needs. And in addition to the abilities God has given us to live our life and to share with others, He has also given us special skills that can be used in special times of need. The duodenum "understands" the necessity for digestion for life. But also recognizes the dangers that lurk in this process. God understands our physical needs that are a necessary for life. But He also recognizes the dangers associated with everyday living and knows what is best for us and has given us the tools and skills to help ourselves and others in times of need.

The bolus of food now moving through the small intestines has all the enzymes and substances needed for the chemical breakdown carbohydrates, fats and protein. The absorption process of these digesting molecules can now begin as the food begins its journey through the remaining length of the digestive system.

The next portion of the small intestines is called the jejunum. It is about eight feet long. It is within this portion of the small intestine that enzymes and other substances continue the breakdown of the food into the smaller "food" molecules that can be more readily absorbed and utilized by the body. Like the stomach, the surrounding tissue of the small intestines is also muscular. The muscular arrangement is such that the muscles can "squeeze" or push the digesting food further along the intestine tube or tract. This controlled movement is referred to as peristalsis. Food can then travel along the digestive tract in a timely and effective manner.

The final segment of the small intestine is the ilium. It is about twelve feet long, and this is where most of the smaller carbohydrate, fat and protein "food" molecules are absorbed by the body. Within the central lumen of the small intestines are millions of small, fingerlike projections called villi. These villi give the lining of the small intestine a velvet-like appearance and texture and gives a tremendous increase in the absorptive surface area of the inner lining of the mall intestine. This makes it much easier for the smaller "food" molecules to be absorbed and enter the body for use. In addition to the villi, goblet cells are nestled within the inner lining of the small intestines. The goblet cells add mucous to the digesting "food", to better aid in the moving of it down the digestive tract.

As certain foods are absorbed by the body and gives nourishment and strength to the body, absorbing "God's Word" also helps determine our "spiritual health". As previously mentioned, there are some foods such as proteins and fats that need special enzymes and acids to break down and absorb. This take special effort and time for the "food" to be properly utilized by the body. So it is with God's Word. Some of it requires special effort and time to be properly consumed and utilized by the spiritual "body". We have been given good Sunday school teachers, pastors, and other biblical scholars and leaders to help and properly discern God's Word for our life. And we need to take advantage of it in order to grow in strength and stature in the Lord.

Now that the food has been eaten, chewed, and digestive enzymes and other substances added, and it has been chemically broken down further and absorbed by the body, the remaining non-utilized waste must be prepared to be eliminated.

Large Intestine

The large intestines are about six feet long and about two and a half inches in diameter. The main function of this portion of the digestive tract is to absorb water and prepare the "waste" for elimination.

"Do you not yet understand that whatever enters your mouth goes into the stomach and is eliminated? But those things that proceed out of the mouth come from the heart, and they can defile a man. For out of the heart proceed evil thoughts, murders, adulteries, fornication, thefts, false witness, blasphemies. These are the things which defile a man. But to eat with unwashed hands does not defile a man" (Matthew 15:17–20).

Have you ever considered the things that come OUT of the human body? Urine, fecal matter, vomit, puss, mucous. It is all gross! These things come from INSIDE the body. But God uses this concept to describe a man's inward feelings and thoughts. And since the "heart" is the seat of human emotion, God uses this opportunity to express the attitude of the heart, and thus the inward feelings and thoughts of man. The heart will be discussed later. But regardless of how "wonderful" the things we eat may be, what comes OUT of the body is not so wonderful. And Scripture uses this analogy to describe our behavior, in that our behavior is driven by our thoughts, which come from within. Although we may understand that some of our actions may not be good, we often think that MOST of what we do IS good.

There are those who claim to always try to find the good that is in people. And this attitude is admirable. However, human history has shown just the opposite to be true, and the Bible is clear. "Even so you also outwardly appear righteous to men, but inside you are full of hypocrisy and lawlessness" (Matthew 23:28). "As it is written: there is none righteous, no not one" (Romans 3:10). "But we are all like an unclean thing. And all our righteousness are like filthy rags" (Isaiah 64:6). Scripture uses examples of what comes out of the body to exemplify the idea that what is INSIDE man (spiritually, speaking), is not good. And although it is clearly described that what is on the inside bad, it is interesting that this is where Jesus wants to reside! Only in Christ can we be "good". "Behold, I (Jesus) stand at the door and knock. If anyone hears my voice and opens the door, I will come IN to him and dine with him and he with me" (Revelations 3:20).

Mesentery, Hepatic Portal System, and Liver

If one considers the total length of the digestive tract, which is about 28 feet of "tubing", one also must consider how this continuous tube never gets tangled or "knotted up". Can you imagine if even one small area of this long digestive tract were to get twisted or snarled, what would happen? But the body has a design which sees that this does not happen. It is called the mesentery. The mesentery is like cellophane or clear plastic food storing wrap, such as Saran Wrap (trademark name, SC Johnson and Son, Inc.) or Glad ClingWrap (trademark name, The Glad Products Company).

It is part of the peritoneum within the abdomen that not only holds the intestines in its place, but also serves to house an elaborate yet intricate vascular system that is being used to absorb the digested food molecules. Keeping these blood vessels intact and maintaining position of the 28 feet of intestinal tubing is critical, and this mesentery is up to the task. Without it, the blood vessels would break and there would be twisting and knotting of the intestines.

All the digested food molecules in the small intestines are absorbed into this elaborate, intricate vascular system. But before the digested food molecules can be transported throughout the body, it FIRST must go to the liver. This relationship of intestine, blood vessels and liver relationship is called the hepatic portal system. Once there, the **liver** then "processes" and determines the disposition of the absorbed food molecules. This is why the liver is so critical in the health of a human. All food that is eaten and digested must pass through the liver before it can be forwarded on the rest of the body. The food that was once on the dinner table but is now broken down into its smallest molecular form, must now be organized and "processed" before the body can utilize it.

The liver can "cleanse" the blood of bacteria and toxins before going to the tissues of the body that need the life-giving nutrients. One example of how this occurs are Kupffer cells. Kupffer cells act as macrophages in the liver that can attack and engulf a single bacterium in less than 1/100 second and each Kupffer cell can engulf more than 100 bacteria.

More than 500 vital functions have been identified with the liver. Some of the more important functions include:

1. The clearing of drugs and other substances from the blood.
2. The making of immune factors and removing bacteria from the blood.
3. The production of bile, which breaks down fat and helps carry nutrients away from the small intestines.
4. The production of cholesterol and special proteins to help carry fats throughout the body.
5. The regulation of blood levels of certain amino acids (protein building blocks).
6. The production of certain proteins for blood plasma.
7. The regulation of blood clotting.
8. The storage of iron and processing blood hemoglobin.
9. The conversion of poisonous ammonia to urea (which is excreted in the urine).
10. Conversion of excess glucose into glycogen for storage.

Obtaining all the nutrients and energy supply by the Digestive System, and then breaking it down for use, yet at the same time protecting the body from harmful things that can enter and destroy the body is a complicated and ever continuing process. Studying the Bible and "feeding" on God's Word is not dissimilar.

To be sure the Bible is an enormous text, but there is a lot of it that can easily be understood. However, there are places of Scripture that can easily be taken out of context or otherwise "misconstrued". Thus, proper study and "processing" is needed. "You believe there is one God. You do well. Even the demons believe and tremble!" (James 2:19). When Satan was tempting Jesus, "And (Satan) said, if you are the Son of God, throw Yourself down. For it is written: 'He shall give charge over You and in their hands, they shall bear You up, lest You dash your foot against a stone'" (Matthew 4:6). Satan was quoting from Psalm 91:11. Thus, even Satan can quote Scripture.

It does no good for the physical body to just see good, nourishing food on the table. It does no good for the physical body to eat the food if there is no digestion. It does no good for the physical body to digest the food if it is not properly absorbed and distributed. So it is with God's Word. It does no good to the spiritual "body" for the Bible (spiritual food) to just sit on the table. It does no good to the spiritual "body" to sporadically read the Bible and try to digest its entirety. It does no good to read the Bible with a personal agenda, or out of context scheme that one may have in mind. Pure Bible study is important for spiritual growth, and it cannot be taken for granted.

The Urinary System

Man is a dynamic creature, meaning that man's life is a cycle of movements and activities, combined with periods of rest. However, regardless of the state of physical activity, certain physiological processes are occurring within the body to maintain a homeostasis. Homeostasis is the state of relative stability of the body's inner working physiology. For the body to remain healthy, a chemical balance must be maintained. The urinary system is major system of the body that helps regulate body homeostasis.

It has been shown that man is obliged to take in food and water if he is to remain alive. And it has also been shown that the human body must eliminate wastes. Although removal of waste such as fecal matter is done from the digestive system, there are considerably more waste products that must be removed from the body, or else death can ensue. The breakdown and use of proteins, for example, produce nitrogenous wastes such as ammonia and urea. Certain elements and ionic material such as hydrogen, sodium, chlorine, sulfates and phosphates, can accumulate to excess and be toxic to the nature and life of the body. Thus, these toxic materials must be eliminated from the body and the urinary system consisting of the kidneys, ureters, urinary bladder, and urethra are the parts of the body that does this.

Kidney

As previously mentioned, there are approximately 50 trillion cells in the body, and each one is undergoing and doing their various metabolic activities. And with this metabolic activity there are considerable metabolic waste and biproducts that are released into the surrounding interstitial fluids. These biproducts are toxic to the body and must be eliminated.

The cells receive their nutrients via the blood, and in return give off their waste products. These waste products are eventually picked up by the blood and transferred for processing and elimination. The kidneys are responsible for this processing, and the human body has two kidneys. Both kidneys are located in the upper, back part of the abdomen, protected by the most bottom two ribs.

The functional unit of the kidney is the nephron. There are approximately 1 million nephrons in each kidney. The specific anatomy of the nephrons ensures the processes of glomerular filtration, tubular reabsorption and tubular secretion, which are the mechanisms by which the wastes products in the circulating blood are removed. In the lifetime of an individual, the kidneys will process over 11 million gallons of blood and produce over 9,000 gallons of urine.

In addition to removing unwanted substances from the blood, the kidney is also responsible for maintaining a "normal" pH acid-base relationship. The pH of a substance is essentially a logarithmic scale of a hydronium ion (H_3O^+) concentration. The scale runs from 1–14, where numbers 1–6 are acidic concentrations and 8–14 are basic concentrations. The number 7 is neutral, neither basic or acidic. Normal pH values for circulating blood should be between 7.35 and 7.45, which is a narrow range. Any values above or below this value would spell eventual doom to the body. But the kidneys can increase alkalinity if the blood becomes too acidic, and it is able to increase acidity if the blood becomes too basic.

The speed of the work by the kidney can vary. And justly so. At night, while we are asleep, the kidneys may work "slow", so that it will not make too much urine during the night. If a lot of urine was produced during the night, we would have to wake up and void the bladder and this would interfere with much needed rest. Also, when exercising, the kidneys "alter" their work by making a more concentrated urine, thus keeping much needed fluids as one exercises.

Ureter, Urinary Bladder, Urethra.

As the toxins are removed from the blood, they are placed in surrounding fluid, forming urine. The urine then passes from the kidney through the **ureter** to the **urinary bladder** for storage in the form of urine, until there is an "appropriate" time for elimination. Each kidney has its own ureter. The urinary bladder is a muscular container that lies at the base of the pelvic cavity. It usually accumulates about a third of a pint of urine before being emptied, though it can expand and hold twice as much. From the urinary bladder, the urine then passed through a tube called the **urethra**, to outside the body.

As man lives his normal life in today's world, there are things that "naturally" occur. But in this process, certain life "toxins" may develop. For example, we can live such a busy life, working our jobs, going to Little League games or watching other sporting events, fishing and hunting, that we can miss out on worship and seeing the good things that God has presented to us in our life. It is not that these life things are not important. Watching my children and grandchildren participating in school sporting events and functions are important. But if left unchecked, they can unexpectedly consume us, and then we fail to see what God desires for us to do. Just like God created the Urinary System to help our bodies maintain a chemical balance in our physiological make up, He also made us to have a "balance" in our physical and spiritual lives.

As these "toxins" can build up over time, we may fail to see the blessings God wanted us to have, including salvation through His Son, until it is too late "And it is appointed unto men to die once, but after this the judgment" (Hebrews 9:27). Thus, in order to keep from getting caught up and worldly "toxins" consume us, we must continually be on guard and repeatedly checked our life and eliminate those things in our life that would eventually do us harm. God wants us to have a relationship with Him all the time. Not just on Sunday!

The Immune (Lymphatic) System

There are five kingdoms in the biological classification of life. These include Animalia, Plantae and Fungi, but also Protista, and Monera. (The Kingdom Monera has recently been divided further into Archaebacteria and Eubacteria). It is interesting that it is the smallest of these organisms from the Phyla Protista, which include single celled microorganisms and parasitic pathogens, and the Phyla Monera, which include bacteria, are responsible infectious and parasitic diseases, and account for the single most cause of deaths in humans.

The plague of Justinian in Europe in the middle sixth century killed upward to 60% of the population of London and Florence. The Black Death plague of the middle 1300's killed between 25 million and 100 million in Europe and Asia.[5] It is impossible to give a reasonable estimate of the number of human deaths throughout history as a result of infectious and parasitic diseases. Estimates of mortality of low and middle-income countries by 2030 due to infectious and parasitic disease as determined by the World Health Organization is 40%.[6] In other words, 40% of human deaths in these countries can be attributed to the effects of the smallest of all organisms, Protista and Monera!

The Immune (Lymphatic) System protects us from everyday threats of infections from these microorganisms and disease-causing pathogens. Without the immune system, even the simplest of illness can lead to death. A healthy immune system can distinguish between the body (self) and an invading foreign substance (non-self). This ability to distinguish "self" from "non-self" is central to the immune system. Recognizing what organisms cause harm to the body is important. However, we may live our life and never recognize the dangers that lurk.

"Be sober, be vigilant; because your adversary the devil walks about like a roaring lion, seeking whom he may devour" (1 Peter 5:8). A lion may be great in strength and should be feared. But even this mighty creature uses stealth to surprise its prey in their attacks. Satan is no different. This Scripture text uses a lion to describe Satan. Like a lion, Satan is a formidable foe. However, also like a lion, he "sneaks" and "deceives", devouring and destroying in the process. For a prey to escape a lion's snare, that prey must constantly be on the lookout and be on guard against being attacked and eaten by a lion.

We must also be on continual guard and look out for Satan's harm. As Satan goes about trying to "devour" us, our only salvation is in God. "I will lift up my eyes to the hills from whence comes my help? My help comes from the LORD, who made heaven and earth ... The LORD shall preserve you from all evil; He shall preserve your going out and your coming in from this time forth, and even forevermore" (Psalm 121:1, 8).

So it is with man. There are considerable outside organisms that can cause sickness and even death. We may be unaware of their existence and danger. And we need something to recognize and attack these outside agents of sickness and death. Our bodies are designed with an immune system, to do just that

Whether the danger be immediate and acute, or chronic and long term, the body has a defense mechanism available to help prevent sickness and even death to the body. There is a *nonspecific defense* that, although does not specifically recognize the invading pathogen, it still able to destroy foreign substances that has entered the body. Oftentimes this mechanism is used in an acute, inflammatory response, usually following an injury or breach of the body by an invading microorganism, such as a cut or infectious sore. In most cases, the number of invading microorganisms can be destroyed, and further infection is avoided.

There is also a *specific defense* that specifically recognizes certain foreign or unfamiliar substances and develop specific means to destroy that foreign substance. This mechanism is usually reserved for chronic or long-term effects and is the basis for vaccines and "inoculations". Vaccines take advantage of the body's natural ability to combat these foreign or unfamiliar pathogens. Either dead or denatured pathogens are placed in the body. Since the pathogen is dead or denatured, the person will not actually get the disease. However, the body responds by producing specific antibodies, in great numbers, which have been designed and made to target this particular pathogen. If the real, live pathogen does enter the body, the body is already prepared to attack and destroy this pathogen before the disease can set in. In effect, the body is stimulated to make ample antibodies to resist something that is real, by being exposed to something that is not real. Such vaccines have included the small pox and polio vaccines, diphtheria, rubella, tetanus, shingles, and numerous others.

Unfortunately, sometimes this can happen to the spiritual body. Sometimes individuals can get "inoculated" with "religion". For some, "religion" is a "foreign matter" to their life. They go to church and "pretend" they are Christians. Regrettably they may believe that they are "Christian", but in fact are not. They have just "gone through the motions" and have stimulated their spiritual antibodies to push aside the teachings of Christ. Essentially, church life is not part of their life but is extraneous. Because they may not have a personal relationship with Christ, Bible study and church attendance are not meaningful. Over time they become "immune", and ultimately it may prevent them from getting the real thing and having a relationship with the one true God. "Not everyone who says to Me (Jesus) Lord, Lord, shall enter the kingdom of heaven, but he that does the will of My Father in heaven. Many will say to Me in that day, Lord, Lord, have we not prophesied in Your name, cast out demons in Your name, and done many wonders in Your name? And then I (Jesus) will declare to them, I never knew you, depart from Me, you who practice lawlessness" (Matthew 7:21–23).

Antibodies

An antibody is any one of millions of distinct protein structures that are capable of "inactivating" specific microorganisms, virus, cancer cells, or other foreign microbes and bacteria. This process of "inactivating" these foreign bodies is called immunity. It is this immunity that protects the body by providing long term protection against reinfection by the same microorganisms.

The Immune or Lymphatic System has several functions. It does indeed play the major role in our "immunity" and disease fighting capabilities. But these immune defense mechanisms are intricately entwined. One function of the Immune (Lymphatic) System is to return interstitial fluid and other capillary effluents back into the cardiovascular system. It is kind of like a shower drain. When we wash ourselves, the "dirty" rinse water goes down the drain and runs into the septic tank or sewer line (for "processing" and return to "nature"). However, the body cannot "hook up" to a sewer line. Instead the body has its own system of pipes and cleaners to help collect this "rinse water".

The cardiovascular capillaries surround and perfuse body tissue like a shower, flooding the tissue with life giving nutrients and fluids. The cells absorb and take in these nutrients and in return give off metabolic wastes. These metabolic wastes make their way into the surrounding interstitial fluid and is like what was described as dirty "rinse water". Venous return of this fluid via the cardiovascular system capillaries is too slow to return directly back into the pipes of the cardiovascular system. If this venous return could not keep up and return the fluid to the cardiovascular system, there would eventually be a collective buildup of interstitial fluid, causing swelling, bloating and eventually death. But there is a system of lymphatic capillaries and veins (pipes) that additionally collect and return this fluid back into the body's cardiovascular system. The system of "pipes" is called the Lymphatic System and the fluid is called Lymph.

Lymph

Lymph is a clear, watery fluid. It is like blood, but without the red cells and most other plasma proteins that are found in blood. Not all the fluid that exudes from the capillaries of the cardiovascular system re-enters the cardiovascular system. In a 24-hour period, almost a gallon of cardiovascular "fluids" is picked up by lymphatic vessels and eventually makes its way back into the cardiovascular system.

In the meantime, this fluid will continually bathe surrounding body tissues. Within this fluid we will find certain leukocytes or "white" cells. Leukocytes are produced in the bone marrow and are also found in blood. One class of leukocytes is *monocytes*. These cells seek out and can ingest certain pathogenic microorganisms, cancer cells, cellular debris, and other matter found in lymph.

A second class of leukocytes is *lymphocytes*. There are B lymphocytes and T lymphocytes. There are as many as 2 trillion B lymphocytes in the body and are considered the basis of the immune response. These are responsible for producing over 100 million trillion antibodies in a lifetime![7] And what is most impressive is that most of these antibodies do not even look alike, responding to the many different antigens and foreign substances that can destroy the body.

Lymphatic Capillaries and Ducts

Lymphatic capillaries are similar to cardiovascular capillaries. They enhance recovery of excess interstitial fluids and waste material surrounding the cells of the body tissue. Thus, one function of the lymphatic system is to assist in the return of fluids or lymph back to the cardiovascular system. And in this process, it will also assist in transporting certain fat and protein molecules back to the cardiovascular system for circulation throughout the body.

But the major function of the Lymphatic System is body surveillance and defense. It protects the body from foreign cells, microbes, cancer cells, or other microbial agents that seek to do the body harm and even death. These microscopic parasitic and infectious disease producing organisms are called pathogens and come from the kingdoms Protista and Monera. It is the purpose of the Lymphatic System to locate and destroy these pathogens.

The lymphatic capillaries eventually dump lymph into larger pipes called lymphatic ducts. These ducts are very similar in size and structure to cardiovascular veins, except, scattered along these lymphatic ducts are areas like a strainer or filter. These areas are called lymph nodes. These lymph nodes catch these small foreign microbes and bacteria, essentially collecting or "rounding them up" in a close area. After they are collected, they can be destroyed. These lymphatic ducts are scattered throughout the body and eventually ties back into the cardiovascular system near the heart. Most lymph nodes are found within the trunk of the body, with concentrated areas under the arm pit and in the inguinal area.

This is why oncologists are interested in lymph nodes for cancer treatment. A greater number of lymph nodes showing cancer cells indicates a greater extent of the spread of the cancer.

There are other areas of lymphatic tissues. These include the tonsils, duodenum, appendix, spleen and thymus gland. These lymphatic tissues of the Immune System work with other body systems such as the Cardiorespiratory and Digestive systems to seek and destroy the smallest of infection causing pathogens.

Tonsils

Airborne pathogens may think that they can enter the body via the air that is breathed into the lungs. However, the body has a defense for that. It is called the tonsils. Tonsils are essentially a strategically arranged ring of lymphatic nodules that surround the junction of the oral cavity and the pharynx at the back of the throat. Airborne pathogens, including those that may be in food and are eaten, must pass by the tonsils. These pathogens are collected and attacked by the lymphatic tissue of the tonsils.

Oftentimes the tonsils may be overwhelmed by pathogens and become infected. In the "old days" tonsils had to be removed as such infections were too great for the body to fight alone. But today, there are modern antibiotics that can assist in destroying the bacteria that seeks to do our body harm.

Duodenum

The first part of the small intestines is the duodenum. If a pathogen has passed the tonsils without being destroyed, it will enter the stomach, then pass into the duodenum. But a function of the duodenum is lymphatic. Like the tonsils, it contains lymphatic tissue that seeks and destroys pathogens that may enter the digestive tract. However, even if a pathogen has made it all the way to the large intestine, the body still has an additional defense mechanism, the appendix.

Appendix

The final segment of the small intestine is the ilium. Instead of the ilium simply becoming a larger diameter and beginning the large intestine, the ilium merges with the large intestine about an inch from the beginning at a 90° angle. This forms a sac or pouch called the cecum. As the remaining waste material enters the large intestines from the ilium, it must make this 90° turn to begin its journey through the large intestine. It is at this point that existing pathogens can be trapped in the cecum and then destroyed by the lymphatic tissue of the appendix. And like the tonsils, in the early days when the appendix could be overwhelmed and become infected, oftentimes it had to be removed. But today, antibiotics can help in destroying the bacteria that is set to destroy the body.

Spleen

The spleen is the largest lymphatic organ in the body. The main function of the spleen is a revitalization of blood by removing dead red blood cells, platelets, microorganisms and other debris from the blood. It also aids in the production of Monocytes and certain Lymphocytes. And because it contains so much blood it also serves as a reservoir of blood to the general blood circulation in the case of trauma or accident.

Thymus Gland

The thymus gland is a ductless gland located in the chest, overlying the heart. It secretes its products into the surrounding tissue to be picked by the cardiovascular and lymphatic capillaries. It is greatest in size at birth and diminishes in size with age. After puberty it essentially atrophies and is involved very little in the immune system in adulthood. However, during early child hood it is most active, producing antibodies. It is during this early time in life when these antibodies are produced to fight against disease pathogens and maintain its strength against future attacks.

Thus, it is during the early stages of life that one can garnish the greatest effect of the immune system. "Remember now your Creator in the days of your youth before the difficult days come ..." (Ecclesiastes 12:1). It is much easier to learn of God's amazing grace early in life and grow from it, than to live a life of many years and not experience it. "LORD, my heart is not haughty, nor my eyes lofty. Neither do I concern myself with great matters, or with things too profound for me. Surely I have calmed and quieted my soul, like a weaned child with his mother; like a weaned child is my soul within me" (Psalm 131:1–2). "Rejoice O young man, in your youth, and let your heart cheer you in the days of your youth" (Ecclesiastes 11:9).

When we are young, it is easier to accept God's word. And oftentimes because we are young, we do not understand God's Word, but we accept it in faith. It is then that over time we become stronger and mature into what God wants us to become.

"Then Jesus called a little child to Him, set him in the midst of them and said, 'Assuredly, I say to you, unless you are converted and become as a little child, you will by no means enter the kingdom of heaven. Therefore, whoever humbles himself as this little child is the greatest in the kingdom of heaven'" (Matthew 18:2–4). It is because of this youthful innocence that one can more easily receive the message of the Bible.

Once an individual has become older and has not already accepted the gift of life through Jesus, the chances of the "Disease of ME" can set in and take a solid grip on the life of the individual. The main symptom of the Disease of Me is that of self-centeredness. The individual succumbs to Satan's lies. ME becomes most important in the world and the pathogens of selfish pride and egotistical self-interest invade the spiritual body. The Disease of Me can easily set in, because there are no spiritual antibodies immediately available to fight against such lethal agents.

Besides the "Disease of Me", there is another scenario that can occur. It is that of being "Inoculated with Religion". We may get "excited" about "religion", claim to know Christ as our Savior, and even get "involved" in a church. Using the same analogy of inoculation and the effects of the immune system, we may gain a limited amount of biblical knowledge and understanding of Christ and the Church. But this lack of depth in knowledge and understanding can keep us from getting the real thing. We are deceived that we know enough and may even develop our own philosophy and theology regarding God and His laws and His plan of salvation. Thus, we become "inoculated" with our "religious" thoughts and ideas, and it prevents us from getting the Truth, as presented in Scripture. Regarding both scenarios, if left untreated, the individual will perish.

But given the right treatment, recovery is possible. "The Lord is not slack concerning His promise, as some count slackness, but is longsuffering toward us, not willing that any should perish, but that all should come to repentance" (2 Peter 3:9). "I tell you no; but unless you repent you will all likewise perish" (Luke 13:3).

There is a "true" story of long ago, but like many stories, the authenticity and accuracy of the truth may be debated. But there is a story of a young boy, born of an aristocratic family in the late 1800's in England. This boy fell into a creek but was saved by another young boy who was of a peasant background. The aristocratic father was so pleased and thankful that his son had been saved, he offered a reward to the peasant boy's father. But he refused.

However, not to let this deed go unnoticed and rewarded, the aristocratic father paid for the private education of the peasant father's son. That young boy grew up, interested in science and medicine, and went on to propose the germ theory of disease and the concept of sterilization. He developed the first vaccines for anthrax and rabies. He established an infectious diseases research and training institute and became known as the father of microbiology. This boy's name was Louis Pasteur. The name of the aristocratic son that fell in to the creek was Winston Churchill. Of course, he went on to become Prime Minister of England and became a key figure during World War II.

Man had to study and learn and experiment in order to understand and utilize the effects of Immune (Lymphatic) System. As we witness the wonders of modern medical technologies and medicines, it amazing how God can weave such a special, unique web of life for each individual in this world. We fail to see the larger picture that is there, but the Lord can certainly see. In fact, God's immune system for us has been there the whole time.

The Respiratory (Pulmonary) System

There is little doubt as to the importance of the respiratory system. The human body can survive without food for several weeks and without water for several days. But the human body can survive only a few minutes without oxygen. It is this oxygen that is used in the respiration equation described in Chapter 1. It is interesting that God used this principle in the creation of man. "And the LORD God formed man of the dust of the ground, and breathed into his nostrils the breath of life; and man became a living soul" (Genesis 2:7). A breathless body certainly indicates a lifeless body.

It is interesting that the gospel writer Mark, described Jesus' death on the cross, "And Jesus cried with a loud voice and breathed His last" (Mark 15:37). Jesus was totally man, needing to eat, sleep, breathe. In Bethlehem on the first Christmas morning, he had the "breath of life". At the time of the Passover, while on the cross, He breathed His last breath. Fortunately, the story does not end there as Jesus conquered death and rose again. But it gives the significance of breathing.

Almost 80% of the earth atmosphere is nitrogen. Only about 20% of the earth atmosphere is oxygen. The nitrogen serves as a "filler gas" or material that the oxygen can diffuse through and spread out throughout the earth's atmosphere. When breathed in, nitrogen is inert and is not involved in any chemical reactions in our body. Although it cannot support life, it does no harm to the body to breathe in.

Oxygen on the other hand is very chemically reactive. In addition to giving life, oxygen supports combustion. No sparks or open flame signs may be posted around oxygen tanks because of the danger of explosion. If the earth's atmosphere contained more oxygen, even one small spark from somewhere overseas could ignite the entire atmosphere. Extracting this oxygen for use in the human body is remarkable. For some living organisms, oxygen simply diffuses into the body of the organism. This mechanism of obtaining lifegiving oxygen severely limits the physical abilities of the organism.

The human body is designed to do so much more, and the need for oxygen is so much more. Therefore, the mechanism to extract the oxygen from the air is not only important, but is an elaborate process for which the body is adequately prepared. The components of the respiratory system are uniquely designed to take in and absorb atmospheric oxygen. The nose, pharynx, larynx, trachea, bronchi and bronchioles, as well as the lungs, all contribute to the process of taking oxygen out of the air and putting it in the body. At the same time, the respiratory system collects and releases certain compounds such as carbon dioxide that are lethal to the body.

Our body uses the lungs by filling them with air (oxygen) that is needed for life. Thus, we "take in" oxygen, and it provides us with life. But sometimes our life can be enhanced and fulfilled by things that "take our breath away". I recall the sight of my bride on my wedding night. I recall the first sight of my first born. I recall my first sight of the city of Jerusalem, the great wall of China, the Grand Canyon, my daughter making a game winning basket (in basketball), my granddaughter catching a large redfish. (This list could easily continue.) There are many things that contribute to the enjoyment and pleasure of life, that ironically, instead of breathing in oxygen, it "takes your breath away". "When I consider Your heavens, the work of Your fingers, the moon, the stars, which You have ordained, what is man that you are mindful of him" (Psalm 8:3–4).

The diaphragm is a curved muscle that separates the abdomen from the chest. As the diaphragm contracts, it shortens, creating a negative pressure in the lungs, where air then, rushes in.

Nose

The nose has several functions. It warms and moisturizes the inspired air, detects odor in the airstream, and serves as a resonating chamber that amplifies voice. The nasal cavity has a mucosal lining. Inhaled dust, pollen, bacteria, and other foreign material stick to the mucus and are swallowed (for destruction and elimination) rather than contaminating the lungs. This mucosal lining also helps to warm and moisturize the air before it enters the lungs. This tissue responds to blood flow. Every 30–60 minutes, this tissue on one side of the nose swells and restricts airflow through that nostril. Most air is then directed through the other nostril, allowing this side of the nostril to recover from drying. Thus, the preponderance of air flow shifts from one side of the nostrils to the other once or twice each hour, preventing overuse damage to the mucosal lining of the nose.

Pharynx

The pharynx is a muscular channel which sits at the beginning of the esophagus. It has three parts, each of which is important. The first part receives the Eustachian tube from the ear. This serves as the opening to balance the air pressure within the inner ear. The second part is where the palatine tonsils are located. They are well positioned to respond to airborne pathogens. The third part is this is where the esophagus begins.

Larynx

The larynx is the "voice box". It is a cartilaginous chamber that also contains the epiglottis, which is used to block the esophagus when swallowing. The walls of the larynx are quite muscular, and are used in swallowing and for speech. The inside wall of the larynx has folds of cartilage that are referred to as the vocal cord. When air is forced pass these folds, sound is produced.

Trachea, Bronchi, Bronchioles, Alveoli

The trachea is a tube about four and a half inches in length. The tube is C-shaped with cartilage, meaning that most of the circumference of the tube is cartilage. But running along the backside and the length of the trachea is the esophagus. The esophagus is a soft, collapsed tube that only opens when a bolus of food is passing down to the stomach. It is along this region that the back portion of the trachea is not cartilage, but mainly soft tissue, attaching to the esophagus for its support but also allowing for a large bolus of food that is passing down the esophagus to protrude into the trachea somewhat.

The outer part of the trachea may be rigid cartilage, but the inner lining is columnar epithelial cells which are ciliated, or have small hairs. These cells secrete mucous that can trap inhaled particulates and move them upward and out of the trachea, keeping these particulates out of the lungs. The trachea enters the lungs, where it branches into smaller and smaller bronchi and bronchioles. These bronchioles eventually terminate into small, grape-like clusters called alveolar sacs. Each alveolar sac will terminate with the final anatomy of the lung, the alveoli. It is at the surface of the alveoli that gas exchange takes place. Essentially oxygen is absorbed and carbon dioxide is released.

Lungs

Although bronchioles spread throughout the lungs, the bulk of lung tissue is the alveoli. Each lung contains about 150 million alveoli. The combined surface area that these alveoli have is equal to the surface of a tennis court! In addition, there are alveolar macrophages roaming the spaces of the lungs, trapping dust and debris that may have reached the final depths of the lungs. They also trap bacteria and loose blood cells, keeping the surface of the alveoli as clean as possible. As many as 100 million alveolar macrophages die each day as they ride up the trachea elevator to be swallowed and digested, thus ridding the lungs of any debris that may hinder the necessary exchange of gasses in the alveoli.[8]

With normal inspiration, about a pint of air is inhaled and moves into the lung for gas exchange. Minimal workloads performed by the body require only a minimal amount of oxygen. However, when the body is under a greater workload and more oxygen is needed, the lungs can accommodate up to one and a half gallons of air, or roughly 10 times more air! Since oxygen that is in the air is required by man in order to live, a lot of breathing must take place. Three hundred million breaths in a lifetime is a lot of breathing. The body goes to great lengths to exchange carbon dioxide and other by-products of metabolism with oxygen from the air, and it does not have a true air filter that can be removed and replaced. The Respiratory (Pulmonary) System is "fitly framed together" in its own right.

The Cardiovascular System

The Cardiovascular System has long been a topic of life and life systems of the human body. In order to maintain the body, a continual supply of food, oxygen, vitamins and other nutrients are necessary and must traverse throughout the body. The Cardiovascular System delivers the life-giving needs to the body while removing the waste and by-products of cellular metabolism. Blood is the river of life that flows within the body, yet a pump must push the blood and there must be a network of vascular "pipes" to carry the life-giving blood.

Blood

Blood has long since been viewed as important and a necessary part of life. Blood is not merely a "fluid" that carries nutrients throughout the body. It represents life itself. To shed blood implies that death occurs. There is a trail of blood throughout the Bible. There are over 200 references to blood in the Bible.

> But you shall not eat flesh with its life that is its blood. (Genesis 9:4)

> And He (God) said, "what have you done? The voice of your brother's blood cries out to Me from the ground." (Genesis 4:10)

> For the life of flesh is in the blood, and I have given it to you upon the altar to make atonement for your souls; for it is the blood that makes atonement for the

soul … for it is the life of all flesh. Its blood sustains its life …. (Leviticus 17:11–14)

And Moses took the blood, sprinkled it on the people, and said, this is the blood of the covenant which the LORD has made with you according to all these words. (Exodus 24:8)

And from Jesus Christ, the faithful witness, the firstborn from the dead, and the ruler over kings of the earth. To Him who loved us and washed us from our sins in His own Blood …. (Revelation 1:5)

Blood has a purpose and within the body it travels in one direction only. It does not ebb and flow or "slosh" around. Life, too, has direction and purpose. Whatever is in the blood directs our life. Nutrients, vitamins, drugs, anything that is in the blood affects the body. The basic tenet of Christian faith is that Jesus shed His blood and died on the cross as payment for our sins. Since Jesus was physical, His blood was also physical, and as such was "given" and accepted as the ultimate payment for the redemption of our sins. But if it were blood that was needed, why could not Jesus just cut His arm or something and "bleed". The answer is that blood IS life. And the sacrifice of Jesus' blood was sufficient payment for man's sin and resulting death.

And according to the law almost all things are purified with blood, and without the shedding of blood, there is no remission (of sin). (Hebrews 9:22)

…having now been justified by His (Jesus') blood, we shall be saved from wrath through Him. (Romans 5:9)

In Him (Jesus) we have redemption through His blood, the forgiveness of sins, according to the riches of His grace. (Ephesians 1:7)

...in whom we have redemption through His (Jesus') blood, the forgiveness of sins. (Colossians 1:14)

...to Jesus the Mediator of the new covenant, and to the blood of sprinkling that speaks better things than of Abel. (Hebrews 13:24)

Therefore Jesus also, that He might sanctify the people with His own blood, suffered outside the gate. (Hebrews 13:12)

It is interesting that as God prepared the Hebrews to leave Egypt, the first "plague" upon Egypt was the turning of water to blood. The final "plague" was the death of the first born. And as a focus of the Passover, God instructed the Hebrews to spread the blood (of a sacrifice) on the two door posts and lintel" (Exodus 12:7). As the Death Angel "passed over" the household, families were spared and death did not happen. However, if the Death Angel did not see the blood, death was certain. "Now the blood shall be a sign for you on the houses where you are. And when I see the blood, I will pass over you; and the plague shall not be on you ..." (Exodus 12:13). When God sees a "born-again believer" (Christian), He does not see the sins of the individual, but rather sees the blood of Christ and "passes over" and the individual is spared eternal death.

It is because of God's love for man that He was willing to sacrifice Himself with His blood. "For God so loved the world that He gave His only begotton Son, that whosoever believes in Him should not perish but have everlasting life" (John 3:16). "But God demonstrated His love toward us in that while we were still sinners, Christ died for us. Much more then, having now been justified by His blood, we shall be saved from wrath through Him" (Romans 5:8–9). "...I live by faith in the Son of God, who loved me and gave Himself for me" (Galatians 2:20).

We talk about love, but many times do not truly understand its meaning. There is a story of a 12-year-old boy and his 8-year-old sister. During the Viet Nam war their parents were killed and the little girl was wounded, and in need of blood. As this emergency presented itself, a nurse, in a moment of quick decision, found out that the little girl and her brother had the same blood type and decided to take a little blood from the boy and do a transfusion with his sister. Not much blood would be needed and the procedure would not be too invasive on the boy, yet it might save the life of the little girl. The boy willingly wanted to be a part of that and eagerly submitted to the "needle stick".

After a few moments, the nurse noticed the boy, sniffling and subtly crying. Thinking that the needle was hurting the boy's arm she asked him what was wrong. He replied, "When am I to die?" Not fully understanding the procedure, the boy thought that he was going to die while giving blood to his sister. He loved his sister so much that he was willing to sacrifice his life for her. Man can only imagine the love God has for us.

There is a little over a gallon of blood in the human body. The liquid portion of blood is plasma. Although about 90% of it is water, plasma contains over 100 different dissolved solutes, including nutrients, gases, hormones, wastes. Larger proteins and other molecules are also found in the plasma.

About 45% of blood by volume are red blood cells. There are approximately 25, 000 million red blood cells in the blood, or about 5 million red blood cells per cubic centimeter (cc). Red blood cells are essentially a bag containing molecules called hemoglobin. Hemoglobin is a protein that has not only can carry oxygen, but is also able to "swap it" for carbon dioxide. There is not a nucleus and DNA in red blood cells, there is only hemoglobin. Each red blood cell can contain as many as 250 million hemoglobin molecules.

The reason hemoglobin is contained in the sac-like red blood cells instead of just free floating in the plasma is that the hemoglobin molecules would break in smaller fragments and leak into the tissue and not be able to return to the circulation. Therefore, they are nicely bound within the red blood cell. Red blood cells have a useful lifespan of about 120 days, or four months. The bone marrow makes about an ounce of blood containing about 1,000 million (1 billion) red blood cells each day or about 2.5 million per second![8]

Blood also contains white blood cells and platelets. White blood cells or leukocytes, serve as non-specific defense scavengers that seek and destroy microorganisms at infection sites, and help remove debris and dead or injured cells. Between 4,000 and 1,000 white blood cells are in one cubic centimeter (cc) of blood. There are five types of white blood cells. They are: Basophils, Eosinophil, Lymphocytes, Monocytes, Neutrophils. Each has its own function. While most white blood cells last only a few days, lymphocytes may last for up to a year. During an infection, some white blood cells may last only a few hours until they are replaced.

Platelets are not cells in the strict sense, but rather small sacs (about one-fourth the size of white blood cells). Platelets are used in the clotting mechanism of blood. There are about 150,000–400,000 platelets per cc of blood. Most platelets degenerate within ten days. Roughly 30,000 must be replaced every day for each cc of blood.

Plasma, red blood cells, white blood cells, platelets, all tirelessly working in the blood for the body and are actively replaced as needed by the body.

Heart

Since ancient times, the heart has been thought of as the center of intelligence and source of emotion. During times of stress and extreme excitement, the heartbeat in the chest beats strong and fast. Around Valentine's day we are reminded of a familiar shape of the heart. But stripped of its mysterious and romantic cloak, the heart is nothing more than a muscular pump, pushing blood throughout the body. And although we can study the heart as an anatomical organ, we still describe it as the seat of our emotions.

God chose the "heart" as the focus of man's thoughts, emotions and behavior.

> So that you incline your ear to wisdom, and apply your heart to understanding. (Proverbs 2:2)

> When wisdom enters your heart, and knowledge is pleasant to soul .... (Proverbs 2:10)

My son, forget not my (God's) law; but let your heart keep my commandments; (Proverbs 3:1)

But sanctify the Lord God in your heart .... (1 Peter 3:15)

Then He (Jesus) opened his mouth and taught them, saying ... "Blessed are the pure in heart, for they shall see God." (Matthew 5:2, 8)

For it is the God who commanded light to shine out of darkness, who has shone in our hearts to give light of the knowledge of the glory of God in the face of Jesus Christ. (2 Corinthians 4:6)

The Bible links our thoughts and behavior to the heart, and most of the time, man's thoughts and behavior are bad.

Then the LORD saw that the wickedness of man was great in the earth, and that every intent of the thoughts of his heart was only evil continually. (Genesis 6:5)

The heart is deceitful above all things, and desperately wicked: who can know it? (Jeremiah 17:9)

So the LORD said to Moses, Pharaoh's heart is hard, he refuses to let the people go. (Exodus 7:14)

And when He (Jesus) looked around at them with anger, being grieved by the hardness of their hearts .... (Mark 3:5)

And Jesus knowing their thoughts said, "Why do you think evil in your hearts?" (Matthew 9:4)

"You have neither part nor portion in this matter, for your heart is not right in the sight of the Lord" (Acts 8:21).

So He (Jesus) said to them, "Are you thus without understanding also? Do you not perceive that whatever enters a man from the outside cannot defile him, because it does not enter his heart but his stomach and is eliminated, thus purifying all foods ...? For from within, out of the heart of men proceed evil thoughts ..." (Mark 7:18–19, 21).

Considering all the evil that goes on in this world today, it could be said that the heart of the problem is the heart. There is a medical condition called arteriosclerosis, where the arteries of the body become harden with calcium deposits or plaque. It is a serious condition and is the leading cause of heart attacks, stroke and peripheral vascular disease.

There is a similar medical condition of the heart called atherosclerosis. It is where fat deposits occur within the arteries that supply blood to the heart muscle itself. These fatty deposits can be the result of fatty diets and high cholesterol. If these blood vessels become "clogged" with fat, it decreases the amount of blood being pumped to the area. And of course, this can compromise the tissue, leading to muscle death and eventually cardiac failure.

Unfortunately, both conditions do not have any early "symptoms" or warning signs and may not be noticed until it is too late. However, with medical checkups we can be made aware of the potential problems, and with a better diet, exercise, and medication, these conditions can be eliminated or delayed.

In many areas of our life, there are tragic consequences that occur as a result of "poor" behavior and actions. Over time, calloused hands are made from friction and conflict. A heart can also become calloused over time from friction and conflict of life. And many times, these consequences are not noticed until it is too late. But Jesus can change these serious conditions. "Behold I (Jesus) stand at the door (of the heart) and knock. If anyone hears My voice and opens the door, I will come in to him and dine with him, and he with Me" (Revelation 3:20).

There is a story about a little 9-year-old girl who needed open heart surgery. When the surgeon was explaining the surgery to the little girl, saying he would have to open the chest in order to see the heart, the little girl said, "Then you can see Jesus. He's in my heart." To be sure, the only one who can satisfy the heart is the one who made it. "He (God) heals the broken in heart, and binds up their wounds" (Psalm 147:3).

A lot can be said of the heart and the emotional and behavioral characteristics that surround its nature. King David of Israel was a man described as a man after God's own heart. "...the LORD has sought for Himself a man after His own heart ..." (1 Samuel 13:14). "...I have found David the son of Jesse, a man after My own heart, who will do all My will" (Acts 13:22). As a young boy, David confronted the great giant Goliath of the Philistine army. But his brother, and others, doubted David's ability to fight and defeat the giant. "Now Eliab his (David's) older brother heard when he (David) spoke to the men; and Eliab's anger was aroused against David, and he said, why do you come down here? And with whom have you left those few sheep in the wilderness? I know your pride and the insolence of your heart, for you have come down to see the battle?" (1 Samuel 17:28). David had not come to "see" the battle but to be the victorious hero of it.

His brother(s) could not see inside of David and see his heart. All they could see was what they saw on the outside. And what they saw was a young, inexperienced boy, thinking that he was a warrior. But the results of what happened later was a great event. David killed Goliath and helped the Israelite army defeat the Philistines. God can see our hearts. The accomplishments of our hearts are immeasurable. "I can do all things through Christ who strengthens me" (Philippians 4:13). David certainly accomplished a lot!

The physical anatomy of the human heart is remarkable. It is about the size of a fist and weighs less than a pound. It has four chambers and has two parts of a "beat". The upper chambers of the heart are the atrium. Like the atrium of a building, it receives. The right atrium receives unoxygenated blood from the body while the left atrium receives oxygenated blood from the lungs.

When we listen to a single heartbeat, we hear two sounds, or a "lub-dub" sound. These are the sounds of the tricuspid and bicuspid valves (valves between the chambers of the atria and ventricles) that together, give a sound when "slapping shut", and alternating with the pulmonary valve and aortic valve (valves at the entrance of the pulmonary artery and aorta (artery) that together, give a sound when "slapping shut". During the first phase of the heart "beat", the heart muscles of the atrium contract and squeeze blood down into the ventricles. Unoxygenated blood from the right atria moves into the right ventricle and oxygenated blood from the left atrium moves into the left ventricle.

Once both ventricles are filled with blood, the second phase of the heart "beat" takes place. The muscles of the ventricles contract, expelling blood from the ventricles. The unoxygenated blood from the right ventricle goes to the lungs for oxygenation, while the oxygenated blood of the left ventricle goes to the rest of the body for use. Thus, there is a unique mechanism of stimulation of the heart muscle for a controlled, rhythmic contraction, moving blood in a single direction only. There is a built in "pacemaker" that not only controls the rate of the heartbeat, but the direction of contraction by the atrial and ventricle muscles. Blood is squeezed "downward" into the ventricles, then blood is squeezed "upward", out into the arteries to the lung and body. It is an amazing process that occurs (on average) 70 times per minute 4,200 times per hour, 100,800 times per day!

In other words, blood from the body enters the right atrium, then is moved to the right ventricle, where it is pumped to the lungs for oxygenation. The oxygenated blood returns to the heart, entering the left atrium, which then moves into the left ventricle, and is then pumped to the far reaches of the body.

The amount of blood pumped by the heart per "beat" is called the stroke volume. The average stroke volume is about 70 milliliters (ml) or 2.5 ounces. A canned soft drink is 355 ml or 12 ounces. Thus, in five heartbeats, the heart will pump the equivalent of a volume in a canned soft drink. In an hour it will pump about 73 gallons and in a day, it will pump over 1,700 gallons. In a year that works out to be nearly 650,000 gallons of blood, and in a lifetime over 45 million gallons of blood!

The amount of blood pumped out by the heart per minute is referred to as the cardiac output and can be calculated by multiplying the stroke volume by the heart rate. Thus, a stroke volume of 70 ml a heart rate, times a heart rate of 70 beats/minute, equals 4,900 ml or 4.9 liters or a little over a gallon. The maximum heart rate can be estimated by subtracting your age from 220. Therefore, a person, aged 30 will have a maximum heart rate of 190 beats per minute (220 − 30 = 190). A good exercising heart rate is generally 80–85 maximum heart rate, or in this case 152 (80% of 190).

When heart rate increases with exercise, stroke volume also increases, as the ventricles stretch to receive more blood and squeeze more blood out of the ventricles. An exercising stroke volume can increase up to 130 ml. Therefore, a stroke volume of 130 ml combined with a heart rate of 152 beats/minute will result in a cardiac output of 19,760 ml or 19.7 liters or a little over five gallons. In other words, when the heart is at rest and under "normal" conditions, it will deliver a little over a gallon of blood to the body each minute. But with exercise, it can deliver over five gallons per minute!

Although the body needs the nutrients that the blood carries, it is the oxygen that it needs most. Lack of oxygen to body parts, especially the brain, could result in permanent damage or death in only a few minutes. The $VO_{2\,max}$ is a measurement of the maximum amount of oxygen the body can "sniff in", diffuse into the lungs and into the blood, be pumped out by the heart, transported to the body (muscles) by the blood vessels, enter the muscle, diffuse into the cell, and be utilized in the metabolic equations. In other words, it is the body's ability to take in oxygen and use it. There is a lot involved.

The $VO_{2\,max}$ can be used to judge the general cardiovascular health of an individual. People who smoke or have other pulmonary or cardiovascular issues have a lower $VO_{2\,max}$ while athletes generally have a higher $VO_{2\,max}$. A person with a $VO_{2\,max}$ of 30 ml O_2 per minute per kilogram (kg)body weight, would probably have to "huff and puff" walking across a parking lot, while a person with a $VO_{2\,max}$ of 80 ml O_2 per minute per kilogram body weight could probably run a marathon in three hours!

Aerobic or cardiovascular training can increase the body's $VO_{2\,max}$.

For example, an individual with a VO_{2max} of 40 ml/min/kg can train aerobically and increase the VO_{2max} to 50 ml/min/kg or more. Our spiritual training is not much different. How much "spiritual training" is done in the average Christian's life? Is the ability to enhance our Biblical knowledge and its principles increase, or does it remain stagnant in our daily lives? Paul, in his letter to Titus, expounded on the qualities of a sound church. " ...in all things showing yourself to be a pattern of good works; in doctrine showing integrity, reverence, incorruptibility, sound speech that cannot be condemned, that on who is an opponent may be ashamed, having nothing evil to say of you ... that they may adorn the doctrine of God our Savior in all things" (Titus 2:7–8, 10).

I have had conversations with many non-Christians in my life. And many times, I have been told that when they have spoken with other "Christians", they have perceived that many of those "Christians" did not know much about God, the gospel, and the Bible in general. And because those "Christians" lack knowledge and spiritual growth, they are a detriment and deterrent to any witness or testimony I may have. Though I do not claim to be a Bible scholar, I do try to "train" and increase my VO_{2max}, or rather, my ability to learn and gain knowledge, and grow in Christ. Though someone with a high VO_{2max} may never run a marathon, they are still much healthier than an individual with a low VO_{2max}.

There are no ligaments that can hold the beating heart in place as it incessantly beats throughout the life of an individual. Any ligament or structure that would hold the heart in place as the heart continually beats would eventually break as a result of the forces generated during the physical heartbeat. The pipes, or the arteries and veins leading to and coming from the heart are not capable of holding the heart in place either. Instead, the heart is inside a stable sac, called the pericardial sac (peri, as in perimeter, meaning around). Within this sac is a fluid referred to as the pericardial fluid. The sac and fluid help protect the heart and keeps the heart in place during its physical beating and movement.

There are five major "coronary" arteries, and other secondary arteries, that envelop the heart and supply the heart itself with rich, oxygenated blood. Surrounding these arteries is fat, which have the appearance as they encircle the heart, of a king's crown. Thus, the name "coronary" is derived from a "coronation" of royalty.

Arteries, Veins, Capillaries

Blood vessels are sometimes compared to pipes that are scattered throughout the body, delivering life giving blood to the tissues. However, blood vessels are dynamic structures that pulsate, constrict, relax, and even proliferate. There are three types of blood vessels. Arteries carry blood away from the heart and to the tissue. Arteries are generally thick walled and elastic, expanding with each heartbeat. As blood is expelled into the arteries, the volume of blood in the arteries increase, expanding the walls of the arteries. The expanded walls then can further "squeeze" the blood toward their intended destination.

Therefore, there are two numbers in the blood pressure measure measurement. The first number is the maximum pressure in the artery that is generated when the new amount of blood enters the arteries. This occurs when the heart beats and pumps the blood into the arteries. We can feel the "pulse" of the heart beat at strategic places as the arteries momentarily expand. The second number is the amount of pressure still left in the arteries after the arterial walls have compressed the blood and keeps it moving in the arteries. Arteries do not need valves as the pressure from the heart keeps the blood flowing away from the heart.

Once the blood reaches the smaller diameter capillaries (arterioles), much of the blood plasma is squeezed out of the capillary and literally bathes the tissue in nutrient, oxygen rich fluids that diffuse into the cells, delivering the life-giving essentials. Cellular and metabolic wastes then, diffuse into the fluid, which then is picked up by the capillary (venules) and begins its journey back to the heart.

Blood from the venules find their way into larger veins. Veins are the blood vessels that carry blood back to the heart. There is very little pressure in veins. There is not a "pump" at the beginning of the veins to push blood back to the heart. Therefore, there are generally twice as many veins as arteries and there are valves that are scattered throughout the length of veins.

If blood is squeezed or pushed at all, it must move in one direction. This is why body movement and muscular contractions are important to blood flow. As the veins travel back to the heart, skeletal muscles contract around them and press upon the veins, compressing it and squeezing the blood (within the veins) in the direction of the heart. Blood flow back to the heart is equally as important as blood flow out of the heart. The heart can only pump out what comes in. If very little blood is returning to the heart, the heart does not have much blood to pump out. Therefore, exercise and movement are key to essential blood flow throughout the body.

On the Death of Jesus Christ by Crucifixion

There has always been a question of whether Jesus actually died on the cross, or was just in a comatose state. And, if the crucifixion truly brought on the death of Jesus, what was the actual cause of death. There should be little debate as to whether Jesus literally, physically died on the cross as a result of His crucifixion. The weight of historical and medical evidence clearly indicates that Jesus did indeed die, and that He was already dead when Roman soldiers pierced His side with a spear. "But one of the soldiers pierced His side with a spear, and immediately blood and water came out" (John 19:34). There have been many scientific and medical articles on the subject.[9, 10, 11, 12, 13]

There are two aspects of Jesus' death that are worthy of note. First, after the death of Jesus, The Gospel of John describes the piercing of Jesus' side by a soldier with a spear and emphasizes that the spear probably perforated His lung, and the pericardium and heart. The blood seems obvious as the spear penetrated the cardiac region of the chest. The water probably denotes a considerable amount of serous pleural and pericardial fluid. As a result of the impending acute heart failure, pleural and pericardial effusions would have developed and become quite prominent upon the rupture of the heart area with the soldier's spear.

As Jesus hung on the cross, it was difficult for Him to lift Himself to breathe effectively. The weight of His body pulled downward, and His ability to lift Himself upward in order to take deep breaths was limited. As a result of diminished air flow to His lungs, and the diminished amount of blood in His body following the severe beatings He had taken, his heart was having to work in overdrive in order to keep up with His body's demand for oxygen.

As His heart began to work harder and harder, an overuse, inflammation condition known as pericarditis set in and began to affect the pericardium. And as the inflammation grew worse, more pericardial fluid developed. And the more the pericardial fluid increased, the greater the inflammation became. And from this developed a cycle from which there was no recovery. The greater amount of pericardial fluid within the pericardial sac created additional pressure upon the heart, making it even more difficult for His heart to keep up with His oxygen demands. It was this excessive amount of pericardial fluid, along with other fluids from the lungs, that was most likely seen when the soldier pierced Jesus' side.

A second important aspect of the death of Jesus was that Jesus' death occurred after only six hours on the cross. To be frank, I doubt anyone would desire to hang on a cross for any amount of time. But the fact is that most criminals that were crucified took much more time, even days before their death took place. It could be said that Jesus was a healthy man, with no diseases or physical issues. And for a healthy man such as Jesus to die within only six hours would seem unlikely. Jesus had indicated that no one would take His life from him. "No one takes it (life) from Me, but I lay it down myself. I have the power to lay it down, and I have the power to take it again" (John 10:18).

But in the case of Jesus, it is recorded that Jesus cried with a loud voice and died on purpose. "And Jesus cried out again with a loud voice, and yielded up His spirit" (Matthew 27:50). By His own volition and ability, Jesus did indeed die, but was not "technically" killed by the Roman soldiers (and the Jews). Although, like other crucified victims, the actual cause of Jesus' death was multifactorial, including exhaustion, hypovolemic shock, asphyxia, pericarditis, transmural myocardial infarction, cardio-respiratory failure, and acute heart failure. Though not common, rupture of the left ventricular wall has occurred in the first few hours following a cardiac infarction.

Although the actual "cause" of death of Jesus can be a topic of interest, there is supporting evidence that the literal, physical death of Jesus resulted from a fatal cardiac arrhythmia and subsequent sudden catastrophic, terminal heart event. It could be said that physical death of Jesus was caused by a broken heart!

There is little doubt as to the importance of the heart. Whether discussion is anatomical and physical, or emotional and behavioral. And although the heart resides inside our body, it does not necessarily belong to us. Think of our loved ones, our spouses, children, grandchildren, friends. And if it is that important to them, imagine how important our heart is to the God who created it!

REFERENCES

1. Newport, F. "Most Americans Still Believe in God." Newsgallup. com. June 29, 2016. https://news.gallup.com/poll/193271/ americans-believe-god.aspx (accessed April 30, 2018)

2. "Three-quarters of Americans Believe Jesus Rose From the Dead." Rasmussenreports.com. March 24, 2016. http://www. rasmussenreports.com/public_content/lifestyle/general_lifestyle/ march_2016/three_quarters_of_americans_believe_jesus_rose_ from_the_dead (accessed April 30, 2018).

3. Holms, M. "What Would Happen if the Church Tithed?" *Relevant.* March 8, 2016. https://relevantmagazine.com/love-and-money/ what-would-happen-if-church-tithed/ (accessed April 30, 2019)

4. "The State of the Church 2016." Barna.com. September 15, 2016. https://www.barna.com/research/state-church-2016/ (accessed April 30, 2018).

5. Filip, J. "Avoiding the Black Plague Today." *The Atlantic.* https:// www.theatlantic.com/health/archive/2014/04/avoiding-black-plague-t.oday/360475/ (accessed April 30, 2018)

6. "Global Health and Aging." World Health Organization Report. 2004. (Pg. 10) Https://www.who.int/ageing/publications/global_ health.pdf (accessed April 30, 2018)

7. Wynsberghe, DV, Noback, CR, and Carola, R. *Human Anatomy and Physiology* (3rd ed.) McGraw-Hill, 1995.

8. Salidin, KS. *Anatomy and Physiology: The Unity of Form and Function* (5th ed.) McGraw-Hill, 2010.

9. Edwards, WD, Gabel, WJ, Hosmer, FE. "On the Physical Death of Jesus Christ." *Journal of the American Medical Association* 255, no. 11 (1986): 1455–1463.

10. Lumpkin, R. "The Physical Suffering of Christ." *Journal of Medical Association of Alabama* 47 (1978): 8–10.

11. Davis, CT. "The Crucifixion of Jesus: The Passion of Christ from a Medical Point of View." *Arizona Medicine* 22 (1965): 183–187.

12. Tenney, SM. "On Death by Crucifixion." *American Heart Journal* 68 (1964): 286–287.

13. Clark, CCP. "What was the Physical Cause of the Death of Jesus Christ?" *Medical Review* 38 (1890): 543.

[The author notes that there are many internet sites that cite quotations from others. And some of these quotations are questioned by current groups for various reasons and intents.]

[The author also notes that many internet sites quote statistics of all types, collected by polling services, including Barna Group, Gallup, Rasmussen and USA Today.]

CHAPTER 6

REPRODUCTION

So God created great sea creatures and every living thing that moves, which the waters abounded, according to their kind, and every winged bird according to its kind. And God saw that it was good. And God blessed them saying; "Be fruitful and multiply, and fill the waters in the seas, and let birds multiply on the earth." – Genesis 1:21-22

From the beginning of creation, it was intended that any life form reproduce its same life form. For example, a cow reproduces a cow and not a goat. From a dog comes from a dog and not a cat. And from a human comes another human. Many simple organisms such as algae reproduce by simple mitosis and single cell replication. Other animals may produce millions upon millions of offspring with the hopes that a few can survive and perpetuate the species. But of all of God's creation, it has been shown that man is the ultimate creation. Therefore, the reproduction and perpetuation of mankind is most special.

When we examine Scripture, following the story of the murder of Abel by Cain, we see than Adam and Eve were 130 years old when they had Seth. Methuselah, who was the oldest man to ever live, had Lamech at the age of 187. Lamech was 182 years old when he had Noah. Noah was 600 years old at the time of the Flood. Thus, in "biblical days" when men (and women) lived a long time, and were older when they had children. And, in their long lifetime, could have many children.

However, after the Flood, the lifespan of man decreased, although Abraham was 100 years old when Isaac was born. Even after his wife Sarah died, he still fathered six more sons with Keturah after the age of 140. Abraham died at the age of 175. But closer to "modern times", the oldest male to father a child is ninety-six (in 2012). His wife was fifty-two. They had even had a son two years earlier![1] A 70-year-old woman gave birth to twins in 2008. She already had five grandchildren.[2] From the early to mid-1700's a woman had sixty-nine children in twenty-seven pregnancies. She had sixteen sets of twins, seven sets of triplets and four sets of quadruplets. However, in the late 1800's a woman gave birth to thirty-nine children in thirty-eight pregnancies![3] There is little doubt as to the proliferation and reproductive abilities of mankind.

Before construction of a building can begin, there must be a blueprint. Specific and detailed instructions are required to properly build such a structure. And the building that is constructed has a particular purpose. There are hospitals, apartments, factories, retail stores, business, houses, all constructed with intended purposes. And, of course, there would be corresponding physical aspects of those buildings to meet the need of those purposes for which they were constructed in the first place. And, therefore, there would be a corresponding need for an exact blueprint to build those physical aspects of those buildings.

Within the scheme of God's creation, it has been stated that there is a reason and purpose of man. And thus, there is a blueprint for the "construction" of man, with its godly purpose. "Blessed be the God and Father of our Lord Jesus Christ, who has blessed us with every spiritual blessing in the heavenly places in Christ, just as He chose us in Him before the foundation of the world, that we should be holy and without blame before Him in love, having predestined us to adoption as sons by Jesus Christ to Himself according to the good pleasure of

His will, to the praise of the glory of His grace, by which He made us accepted in the beloved" (Ephesians 1: 3-6).

When God created man, He created two distinct genders, male and female. "So God created man in His own image; in the image of God He created him; male and female He created them" (Genesis 1:27). Later we find that "LORD God said, 'It is not good that man should be alone; I will make him a helper comparable to him'" (Genesis 2:18). Thus, God made Adam first, THEN He made Eve. "And the LORD God caused a deep sleep to fall on Adam, and he slept, and He (God) took one of the ribs, and closed up the flesh in its place. Then the rib which the Lord God had taken from man He made into a woman, and He brought her to the man" (Genesis 2:22–23). Though God made woman from man, this does not imply that the woman is "inferior" to man. God chose the rib, which is in the middle of the human body. He did not choose anything higher or lower. Thus, she was made as an equal.

However, many in today's world have their own idea and definition as to what the word "equal" means. Equal does not mean "identical". It is interesting that in Genesis 2 woman came from man but in Genesis 4 man came from woman. "Now Adam knew his wife, and she conceived and bore Cain, and said, I have acquired a man from the LORD" (Genesis 4:1). Obviously, men cannot have children. Thus, in this regard, women seem to have the upper hand. God designed the union or "marriage" between a man and a woman (different genders) for a purpose.

There are three reasons for the design and purpose of two distinct genders. The first is companionship that is developed through marriage. As mentioned in Genesis 2:18, "It is not good for man to be alone." One of the worst feelings a human can sense is loneliness. God made a counterpart, a "female" to fill the void of loneliness. One might think, "Well, what about another male as a "companion?" It should be noted that God made Adam and Eve, not Adam and Steve. The depth of feelings and intimacy were intended to run deep. "Therefore a man shall leave his father and mother and be joined (married) to his wife, and they shall become one flesh" (Genesis 2:24). It says "become one flesh", not become "as one flesh". In other words, one plus one equals one.

A second reason for the design and purpose of two distinct genders within this marriage is procreation (reproduction), and this can only take place between a male and a female. Obviously two males (or two females) cannot procreate. "...in the image of God, He (God) created him; male and female He created them. Then God blessed them, and God said to them (male AND female), be fruitful and multiply; fill the earth and subdue it ..." (Genesis 1:27–28). The word "him" may be masculine, but it simply refers to "all mankind", as in "humankind", or people. God created "people", but He created two distinct genders. Only a male and a female having intercourse can reproduce. [The author notes that "reproduction" can occur in today's modern world through medical technologies such as in-vitro fertilization, surrogacy and cloning. However, cloning produces no males, and with in-vitro fertilization and surrogacy, males are still required.] "Behold, children are a heritage from the Lord. The fruit of the womb is a reward. Like arrows in the hand of a warrior, so are the children of one's youth" (Psalm 127:3-4).

Aside from engaging in medical advances of in-vitro fertilization, sexual relation (intercourse) is needed for humans to reproduce. And it is interesting that in this fashion, the offspring gets genetic material from both parents. But God did not create "sex" for procreation only. To be sure, the "sex drive" and "hunger" are the two most formidable human feelings and sensations that exist. Scripture is clear that sexual intimacy within the confines of marriage is good and "normal".

> Let your fountain be blessed, and rejoice with the wife of your youth. As a loving deer and graceful doe, let her breasts satisfy you at all times; and always be enraptured with her love. (Proverbs 5:18–19)

> Nevertheless, because of sexual immorality, let each man have his own wife, and let each woman have her own husband. Let the husband render to his wife the affection due her, and likewise also the wife to her husband. The wife does not have authority over her own body, but the husband does. And likewise the

husband does not have authority over his own body, but the wife does. (1 Corinthians 7:2–4)

A third crowning purpose of two distinct genders and marriage between a male and female is that God uses the marriage relationship to describe His intimate relationship with believers. In Scripture, there is an example of Isaac "playing around" with his wife, Rebekah. In response to a famine, Isaac had gone to Gerar and to Abimelech, king of the Philistines. "So Isaac dwelt in Gerar. And the men of the place asked about his wife (Rebekah). And he (Isaac) said, she is my sister, for he was afraid to say she was his wife, because he thought lest the men of that place kill me for Rebekah, because she is beautiful to behold. Now it came to pass when he had been there a long time that Abimelech the king of the Philistines looked through a window and saw, and there was Isaac, showing endearment (sporting, playing) to Rebekah, his wife" (Genesis 26:6–8).

Many view God as "some old man" sitting on a throne "out there somewhere", just waiting to dispense His "wrath" upon all the people who "commit great sin"! This could not be farther from the truth. The Church (or believers, Christians) is represented in the Bible as a Bride and Jesus is represented as a Groom. At the "end times" when Christ returns, the following is mentioned. "Let us be glad and rejoice and give Him glory, for the marriage of the Lamb has come, and His wife has made herself ready. And to her it was granted to be arrayed in fine linen, clean and bright, for the fine linen is the righteous acts of the saints. Then he said to me (John), write, blessed are those who are called to the marriage supper of the Lamb. And He said to me, these are the true sayings of God" (Revelation 19:7–9).

Thus, marriage is a reflection on the relationship between Christ and His church. It is a joyful and intimate relationship, and faithful believers will "spread the gospel" and reproduce and advance the message of Christ. "For as the rain comes down and the snow from heaven, and do not return there, but water the earth, and make it to bring forth bud that it may give seed to the sower and bread to the eater, so shall My word be that goes forth from my mouth; it shall not return void, but it shall accomplish what I please and it shall prosper in the thing for which I sent it" (Isaiah 55:10–11). To be sure, humans use sex to continue the human species (reproduction). However, sexual activity and intimacy is also intended to be incorporate into the life of a human.

Other species of animals use sex "activities" as only a means to reproduce. Some species have only a small window of their life span in which to reproduce. Their sexual "activities" are merely used to reproduce and perpetuate their species. Humans, on the other hand, can use "sex" for purposes other than just reproduction. There is little doubt as to the intensity and sensations of sexual "activities". However, when engaging in sexual "activities", there is also a high level of intimacy and closeness between partners. Humans greatly desire those feelings and the emotional state of mind that engaging in sexual "activity" can bring. Imagine feeling that close to God! God intended intimacy in marriage. Sex, after all was part of the overall plan of creation. Commitment and intimacy are deep rooted parts of marriage.

The essence of human reproduction is that it is biparental. That is, the offspring receives genes from each parent and are therefore not genetically identical to either one. The purpose of the male gender is to produce and deliver sperm to the female. The purpose of the female is to be able to receive these sperm, deliver them to an egg, and be able to house the developing human until birth.

Sexual reproduction among certain organisms can be interesting. Many male spiders simple "wrap up" their sperm in a "package" and "give it" to the female. The female then keeps the sperm until that time she desires to fertilize her eggs. When that time comes, she kills the male, and places the fertilized eggs into the carcass of "dear ol' dad". When the eggs hatch, the tiny, baby spiders instantly have something to eat and from which to grow and develop, until they are old enough to venture out into the world on their own. One such spider that does this is the "Black Widow".

Humans however do not, and cannot do this. Once sperm leave the male's body, they can only survive for about twenty-four hours or so. And considering the female's body, which include milk-giving breasts, the new-born baby has a means of life-support. In addition, the very act of coitus is different for humans, even among the mammals.

Reproductive acts performed by most mammals is "rear-entry". That is, the genitalia of the female point more toward the "rear" of her body, making it more accessible to the male. In this position, and for the purpose of mere procreation, there is little need for emotional response and feelings of intimacy by either the male or female. To be sure the females may be "picky" in their choice of males, and males may be aggressive and fight other males to "be the winner" and the one who gets to "mate" with the female. But considering biology, these behaviors are simply for the purpose of the "strongest survive", and thus ensuring the continuance of the species into another generation.

But having children is more than just perpetuating the human species. Since humans are bipedal and not "four-legged" animals, the genitalia of the human female are not positioned the same way. To be sure, coitus can be achieved from the rear by humans, but sexual relations from the front provide for a more meaningful, intimate, and private way to engage is this sexual activity. Love between the male and female can be better expressed. And this expression of love can be strong.

"Love is an act of faith, and whoever is of little faith is also of little love."[4] The bond of love in a marriage is based upon faith. It is the cement that binds the commitment to each other. God used the relationship of Jesus as the groom and the Church as the bride and a faith-commitment relationship. Christ loves and is forever faithful. God also used the book of Hosea to expound upon this relationship. Multiple partners, mere self-indulgence and non-committal behavior fosters not only limits of faith, but can bury faithfulness. There is little doubt as to the love God has for mankind. Afterall, He did give Himself as a ransom and atonement for our sins.

The love between a husband and wife surpasses all other human emotions. Human love is stronger than muscle. We may train our muscles to become stronger with weight training. But the love of a human can be stronger. The Song of Solomon in the Bible is a book of love. It describes loves longing, loves celebration, loves anxiety and peace and loves commitment. "Behold you are fair my love. You are fair … You are fair my love, and there is no spot in you … Set me as a seal upon your heart, as a seal upon your arm; for love is as strong as death … Many waters cannot quench love, nor can floods drown it." (Song of Solomon 4:1, 7; 8:6, 7). Christian love is simply the overflow of joy in God.

The Male Reproductive System

"Behold, children are a heritage from the LORD, the fruit of the womb is a reward. Like arrows in the hand of the warrior, so are the children of one's youth. Happy is the man who has his quiver full of them" (Psalm 127:3–5). God is our Father. He has no grandchildren. I have three daughters and when each one was born there was a sense of pride and happiness and joy that I could not explain. But when they begin to have children of their own, and my wife and I became grandparents, there was a sense of pride and happiness and joy that superseded any emotion I had ever experienced. I always joke with our friends that if I had known how wonderful it was to have grandchildren, I would have had them first! It has been said that grandchildren are God's way of compensating us for growing old. "Children are the crown of old men, and the glory of children is their father" (Proverbs 17:6).

But God the Father does not have grandchildren. There are no second, third, fourth, fifth, etc. generations. His generation is one. We are all one; brothers and sisters in Christ, and God is our Father. One thing about being a grandfather, I receive and "play" with my grandkids, "spoil" them and send them home. Although I may provide for them on occasions and teach them ways to live a Godly life, and I am not responsible for raising them, teaching them, and providing for them. Their parents are responsible for that. In other words, basically, I really am not responsible for them. They have parents.

With God, however, He IS responsible for us. He cares for us. He teaches us. He guides us and directs us. He saved us from our own sins and death. He created us and he provides for us. "The Spirit Himself bears witness with our spirit that we are children of God, and if children, then heirs - heirs of God and joint heirs with Christ …" (Romans 8:16–17). The book of Isaiah depicts God as a loving parent who has done everything possible to raise His child (Israel) well. Yet, Israel stilled rebelled.

There are those who refute the existence of Israel and even the existence of God. But the fact remains that although Israel is not righteous, they were chosen. "Israel is the only nation on earth that inhabits the same land, bears the same name, speaks the same language, and worships the same God that it did 3,000 years ago."[5] There was a three-fold purpose for using Israel like God did.

First, the people of the world could view Israel and see how to discern matters of life more accurately. No doubt the Hebrews had many ups and downs in their history, and there were specific reasons for each. All one had to do is study the kingships of Israel even past the splitting of the kingdom into two nations. The "good" and evil" acts and behavior of the kings and the people are clearly stated. Factors that play into a "good life" and into a "bad life" can be clearly seen.

Second, it could be seen by the world that although God is an almighty and most powerful God, He can easily establish an intimate relationship with His people. And although Israel certainly did things that were terribly displeasing to God, He never abandoned nor forsook them. "As a father pities his children, So the LORD pities those who fear Him" (Psalm 103:13). "When you pass through the waters, I will be with you; and through the rivers, they shall not overflow you. When you walk through the fire, you shall not be burned. Nor shall the flame scorch you. For I am the LORD your God, the Holy One of Israel, your Savior ... And I have loved you" (Isaiah 43:2–4).

And finally, the nation of Israel could reflect the moral righteousness and justice that represents the very nature of God. There was the formation of "the world", but there was also the formation of Israel, to reflect the characteristics of the most-high God. God used their existence and His commitment to them to express His commitment to man, even though man is not righteous and is unfaithful to God.

The following is a true story of commitment of a father to his son. Shortly after the birth of his son, a man's wife, the boy's mother passed away. The father made a commitment that as his son grew up, he would be faithful to his son and always be there for him. When the boy was eight years old, there was a great earthquake and the city was destroyed by the effects of the earthquake. Destruction and desolation were everywhere. The father survived and ran to the school house where his son attended school. The school building was in ruin. His eyes saw a pile of rubble.

Undeterred the father began to go through the rubble, digging with his bare hands, removing the debris piece by piece. Local firemen told him to leave, that there was nothing left to do. Twelve hours later the man was still digging through the rubble, removing each fragment of ruin by hand. Local police asked to give it up and leave, but the young father continued. Twenty-four hours passed and the young father kept digging. The people begged him to stop. "There is nothing more you can do," they pleaded. But he continued.

Thirty-six hours later, as he was digging, he heard a sound. It was the voice of his son. Elated and overjoyed the father continued to work until he could see his son. "I am here," he told his son. I am here for you." "I knew you would come, father. I knew you would find us," answered the boy. "Us?" the father replied. "Yes," the boy said. "There are twelve of us, here." The great love and unfailing commitment the father had for his son not only saved his son, but eleven other young children that were trapped because of the earthquake.

This is the love of Christ toward His bride, the Church. So it should be between the man and the woman, husband and wife. Unabated and total commitment.

The reproductive role of man is to produce sperm and to deliver them to the female. There are four different types of structures that help do this.

1. **Testes** – A structure located in a sac called the "scrotum" that hangs at the base of the male torso. It produces sperm. Normally, 300 to 500 million sperm are released during a single sex act or ejaculation. The scrotum hangs outside the body for cooling purposes. Normal body temperature of about 98.6° F, which is too hot an environment for developing sperm.

2. **Penis** – The penis has two functions. First, it contains the urethra, which carries urine away from the urinary bladder. But its design and structure are to deliver sperm to inside the

female for fertilization of her egg. In addition to containing the urethra, the penis contains three cylindrical strands of erectile tissue: two corpora cavernosa and the corpus spongiosum. They both run the length of the penis. The corpus spongiosum surrounds and envelops the urethra. During sexual excitement the tissue of the corpora cavernosa become engorged with blood, causing the penis to become rigid and stiff (erection). The corpus spongiosum which surrounds the urethra prevents the urethra from being "squeezed" and closed off. This tube will be needed for the sperm to pass through. The skin around the penis is loosely fitting, permitting it to move or "slide" up and down over the underlying corpora cavernosum, the length of the penis. This characteristic allows for further stimulation of the erect penis in order to stimulate the release of the sperm.

3. **Accessory glands** – Sperm is not the only substance emitted during ejaculation. In addition to the sperm, the average ejaculation produces about a teaspoon of a substance called semen. The emitted sperm will have a great task in trying to fertilize the female's egg and will need the "additives" that are in the semen.

    Bulbourethral (Cowper's) gland: Located at the beginning or base of the penis, this gland secretes a clear, slippery fluid during sexual arousal. This slippery fluid helps to lubricate the vagina for easy entry and comfort of the penis. But a greater function is that it increases the pH of the vaginal environment. In order to kill bacteria that can potentially enter the female's birth canal and cause life threatening infection, the pH of the female vagina can be as low as three and a half or four (seven is neutral). This acidic environment is low enough to kill bacteria, but it is low enough to kill sperm, too. Thus, during coitus, the introduction of the fluid produced by the bulbourethral gland raises the pH to close to seven, where sperm can survive. It also can neutralize any acidity that is in residual urine that is in the urethra.

Prostate gland: Located at the base of the urinary bladder and surrounding the urethra, the prostate gland is about the size of a walnut and secretes a thin, milky fluid, which constitutes about 30% of the volume of semen. In addition to the volume of fluid needed for sperm to "swim", it also secretes a clotting enzyme.

Seminal Vesicles: Located either side of the beginning of the prostate at the base of the urinary bladder, the seminal vesicles are about the size and shape of a small pea. The seminal vesicles secrete about 60% of the volume of semen. This fluid contains fructose, other carbohydrates and prostaglandins, which nourish and assist the sperm as they journey to fertilize the female egg. But it also secretes a protein called proseminogelin. A well-known property of semen is its stickiness, which is actually an adaptation that promotes fertilization. When the clotting enzyme secreted by the prostate combines with this protein, the proseminogelin is converted to seminogelin, which entangles the sperm and attaches to the walls of the vagina and cervix. This limits the amount of semen that can "leak" and drain back out of the vagina. However, if the semen was already thick and sticky inside the male before ejaculation, it would have difficulty in even getting get out of the male. But it is as ejaculation is occurring that the clotting enzyme of the prostate combines with the proseminogelin of the seminal vesicle. The semen is more fluid as it leaves the penis but then quickly "clots", and becomes sticky at the moment of coitus. However, after about twenty minutes, the seminogelin protein begins to breakdown, causing the semen to liquify. The fluid environment makes it easier for the sperm to migrate from the vagina into the uterus and beyond. The prostaglandins help stimulate peristaltic waves of rhythmic muscular contractions of the uterus and uterine tube. This helps to spread the semen through the female reproductive tract.

4. **Accessory ducts** – Sperm that are produced in the testes are carried to the outside must travel through a system of ducts. These ducts lead from the testes that are in the scrotum, up into the abdominopelvic cavity and out of the penis.

Epididymis: Located atop of the testes, the epididymis is a coiled duct that if straightened out would be about twenty feet long. It stores sperm until they are mature and ready to be ejaculated. It contains a muscular wall that helps propel mature sperm toward the penis. Maturing sperm leave the testes through several ducts at the beginning of the epididymis. The sperm may stay in the epididymis for as long as four weeks and as short as ten days. Mature sperm can remain fertile in the epididymis for about a month. If they are not ejaculated during that time they degenerate and are absorbed back into the body.

Ductus Deferens: The epididymis eventually becomes the ductus deferens (also called the vas deferens). As this duct leaves the testes it enters the lower abdomen. It becomes surrounded by a network of arteries, veins, nerves and other supporting tissue that is called the spermatic cord. The ductus deferens is the main carrier of sperm from the testes to the penis. A form of male birth control is the cutting and tying of these cords (for each testes), preventing sperm from ever reaching the penis.

Ejaculatory duct: The end of the ductus deferens is joined by the ejaculatory duct. The ejaculatory duct comes from the seminal vesicles and both the ductus deferens and ejaculatory duct empty into the urethra at the base of the urinary bladder and the beginning of the prostate gland.

Urethra: The urethra is the tube that empties the urinary bladder. It leaves the bladder and ends at the end of the penis. The contents of the ductus deferens and ejaculatory ducts are emptied into the urethra. The prostate gland secretes its products through multiple small pores into the urethra. The entire contents of semen then flow through the urethra, which is then forcefully expelled via muscular contractions along the epididymis, ductus deferens and prostate.

This design and arrangement of male anatomy allows the male to be able to produce and deliver sperm at any time (after puberty). Sperm are made and delivered to the female, with additional "additives" and helps that assist the sperm in fertilizing the female egg. It is a very effective anatomy and means of sexual reproduction. But the simple anatomy can be described with a deeper association.

The loosely fitting skin around the penis serves to help stimulate the erect penis during intercourse. This loose-fitting skin folds forward at the end of the penis, forming a prepuce or foreskin. Circumcision is the removal of this prepuce. Circumcision was instituted by God as He instructed Abraham and his future descendants to be circumcised (Genesis 17:10–14). Later, it was performed eight days after the birth of a son, and the naming of the child was done at that time (Luke 1:59). It was viewed as a seal of righteousness. "And he (Abraham) received the sign of circumcision, a seal of righteousness of the faith which he had while still uncircumcised, that he might be the father of all those who believe" (Romans 4:11).

But the question of why God initiated the act of circumcision has long been a topic of discussion. Following the Creation and man's original sin which resulted in death, God established His covenant with man. In His covenant with man, God essentially said that He would redeem man and restore unto man the righteousness that was in the original Creation. Of course, if one reads and studies the Bible, this covenant came to fruition at the birth, death, burial, and resurrection of Jesus. God "promised" (as contained within His statement or covenant with man), that He and He alone would do this. Man is unable to perform such an act. The price is too great for man. But God would be able (and desires) to do it. To bear "witness" as to the hearing and receiving of this promise or covenant, God basically said, "If you believe that I am God, and that I can do such a thing and will do such a thing, then all I ask is that you believe that I can. "… Believe on the Lord Jesus Christ and you will be saved…" (Acts 16:31).

In today's legal world, when a contract is agreed upon and "signed", one or more "witnesses" also signs the document. This is to ensure that all that are involved directly with the contract (covenant) know exactly what it is about and know the implications of entering into the agreement, and that they are the ones entering into the contract not someone else who is staging or faking the agreement. In other words, the contract becomes real and valid with the signing of the witness or witnesses.

Of course, the foreskin covered that part of the penis that lay beneath it. Removal of it reveals this anatomy, which can now, literally be seen. Analogous references can now be made regarding circumcision. "...if their uncircumcised hearts are humbled, and accept their guilt, then I will remember My covenant with Jacob, and my covenant with Isaac and my covenant with Abraham I will remember" (Leviticus 26:41–42). In "biblical days", covenants contained similar "witnesses" to verify the terms and arrangements of the covenant. In the case of God's covenant with man, which was a permanent, everlasting covenant, circumcision was to be a permanent reminder of that covenant. At the time, it showed a submissiveness to God's will and as a distinction between the Hebrews and the other peoples of the earth and was important to distinguish those who were "God's people", or not.

God created the male first, THEN He created the female. Although as husband and wife, the male and female are one, it was the intent of God to make the male the head of the household and spiritual leader of the family. The covenant "witness" was the circumcision of the male. Nothing is said of the female. In Luke's account of the circumcision of Jesus, He eluded to Old Testament law (Numbers 3:13). "Now when the days of her (Mary's) purification (following childbirth) were completed, they brought Him (Jesus) to Jerusalem to present Him to the Lord as it is written in the law of the Lord, Every male who opens the womb shall be called holy to the LORD" (Luke 2:22–23).

However, circumcision is not part of God's covenant with New Testament Christians. The death, burial, and resurrection of Jesus ushered in the fulfillment of God's covenant and His redemptive plan of salvation.

> Therefore remember that you, once Gentiles in the flesh, who are called uncircumcised by what is called the circumcision made in the flesh by hands, that at that time you were without Christ, being aliens from the commonwealth of Israel and strangers from the covenant of promise, having no hope and without God in the world. But now in Christ Jesus you who once were far off have been brought near by the blood of Christ. (Ephesians 2:11–13)

> And I (Paul) testify to every man who becomes circumcised that he is a debtor to keep the whole law … For in Christ Jesus neither circumcision nor uncircumcision avails anything, but faith working through the love. (Galatians 5:3, 6)

> Where there is neither Greek nor Jew, circumcised nor uncircumcised, barbarian, Scythian, slave or free, but Christ is all in all. (Colossians 3:11)

There is little doubt of the importance of the male within the context of God's creation, and certainly the necessity of a male in the procreation of mankind.

The Female Reproductive System

The reproductive anatomy of the female is far more complex than that of the male. We found earlier that the entire musculoskeletal systems were arranged with the sole purpose of the female being the one to become pregnant and give birth. The skeletal system had to be arranged differently from that of the male. All the male reproductive system must do is develop and deliver sperm to the female egg.

The female anatomy, on the other hand, must make the egg, receive the sperm in such a way as to fertilize the egg, then provide safe harbor and nutrition during fetal development, and give birth. In addition, even after birth, the female is the one who provides continual nourishment through milk that is made in the breasts. It can be safely said that the body of the female is centered around reproduction and child birth.

Of course, for Jesus to be made flesh, He had to "be born". "And she brought forth her firstborn son ..." (Luke 2:7). "For unto you is born this day in the city of David a Savior, who is Christ the Lord" (Luke 2:11).

But Jesus had to be born of a virgin. Theologically, the sin nature of man (DNA) comes from the male. Since at the time of conception, half of the genetic material comes from the father, Joseph could not be the literal father of Jesus. "And the angel answered and said to her (Mary), 'The Holy Spirit will come upon you, and the power of the Highest will overshadow you; therefore, also that Holy One who is to be born will be called the Son of God'" (Luke 1:35). The heavenly father had to be the literal father of Jesus, so the nature of sin could not be in Jesus. Jesus was MADE sin, to take the sins of the world. "The next day John (the Baptist) saw Jesus coming toward him, and said, behold! The lamb of God who takes away the sin of the world" (John 1:29).

The female reproductive system consists of essentially six structures with specialized functions.

1. **Ovaries** – There are a pair of ovaries, located on either side of the uterus. It is the responsibility of the ovary to produce the egg. By puberty, (usually between ten and fourteen years of age) each ovary may contain as many as 200,000 oocytes, or potential eggs. However, only about 400 will be developed during the lifetime of the female. The ovary is also responsible for secreting "female" hormones (previously described in chapter 4) which control the development and maintenance of feminine characteristics and the monthly "period" or menstrual cycle.

2. **Uterine tubes** – Coming from the ovary and going to the uterus are the uterine tubes, also called Fallopian tubes. They are about four inches in length. Each month an egg is produced

and leaves the ovary and enters the uterine tube. Unlike sperm, the egg is unable to move on its own. Instead it is carried along the uterine tube toward the uterus by rhythmic contractions of tube and waving movements of cilia or small hair like structures within the tube. The process of the egg leaving the ovary and entering the uterine tube is called ovulation. It is inside the uterine tube where fertilization takes place. If the egg is not fertilized within twelve to twenty-four hours it simply dies and degenerates. But if sperm are present, the egg can become fertilized, and the time that it takes the fertilized egg to complete the journey down the uterine tube and enter the uterus may take four to seven days. It is this "timing" of when the egg is produced and when the sperm will fertilize it that is called the "rhythm method" of birth control. A female's monthly "period" or menstrual cycle is (on average) twenty-eight days. On day one, the menstrual blood flow starts, and on day fourteen the egg from the ovary is released. The egg survives only one or two days. Sperm can survive only one or two days. Sperm that is already waiting in the uterine tube can fertilizes the egg. Thus, if intercourse takes place within twelve to forty-eight hours of ovulation, fertilization can occur. Having sex at other times would not necessarily result in pregnancy. However, the key is knowing exactly when the egg is released from the ovary and ovulation occurs. If ovulation varies, then the timing of fertilization would correspondingly very.

3. **Uterus** – the uterine tubes terminate in the uterus. Located in front of the rectum and behind the urinary bladder, the uterus is a muscular structure that is pear shaped and pear size. The uterus is attached to the wall of the pelvis by two major ligaments. The entrance of the uterus from the vagina is called the cervix. During sexual stimulation, the tissue of the cervix secretes an alkaline fluid which helps neutralize the acidic environment that would be detrimental to the life of sperm, which is deposited in this area during coitus. The inner lining of the uterus is called endometrium, and thickens in preparation

for pregnancy during the menstrual cycle. However, after ovulation and if the egg is not fertilized, the endometrium begins to deteriorate and, within a couple of weeks, will begin to slough off and exit the body through the entrance of the uterus called the cervix, and then out the vagina. This breakdown and outflow of endometrium and accompanying blood is called menstrual flow. The outflow of the endometrium lasts (on average) 3-5 days, and is considered the menstrual "period". However, if pregnancy does occur, the endometrium continues to build and develop as it prepares to house and nourish the developing fetus. During a normal pregnancy the uterus may expand to more than six times its normal size.

4. **Vagina** – The vagina is a muscle lined sheath about three or four inches long. It connects the uterus to the outside. It serves as a birth canal for the baby, but also acts as a receiving tube for the semen as well an exiting structure for the menstrual flow. The wall of the vagina ordinarily is collapsed, but it can expand and enlarge to accommodate an erect penis during sexual intercourse and accommodate the passage of a baby during child birth. The lining of the vaginal walls secretes mucous that lubricates the vagina and keeps it moist. But it also has another important function. Bacteria, that may be able to enter the vagina and move up the birth canal and eventually into the open spaces of the female abdomen become trapped in the mucous. The pH of this mucous environment is acidic enough to kill most bacteria that would be in the area and cause infection. However, with sexual stimulation the vaginal walls become engorged with blood. Most vaginal lubrication comes from a blood plasma seepage known as transudate. This initially forms as sweat-like droplets on the inner walls of the vagina.

5. **External genital organs (structures)** – These organs or structures collectively have protective functions and play a role in sexual arousal.

Greater Vestibular (Bartholin's) glands: Located on each side and toward the bottom of the vagina, the greater vestibular glands are a pea-size gland which is homologous to the bulbourethral gland of the male. Its main function is to secrete mucous. This mucous will help provide vaginal and vulvar lubrication during sexual excitement and intercourse. The fluid produced by the Bartholin's glands is slippery, yet thin in order to spread more easily in the vagina during sexual intercourse. There are also numerous *lesser vestibular glands* surrounding the vagina that also provide additional lubrication for not only the vagina, but the surrounding area of the vulva.

Paraurethral (Skene's) glands: The openings of Skene's glands are actually at the entrance of the urethra (hence the name "para" urethral gland), and are analogous to the male prostate gland. The fluid secretion of Skene's is a thin, white substance whose composition is like that of the male prostate. During sexual excitement, there is stimulation of the vestibular gland, which is located on each side at the entrance of the vagina. The vestibular glands secrete an alkaline fluid that can also neutralize the acid that is in the vagina.

Vulva: The vulva is generally recognized as the external genitalia of the female. It consists of the *mons pubis*, and the *major* and *minor labia*. The opening of the vagina would ordinarily open out into the environment, where it would be exposed to harmful bacteria. Passage from the outside environment to within the abdominal cavity is unimpeded. It has already been discussed how the pH of the female reproductive tract is acidic to kill intruding bacteria. However, an outer, protective barrier will also help protect this important reproductive tract. The *minor labia* or smaller lips, is a small fold of skin, that contain oil glands and blood, but not hair. The minor labia form the inner lips of the female genitalia. When "closed", these two folds of skin touch each other and form a physical barrier to the entrance of the vagina. The *major labia*, or major lips, form the inner wall or border of the *mons pubis.* The major labia are the outer lips that make up the female genitalia. The fat laden mons forms a mitten-like structure which pushes against the inner lips or minor labia, closing it and forming the physical barrier to the entrance of the vagina.

Clitoris: Located at the upper end of the vulva, just beneath the mons pubis is the clitoris. The clitoris is analogous to the male penis. It is the major source of sexual stimulation and subsequent sexual arousal. Like the male penis, it too, has two corpora cavernosa that can fill with blood during sexual stimulation and become enlarged.

6. **Mammary Glands** – Within the paired breasts of a female are modified sweat glands which can produce and secrete milk. Depending on genetic predisposition and general amount of body fat, the breasts contain a varying amount of fat. Within this fatty deposit are fifteen to twenty lobes of glandular tissue (exocrine gland that are like sweat glands). These glands look like clusters of grapes which have ducts which drain the milk into lactiferous sinuses, which drain into the nipple. The breasts only produce milk during lactation following child birth. A normal amount of time a mother may breastfeed her baby is from eight to twenty-four months. However, as long as she can expel milk from her breasts, her breasts may be able to produce milk for twenty to thirty years! Just so long the breasts are emptied of the milk, the breasts will replenish it. Some women, called "wet nurses" can literally move from family to family, breast feeding other parents' babies, either for a fee or for a service. Incidentally, there is no relationship between the size of breasts and the amount of milk they can produce. Large breasts do not necessarily produce more milk. But it is not uncommon for one breast to produce more milk than the other.

There has been a great deal of discussion, especially among women, as to why the menstrual cycle and menstrual period are needed. It can be answered this way. Any living cell in the body must be supported. The body already has about 50 trillion or so, so adding to this will require greater amounts of energy and resources. Remember the neuron and its ability to propagate an impulse? Schwann's cells were needed on the neurons that were out in the long extremities of the arms and legs (to help speed up the impulse), but not inside the brain. Each of the living Schwann's cell needs life support by the body, which takes up energy and resources of the body.

Remember the oil gland? It is a holocrine gland which means the cells that make the oil die in the process of making the oil. The body must have the additional energy and resources to replenish these cells. Thus, the hair, which effectively spreads the oil around, can minimize the production of oil, which minimizes death to the cells, which minimizes the energy and resources the body needs to sustain that body function.

The same course that the Schwann's cells, and the cells of the oil gland (and many other similar scenarios), is behind the process of the menstrual cycle. The inner lining of the uterus (endometrium) is very important. If the egg has been fertilized it must be able to support and maintain a developing fetus. Thus, at the time of making the egg, the endometrium must be ready to support a pregnancy. However, if the egg is not fertilized there is no need to continue to support and maintain the endometrium. It no longer has a function because there is no fetus to support. So, the body decides to stop supporting the endometrium, and the endometrium dies. It takes about two weeks for the endometrium to deteriorate and begin sloughing off as the menstrual period begins. It normally takes three to five days for this process to complete.

Meanwhile the body can begin another "pregnancy process", making an egg and creating another viable endometrium. If this egg is fertilized, the endometrium is ready to support the pregnancy. But if this egg is not fertilized, the whole process begins again, and again, and again. This process, or monthly cycle, will continue until an egg is eventually fertilized and pregnancy occurs, or old age (menopause) sets in. In this fashion, the body does not have to support and maintain the cells of the endometrium for every month and the duration of life. This would require a tremendous amount of extra energy and resources. Therefore, the body only supports the needs of the cells of the endometrium for less than half that time and thus less than half of that extra energy. Of course, if pregnancy does occur, the endometrium is supported and maintained until birth.

After a period following birth, the menstrual cycle and "monthly" periods will begin again, possibly as early as four to six weeks. Breast feeding may delay the onset of the menstrual cycle, and a subsequent pregnancy may not occur. However, breast feeding is not a reliable means of birth control. About 5-10% of breastfeeding mothers become pregnant again while still breast feeding their baby.

The growth and development of the fetus is remarkable and wonderful. When the egg is fertilized, it is one cell. This one cell is called a zygote. This single cell will divide again and again and again in a series of mitotic divisions called cleavage. The one cell becomes two. Then two cells become four. Four cells become eight, then sixteen, then thirty-two, then sixty-four and so on. The first cleavage division takes place about thirty-six hours after fertilization has occurred.

About four to five days after fertilization, this one cell is now a ball of many cells called a blastula. The blastula enters the uterus and attaches to the uterine wall. Clinical pregnancy has now begun. The total length of pregnancy is forty weeks. The developing human is now called an embryo. The placenta begins to develop, transferring nutrients from the mother to the embryo.

Rapid development of the embryo continues. By the third week the head and body can be distinguished. Since growth and development is dependent on oxygen and nutrients delivered by circulating blood, the cardiovascular system is one of the first organ systems to differentiate and develop. By day twenty-two, the embryonic heart begins to beat. By day twenty-eight, the eyes, ears and limb buds are visible.

After eight weeks, the embryo is now called a fetus. All organ systems are at some point of development. There is some bone formation and muscles of the trunk, limbs and head are present. The fetus is now capable of some movement. In only twelve weeks, the single cell zygote has become a developing human one and half inches long with fully distinguishable body parts. Eyelids, lips, fingernails, toenails are clearly recognizable. By week sixteen, the face looks human and all vital organs have been formed. The kidneys are fully functional and urination is now possible. The fetus is now about two and a half inches long.

By the twentieth week, the fetus has grown to six and a half inches! The gripping reflex of the hand has developed and kicking movements may be felt by the mother. The lungs are the final organ to be formed, but of course do not function. By twenty-forth weeks, thumb sucking may begin. By week twenty-eight, the nervous system has developed enough so that the fetus can practice controlled breathing and swallowing movements. If delivery were to happen now, there would be at least a 10% chance of survival. But with just four more weeks of development, chances of survival at delivery has increased to over 70%.

By week forty, no more development within the mother is needed. All vital organ systems are functional and the fetus is ready for birth. To be sure the fetus is nowhere near ready to care for themselves, and in a sense, are always born premature. But if the fetus was to continue to grow and develop for longer than nine or even ten months, the baby would be too large to pass through the vaginal (birth) canal. Therefore, the timing of the birth is just right.

Following birth, the mother may nurse the child. At birth, the breasts produce a substance called colostrum, not milk. Colostrum is similar to milk, but contains far less fat. The amount of colostrum produced by the breasts is also far less than that of milk production, which will begin about three days later. Since the baby has a considerable amount of fat and excess body water, colostrum is better than milk at this point, as the baby can more effectively lose the excess body fluids and use the fat for calories.

However, after about three days the breasts begin to produce milk. After a couple of weeks, a mother nursing one baby can produce as much as two pints of milk a day, although the growing infant will not need more, even as the infant gets larger. Human milk is much better than cow's milk at this point. Cow's milk has one-third less lactose (milk sugar) but three to five times more protein and minerals compared to human milk. This excess protein can form a hard curd in the baby's stomach and is not absorbed easily. And because of the high protein content, cow's milk also increases the infant's nitrogenous waste excretion, which can increase the frequency and severity of diaper rash. Breast milk also promotes the colonization of beneficial bacteria in the intestines and supplies antibodies that help fight potential pathogens. Incidentally, the documented record for human milk production is 53,081 ounces of milk produced in 1168 days.[6] That is a total of 415 gallons or almost one and a half quarts per day! This woman donated her milk to a milk bank. Milk banks use pasteurized breast milk in high risk and neonatal intensive care units and for other health care needs of infants in hospitals. Some nursing women have produced as much as 100 ounces of milk per day.[7]

In Psalm 139, David proclaims God's perfect knowledge of man, regarding a human being even before that human being is even born.

> For You formed my inward parts: You covered me in my mother's womb. I will praise You, for I am fearfully and wonderfully made; Marvelous are Your works, and that my soul knows well. My frame was not hidden from you when I was made in secret, and skillfully wrought in the lowest parts of the earth. Your eyes saw my substance, being yet unformed. And in Your book they were all written, the days fashioned for me, when as yet there was none of them How precious are you to me O God! How great is the sum of them! If I should count them, they would be more than the sand .... (Psalm 139:13–18)

It is amazing that God, in His infinite wisdom and foreknowledge (and since He created us), actually knew us before we were even conceived, and especially while we were developing in our mother's womb. This Scripture affirms three things in the conception and gestation of preborn babies. It goes beyond "pro-choice" rationale, thinking that a mother considering an abortion actually has "a choice".

First, it affirms that the preborn baby is God's creation (not the mother's). There are many stories of pregnancies and births in Scripture. The birth of Ishmael to Abraham was no surprise to God. But Ishmael was not in God's plan in lineage to Jesus, God's plan of salvation. That fell to Isaac, Abraham's son from Sarah, his wife. God chose Israel, not Egypt, Assyria, Babylon, Persia, Greece or Rome. Israel is not righteous, just chosen.

> This is the genealogy of Isaac. Abraham's son. Abraham begat Isaac. Isaac was forty years old when he took Rebekah as his wife … Now Isaac pleaded with the Lord for his wife, because she was barren, and the Lord granted his plea, and Rebekah, his wife conceived. But the children struggled together within her (she was to give birth to twins); and she said "If all is well, why am I like this?" So she went to inquire of the Lord. And the Lord said to her, "Two nations are in your womb. Two peoples shall be separated from one body; One people shall be stronger than the other; and the older shall serve the younger. (Genesis 25:19–23)

God not only knew and used the descendants of this conception, but He had already ordained it from the beginning of time, to establish His plan of salvation through Jesus, which came through Abraham, Isaac and Jacob (the younger or second born of the twins). It is more than just a mother "getting pregnant". It is God's creation.

Second, it affirms that God communes with us, even before we are born. Although a fetus does not have a fully developed physical body, according to God's Word, they may know more than we think. "…Elizabeth, your relative has also conceived a son in her old age; and this is now the sixth month for her who was called barren … And it happened, when Elizabeth heard the greeting of Mary, that the babe leaped in her womb, and Elizabeth was filled with the Holy Spirit" (Luke 1:36, 41). To be sure, unborn babies growing in their mother's womb cannot speak, but God knows the baby's person (character) even before birth, and that is reassuring long after we are born, to know that we are that special to the One who created us.

A final affirmation of conception and gestation of preborn babies is that there is continuity of God's creation from the beginning until the end. From the beginning of time until the end of time, and from conception before birth, and after birth and through life until the end of physical life, there is continuity of Life in God's creation. It is interesting in the life of my wife and I, as we consider our ancestors. Over 250 years ago my set of parents came from Ireland and my wife's ancestors came from Germany. Then, as time passed, her family eventually settled down, and her parents subsequently came into being, and finally, her.

My family did the same thing, eventually settling in the same area, and I eventually came into being. But if there had been any changes or altering of the coming together of a mother and father, there would have been a change in the subsequent births of offspring's, and we would not even come into being, and obviously our paths would have never crossed. But even before time, God had a plan for my wife and myself. And that is amazing to think that such an almighty, omnipotent, holy God, creator and sustainer of all, knew me, and thought of ... ME (even before I was born)!

> Then the word of the Lord came to me saying; Before I formed you in the womb I knew you; before you were born I sanctified; I ordained you a prophet to the nations. (Jeremiah 1:4-5)

> But when it pleased God, who separated me from my mother's womb and called me through His grace. (Galatians 1:15)

> Thus says the LORD who made you and formed you from the womb, who will help you: 'Fear not, O Jacob .... (Isaiah 44:2)

> ...the Lord has called me from the womb; from the matrix of my mother he has made mention of my name. (Isaiah 49:1)

> Can a woman forget her nursing child, and not have
> compassion on the son of her womb? (Isaiah 49:15)

The birthing process of a physical human is manifest in the coming into being of a new person ... a little baby. A baby can be seen, heard, and felt. In addition, we may even say that it has certain features of the parents, like the shape of the nose or mouth. Sometime we may even say that old expression, "The apple does not fall far from the tree," implying that the offspring is just like the parent.

But what about a "born again" Christian? The term, "born again" Christian, seems redundant. A Christian is "born again". However, there are many professing Christians who, in fact, really are not Christian. They are not "born again".

> There was a man of the Pharisees named Nicodemus, a
> ruler of the Jews. This man came to Jesus by night and
> said to Him, "Rabbi, we know that You are a teacher
> come from God; for no one can do these signs that
> You do unless God is with Him." Jesus answered and
> said to him, "Most assuredly, I say to you, unless one
> is born again, he cannot see the kingdom of God."
> Nicodemus said to him, "How can a man be born
> again when he is old? Can he enter a second time
> into his mother's womb and be born?" Jesus answered,
> "Most assuredly, I say to you, unless one is born of
> water and the Spirit, he cannot enter the kingdom of
> God. That which is born of the flesh is flesh and that
> which is born of the Spirit is spirit. Do not marvel that
> I said, to you, 'You must be born again.'" (John 3:1–7)

Every "born again" believer has a threefold proof of a new birth. It can be described as an inward proof, an outgoing proof, and an outward proof. "Whoever believes that Jesus is the Christ, born of God, and everyone who loves Him who begot also loves him who is begotten of Him. By this we know that we love the children of God, when we love God and keep His commandments. For this is the love of God, that we keep His commandments ... For whatsoever is born of God overcomes the world. And this is the victory that has overcome the world, our faith" (1 John 5:1–4).

Whoever believes that Jesus is the Christ and is born of God must have enough personal evidence to believe such, and that they are a "born again" Christian. This can be described as an inward proof of being "born again". However, an outgoing proof of being born again can be seen when a "born again" Christian loves his fellow man, even when we are not capable of doing so in the flesh. "...love is of God, and every one that loves is born of God and knows God" (1 John 4:7). And although we still may fail in our efforts, if we love God and love our fellow man, we will practice and make a habit of doing those things that please God who loves us and we Him. "Therefore, if any man be in Christ, he is a new creation; old things have passed away; behold all things have become new ... now we are ambassadors for Christ ..." (2 Corinthians 5:17, 20). This, then, is the outward proof, that we can be called a child of God, "born again".

A child is born with a will to do wrong. It is the responsibility of the parent to discipline and break the will of that part of the child that wants to do wrong and conform to the parent's good will. The parent should break the spirit of the child, but only that which would bring harm to the child. God is our heavenly Father and we are His children. It is His responsibility to lead us and guide us in His good will. And, of course, He does that through His Word and the Holy Spirit. The unbeliever has difficulty in understanding the phenomenon of spiritual birth. Yet, they cannot deny the existence of the wind just because they cannot see it. Even things of the earth are not easy to grasp for the non-Christian and Christian alike.

REFERENCES

1. "Ten Oldest Fathers in the World." Oldest.org. http://www.oldest. org/people/men/ (accessed February 7, 2019).
2. "World's Oldest Mothers; Story of the Oldest Woman to Give Birth." Motherhow.com. https://motherhow.com/oldest-woman-to-give-birth/ (accessed February 7, 2019).
3. "Most Prolific Mother Ever." Guinessworldrecords.com. http://www.guinnessworldrecords.com/world-records/most-prolific-mother-ever (accessed February 2, 2019).
4. Fromm, E. "Beliefnet's Inspirational Quotes." Beliefnet.com. https://www.beliefnet.com/quotes/inspiration/e/erich-fromm/love-is-an-act-of-faith-and-whoever-is-of-little.aspx (accessed February 2, 2019).
5. Krauthhammer, C. *The Weekly Standard*, May,11, 1998. https://www.weeklystandard.com/charles-krauthammer/at-last-zion (accessed February 2, 2019)
6. "Most Breastmilk Donated." Guinessworldrecords.com. 2014. http://www.guinnessworldrecords.com/world-records/most-breastmilk-donated (accessed February 9, 2019)
7. Cassidy, Suzanne, "Landisville Woman No Longer Has Breast Milk World Records, But Intends to Keep Pumping." LancasterOnline. com. August 5, 2010. https://lancasteronline.com/news/local/landisville-woman-no-longer-has-breast-milk-world-record-but/article_7f3ffe7c-1ce6-11e4-bc71-0017a43b2370.html (accessed February 9, 2019).

CHAPTER 7

EPILOGUE

ᛘ

Let us hear the conclusion of the whole matter: Fear God, and keep his commandments: for this is the whole duty of man. – Ecclesiastes 12:13

God created man in His own image. Not even the angels of heaven can boast that claim! But like angels, man was indeed created for God's purpose. But even with a greater understanding of the human body and its physical and spiritual nature, it is difficult to understand the status and value of man, and his place in this vast universe. Oftentimes we place a greater emphasis to the importance of man, rather than the importance of God who created man. We think more of ourselves than God. Man like to think of himself as a beautiful, significant flower, growing out of a flower pot. Others, who view the flower in the pot see the beauty and glory of the flower as it emerges from out of the pot. It is the flower that gets the "attention", not the pot.

However, the fact of the matter is, that man is not the flower, but rather, the flower pot! Regardless of how impressive our anatomy and physiology may be, we are the pot, and not the flower. It is the intent of God that the greatness and glory of God grows out of us! It is God that deserves the emphasis, not man. There is little doubt that man is God's ultimate creation and was important enough to Him that He gave His only begotten son as a ransom for our sins. Therefore, we should glorify God in our body. "Or do you not know that your body is the temple of the Holy Spirit, who is in you, whom you have from God, and you are not your own? For you were bought with a price; therefore glorify God in your body and in your spirit, which are God's" (1 Corinthians 6:19–20). "Now you are the body of Christ, and members in particular" (1 Corinthians 12:27). Indeed, our body is the flower pot where the Holy Spirit of God resides. Thus, the conclusion of the matter is ... the glory of God in us!

There is a beginning book of the Bible, Genesis. It tells of a beginning and provides the foundation for understanding life's meaning and finding abundant life. There is also an ending book of the Bible, the Revelation. It implies that there will be and ending to the physical creation. One of the things that struck Einstein as he developed his Theory of Relativity, was that since there was a beginning, and there will be an end. Nothing physical lasts forever!

There has always been great discussion and debate as to the events leading up to the "end of the world." "And Jesus answered and said to him, 'Do you see these great buildings? Not one stone shall be left upon the other, that shall not be thrown down.' Now as He sat at the Mount of Olives opposite the temple, Peter, James, John and Andrew asked Him privately, 'Tell us, when will these things be?'" (Mark 13:2–4).

> But someone will say, "How are the dead raised up? And with what body do they come?" Foolish ones, what you sow is not made alive unless it dies. And what you sow that body that shall be, but mere grain, perhaps wheat or some other grain. But God gives it a body as He pleases, and to each seed its own body. All flesh is not the same flesh, but there is one kind of flesh of men, another flesh of animals, another flesh of fish, and another of birds. There are celestial bodies and terrestrial bodies; but the glory of the celestial is one, and the glory of the terrestrial is another. There

is the glory of the sun, and the glory of the moon, and another glory of the stars; for one star differs from another star in glory. See also the resurrection of the dead. The body is sown in corruption, it is raised in incorruption. It is sown in dishonor, it is raised in glory. It is sown in weakness, it is raised in power. It is sown a natural body, it is raised a spiritual body. There is a natural body, and there is a spiritual body. And so it is written, "The first man Adam became a living being." The last Adam (Jesus) became a life-giving Spirit. However, the spiritual is not the first, but the natural (physical), and afterward the spiritual. The first man was of the earth, made of dust, the second Man is the Lord from heaven. As was the man of dust, so also are those who are made of dust; and as is the heavenly Man, so also are those who are heavenly. And as we have borne the image of the man of dust (physical), we shall also bear the image of the heavenly Man. (1 Corinthians 15:35–49)

However, in the meantime, God created us in His image for His purpose. And in His image means He gave us free will. We are not like robots who MUST do what God wants. We are given free choice to do as WE will. Of course God would like for us to do His will, we still can choose our own path. An artist may use a brush and various colored paint to create a beautiful picture on canvas. We make decisions. Those decisions are the brush strokes on canvas of our life. It eventually will become a portrait of our life, and what we paint is what others will see!

As a narrative to illustrate His power and glory, and love and grace, God chose the physical. Man has always been subject to the physical "laws of nature". Humans cannot defy gravity and overcome it on our own and live as though it does not exist. However, we can understand the law of gravity and make airplanes and other devices that can work in the presence of gravity. Like a coin drops because of gravity, a hand can reach out and catch it and keep it from hitting the floor. So it is with our salvation. We cannot defy and overcome sin and death. We fall and succumb to the effects of sin and death. However, through God's plan of salvation in Jesus Christ, He reaches his hand out and "catches" us, and we are saved. And God uses example after example of the physical nature of man to describe and declare His creation, His salvation, and His glory.

The Hebrews were not brought out of bondage in Egypt just to wonder around in the desert. They were brought from one place to go to another place and serve God. So it is with physical man, to be created and placed to serve the Lord. Christians are not just "saved" from Hell, but are "saved" to do something, and that is to serve and glorify God. He did not come into the world just to be Savior, but to be Sovereign. Christians are to live a life of participation, not imitation. We were created in the image of God and therefore Christians are to reflect God and not mirror the world.

Scripture says all knowledge is ascribed to God. "Great is our Lord and mighty is His power; His understanding is infinite" (Psalm 147:5). Scripture says that all power is ascribed to God. "And I heard, as it were the voice of a great multitude, as the sound of many waters and as the sound of mighty thunderings, saying, 'Alleluia! For the Lord God Omnipotent reigns!'" Revelation 19:6). And Scripture says that all life is ascribed to God. "Most assuredly, I say to you, 'The hour is coming and now is, when the dead will hear the voice of the Son of God; and those who hear will live, For as the Father has life in Himself, So He has granted the Son to have life in Himself'" (John 5:25–26).

When we take God out of the narrative, man is in trouble. It should be easy to understand that man cannot control the physical world. In this day and age of "global warming" and "climate change", it is vain to think that man can elevate himself within creation and control the creation. There is too much in the world and too little man can do. To be sure, there is a lot man can do, and in the beginning, he was asked to "tend and keep" it (Genesis 2:15). But even as Satan tried to elevate himself above God, man also thinks he has more power than he actually does and attempts to win control of things he does not have the power to do. Man eventually winds up "spinning his wheels" and cannot accomplish what the flesh desires. And anytime the outflow exceeds the intake, the upkeep will be the downfall. Sin appeals to the nature of the flesh. However, because of who God is and what He did in His creation of man, we should strive to be all that we are to all that He is.

It is interesting to think that throughout history, has formed many images of pagan gods. Yet it was God who formed man, and in the image and likeness of Himself! Instead of man trying to look "up" to A god, it was THE God who was looking down on man, and loved us enough to give Himself for us.

The Bible teaches that we should pray. We certainly should pray for one another. But among the many reasons and objects for which to pray for, none are more precious than praying for our children. We should pray for our children from **"Head to Foot"**.[1]

1. "…And lift up your voice for understanding, if you seek her as silver, and search for her as for hidden treasures; Then you will understand the fear of the LORD, and find the knowledge of God. For the Lord gives wisdom; from His mouth comes knowledge and understanding. He stores up sound wisdom for the upright" (Proverbs 2:3–7). Therefore, we should pray for the **minds** of our children. We should pray that our children would earnestly seek wisdom and understanding from the Lord. We should pray that their thoughts would stay centered on the truths of God's Word.

2. "Let your eyes look straight ahead, and your eyelids look right before you. Ponder the path of your feet" (Proverbs 4: 25–26). We should pray that God would protect our children's **eyes** and protect their innocence. We should pray that they would keep their eyes focused on where they are going and what they are doing and be able to see what is right and truth.

3. "Put away from you a deceitful mouth, and put perverse lips far from you" (Proverbs 4:24). We should ask God to keep their **mouths** from speaking evil and lies, and that the words spoken by our children would be pleasing to Him and edifying others.

4. "Incline your ear and come unto Me. Hear, and your soul shall live; and I will make an everlasting covenant with you" (Isaiah 55:3). We should pray that our children would be quick to hear and incline their **ears** to the Lord and listen for His instruction and guidance in their life.

5. "The Lord is my strength and my shield; my heart trusted in him, and I am helped: therefore my heart greatly rejoices; and with my song will I praise him" (Psalm 28:7). We should ask God to give our children a happy and cheerful **heart**. A heart that will come to faith in the Lord and trust in Him.

6. "Whatever your hand finds to do, do it with your might; for there is no work or device or knowledge or wisdom in the grave where you are going" (Ecclesiastes 9:10). We should pray that the **hands** of our children would not be idle and that they would be diligent in their work, and that God would bless, confirm, and establish the work of their hands.

7. "Blessed is the man who walks not in the council of the ungodly, nor stands in the path of sinners" (Psalm 1:1). Our **legs** provide us with mobility, to move in any direction. We should pray that our children would not walk in step with the wicked, nor stand in the way of sinners. We should ask God to provide them with wise and godly companions along life's journey.

8. "Uphold my steps in Your paths, that my footsteps may not slip" (Psalm 17:5). We may use our legs for movement, but it is our **feet** that provide us with the foundation for stable footing as we walk. We should ask God to direct the steps of our children and help them stand fast and protect them from stumbling.

The various organs systems of the body work together to give us life. There are great benefits when things work together for a common good. God does not want us to just have a life, however. "I (Jesus) have come that they may have life, and that they may have it more abundantly" (John 10:10). There are many aspects of a Christian's life that can give us a more abundant life. "Oh magnify the LORD with me. And let us exalt His name together" (Psalm 34:3). "...That their hearts may be knit together in love" (Colossians 2:2). "And we know that all things work together for good to them that love God, to those who are called according to His purpose" Romans 8:28). Even as the organ systems of the body work together to glorify the body, Christians should work together to glorify God.

Our bodies are physical, and it is good to know that our tissues and organ systems work together for our better physical good. But even though the physical will come to an end, and our body gets old and will eventually die, it is good to know that there is something much better in store for us. "...who will transform our lowly body that it may be conformed to His glorious body, according to the working by which He is able even to subdue all things to Himself" (Philippians 3:21). God can transform a nobody to a somebody. You are truly somebody in God's body!

Will Rogers once said, "Its great being great, but it's greater being Human."[2] Isaac Newton said, "Live your life as an exclamation rather than an explanation."[3] We may fail to wonder at the intricate details of the twelve organ systems of the human body and take many aspects of them for granted. But praise God, He did not! There are many unseen realities in the world. For example, we cannot see the wind but we can experience it. Or seeing a footprint on the beach of a "deserted" island, knowing that the footprint is not yours. The reality is that God created all things, including man, and made man for a purpose. Understanding the reality and the purpose is only the beginning. God not only gave us life, but He gave it that we may have it and enjoy it more abundantly. Amen.

REFERENCES

1. Adapted from "Pray for Your Children from Head to Toe". Lovinglifeathome.com. https://lovinglifeathome.com/2014/01/21/pray-for-your-children-from-head-to-toe/ (accessed February 12, 2019).
2. Mancini, M. "Eighteen Timeless Will Rogers Quotes". *Mental Floss.* Mentalfloss.com. http://mentalfloss.com/article/59855/18-timeless-will-rogers-quotes-his-135th-birthday (accessed February 11, 2019).
3. "Quotes from Isaac Newton". Goodreads.com. https://www.goodreads.com/quotes/110156-live-your-life-as-an-exclamation-rather-than-an-explanation (accessed April 30, 2018)

[The author notes that there are many internet sites that cite quotations from others. And some of these quotes are questioned by current groups for various reasons and intents.}

CONCORDANCE

This concordance has been prepared specially for this text for use in finding various body parts mentioned in the Bible. For this purpose, the King James version of the Bible has been used for this concordance. The author does not claim a complete listing of all body parts or all Scripture references. In order to save space and give the reader the greatest possible number of important references, the various books of the Bible have been referred to with the shortest abbreviation possible.

Ankle
Acts 3:7: and immediately his feet and a. bones received strength.

Arm
Ex 6:6: and I will redeem you with a stretched out a.
Ex 15:16: by the greatness of thine a. they shall be as still as a stone;
Deut 4:34: and by a stretched out a.
Deut 5:15: and by a stretched out a.
Deut 7:19: and the stretched out a.,
Deut 9:29: and by thy stretched out a.

Deut 11:2: and his stretched out a.
Deut 26:8: and with an outstretched a.
Deut 33:20: and teareth the a. with the crown of the head.
1 Sam 2:31: Behold, the days come, that I will cut off thine a., and the a. of thy father's house
2 Sam 1:10: ... and the bracelet that was on his a.,
1 Kgs 8:42: of thy stretched out a.
2 Kgs 17:36: and a stretched out a.
2 Chron 6:32: and thy stretched out a.;

2 Chron 32:8: With him is an a. of flesh;
Job 26:2: how savest thou the a. that hath no strength?
Job 31:22: and mine a. be broken from the bone.
Job 35:9: they cry out by reason of the a.
Job 38:15: and the high a. shall be broken.
Job 40:9: Hast thou an a. like God?
Ps 10:15: Break thou the a. of the wicked and the evil man
Ps 44:3: neither did their own a. save them: but thy right hand, and thine a.
Ps 77:15: Thou hast with thine a. redeemed thy people.

Ps 89:10: thou hast scattered thine enemies with thy strong a.
Ps 89:13: Thou hast a mighty a.
Ps 89:21: mine a. also shall strengthen him.
Ps 98:1: his right hand, and his holy a.,
Ps 136:12: a stretched out a.
Song 8:6: as a seal upon thine a. for love is strong as death
Isa 9:20: they shall eat every man the flesh of his own a.
Isa 17:5: reapeth the ears with his a.
Isa 30:30: and shall shew the lighting down of his a.
Isa 33:2: be thou their a. every morning, our salvation also in the time of trouble.
Isa 40:10: and his a. shall rule for him ...
Isa 40:11: he shall gather the lambs with his a.
Isa 48:14: and his a. shall be on the Chaldeans.
Isa 51:9: Awake, awake, put on strength, O a. of the LORD
Isa 52:10: The LORD hath made bare his holy a. in the eyes of all the nations
Isa 53:1: ... and to whom is the a. of the LORD revealed?
Isa 59:16: ... therefore his a. brought salvation unto him
Isa 62:8: The LORD hath sworn by his right hand, and by the a. of his strength
Isa 63:5: ... therefore mine own a. brought salvation unto me
Isa 63:12: That led them by the right hand of Moses with his glorious a.
Jer 17:5: and maketh flesh his a., and whose heart departeth from the LORD.
Jer 21:5: with a strong a.
Jer 27:5: by my great power and by my outstretched a.

Jer 32:17: by thy great power and stretched out a.
Jer 32:21: and with a strong hand, and with a stretched out a.
Jer 48:25: and his a. is broken, saith the LORD.
Ezek 4:7: and thine a. shall be uncovered, and thou shalt prophesy against it.
Ezek 20:33: and with a stretched out a., Ezek 20:34: and with a stretched out a.
Ezek 30:21: Son of man, I have broken the a. of Pharaoh king of Egypt
Ezek 31:17: and they that were his a.,
Dan 11:6: shall not retain the power of the a.; neither shall he stand, nor his a.
Zech 11:17 his a. shall be clean dried up,
Lk 1:51: He hath shewed strength with his a.;
Jn 12:38: and to whom hath the a. of the Lord been revealed?
Acts 13:17: and with an high a. brought he them out of it.
1 Pt 4:1: Christ hath suffered for us in the flesh, a. yourselves likewise

Belly
Gen 3:14: upon thy b. shalt thou go, and dust shalt thou eat all the days of thy life:
Lev 11:42: Whatsoever goeth upon the b. ... they are an abomination.
Num 5:21: when the LORD doth make thy thigh to rot, and thy b. to swell;
Num 5:22 to make thy b. to swell, and thy thigh to rot:
Num 25:8: and the woman through her b
Judg 3:21: and thrust it into his b.:
Judg 3:22: so that he could not draw the dagger out of his b.;

1Kgs 7:20: over against the b. which was by the network:
Job 3 11: why did I not give up the ghost when I came out of the b.?
Job 15:2: and fill his b. with the east wind?
Job 15:35: and their b. prepareth deceit.
Job 20:15: God shall cast them out of his b.
Job 20:20: Surely he shall not feel quietness in his b.,
Job 20:23: When he is about to fill his b., God shall cast the fury of his wrath upon him
Job 32:19: Behold, my b. is as wine which hath no vent;
Job 40:16: his force is in the navel of his b.
Ps 17:14: and whose b. thou fillest with thy hid treasure:
Ps 22:10: thou art my God from my mother's b.
Ps 31:9: yea, my soul and my b.
Ps 44:25: For our soul is bowed down to the dust: our b. cleaveth unto the earth.
Prov 13:25: but the b. of the wicked shall want.
Prov 18:8: and they go down into the innermost parts of the b.
Prov 18:20: A man's b. shall be satisfied with the fruit of his mouth;
Prov 20:27: searching all the inward parts of the b.
Prov 20:30: so do stripes the inward parts of the b.
Prov 26:22: and they go down into the innermost parts of the b.
Song 5:14: his b. is as bright ivory overlaid with sapphires.
Song 7:2: thy b. is like an heap of wheat set about with lilies.
Isa 46:3: house of Israel, which are borne by me from the b.
Jer 1:5: Before I formed thee in the b. I knew thee ....

Jer 51:34: he hath filled his b. with my delicates,

Ezek 3:3: cause thy b. to eat, and fill thy bowels with this roll that I give thee.

Dan 2:32: his b. and his thighs of brass

Jonah 1:17: And Jonah was in the b. of the fish three days and three nights.

Jonah 2:1: Then Jonah prayed unto the LORD his God out of the fish's b.

Jonah 2:2: and he heard me; out of the b, of hell cried I, and thou heardest my voice.

Hab3:16: When I heard, my b. trembled;

Mt 12:40: For as Jonas was three days and three nights in the whale's b.; so shall the Son of man be three days and three nights in the heart of the earth.

Mt 15:17: that whatsoever entereth in at the mouth goeth into the b.,

Mk 7:19: Because it entereth not into his heart, but into the b.,

Lk 15:16: fain have filled his b. with the husks that the swine did eat:

Jn 7:38: as the scripture hath said, out of his b. shall flow rivers of living water.

Rom 16:18: they that are such serve not our Lord Jesus Christ, but their own b.

1 Cor 6:13: Meats for the b., and the b. for meats:

Phil 3:19: Whose end is destruction, whose God is their b.,

Rv 10:9: and it shall make thy b, bitter, Rv 10:10: and as soon as I had eaten it, my b, was bitter.

Blood

Gen 4:10: the voice of thy brother's b. crieth unto me from the ground.

Gen 4:11: to receive thy brother's b. from thy hand;

Gen 9:4: But flesh with the life thereof, which is the b. thereof, shall ye not eat.

Gen 9:5: And surely your b. of your lives will I require;

Gen 6: Whoso sheddeth man's b., by man shall his b. be shed:

Gen 37:22: Shed no b., but cast him into this pit

Gen 37:26: if we slay our brother, and conceal his b.?

Gen 37:31: and dipped the coat in the b.;

Gen 42:22: therefore, behold, also his b. is required.

Gen 49:11: he washed his garments in wine, and his clothes in the b. of grapes:

Ex 4:9: water which thou takest out of the river shall become b. upon the dry land.

Ex 7:17: and they shall be turned to b.

Ex 7:19: and upon all their pools of water, that they may become b.; and that there may be b. throughout

Ex 7:20: and all the waters that were in the river were turned to b.

Ex 7:21: and there was b. throughout all the land of Egypt.

Ex 12:7: And they shall take of the b., and strike it on the two side posts ....

Ex 12:13: And the b. shall be to you for a token ... when I see the b., I will pass over you.

Ex 12:22: and dip it in the b. that is in the bason, and strike the lintel and the two side posts with the b. that is in the bason;

Ex 12:23: and when he seeth the b. upon the lintel, and on the two side posts, the LORD will pass over the door,

Ex 22:2: there shall no b. be shed for him.

Ex 23:18: Thou shalt not offer the b. of my sacrifice with leavened bread;

Ex 24:6: And Moses took half of the b., and put it in basins; and half of the b. he sprinkled on the altar.

Ex 24:8: And Moses took the b., and sprinkled it on the people, and said, Behold the b. of the covenant

Ex 29:12: And thou shalt take of the b. of the bullock and put it upon the horns of the altar with thy finger and pour all the b. beside the bottom of the altar.

Ex 29:16: and thou shalt take his b. and sprinkle it round about upon the altar.

Ex 29:20: Then shalt thou kill the ram, and take of his b., and put it upon the tip of the right ear of Aaron ... and sprinkle the b. upon the altar round about.

Ex 29:21: And thou shalt take of the b. that is upon the altar

Ex 30:10: shall make an atonement upon the horns of it once in a year with the b. of the sin offering of atonements:

Ex 34:25: Thou shalt not offer the b. of my sacrifice with leaven;

Lev 1:5: Aaron's sons, shall bring the b., and sprinkle the b. round about upon the altar

Lev 1:15: and the b. thereof shall be wrung out at the side of the altar:

Lev 3:17: It shall be a perpetual statute for your generations throughout all your dwellings, that ye eat neither fat nor b.

Lev 4:5: And the priest that is anointed shall take of the bullock's b.,

Lev 4:6: And the priest shall dip his finger in the b., and sprinkle of the b. seven times before the LORD

Lev 4:7: the priest shall put some of the b. upon the horns of the altar of sweet incense … and shall pour all the b. of the bullock at the bottom of the altar

Lev 4:16: And the priest that is anointed shall bring of the bullock's b. to the tabernacle of the congregation:

Lev 6:27: and when there is sprinkled of the b. thereof upon any garment,

Lev 6:30: whereof any of the b. is brought into the tabernacle

Lev 7:14: and it shall be the priest's that sprinkleth the b. of the peace offerings.

Lev 7:26: Moreover ye shall eat no manner of b.

Lev 7:27: Whatsoever soul it be that eateth any manner of b., even that soul shall be cut off from his people.

Lev 7:33: He among the sons of Aaron, that offereth the b. of the peace offerings

Lev 10:18: Behold, the b. of it was not brought in within the holy place:

Lev 12:4: she shall then continue in the b. of her purifying three and thirty days;

Lev 12:5: and she shall continue in the b. of her purifying threescore and six days.

Lev 12:7: and she shall be cleansed from the issue of her b.

Lev 14:6: living bird in the b. of the bird that was killed over the running water:

Lev 14:25: and the priest shall take some of the b. of the trespass offering

Lev 14:51: and the living bird, and dip them in the b. of the slain bird

Lev 14:52: And he shall cleanse the house with the b. of the bird

Lev 15:19: and her issue in her flesh be b., she shall be put apart seven days:

Lev 15:25: And if a woman have an issue of her b.

Lev 16:14: And he shall take of the b. of the bullock, and sprinkle it

Lev 16:15: and bring his b. within the vail, and do with that b. as he did with the b. of the bullock

Lev 16:18: and shall take of the b. of the bullock, and of the b. of the goat, and put it upon the horns of the altar round about.

Lev 16:19: And he shall sprinkle of the b. upon it with his finger seven times,

Lev 16:27: and the goat for the sin offering, whose b. was brought in to make atonement

Lev 17:4: b. shall be imputed unto that man; he hath shed b.;

Lev 17:6: And the priest shall sprinkle the b. upon the altar of the LORD …

Lev 17:10: that eateth any manner of b.; I will even set my face against that soul that eateth b.

Lev 17:11: life of the flesh is in the b.; for … blood that maketh an atonement

Lev17:12: No soul of you shall eat b., neither shall any stranger that sojourneth among you eat b.

Lev 17:13: he shall even pour out the b. Lev 17:14: the b. of it is for the life thereof: … Ye

shall eat the b. of no manner of flesh: for the life of all flesh is the b. thereof:

Lev 19:16: neither shalt thou stand against the b. of thy neighbour:

Lev 19:26: Ye shall not eat any thing with the b.

Lev 20:9: his b. shall be upon him.

Lev 20:11: both of them shall surely be put to death; their b. shall be upon them.

Lev 20:13: their b. shall be upon them.

Lev 20:16: their b. shall be upon them.

Num 23:24 and drink the b. of the slain.

Num 35:19: The revenger of b. himself shall slay the murderer:

Num 35:21: for he is a murderer: the revenger of b. shall slay the murderer

Num 35:24: Then the congregation shall judge between the slayer and the revenger of b.

Num 35:25: And the congregation shall deliver the slayer out of the hand of the revenger of b.

Num 35:27: And the revenger of b. find him without the borders of the city of his refuge, and the revenger of b. kill the slayer; he shall not be guilty of b.

Num 35:33: for b. it defileth the land: and the land cannot be cleansed of the b. that is shed therein, but by the b. of him that shed it.

Deut 12:16: Only ye shall not eat the b.

Deut 12:23: Only be sure that thou eat not the b.: for the b. is the life;

Deut 12:27: the flesh and the b., upon the altar of the LORD thy God: and the b. of thy

sacrifices shall be poured out
upon the altar of the LORD
Deut 15:23: Only thou shalt
not eat the b. thereof;
Deut 17:8: If there arise a
matter too hard for thee in
judgment, between b. and b.
Deut 19:6: Lest the avenger of
the b. pursue the slayer
Deut 19:10: That innocent b.
be not shed in thy land ... and
so b. be upon thee.
Deut 19:12: and deliver him
into the hand of the avenger of
b., that he may die.
Deut 19:13: but thou shalt put
away the guilt of innocent b.
from Israel
Deut 21:7: Our hands have not
shed this b., neither have our
eyes seen it.
Deut 21:8: and lay not
innocent b. unto thy people
of Israel's charge. And the b.
shall be forgiven them.
Deut 21:9: So shalt thou put
away the guilt of innocent b.
from among you Deut 22:8:
that thou bring not b. upon
thine house
Deut32:14: and thou didst
drink the pure b. of the grape.
Deut 32:42: I will make mine
arrows drunk with b ... and
that with the b. of the slain
Deut 32:43: Rejoice, O ye
nations, with his people: for
he will avenge the b. of his
servants,
Josh 2:19: his b. shall be upon
his head ... his b. shall be on
our head,
Josh 20:3: and they shall be
your refuge from the avenger
of b.
Josh 20:5: And if the avenger
of b. pursue after him,
Josh 20:9: and not die by the
hand of the avenger of b.,
Judg 9:24: and their b. be laid
upon Abimelech their brother

1 Sam 14:32: and the people
did eat them with the b.
1 Sam 14:33: in that they eat
with the b.
1 Sam 14:34: and sin not
against the LORD in eating
with the b.
2 Sam 1:16: Thy b. be upon
thy head;
2 Sam 1:22: From the b. of
the slain, from the fat of the
mighty
2 Sam 3:27: that he died, for
the b. of Asahel his brother.
2 Sam 3:28: for ever from the
b. of Abner.
2 Sam 4:11: shall I not
therefore now require his b. of
your hand,
2 Sam 14:11: thou wouldest
not suffer the revengers of b. to
destroy any more,
2 Sam 16:8: The LORD hath
returned upon thee all the b.
of the house of Saul,
2 Sam 20:12: And Amasa
wallowed in b.
2Sam 23:17: is not this the
b. of the men that went in
jeopardy of their lives?
1 Kgs 2:5: and shed the b. of
war in peace, and put the b. of
war upon his girdle that was
about his loins,
1 Kgs 2:9: but his hoar head
bring thou down to the grave
with b.
1 Kgs 2:31: that thou mayest
take away the innocent b.,
which Joab shed, from me,
1 Kgs 2:32: And the LORD
shall return his b. upon his
own head,
1 Kgs 2:33: Their b. shall
therefore return upon the
head of Joab,
1 Kgs 2:37: thy b. shall be upon
thine own head.
1 Kgs 18:28: till the b. gushed
out upon them.
1 Kgs 21:19: In the place where
dogs licked the b. of Naboth

shall dogs lick thy b., even
thine.
1 Kgs 22:35: and the b. ran out
of the wound into the midst of
the chariot.
1 Kgs 22:38: and the dogs
licked up his b.;
2 Kgs 3:22: and the Moabites
saw the water on the other
side as red as b.:
2 Kgs 3:23: And they said, This
is b.: the kings are surely slain,
2Kgs 9:7: that I may avenge
the b. of my servants the
prophets, and the b. of all the
servants of the LORD,
2Kgs 9:26: Surely I have seen
yesterday the b. of Naboth,
and the b. of his sons,
2Kgs 9:33: and some of her b.
was sprinkled on the wall, and
on the horses:
2Kgs 16:13: and sprinkled the
b. of his peace offerings, upon
the altar.
2Kgs 16:15: and sprinkle
upon it all the b. of the burnt
offering, and all the b. of the
sacrifice:
2Kgs 21:16: Moreover
Manasseh shed innocent b.
very much,
2Kgs 24:4: And also for the
innocent b. that he shed:
for he filled Jerusalem with
innocent b.;
1 Chron 11:19: shall I drink
the b. of these men that have
put their lives in jeopardy?
1 Chron 22:8: Thou hast shed
b. abundantly ... because thou
hast shed much b. upon the
earth in my sight.
1 Chron 28:3: because thou
hast been a man of war, and
hast shed b.
2 Chron 19:10: between b.
and b., between law and
commandment,
2 Chron 24:25: his own
servants conspired against

him for the b. of the sons of
Jehoiada the priest,
2 Chron 29:22: and the priests
received the b., and sprinkled
it on the altar: likewise, when
they had killed the rams,
they sprinkled the b. upon
the altar: they killed also the
lambs, and they sprinkled the
b. upon the altar.
2 Chron 29:24: they made
reconciliation with their b.
upon the altar,
2 Chron 35:11: and the priests
sprinkled the b. from their
hands,
Job 16:18: O earth, cover not
thou my b.,
Job 39:30: young ones also
suck up b.:
Ps 9:12: he maketh inquisition
for b.,
Ps 16:4: their drink offerings of
b. will I not offer,
Ps 30:9: What profit is there
in my b.,
Ps 50:13: Will I eat the flesh of
bulls, or drink the b. of goats?
Ps 58:10: he shall wash his feet
in the b. of the wicked.
Ps 68:23: That thy foot may
be dipped in the b. of thine
enemies,
Ps 72:14: and precious shall
their b. be in his sight.
Ps 78:44: And had turned
their rivers into b.;
Ps 79:3: Their b. have they
shed like water round about
Jerusalem;
Ps 79:10: let him be known
among the heathen in our
sight by the revenging of the b.
of thy servants which is shed.
Ps 94:21: and condemn the
innocent b.
Ps 105:29: He turned their
waters into b.,
Ps 106:38: And shed innocent
b., even the b. of their sons and
of their daughters, ... and the
land was polluted with b.

Prov 1:11: If they say, Come
with us, let us lay wait for b.,
Prov 1:16: For their feet run to
evil, and make haste to shed b.
Prov 1:18: And they lay wait
for their own b.;
Prov 6:17: A proud look, a
lying tongue, and hands that
shed innocent b.,
Prov 12:6: The words of the
wicked are to lie in wait for b.:
Prov 28:17: A man that doeth
violence to the b. of any person
shall flee to the pit;
Prov 30:33: and the wringing
of the nose bringeth forth b.:
Isa 1 11: and I delight not in
the b. of bullocks, or of lambs,
or of he goats.
Isa 1 15: I will not hear: your
hands are full of b.
Isa 4:4: and shall have purged
the b. of Jerusalem ....
Isa 9:5: and garments rolled
in b.;
Isa 15:9: For the waters of
Dimon shall be full of b.:
Isa 26:21: the earth also shall
disclose her b., and shall no
more cover her slain.
Isa 33:15: that stoppeth his
ears from hearing of b.,
Isa 34:3: and the mountains
shall be melted with their b.
Isa 34:6: The sword of the
LORD is filled with b., it is
made fat with fatness, and
with the b. of lambs and goats,
Isa 34:7: and their land shall
be soaked with b.,
Isa 49:26: and they shall be
drunken with their own b.,
Isa 59:3: your hands are
defiled with b.,
Isa 59:7: Their feet run to evil,
and they make hast to shed
innocent b.:
Isa 63:3: and their b. shall be
sprinkled upon my garments,
Isa 66:3: as if he offered
swine's b.;

Jer 2:34: Also in thy skirts is
found the b. of the souls of the
poor innocents:
Jer 7:6: shed not innocent b. in
this place,
Jer 18:21: and pour out their b.
by the force of the sword;
Jer19:4: and have filled this
place with the b. of innocents;
Jer 22:3: neither shed innocent
b. in this place.
Jer 22:17: and for to
shed innocent b., and for
oppression, and for violence,
to do it.
Jer 26:15: that if ye put me to
death, ye shall surely bring
innocent b. upon yourselves,
Jer 46:10: and made drunk
with their b.:
Jer 48:10: and cursed be he
that keepeth back his sword
from b.
Jer 51:35: and my b. upon the
inhabitants of Chaldea,
Lam 4:13: that have shed
the b. of the just in the midst
of her,
Lam 4:14: they have polluted
themselves with b.,
Ezek 3:18: the same wicked
man shall die in his iniquity;
but his b. will I require at
thine hand.
Ezek 3:20: but his b. will I
require at thine hand.
Ezek 5:17: and pestilence and
b. shall pass through thee;
Ezek 9:9: and the land is full
of b.,
Ezek 14:19: and pour out my
fury upon it in b.,
Ezek 16:6: and saw thee
polluted in thine own b., I said
unto thee when thou wast in
thy b., Live; yea, I said unto
thee when thou wast in thy b.
Ezek 16:9: I thoroughly
washed away thy b. from thee,
Ezek 16:22: when thou wast
naked and bare, and wast
polluted in thy b.

Ezek 16:36: and by the b. of
thy children, which thou didst
give unto them;
Ezek 16:38: as women that
break wedlock and shed b. are
judged; and I will give thee b.
in fury and jealousy.
Ezek 18:10: If he beget a son
that is a robber, a shedder
of b.,
Ezek 18:13: his b. shall be
upon him. Ezek 19:10: Thy
mother is like a vine in thy b.,
Ezek 21:32: Thou shalt be for
fuel to the fire; thy b. shall be
in the midst of the land;
Ezek 22:3: The city sheddeth b.
in the midst of it,
Ezek 22:4: Thou art become
guilty in thy b. that thou hast
shed;
Ezek 22:6: every one were in
thee to their power to shed b.
Ezek 22:9: In thee are men
that carry tales to shed b.:
Ezek 22:12: In thee have they
taken gifts to shed b.;
Ezek 22:13: and at thy b.
which hath been in the midst
of thee.
Ezek 22:27: to shed b., and to
destroy souls, to get dishonest
gain.
Ezek 23:37: That they have
committed adultery, and b. is
in their hands,
Ezek 23:45: and after the
manner of women that
shed b.; because they are
adulteresses, and b. is in their
hands.
Ezek 24:7: For her b. is in the
midst of her;
Ezek 24:8: I have set her b.
upon the top of a rock, that it
should not be covered.
Ezek 28:23: For I will send
into her pestilence, and b. into
her streets;
Ezek 32:6: I will also water
with thy b. the land wherein
thou swimmest,

Ezek 33:4: if the sword come,
and take him away, his b.
shall be upon his own head.
Ezek 33:5: He heard the sound
of the trumpet, and took
not warning; his b. shall be
upon him.
Ezek 33:6: but his b. will I
require at the watchman's
hand.
Ezek 33:8: but his b. will I
require at thine hand.
Ezek 33:25: Ye eat with the b.,
and lift up your eyes toward
your idols, and shed b.: Ezek
35:5: and hast shed the b. of
the children of Israel
Ezek 35:6: I will prepare thee
unto b., and b. shall pursue
thee: since thou hast not hated
b., even blood shall pursue
thee.
Ezek 36:18: Wherefore I
poured my fury upon them for
the b. that they had shed upon
the land,
Ezek 38:22: And I will plead
against him with pestilence
and with b.;
Ezek 39:17: that ye may eat
flesh, and drink b.
Ezek 39:18: Ye shall eat the
flesh of the mighty, and drink
the b. of the princes of the
earth, Ezek:39:19: And ye
shall eat fat till ye be full, and
drink b. till ye be drunken,
Ezek 43:18: to offer burnt
offerings thereon, and to
sprinkle b. thereon.
Ezek 43:20: And thou shalt
take of the b.
Ezek 44:7: the fat and the b.,
Ezek 44:15: and they shall
stand before me to offer unto
me the fat and the b.,
Ezek 45:19: And the priest
shall take of the b. of the sin
offering,
Hosea 1:4: and I will avenge
the b. of Jezreel
Hosea 4:2: and b. toucheth b.

Hosea 6:8: and is polluted
with b.
Hosea 12:14: therefore shall he
leave his b. upon him,
Joel 2:30: And I will shew
wonders in the heavens and in
the earth, b., and fire,
Joel 2:31: and the moon
into b.,
Joel 3:19: because they have
shed innocent b. in their land.
Joel 3:21: For I will cleanse
their b. that I have not
cleansed:
Jonah 1:14: lay not upon us
innocent b.:
Micah 3:10: They build up
Zion with b.
Micah 7:2: they all lie in wait
for b.;
Hab 2:8: because of men's b.,
Hab 2:12: Woe to him that
buildeth a town with b.,
Hab 2:17: because of men's b.,
Zeph 1:17: and their b. shall
be poured out as dust, and
their flesh as the dung.
Zech 9:7: And I will take away
his b. out of his mouth,
Zech 9:11: by the b. of thy
covenant I have sent forth thy
prisoners.
Mt 9:20: with an issue of b.
twelve years,
Mt 16:17: flesh and b. hath not
revealed it unto thee,
Mt 23:30: we would not have
been partakers with them in
the b. of the prophets.
Mt 23:35: the righteous b.
shed upon the earth, from the
b. of righteous Abel unto the b.
of Zacharias
Mt 26:28: For this is my b. of
the new testament,
Mt 27:4: Saying, I have sinned
in that I have betrayed the
innocent b.
Mt 27:6: because it is the price
of b.
Mt 27:8: was called, The field
of b., unto this day.

Mt 27:24: I am innocent of the b. of this just person:
Mt 27:25: His b. be on us, and on our children.
Mk 5:25: had an issue of b. twelve years,
Mk 5:29: And straightway the fountain of her b. was dried up;
Mk 14:24: This is my b. of the new testament,
Lk 8:43: And a woman having an issue of b. twelve years,
Lk 8:44: and immediately her issue of b. stanched.
Lk 11:50: That the b. of all the prophets,
Lk 11:51: From the b. of Abel unto the blood of Zacharias,
Lk 13:1: whose b. Pilate had mingled with their sacrifices.
Lk 22:20: This cup is the new testament in my b.,
Lk 22:44: as it were great drops of b. falling down
Jn 1:13: Which were born, not of b.,
Jn 6:53: and drink his b., ye have no life in you.
Jn 6:54: Whoso eateth my flesh, and drinketh my b.,
Jn 6:55: and my b. is drink indeed.
Jn 6:56: He that eateth my flesh, and drinketh my b.,
Jn 19:34: and forthwith came there out b. and water.
Acts 1:19: that is to say, The field of b.
Acts 2:19: b., and fire, and vapor of smoke:
Acts 2:20: and the moon into b.,
Acts 5:28: and intend to bring this man's b. upon us.
Acts 15:20: and from things strangled, and from b.
Acts 15:29: and from b., and from things strangled,
Acts 17:26: And hath made of one b. all nations of men

Acts 18:6: Your b. be upon your own heads;
Acts 20:26: that I am pure from the b. of all men.
Acts 20:28: which he hath purchased with his own b.
Acts 21:25: keep themselves from things offered to idols, and from b.,
Acts 22:20: And when the b. of thy martyr Stephen was shed,
Rom 3:15: Their feet are swift to shed b.:
Rom 3:25: to be a propitiation through faith in his b.,
Rom 5:9: Much more then, being now justified by his b.,
1 Cor 10:16: is it not the communion of the b. of Christ?
1 Cor 11:25: This cup is the new testament in my b.:
1 Cor 11:27: shall be guilty of the body and blood of the Lord.
1 Cor 15:50: flesh and b. cannot inherit the kingdom of God;
Gal 1:16: immediately I conferred not with flesh and b.:
Eph 1:7: In whom we have redemption through his b.,
Eph 2:13: were far off are made nigh by the b. of Christ.
Eph 6:12: For we wrestle not against flesh and b.,
Col 1:14: In whom we have redemption through his b.,
Col 1:20: And, having made peace through the b. of his cross,
Heb 2:14 as the children are partakers of flesh and b.,
Heb 9:7: not without b., which he offered for himself,
Heb 9:12: Neither by the b. of goats and calves, but by his own b.
Heb 9:13: For if the b. of bulls and of goats,
Heb 9:14: How much more shall the b. of Christ,

Heb 9:18: the first testament was dedicated without b.
Heb 9:19: he took the b. of calves and of goats,
Heb 9:20: This is the b. of the testament which God
Heb 9:21: Moreover he sprinkled with b. both the tabernacle,
Heb 9:22: by the law purged with b.; and without shedding of b. is no remission.
Heb 9:25: entereth into the holy place every year with b. of others;
Heb 10:4: it is not possible that the b. of bulls and of goats
Heb 10:19: boldness to enter into the holiest by the b. of Jesus,
Heb 10:29: and hath counted the b. of the covenant,
Heb 11:28: and the sprinkling of b.,
Heb 12:4: have not yet resisted unto b.,
Heb 12:24: and to the b. of sprinkling,
Heb 13:11: whose b. is brought into the sanctuary
Heb 13:12: sanctify the people with his own b.,
Heb 13:20: through the b. of the everlasting covenant,
1 Pt 1:2: unto obedience and sprinkling of the b. of Jesus Christ:
1 Pt 1:19: But with the precious b. of Christ
1Jn 1:7: and the b. of Jesus Christ his Son cleanseth us
1 Jn 5:6: This is he that came by water and b.,
1 Jn 5:8: and the b.: and these three agree in one.
Rv 1:5: and washed us from our sins in his own b.,
Rv 5:9: and hast redeemed us to God by thy b. out of every kindred,

Rv 6:10: dost thou not judge and avenge our b. on them
Rv 6:12: and the moon became as b.;
Rv 7:14: and made them white in the b. of the Lamb.
Rv 8:7: followed hail and fire mingled with b.,
Rv 8:8: and the third part of the sea became b.;
Rv 11:6: and have power over waters to turn them to b.,
Rv 12:11: And they overcame him by the b. of the Lamb,
Rv 14:20: and b. came out of the winepress,
Rv 16:3: and it became as the b. of a dead man:
Rv 16:4: and they became b.
Rv 16:6: For they have shed the b. of saints and prophets,
Rv 17:6: drunken with the b. of the saints, and with the b. of the martyrs of Jesus:
Rv 18:24: And in her was found the b. of prophets,
Rv 19:2: and hath avenged the b. of his servants at her hand.
Rv 19:13: And he was clothed with a vesture dipped in b.:

Body

Lev 21:11: Neither shall he go in to any dead b.
Num 6:6: All the days that he separateth himself unto the LORD he shall come at no dead b.
Num 9:6: And there were certain men, who were defiled by the dead b. of a man,
Num 9:7: We are defiled by the dead b. of a man:
Num 9:10: If any man of you or of your posterity shall be unclean by reason of a dead b.
Num 19:11: He that toucheth the dead b. of any man shall be unclean seven days.
Num 19:13: Whosoever toucheth the dead b. of any man that is dead,

Deut 21:23: His b. shall not remain all night upon the tree
Deut 28:4: Blessed shall be the fruit of thy b.
Deut 28:11: in the fruit of thy b.
Deut 28:18: Cursed shall be the fruit of thy b.
Deut 28:53: And thou shalt eat the fruit of thine own b.
Deut 30:9: in the fruit of thy b.
Judg 8:30: And Gideon had threescore and ten sons of his b begotten
1 Sam 31:10: and they fastened his body to the wall of Beth-shan.
1 Sam 31:12: and took the body of Saul and the bodies of his sons from the wall ....
2 Kgs 8:5: telling the king how he had restored a dead b. to life,
1 Chron 10:12: and took away the b. of Saul,
Job 19:17: though I intreated for the children's sake of mine own b.
Job19:26: And though after my skin worms destroy this b.
Job 20:25: It is drawn, and cometh out of the b.
Ps 132:11: Of the fruit of thy b. will I set upon thy throne.
Prov 5:11: when thy flesh and thy b. are consumed,
Isa 10:18: fruitful field, both soul and b.
Isa 26:19: my dead b. shall they arise.
Isa 51:23: and thou hast laid thy b. as the ground,
Jer 26:23: and cast his dead b. into the graves of the common people.
Jer 36:30: and his dead b. shall be cast out
Ezek 10:12: And their whole b. and their backs, and their hands
Dan 4:33: and his b. was wet with the dew of heaven,

Dan 7:11: and his b. destroyed, and given to the burning flame.
Dan 7:15: I Daniel was grieved in my spirit in the midst of my b.
Dan 10:6: His b. also was like the beryl,
Micah 6:7: the fruit of my b. for the sin of my soul?
Hag 2:13: If one that is unclean by a dead b. touch any of these, shall it be unclean?
Mt 5:29: and not that thy whole b. should be cast into hell.
Mt 6:22: thy whole b. shall be full of light.
Mt 6:23: But if thine eye be evil, thy whole b. shall be full of darkness.
Mt 6:25: Is not the life more than meat, and the b. than raiment?
Mt 10:28: And fear not them which kill the b., but are not able to kill the soul: but rather fear him which is able to destroy both soul and b. in hell.
Mt 14:12: And his disciples came, and took up the b.,
Mt 26:12: For in that she hath poured this ointment on my b.,
Mt 26:26: Take, eat; this is my b.
Mt 27:58: He went to Pilate, and begged the b. of Jesus.
Mt 27:59: when Joseph had taken the b.,
Mk 5:29: and she felt in her b. that she was healed of that plague.
Mk 14:8: she is come aforehand to anoint my b. to the burying.
Mk 14:22: Take, eat: this is my b.
Mk 14:51: having a linen cloth cast about his naked b.;

Mk 15:43: and went in boldly unto Pilate, and craved the b. of Jesus.

Mk 15:45: he gave the b. to Joseph.

Lk 12:4: not afraid of them that kill the b.,

Lk 12:22: Take no thought for your life, what ye shall eat; neither for the b.,

Lk 17:37: Wheresoever the b. is, thither will the eagles be gathered together.

Lk 22:19: This is my b. which is given for you:

Lk 23:55: and beheld the sepulcher, and how his b. was laid.

Lk 24:3: And they entered in, and found not the b. of the Lord Jesus.

Lk 24:23: when they found not his b.,

Jn 2:21: he spake of the temple of his b.

Jn 19:40: Then took they the b. of Jesus, and wound it in linen clothes

Jn 20:12: where the b. of Jesus had lain.

Acts 9:40: and turning him to the b. said, Tabitha, arise.

Acts 19:12: So that from his b. were brought unto the sick handkerchiefs

Rom 4:19: he considered not his own b. now dead,

Rom 6:6: that the b. of sin might be destroyed,

Rom 6:12: Let not sin therefore reign in your mortal b.,

Rom 7:4: ye also are become dead to the law by the b. of Christ;

Rom 7:24: who shall deliver me from the b. of this death?

Rom 8:10: And if Christ be in you, the b. is dead because of sin;

Rom 8:13: but if ye through the Spirit do mortify the deeds of the b., ye shall live.

Rom 8:23: the redemption of our b.

Rom 12:4: For as we have many members in one b.,

Rom 12:5: many, are one b. in Christ,

1 Cor 5:3: as absent in b., but present in spirit,

1 Cor 6:13: Now the b. is not for fornication, but for the Lord; and the Lord for the b.

1 Cor 6:16: What? know ye not that he which is joined to an harlot is one b.?

1 Cor 6:18: Every sin that a man doeth is without the b.; but he that committeth fornication sinneth against his own b.

1 Cor 6:19: What? know ye not that your b. is the temple of the Holy Ghost

1 Cor 6:20: glorify God in your b.

1 Cor 7:4: The wife hath not power of her own b ... and likewise also the husband hath not power of his own b., but the wife.

1 Cor 7:34: that she may be holy b. in body and in spirit

1 Cor 9:27: But I keep under my b.,

1 Cor 10:16: is it not the communion of the b. of Christ?

1 Cor 10:17: For we being many are one bread, and one b.:

1 Cor 11:24: Take, eat: this is my b., which is broken for you

1 Cor 11:27: shall be guilty of the b. and blood of the Lord.

1 Cor 11:29: not discerning the Lord's b.

1 Cor 12:12: For as the b. is one, and hath many members, and all the members of that one b., being many, are one b.:

1 Cor 12:13: For by one Spirit are we all baptized into one b.,

1 Cor 12:14: For the b. is not one member, but many.

1 Cor 12:15: If the foot shall say, Because I am not the hand, I am not of the b.; is it therefore not of the b.?

1 Cor 12:16: And if the ear shall say, Because I am not the eye, I am not of the b.; is it therefore not of the b.?

1 Cor 12:17: If the whole b. were an eye, where were the hearing?

1 Cor 12:18: But now hath God set the members every one of them in the b., as it hath pleased him.

1 Cor 12:19: And if they were all one member, where were the b.?

1 Cor 12:20: But now are they many members, yet but one b.

1Cor 12:22: Nay, much more those members of the b.,

1 Cor 12:23: And those members of the b.,

1 Cor 12:24: but God hath tempered the b. together,

1 Cor 12:25: That there should be no schism in the b.;

1 Cor 12:27: Now ye are the b. of Christ,

1 Cor 13:3: and though I give my b. to be burned,

1 Cor 15:35: and with what b. do they come?

1 Cor 15:37: And that which thou sowest, thou sowest not that b. that shall be,

1 Cor 15:38: But God giveth it a b. as it hath pleased him, and to every seed his own b.

1 Cor 15:44: It is sown a natural b.; it is raised a spiritual b. There is a natural b., and there is a spiritual b.

2 Cor 4:10: Always bearing about in the b. the dying of the Lord Jesus, that the life also of Jesus might be made manifest in our b.

2 Cor 5:6: whilst we are at home in the b., we are absent from the Lord:

2 Cor 5:8: to be absent from the b., and to be present with the Lord.

2 Cor 5:10: that every one may receive the things done in his b.,

2 Cor 12:2I cannot tell; or whether out of the b.,

Gal 6:17: for I bear in my b. the marks of the Lord Jesus.

Eph 1:23: Which is his b., the fulness of him that filleth all in all.

Eph 2:16: And that he might reconcile both unto God in one b. by the cross,

Eph 3:6: That the Gentiles should be fellowheirs, and of the same b.,

Eph 4:4: There is one b., and one Spirit,

Eph 4:12: the edifying of the b. of Christ:

Eph 4:16: From whom the whole b. fitly joined together … maketh increase of the b. unto the edifying of itself in love.

Eph 5:30: For we are members of his b.,

Phil 1:20: Christ shall be magnified in my b.,

Phil 3:21: Who shall change our vile b., that it may be fashioned like unto his glorious b.,

Col 1:22: In the b. of his flesh through death,

Col 1:24: and fill up that which is behind of the afflictions of Christ in my flesh for his b. sake, which is the church:

Col 2:11: in putting off the b. of the sins of the flesh

Col 2:17: but the b. is of Christ.

Col 2:19: from which all the b. by joints

Col 2:23: and neglecting of the b.

Col 3:15: also ye are called in one b.

1 Thes 5:23: I pray God your whole spirit and soul and b. be preserved blameless

Heb 10:5: but a b. hast thou prepared me:

Heb 10:10: sanctified through the offering of the b. of Jesus Christ once for all.

Heb 13:3: being yourselves also in the b.

Jms 2:16: which are needful to the b.;

Jms 2:26: For as the b. without the spirit is dead,

Jms 3:2: able also to bridle the whole b.

Jms 3:3: and we turn about their whole b.

Jms 3:6: that it defileth the whole b.,

1 Pt 2:24: Who his own self bare our sins in his own b. on the tree,

Jude 1:9: he disputed about the b. of Moses,

Bone(s)

Gen 2:23: This is now b. of my b.,

Gen 50:25: and ye shall carry up my b. from hence.

Ex 13:19: And Moses took the b. of Joseph with him … and ye shall carry up my b.

Num 24:8: and shall break their b., and pierce them through with his arrows.

Josh 24:32: And the b. of Joseph,

Judg 19:29: and divided her, together with her b., into twelve pieces,

1 Sam 31:13: And they took their b., and buried them under a tree at Jabesh,

2 Sam 19:12: ye are my b. and my flesh:

2 Sam 21:12: And David went and took the b. of Saul and the b. of Jonathan

2 Sam 21:14: And the b. of Saul and Jonathan his son buried they

1 Kgs 13:2: and men's b. shall be burnt upon thee.

1 Kgs 13:31: lay my b. beside his

2 Kgs 13:21: and touched the b. of Elisha,

2 Kgs 23:14: and filled their places with the b. of men.

2 Kgs 23:16 and took the b. out of the sepulchres,

2Kgs 23:18: let no man move his b.

2 Kgs 23:20: and burned men's b. upon them,

1 Chron 10:12: and buried their b. under the oak in Jabesh,

2 Chron 34:5: And he burnt the b. of the priests upon their altars,

Job 4:14: which made all my b. to shake.

Job 10:11: and hast fenced me with b. and sinews.

Job 20:11: His b. are full of the sin of his youth,

Job 21:24: and his b. are moistened with marrow.

Job 30:17: My b. are pierced in me …

Job 30:30: and my b. are burned with heat.

Job 33:19: and the multitude of his b. with strong pain:

Job 33:21: and his b. that were not seen stick out.

Job 40:18: His b. are as strong pieces of brass; his b. are like bars of iron.

Ps 6:2: for my b. are vexed.

Ps 22:14: and all my b. are out of joint:

Ps 22:17: I may tell all my b.

Ps 31:10: and my b. are consumed.

Ps 32:3: my b. waxed old through my roaring ….

Ps 34:20: He keepeth all his b.

Ps 35:10: All my b. shall say,
LORD, who is like unto thee,
Ps 38:3 neither is there any
rest in my b. because of
my sin.
Ps 42:10: As with a sword in
my b
Ps 51:8: that the b. which thou
hast broken may rejoice.
Ps 53:5: for God hath
scattered the b.
Ps 102:3 and my b. are burned
Ps 102:5: my b. cleave to my
skin.
Ps 109:18: and like oil into
his b.
Ps 141:7: Our b. are scattered
at the grave's mouth,
Prov 3:8: and marrow to thy b.
Prov 12:4: but she that maketh
ashamed is as rottenness in
his b.
Prov 14:30: envy the
rottenness of the b.
Prov 15:30: and a good report
maketh the b. fat.
Prov 16:24: and health to
the b.
Prov 17:22: a broken spirit
drieth the b.
Eccl 11:5: nor how the b. does
grow in the womb
Isa 38:13: so will he break all
my b.
Isa 58:11: and make fat thy b.
Isa 66:14: and your b. shall
flourish like an herb:
Jer 8:1: they shall bring out the
b. of the kings of Judah, and
the b. of his princes, and the
b. of the priests, and the b. of
the prophets, and the b. of the
inhabitants of Jerusalem, out
of their graves:
Jer 20:9: But his word was in
mine heart as a burning fire
shut up in my b.,
Jer 23:9: all my b. shake;
Jer 50:17: Nebuchadrezzar
king of Babylon hath broken
his b.

Lam 1:13: From above hath he
sent fire into my b.,
Lam 3:4: he hath broken my b.
Lam 4:8: their skin cleaveth
to their b.
Ezek 6:5: and I will scatter
your b. round about your
altars.
Ezek 24:4: fill it with the
choice b.
Ezek 24:5: and burn also the
b. under it, and make it boil
well, and let them seethe the
b. of it therein.
Ezek 24:10: and let the b. be
burned.
Ezek 32:27: but their iniquities
shall be upon their b.,
Ezek 37:1: in the midst of the
valley which was full of b.
Ezek 37:3: can these b. live?
Ezek 37:4: O ye dry b., hear the
word of the LORD.
Ezek 37:5: Thus saith the Lord
GOD unto these b.
Ezek 37:7: and the b. came
together, b.to his b.
Ezek 37:11: these b. are the
whole house of Israel: behold,
they say, Our b. are dried,
Dan 6:24: and brake all their
b. in pieces
Amos 2:1: because he burned
the b. of the king of Edom into
lime:
Amos 6:10: to bring out the b.
out of the house,
Micah 3:2: and their flesh
from off their b.
Micah 3:3: and they break
their b.,
Hab 3:16: rottenness entered
into my b.,
Zeph 3:3: they gnaw not the b.
till the morrow.
Mt 23:27: but are within full
of dead men's b.,
Lk 24:39: a spirit hath not
flesh and b.,
Acts 3:7: and immediately
his feet and ankle b. received
strength.

Eph 5:30: and of his b.
Heb11:22: and gave
commandment concerning
his b.

Bowel(s)
Gen 15:4: out of thine own b.
shall be thine heir.
Gen 25:23: and two manner
of people shall be separated
from thy b.;
Gen 43:30: And Joseph made
haste; for his b. did yearn
upon his brother:
Num 5:22: the curse shall go
into thy b.
2 Sam 7:12: shall proceed out
of thy b.,
2 Sam 16:11: which came forth
of my b.,
2 Sam 20:10: and shed out his
b. to the ground,
1 Kgs 3:26: her b. yearned
upon her son
2 Chron 21:15 by disease of
thy b.,
2 Chron 21:18: the LORD
smote him in his b.
2 Chron 21:19: his b. fell
out ....
2 Chron 32:21: they that came
forth of his own b. slew him ....
Job 20:14: Yet his meat in his
b. is turned,
Job 30:27: My b. boiled, and
rested not:
Ps 22:14: my heart is like wax;
it is melted in the midst of
my b.
Ps 71:6: thou art he that took
me out of my mother's b.:
Ps 109:18: come into his b. like
water,
Song 5:4: and my b. were
moved for him.
Isa 16:11: Wherefore my b.
shall sound like an harp
Isa 48:19: and the offspring
of thy bowels like the gravel
thereof;

Isa 49:1: from the b. of my mother hath he made mention of my name.
Isa 63:15the sounding of thy b. and of thy mercies toward me
Jer 4:19: My b., my b.!
Jer 31:20: my b. are troubled for him;
Lam 1:20: my b. are troubled;
Ezek 3:3: fill thy b. with this roll
Ezek 7:19: neither fill their b.:
Acts 1:18: and all his b. gushed out.
2Cor 6:12: are straitened in your own b.
Phil 1:8: I long after you all in the b. of Jesus Christ.
Phil 2:1: if any b. and mercies,
Col 3:12: as the elect of God, holy and beloved, b. of mercies,
Phlm 1:7: because the b. of the saints are refreshed by thee,
Phlm 1:12: that is, mine own b.:
Phlm 1:20: refresh my b. in the Lord.
1Jn:3 17: and shutteth up his b. of compassion from him,

Breast(s)
Gen 49:25: blessings of the b.,
Lev 9:20: they put the fat upon the b.,
Lev 9:21: And the b. and the right shoulder ...
Job 3:12: why the b. that I should suck?
Job 21:24: His b. are full of milk,
Ps 22:9: hope when I was upon my mother's b.
Prov 5:19: let her b. satisfy thee
Song 1:13: lie all night betwixt my b.
Song 4:5: Thy two b. are like two young roes
Song 7:3: Thy two b. are like two young roes

Song 7:7: thy b. to clusters of grapes.
Song 7:8: now also thy b. shall be as clusters of the vine,
Song 8:1: that sucked the b. of my mother!
Song 8:8: she hath no b.:
Song 8:10: and my b. like towers:
Isa 28:9: and drawn from the b.
Isa 66:11: be satisfied with the b. of her consolations;
Ezek 16:7: thy b. are fashioned,
Ezek 23:3 there were their b. pressed,
Ezek 23:8: they bruised the b. of her virginity,
Ezek 23:34: pluck off thine own b.:
Hosea 2:2: and her adulteries from between her b.;
Hosea 9:14: miscarrying womb and dry b.
Joel 2:16: those that suck the b.:
Nahum 2:7: tabering upon their b.
Lk 23:48: smote their b., and returned.
Rv 15:6: having their b. girded with golden girdles.

Brow
Isa 48:4: and thy b. brass;
Lk 4:29: and led him unto the b. of the hill ....

Cheek(s)
Deut 18:3: the shoulder, and the two c., and the maw.
Song 1:10: Thy c. are comely with rows of jewels,
Song 5:13: His c. are as a bed of spices,
Isa 50:6: my c. to them that plucked off the hair:
Lam1:2: her tears are on her c.:
Mt 5:39: smite thee on thy right c.,

Lk 6:29: on the one c. offer also the other;

Ear(s)
Gen 20:8: and told all these things in their e.: and the men were sore afraid.
Gen 35:4: all their earrings which were in their e.;
Gen 44:18: speak a word in my lord's e.,
Gen 50:4: I pray you, in the e. of Pharaoh, saying,
Ex 9:31: for the barley was in the e.,
Ex10:2: tell in the e. of thy son,
Ex11:2: Speak now in the e. of the people,
Ex 15:26: and wilt give e. to his commandments,
Ex 17:14: rehearse it in the e. of Joshua:
Ex 21:6: his master shall bore his e. through with an awl;
Ex 29:20: put it upon the tip of the right e. of Aaron, and upon the tip of the right e. of his sons,
Ex 32:2: in the e. of your wives,
Ex 32:3: which were in their e.,
Lev 8:23: and put it upon the tip of Aaron's right e.,
Lev 8:24: put of the blood upon the tip of their right e.,
Lev 14:14: put it upon the tip of the right e. of him
Lev 14:17: the tip of the right e. of him
Lev 14:25: put it upon the tip of the right e. of him
Lev 14:28: the tip of the right e. of him that
Num 11:18: ye have wept in the e. of the LORD.
Num 14:28: spoken in mine e., so will I do to you:
Deut 1:45: nor give e. unto you.
Deut 5:1: which I speak in your e. this day,
Deut 15:17: thrust it through his e. unto the door,

Deut 29:4: and e. to hear, unto this day.

Deut 31:28: speak these words in their e.,

Deut 31:30: Moses spake in the e. of all the congregation of Israel

Deut 32:1: Give e., O ye heavens,

Deut 32:44: song in the e. of the people,

Josh 20:4: declare his cause in the e. of the elders

Judg 5:3: give e., O ye princes;

Judg 7:3: proclaim in the e. of the people,

Judg 9:2: in the e. of all the men of Shechem,

Judg 9:3: spake of him in the e. of all the men

Judg 17:2: spakest of also in mine e.,

1 Sam 3:11: both the e. of every one that heareth

1 Sam 8:12: set them to e. his ground,

1 Sam8:21: rehearsed them in the e. of the LORD.

1 Sam 9:15: the LORD had told Samuel in his e.

1 Sam 11:4: tidings in the e. of the people:

1 Sam 15:14: of the sheep in mine e.,

1 Sam 18:23: spake those words in the e. of David.

2 Sam 3:19: Abner also spake in the e. of Benjamin:

2 Sam 7:22: we have heard with our e.

2Sam 22:7: my cry did enter into his e.

1 Kgs 13:34: destroy it from off the face of the e.

2 Kgs 18:26: the Jews' language in the e. of the people

2 Kgs 19:16: LORD, bow down thine e.,

2 Kgs 19:28: come up into mine e.,

2 Kgs 21:12: both his e. shall tingle.

2 Kgs 23:2: and he read in their e ...

1 Chron 17:20: have heard with our e.

2 Chron 6:40: let thine e. be attent unto the prayer .

2 Chron 7:15: mine e. attend unto the prayer

2 Chron 24:19: they would not give e.

2 Chron 34:30: he read in their e.

Neh 1:6: Let thine e. now be attentive,

Neh 1:11let now thine e. be attentive

Neh 8:3: the e. of all the people were attentive

Neh 9:30: yet would they not give e.:

Job 4:12: mine e. received a little thereof.

Job 12:11: Doth not the e. try words?

Job 13:1: Lo, mine e. hath seen all this,

Job 13:17: my declaration with your e.

Job15:21: A dreadful sound is in his e.:

Job 28:22: have heard the fame thereof with our e.

Job 29:11: When the e. heard me,

Job 29:21: Unto me men gave e.,

Job 32:11: I gave e. to your reasons,

Job 33:16: Then he openeth the e. of men,

Job 34:2: give e. unto me,

Job 34:3: For the e. trieth words,

Job 36:10: He openeth also their e. to discipline,

Job 36:15: openeth their e. in oppression.

Job 42:5: by the hearing of the e.:

Ps 5:1: Give e.to my words,

Ps 10:17: thou wilt cause thine e. to hear:

Ps 17:1: give e. unto my prayer,

Ps 17:6: incline thine e. unto me,

Ps 18:6: even into his e.

Ps 31:2: Bow down thine e. to me;

Ps 34:15: The e. of the LORD are upon the righteous,

Ps 39:12: and give e. unto my cry;

Ps 40:6: mine e. hast thou opened:

Ps 44:1: We have heard with our e.,

Ps 45:10: incline thine e.;

Ps 49:1: all ye people; give e.,

Ps 49:4: I will incline mine e. to a parable:

Ps 54:2: give e. to the words of my mouth.

Ps 55:1: Give e. to my prayer,

Ps 58:4: deaf adder that stoppeth her e.;

Ps 71:2: incline thine e. unto me,

Ps 77:1: he gave e. unto me.

Ps 78:1: Give e., O my people,

Ps 80:1: Give e., O Shepherd of Israel,

Ps 84:8: give e., O God of Jacob.

Ps 86:1: Bow down thine e.,

Ps 86:6: Give e., O LORD,

Ps 88:2: incline thine e. unto my cry;

Ps 92:11: mine e. shall hear

Ps 94:9: He that planted the e.,

Ps 102:2: incline thine e. unto me:

Ps 115:6: They have e.,

Ps 116:2: he hath inclined his e. unto me,

Ps 130:2: let thine e. be attentive

Ps 135:17: They have e.,

Ps 141:1: give e. unto my voice,

Ps 143:1: give e. to my supplications:

Prov 2:2: incline thine e. unto wisdom,

Prov 4:20: incline thine e. unto my sayings.
Prov 5:1: bow thine e. to my understanding:
Prov 5:13: nor inclined mine e. to them
Prov 15:31: The e. that heareth the reproof
Prov 17:4: a liar giveth ear to a naughty tongue.
Prov 18:15: the e. of the wise seeketh knowledge.
Prov 20:12: The hearing e.,
Prov 21:13: Whoso stoppeth his e. at the cry of the poor,
Prov 22:17: Bow down thine e.,
Prov 23:9: Speak not in the e. of a fool:
Prov 23:12: thine e. to the words of knowledge.
Prov 26:17: that taketh a dog by the e.
Prov 28:9: He that turneth away his e ...
Eccl 1:8: the e. filled with hearing.
Isa 1:2: O heavens, and give e.,
Isa 1:10: give e. unto the law of our God,
Isa 5:9: In mine e. said the LORD of hosts,
Isa 6:10: make their e. heavy ... and hear with their e.,
Isa 8:9: and give e., all ye of far countries:
Isa 11:3: neither reprove after the hearing of his e.:
Isa 22:14: it was revealed in mine e ...
Isa 28:23: Give ye e., and hear my voice;
Isa 30:21: thine e. shall hear a word ...
Isa 32:3: the e. of them that hear ...
Isa 32:9: give e. unto my speech.
Isa 33:15: that stoppeth his e. from hearing of blood
Isa 35:5: the e. of the deaf shall be unstopped.

Isa 36:11: in the e. of the people ...
Isa 37:17: Incline thine e., O LORD,
Isa 37:29: is come up into mine e.,
Isa 42:20: opening the e., but he heareth not.
Isa 42:23: Who among you will give e. to this?
Isa 43:8: and the deaf that have e.
Isa 48:8: thine e. was not opened:
Isa 49:20: shall say again in thine e.,
Isa 50:4: he wakeneth mine e. to hear as the learned.
Isa 50:5: GOD hath opened mine e.,
Isa 51:4: give e. unto me, O my nation:
Isa 55:3: Incline your e.,
Isa 59:1: neither his e. heavy,
Isa 64:4: nor perceived by the e.,
Jer 2:2: Go and cry in the e. of Jerusalem,
Jer 5:21: which have e., and hear not:
Jer 6:10: their e. is uncircumcised,
Jer 7:24: nor inclined their e.,
Jer 7:26: nor inclined their e.,
Jer 9:20: let your e. receive the word
Jer 11:8: nor inclined their e
Jer 13:15: Hear ye, and give e.;
Jer 17:23: neither inclined their e.,
Jer 19:3: his e. shall tingle.
Jer 26:11: as ye have heard with your e.
Jer 26:15: speak all these words in your e.
Jer 28:7: I speak in thine e., and in the e. of all the people;
Jer 29:29: read this letter in the e. of Jeremiah
Jer 34:14: neither inclined their e.
Jer 36:6: in the e. of the people

Jer 36:10: in the e. of all the people.
Jer 36:13: the book in the e. of the people.
Jer 36:14: hast read in the e. of the people,
Jer 36:15: read it in our e. So Baruch read it in their e.
Jer 36:20: told all the words in the e. of the king.
Jer 36:21: read it in the e. of the king, and in the e. of all the princes
Jer 44:5: nor inclined their e.
Lam 3:56: hide not thine e. at my breathing,
Ezek 3:10: and hear with thine e.
Ezek 8:18: they cry in mine e. with a loud voice,
Ezek 9:1: cried also in mine e. with a loud voice,
Ezek 12:2: they have e. to hear,
Ezek 16:12: and earrings in thine e.,
Ezek 23:25: shall take away thy nose and thine e.;
Ezek 24:26: to hear it with thine e.?
Ezek 40:4: hear with thine e.,
Ezek 44:5: hear with thine e.
Dan 9:18: O my God, incline thine e.,
Hosea 5:1: and give ye e.,
Joel 1:2 and give e.,
Amos 3:12: or a piece of an e.;
Micah 7:16: their e. shall be deaf.
Zech 7:11: and stopped their e.,
Mt 10:27: what ye hear in the e.,
Mt 11:15: He that hath e. to hear,
Mt 13:9: Who hath e. to hear,
Mt 13:15: and hear with their e.,
Mt 13:16: and your e., for they hear.
Mt 13:43: Who hath e. to hear,
Mt 26:51: and smote off his e.

Mt 28:14: come to the governor's e.,
Mk 4:9: He that hath e. to hear,
Mk 4:23: If any man have e. to hear,
Mk 7:16: If any man have e. to hear,
Mk 7:33: put his fingers into his e.,
Mk 7:35: straightway his e. were opened,
Mk 8:18: having e., hear ye not?
Mk 14:47: and cut off his e.
Lk 1:44: salutation sounded in mine e.,
Lk 4:21: this scripture fulfilled in your e.
Lk 8:8: He that hath e. to hear,
Lk 9:44: sayings sink down into your e.:
Lk 12:3: which ye have spoken in the e.
Lk 14:35: He that hath e. to hear,
Lk 22:50: and cut off his right e.
Lk 22:51: And he touched his e.,
Jn 18:10: and cut off his right e.
Jn 18:26: kinsman whose e. Peter cut off,
Acts 7:51: uncircumcised in heart and e.,
Acts 7:57: and stopped their e.,
Acts 11:22: these things came unto the e. of the church
Acts 17:20: thou bringest certain strange things to our e.:
Acts 28:27: their e. are dull of hearing,
Rom11:8: and e. that they should not hear;
1 Cor 2:9: nor e. heard,
1 Cor 12:16: And if the e. shall say,
2 Tm 4:3: having itching e.;
2 Tm 4:4: turn away their e. from the truth,

Jms 5:4: are entered into the e. of the Lord ...
1 Pt 3:12: his e. are open unto their prayers
Rv 2:7: He that hath an e.,
Rv 2:11: He that hath an e.,
Rv 2:17: He that hath an e.,
Rv 2:29: He that hath an e.,
Rv 3:6: He that hath an e.,
Rv 13:9: If any man have an e.

Eye(s)
Ex 21:24: E. for e.,
Ex 21:26: the e. of his servant, or the e. of his maid ... let him go free for his e. sake.
Lev 21:20: that hath a blemish in his e.,
Lev 24:20: Breach for breach, e. for e.,
Deut 7:16: thine e. shall have no pity upon them:
Deut 13:8: shall thine e. pity him,
Deut 15:9: thine e. be evil against thy poor brother,
Deut 19:13: Thine e. shall not pity him,
Deut 19:21: And thine e. shall not pity;
Deut 25:12: thine e. shall not pity her.
Deut 28:54: his e. shall be evil toward his brother,
Deut 28:56: her e. shall be evil toward the husband
Deut 32:10: kept him as the apple of his e.
Deut 34:7: his e. was not dim,
2Sam 22:25: according to my cleanness in his e. sight.
Ezra 5:5: the e. of their God was upon the elders
Job 7:7: mine e. shall no more see good.
Job 7:8: The e. of him that hath seen me shall see me no more: thine e. are upon me,
Job 10:18: and no e. had seen me!
Job 13:1: Lo, mine e. hath seen all this,

Job 16:20: mine e. poureth out tears unto God.
Job 17:2: doth not mine e. continue in their provocation?
Job 17:7: Mine e. also is dim by reason of sorrow,
Job 20:9: The e. also which saw him
Job 24:15: The e. also of the adulterer
Job 28:7: which the vulture's e. hath not seen:
Job 28:10: his e. seeth every precious thing.
Job 29:11: and when the e. saw me, it gave witness to me:
Job 42:5: but now mine e. seeth thee.
Ps 6:7: Mine e. is consumed because of grief;
Ps 17:8: Keep me as the apple of the e.,
Ps 31:9: mine e. is consumed with grief,
Ps 32:8: I will guide thee with mine e.
Ps 33:18: the e. of the LORD is upon them
Ps 35:19: with the e. that hate me without a cause.
Ps 35:21: our e. hath seen it.
Ps 54:7: mine e. hath seen his desire ...
Ps 88:9: Mine e. mourneth by reason of affliction:
Ps 92:11: Mine e. also shall see my ...
Ps 94:9: that formed the e.,
Prov 7:2: as the apple of thine e.
Prov 10:10: He that winketh with the e. causeth sorrow:
Prov 20:12: and the seeing e.,
Prov 22:9: a bountiful e. shall be blessed;
Prov 23:6: of him that hath an evil e.,
Prov 28:22: He that hasteth to be rich hath an evil e.,
Prov 30:17: The e. that mocketh at his father,

Eccl 1:8: the e. is not satisfied with seeing,
Eccl 4:8: neither is his e. satisfied with riches;
Isa 13:18: their e. shall not spare children.
Isa 52:8: for they shall see eye to e.,
Isa 64:4: neither hath the e. seen,
Jer 3:2: Lift up thine e. unto the high places,
Jer 5:3: are not thine e. upon the truth?
Jer 5:21: which have e., and see not;
Jer 7:11: a den of robbers in your e.?
Jer 9:1: mine e. a fountain of tears,
Jer 13:17: mine e. shall weep sore,
Jer 13:20: Lift up your e.,
Jer 14:6: their e. did fail, because there was no grass.
Jer 14:17: Let mine e. run down with tears night and day,
Jer 16:9: I put of this place in your e.,
Jer 16:17: For mine e. are upon all their ways:
Jer 20:4: thine e. shall behold it:
Jer 22:17: But thine e.and thine heart
Jer 24:6: For I will set mine e. upon them for good,
Jer 29:21: and he shall slay them before your e.;
Jer 31:16: thine e. from tears:
Jer 32:4: and his eyes shall behold his e.;
Jer 32:19: for thine e. are open upon
Jer 34:3: and thine e. shall behold the eyes of the king of Babylon,
Jer 39:6: slew the sons of Zedekiah in Riblah before his e.:

Jer 39:7: he put out Zedekiah's e.,
Jer 42:2: as thine e. do behold us:
Jer 52:2: which was evil in the e. of the LORD,
Jer 52:10: slew the sons of Zedekiah before his e.:
Jer 52:11: Then he put out the e. of Zedekiah;
Lam 1:16: mine e., mine eye runneth down with water,
Lam 2:4: pleasant to the e. in the tabernacle
Lam 2:11: Mine e. do fail with tears,
Lam 2:18: not the apple of thine e. cease.
Lam 3:48: Mine e. runneth down with rivers of water
Lam 3:49: Mine e. trickleth down,
Lam 3:51: Mine e. affecteth mine heart
Lam 4:17: our e. as yet failed for our vain help:
Ezek 5:11: neither shall mine e. spare,
Lam 5:17: for these things our e. are dim.
Ezek 1:18: were full of e. round about them four.
Ezek 6:9: and with their e., which go a whoring,
Ezek 7:4: mine e. shall not spare thee,
Ezek 7:9: And mine e. shall not spare,
Ezek 8:5: lift up thine e. now the way toward the north. So I lifted up mine e.
Ezek 8:18: mine e. shall not spare,
Ezek 9:5: let not your e. spare,
Ezek 9:10: mine e. shall not spare,
Ezek 10:12: were full of e. round about,
Ezek 12:2: which have e. to see,
Ezek 12:12: see not the ground with his e.

Ezek 16:5: None e. pitied thee,
Ezek 18:6: neither hath lifted up his e.
Ezek 18:12: lifted up his e. to the idols,
Ezek 18:15: lifted up his e. to the idols
Ezek 20:7: the abominations of his e.,
Ezek 20:8: abominations of their e.,
Ezek 20:17: mine e. spared them.
Ezek 20:24: their e. were after their fathers' idols.
Ezek 21:6: bitterness sigh before their e.
Ezek 22:26: have hid their e. from my sabbaths,
Ezek 23:16: she saw them with her eyes,
Ezek 23:27: shalt not lift up thine eyes unto them,
Ezek 23:40: paintedst thy e.,
Ezek 24:16: the desire of thine e.
Ezek 24:21: the desire of your e.,
Ezek 24:25: the desire of their e.,
Ezek 33:25: lift up your e. toward
Ezek 36:23: in you before their e.
Ezek 37:20: in thine hand before their e.
Ezek 38:16: before their e.
Ezek 38:23: I will be known in the e. of many nations,
Ezek 40:4: behold with thine e.,
Ezek 44:5: behold with thine e.,
Dan 4:34: Nebuchadnezzar lifted up mine e. unto heaven,
Dan 7:8: horn were e. like the e. of man,
Dan 7:20: that horn that had e.,
Dan 8:3: Then I lifted up mine e.,

Dan 8:5: a notable horn between his e.
Dan 8:21: between his e. is the first king.
Dan 9:18: open thine e.,
Dan 10:5: Then I lifted up mine e.,
Dan 10:6: his e. as lamps of fire,
Hosea 13:14: shall be hid from mine e.
Joel 1:16: meat cut off before our e.,
Amos 9:4: set mine e. upon them for evil,
Amos 9:8: Behold, the e. of the Lord
Micah 4:11: let our e. look upon Zion.
Micah 7:10: mine enemy shall see it ... mine e. shall behold her:
Hab 1:13: Thou art of purer e.
Zeph 3:20: turn back your captivity before your e.,
Hag 2:3: is it not in your e.
Zech 1:18: Then lifted I up mine e.,
Zech 2:1: I lifted up mine e. again,
Zech 2:8 toucheth the apple of his e.
Zech 3:9: one stone shall be seven e.:
Zech 4:10: they are the e. of the LORD,
Zech 5:1: lifted up mine e., and looked,
Zech 5:5: Lift up now thine e.,
Zech 5:9: Then lifted I up mine e.,
Zech 6:1: and lifted up mine e.,
Zech 8:6: If it be marvellous in the eyes ... should it also be marvellous in mine e.?
Zech 9:1: when the e. of man,
Zech 9:8: now have I seen with mine e.
Zech 11:17: upon his right e.:
Zech 12:4: I will open mine e. upon the house of Judah,

Zech 14:12: their e. shall consume away in their holes,
Mal 1:5: And your e. shall see,
Mt 5:29: And if thy right e. offend thee,
Mt 5:38: An eye for an e.,
Mt 6:22: The light of the body is the e.: if therefore thine e. be single,
Mt 6:23: But if thine e. be evil,
Mt 7:3: mote that is in thy brother's e.,
Mt 7:4: a beam is in thine own e.?
Mt 7:5: beam out of thine own e ... the mote out of thy brother's e.
Mt 9:29: Then touched he their e., saying,
Mt 9:30: And their e. were opened;
Mt 13:15: they should see with their e.,
Mt 13:16: But blessed are your e.,
Mt 17:8: when they had lifted up their e.,
Mt 18:9: And if thine e. offend thee ... enter into life with one e., rather than having two e ...
Mt 20:15: Is thine e. evil,
Mt 20:33: that our e. may be opened.
Mt 20:34: and touched their e.:
Mt 21:42: it is marvellous in our e.?
Mt 26:43: their e. were heavy.
Mk 7:22: an evil e.,
Mk 8:18: Having e., see ye not?
Mk 8:23: when he had spit on his e.,
Mk 8:25: his hands again upon his e.,
Mk 9:47: if thine e. offend thee, enter into the kingdom of God with one e.,
Mk 12:11: it is marvelous in our e.?
Mk 14:40: for their e. were heavy,

Lk 2:30: For mine e. have seen thy salvation,
Lk 4:20: And the e. of all them
Lk 6:20: And he lifted up his e. on his disciples,
Lk 6:41: thy brother's e ... is in thine own e.?
Lk 6:42: mote that is in thine e ... beam that is in thine own e.? the beam out of thine e ... that is in thy brother's e.
Lk 10:23: Blessed are the e.
Lk 11:34: light of the body is the e.: therefore when thine e. is single, thy whole body also is full of light; but when thine e. is evil,
Lk 16:23: And in hell he lift up his e.,
Lk 18:13: as his e. unto heaven,
Lk 19:42: they are hid from thine e.
Lk 24:16: But their e. were holden
Lk 24:31: And their e. were opened,
Jn 4:35: Lift up your e.,
Jn 6:5: When Jesus then lifted up his e.,
Jn 9:6: he anointed the e. of the blind man
Jn 9:10: How were thine e. opened?
Jn 9:11: anointed mine e.,
Jn 9:14: and opened his e.
Jn 9:15: He put clay upon mine e.,
Jn 9:17: he hath opened thine e.?
Jn 9:21: who hath opened his e.,
Jn 9:26: how opened he thine e.?
Jn 9:30: yet he hath opened mine e.
Jn 9:32: opened the e. of one that was born blind.
Jn 10:21: Can a devil open the e. of the blind?
Jn 11:37: which opened the e. of the blind,

Jn 11:41: Jesus lifted up his e.,
Jn 12:40: He hath blinded their e.,
Jn 17:1: lifted up his e. to heaven,
Acts 3:4: fastening his e. upon him ...
Acts 9:8: when his e. were opened,
Acts 9:18: there fell from his e. as ...
Acts 9:40: And she opened her e.:
Acts 11:6: I had fastened mine e.,
Acts 13:9: set his e. on him,
Acts 26:18: To open their e.,
Acts 28:27 their e. have they closed;
Rom 3:18: There is no fear of God before their e.
Rom 1:8: e. that they should not see,
Rom 11:10: Let their e. be darkened,
1 Cor 12:16: Because I am not the e,
1 Cor: 2:17: If the whole body were an e.,
1 Cor: 2:21: And the e. cannot say unto the hand,
1 Cor: 5:52: in the twinkling of an e.,
Gal 3:1 before whose e. Jesus Christ ...
Gal 4:15: ye would have plucked out your own e.,
Eph 1:18: The e. of your understanding being enlightened;
Heb 4:13: opened unto the e. of him
1 Pt 3:12: For the e. of the Lord
2 Pt 2:14: Having e. full of adultery,
1 Jn 1:1: we have seen with our e.,
1 Jn 2:11: darkness hath blinded his e.
1 Jn 2:16: and the lust of the e.,
Rv 1:7: and every e. shall see him;

Rv 1:14: his e. were as a flame of fire;
Rv 2:18: his e. like unto a flame of fire,
Rv 3:18: and anoint thine e. with eye salve,
Rv 4:6: four beasts full of e. before and behind.
Rv 4:8: they were full of e. within:
Rv 5:6: having seven horns and seven e.;
Rv 7:17: God shall wipe away all tears from their e.
Rv 19:12: His e. were as a flame of fire,
Rv 21:4: God shall wipe away all tears from their e.;

Eyebrow(s)
Lev 14:9 he shall shave all his hair off his head and his beard and his e.,

Eyelids
Job 16:16: my e. is the shadow of death;
Job 41:18: his eyes are like the e. of the morning.
Ps 11:4: his eyes behold, his e. try,
Ps 132:4: slumber to mine e.,
Prov 4:25: let thine e. look straight before thee.
Prov 6:4: nor slumber to thine e.
Prov 6:25: neither let her take thee with her e.
Prov 30:13: their e. are lifted up.
Jer 9:18: our e. gush out with waters.

Face
Gen 3:19: In the sweat of thy f. shalt thou eat bread,
Gen 16:6: she fled from her f.
Gen 16:8: I flee from the f. of my mistress Sarai.
Gen 17:3: And Abram fell on his f.:

Gen 17:17: Abraham fell upon his f.,
Gen 19:1: he bowed himself with his f. toward the ground;
Gen 19:13: the cry of them is waxen great before the f. of the LORD;
Gen 24:47: I put the earring upon her f.,
Gen 30:33: it shall come for my hire before thy f.:
Gen 31:21: and set his f. toward the mount Gilead.
Gen 32:20: afterward I will see his f.;
Gen 32:30: I have seen God face to f.,
Gen 33:10: therefore I have seen thy f., as though I had seen the f. of God,
Gen 35:1: when thou fleddest from the f. of Esau thy brother.
Gen 35:7: when he fled from the f. of his brother.
Gen 36:6: went into the country from the f. of his brother Jacob.
Gen 38:15: because she had covered her f.
Gen 43:3: Ye shall not see my f.,
Gen 43:5: Ye shall not see my f.,
Gen 43:31: And he washed his f.,
Gen 44:23: ye shall see my f. no more.
Gen 44:26: we may not see the man's f.,
Gen 46:28: to direct his f. unto Goshen;
Gen 46:30: since I have seen thy f.,
Gen 48:11: I had not thought to see thy f.:
Gen 50:1: And Joseph fell upon his father's f.,
Gen 50:18: and fell down before his f.;
Ex 2:15: Moses fled from the f. of Pharaoh,
Ex 3:6: And Moses hid his f.;

Ex 10:28: see my f. no more;
Ex 10:29: I will see thy f. again no more.
Ex 14:19: cloud went from before their f.,
Ex 14:25: Let us flee from the f. of Israel;
Ex 33:11: And the LORD spake unto Moses f. to f.,
Ex 33:20: Thou canst not see my f.:
Ex 33:23: but my f. shall not be seen.
Ex 34:29: his f. shone while he talked with him.
Ex 34:30: the skin of his f. shone;
Ex 34:33: he put a vail on his f.
Ex 34:35: And the children of Israel saw the f. of Moses, that the skin of Moses' f. shone: and Moses put the vail upon his f. again,
Lev 13:41: part of his head toward his f.,
Lev 17:10: I will even set my f. against that soul
Lev 19:32: and honour the f. of the old man,
Lev 20:3: And I will set my f. against that man,
Lev 20:5: Then I will set my f. against that man,
Lev 20:6: I will even set my f. against that soul,
Lev 26:17: I will set my f. against you,
Num 6:25: The LORD make his f. shine upon thee,
Num 12:14: If her father had but spit in her f.,
Num 14:14: that thou LORD art seen f. to f.,
Num 16:4: he fell upon his f.:
Num 19:3: and one shall slay her before his f.:
Num 22:31: and fell flat on his f.
Num 24:1: he set his f. toward the wilderness.
Deut 1:17: shall not be afraid of the f. of man;

Deut 5:4: The LORD talked with you f. to f.
Deut 7:10: he will repay him to his f.
Deut 8:20: which the LORD destroyeth before your f.,
Deut 9:3: he shall bring them down before thy f.:
Deut 25:2: and to be beaten before his f.,
Deut 25:9: and spit in his f.,
Deut 28:7: to be smitten before thy f.:
Deut 28:31: violently taken away from before thy f.,
Deut 31:5: give them up before your f.,
Deut 31:17: I will hide my f. from them,
Deut 31:18: I will surely hide my f. in that day
Deut 32:20: I will hide my f. from them
Deut 34:10: the LORD knew f. to f.,
Josh 5:14: And Joshua fell on his f. to the earth,
Josh 7:6: and fell to the earth upon his f.
Josh 7:10: thus upon thy f.?
Judg 6:22: I have seen an angel of the LORD f. to f.
Ruth 2:10: Then she fell on her f.,
1 Sam 5:3: Dagon was fallen upon his f. to the earth ...
1 Sam 5:4: Dagon was fallen upon his f. to the ground
1 Sam 17:49: and he fell upon his f. to the earth.
1 Sam 20:41: fell on his f. to the ground,
1 Sam 24:8: David stooped with his f. to the earth,
1 Sam 25:23: fell before David on her f.,
1 Sam 25:41: and bowed herself on her f. to the earth
1 Sam 26:20: before the f. of the LORD:
1 Sam 28:14: and he stooped with his f. to the ground,

2 Sam 2:22: I hold up my f. to Joab thy brother?
2 Sam 3:13: when thou comest to see my f.
2 Sam 9:6: he fell on his f. and did reverence.
2 Sam 14:4: she fell on her f. to the ground,
2 Sam 14:22: And Joab fell to the ground on his f.,
2 Sam 14:24: let him not see my f.
2 Sam 14:28: and saw not the king's f.
2 Sam 14:32: therefore let me see the king's f;
2 Sam 14:33: and bowed himself on his f. to the ground
2 Sam 18:28: he fell down to the earth upon his f. before the king,
2 Sam 19:4: But the king covered his f.,
2 Sam 24:20: bowed himself before the king on his f. upon the ground.
1 Kgs 1:23: before the king with his f. to the ground.
1 Kgs 1:31: Then Bath-sheba bowed with her f. to the earth,
1 Kgs 8:14: And the king turned his f. about,
1 Kgs 13:6: now the f. of the LORD thy God,
1 Kgs 18:7: and fell on his f.,
1 Kgs 18:42: and put his f. between his knees,
1 Kgs 19:13 he wrapped his f. in his mantle,
1 Kgs 20:38: disguised himself with ashes upon his f.
1 Kgs 20:41: ashes away from his f.;
1 Kgs 21:4: and turned away his f.,
2 Kgs 4:29: staff upon the f. of the child.
2 Kgs 4:31: staff upon the f. of the child;
2 Kgs 8:15: and spread it on his f.,

2 Kgs 4:29: staff upon the f. of the child.
2 Kgs 4:31: staff upon the f. of the child;
2 Kgs 8:15: and spread it on his f.,
2 Kgs 9:30: and she painted her f.,
2 Kgs 9:32: lifted up his f. to the window,
2 Kgs 12:17: and Hazael set his f. to go up to Jerusalem.
2 Kgs 13:14: and wept over his f.,
2 Kgs 14:8: look one another in the f.
2 Kgs 14:11: looked one another in the f. at Beth-shemesh,
2 Kgs 18:24: the f. of one captain of the least of my master's servants,
2 Kgs 20:2: he turned his f. to the wall,
1 Chron 16:11: seek his f. continually.
1 Chron 21:21: bowed himself to David with his f. to the ground.
2 Chron 6:3: And the king turned his f.,
2Chron 6:42: turn not away the f. of thine anointed:
2 Chron 7:14: and seek my f.,
2 Chron 20:18: bowed his head with his f. to the ground:
2 Chron 25:17: see one another in the f.
2 Chron 25:21: they saw one another in the face,
2 Chron 30:9: will not turn away his f. from you,
2 Chron 32:21: he returned with shame of f. to his own land.
2 Chron 35:22: Josiah would not turn his f. from him,
Ezra 9:6: to lift up my f. to thee,
Ezra 9:7: and to confusion of f.,
Esth 1:14: which saw the king's f.,

Esth 7:8: they covered Haman's f.
Job 1:11: he will curse thee to thy f.
Job 2:5: he will curse thee to thy f.
Job 4:15: Then a spirit passed before my f;
Job 11:15: lift up thy f. without spot;
Job 13:24: Wherefore hidest thou thy f.,
Job 15:27: Because he covereth his f. with his fatness,
Job 16:8: rising up in me beareth witness to my f.
Job 16:16: My f. is foul with weeping,
Job 21:31: Who shall declare his way to his f.?
Job 22:26: shalt lift up thy f. unto God.
Job 23:17: he covered the darkness from my f.
Job 24:15: and disguiseth his f.
Job 26:9: He holdeth back the face of his throne,
Job 30:10: spare not to spit in my f.
Job 33:26: he shall see his f. with joy:
Job 34:29: when he hideth his f.,
Job 41:14: Who can open the doors of his f.?
Ps 5:8: thy way straight before my f.
Ps 10:11: he hideth his f.;
Ps 13:1: how long wilt thou hide thy f. from me?
Ps 17:15: I will behold thy f. in righteousness:
Ps 21:12: thine arrows upon thy strings against the f. of them.
Ps 22:24: neither hath he hid his f. from him;
Ps 24:6: that seek thy f., O Jacob.
Ps 27:8: Seek ye my f.;
Ps 27:9: Hide not thy f. far from me;

Ps 30:7: thou didst hide thy f.,
Ps 31:16: Make thy f. to shine upon thy servant:
Ps 34:16: The f. of the LORD is against them
Ps 41:12: settest me before thy f. forever.
Ps 44:15: shame of my f. hath covered me,
Ps 44:24: Wherefore hidest thou thy f.,
Ps 51:9: Hide thy f. from my sins,
Ps 67:1: cause his f. to shine upon us;
Ps 69:7: shame hath covered my f.
Ps 69:17: And hide not thy f. from thy servant;
Ps 80:3: cause thy f. to shine;
Ps 80:7: cause thy f. to shine;
Ps 80:19: cause thy f. to shine;
Ps 84:9: look upon the f. of thine anointed.
Ps 88:14: why hidest thou thy f. from me?
Ps 89:14: truth shall go before thy f.
Ps 89:23: I will beat down his foes before his f.,
Ps 102:2: Hide not thy f. from me
Ps 104:15: oil to make his f. to shine,
Ps 104:29: Thou hidest thy f.,
Ps 105:4: seek his f. evermore.
Ps 119:135: Make thy f. to shine upon thy servant;
Ps 132:10: turn not away the f. of thine anointed.
Ps 143:7: hide not thy f. from me,
Prov 7:13: With an imputant f.
Prov 7:15: diligently to seek thy f.,
Prov 21:29: wicked man hardeneth his f.
Prov 24:31: and nettles had covered the f. thereof
Prov 27:19: As in water f. answereth to f.,

Eccl 8:1: a man's wisdom maketh his f. to shine, and the boldness of his f. shall be changed.

Isa 6:2: with twain he covered his f.,

Isa 8:17: that hideth his f. from the house of Jacob,

Isa 16:4: from the f. of the spoiler:

Isa 25:7: the f. of the covering cast over all people,

Isa 28:25: When he hath made plain the f. thereof,

Isa 29:22: neither shall his f. now wax pale.

Isa 36:9: turn away the f. of one captain

Isa 38:2: Then Hezekiah turned his face toward the wall,

Isa 49:23: with their f. toward the earth,

Isa 50:6: I hid not my f. from shame and spitting.

Isa 50:7: have I set my f. like a flint,

Isa 54:8: In a little wrath I hid my f. from thee ...

Isa 59:2: your sins have hid his f. from you,

Isa 64:7: for thou hast hid thy f. from us,

Isa 65:3: provoketh me to anger continually to my f.;

Jer 1:13: the f. thereof is toward the north.

Jer 2:27: and not their f.e:

Jer 4:30: though thou rentest thy f. with painting,

Jer 13:26: I discover thy skirts upon thy f.

Jer 16:17: they are not hid from my f.,

Jer 21:10: I have set my f. against this city for evil,

Jer 22:25: whose f. thou fearest,

Jer 32:31: I should remove it from before my f.,

Jer 32:33: and not the f.:

Jer 33:5: I have hid my f. from this city.

Jer 44:11: I will set my f. against you for evil,

Lam 2:19: like water before the f. of the Lord:

Lam 3:35: the right of a man before the f. of the most High,

Ezek 1:28: I fell upon my f.,

Ezek 3:8: Behold, I have made thy f. strong against their faces,

Ezek 3:23: and I fell on my f.

Ezek 4:3: and set thy f. against it,

Ezek 4:7: thou shalt set thy f. toward the siege of Jerusalem,

Ezek 6:2: set thy f. toward the mountains of Israel,

Ezek 7:22: My f. will I turn also from them,

Ezek 9:8: I fell upon my f.,

Ezek 11:13: Then fell I down upon my f.,

Ezek 12:6: thou shalt cover thy f.,

Ezek 12:12: he shall cover his f.,

Ezek 13:17: set thy f. against the daughters of thy people,

Ezek 14:3: stumblingblock of their iniquity before their f.:

Ezek 14:4: stumblingblock of his iniquity before his f.,

Ezek 14:7: stumblingblock of his iniquity before his f.,

Ezek 14:8: And I will set my f. against that man,

Ezek 15:7: I set my f. against them.

Ezek 20:35: will I plead with you f. to f.

Ezek 20:46: set thy f. toward the south,

Ezek 21:2: set thy f. toward Jerusalem,

Ezek 21:16: whithersoever thy f. is set.

Ezek 25:2: set thy face against the Ammonites,

Ezek 28:21: Son of man, set thy f. against Zidon,

Ezek 29:2: Son of man, set thy f. against Pharaoh ...

Ezek 35:2: Son of man, set thy f. against mount Seir,

Ezek 38:2: Son of man, set thy f. against Gog,

Ezek 38:18: my fury shall come up in my f.

Ezek 39:23: hid I my face from them,

Ezek 39:24: and hid my f. from them.

Ezek 39:29: Neither will I hide my f. any more from them:

Ezek 41:19: the f. of a man was toward the palm tree ...

Ezek 43:3: and I fell upon my f.

Ezek 44:4: and I fell upon my f.

Dan 2:46: Nebuchadnezzar fell upon his f.,

Dan 8:17: and fell upon my f.: but he said unto me,

Dan 8:18: a deep sleep on my f. toward the ground:

Dan 9:3: And I set my f. unto the Lord God,

Dan 9:8: to us belongeth confusion of f.,

Dan 9:17: and cause thy f. to shine upon thy sanctuary ...

Dan 10:6: his f. as the appearance of lightning,

Dan 10:9: then was I in a deep sleep on my f., and my f. toward the ground.

Dan 10:15: I set my f. toward the ground,

Dan 11:17: set his f. to enter with the strength

Dan 11:18: After this shall he turn his f. unto the isles,

Dan 11:19: he shall turn his f. toward the fort

Hosea 5:5: the pride of Israel doth testify to his f.:

Hosea 5:15: and seek my f.:

Hosea 7:2: they are before my f.,

Hosea 7:10: the pride of Israel testifieth to his f.:

Joel 2:6: Before their f. the people shall be much pained: all f. shall gather blackness.
Joel 2:20: with his f. toward the east sea,
Micah 3:4: he will even hide his f. from them
Nahum 2:1: is come up before thy f.:
Nahum 3:5: I will discover thy skirts upon thy f.,
Mt 6:17: anoint thine head, and wash thy f.;
Mt 11:10: I send my messenger before thy f.,
Mt 17:2: his f. did shine as the sun,
Mt 17:6: they fell on their f.,
Mt 18:10: the f. of my Father which is in heaven.
Mt 26:39: and fell on his f., and prayed,
Mt 26:67: Then did they spit in his f.,
Mk 1:2: I send my messenger before thy f.,
Mk 14:65: and to cover his f.,
Lk 1:76: for thou shalt go before the f. of the Lord
Lk 2:31: thou hast prepared before the f. of all people;
Lk 5:12: who seeing Jesus fell on his f.,
Lk 7:27: I send my messenger before thy f.,
Lk 9:51: he stedfastly set his face to go to Jerusalem,
Lk 9:52: And sent messengers before his f.:
Lk 9:53: because his f. was as though he would go to Jerusalem.
Lk 10:1: and sent them two and two before his f. into every city and place,
Lk 17:16: And fell down on his f. at his feet,
Lk 22:64: they struck him on the f.,
Jn 11:44: and his f. was bound about with a napkin.

Acts 2:25: I foresaw the Lord always before my f.,
Acts 6:15: saw his f. as it had been the face of an angel.
Acts 7:45: God drave out before the f. of our fathers,
Acts 20:25: shall see my f. no more.
Acts 20:38: that they should see his f. no more.
Acts 25:16: accused have the accusers f. to f.,
1 Cor 13:12: but then face to f.:
1 Cor 14:25: so falling down on his f. he will worship God,
2 Cor 3:7: behold the f. of Moses for the glory
2 Cor 3:13: which put a vail over his f.,
2 Cor 3:18: with open f. beholding as in a glass.
2 Cor 4:6: glory of God in the f. of Jesus Christ.
2 Cor 11:20: if a man smite you on the f.
Gal 1:22: was unknown by f. unto the churches
Gal 2:11: I withstood him to the f.,
Col 2:1: for as many as have not seen my f. in the flesh;
1 Thes 2:17: to see your f. with great desire.
1 Thes 3:10: that we might see your f.,
Jms 1:23: a man beholding his natural f. in a glass:
1 Pt 3:12: the f. of the Lord is against them that do evil.
2 Jn 1:12: speak f. to f.,
3 Jn 1:14: and we shall speak f. to f.
Rv 4:7: the third beast had a f. as a man,
Rv 6:16: hide us from the f. of him that sitteth on the throne,
Rv 10:1: his f. was as it were the sun,
Rv 12:14: from the f. of the serpent.

Rv 20:11: from whose f. the earth and the heaven fled away;
Rv 22:4: And they shall see his f.;

Feet

Gen 18:4: and wash your f.,
Gen 19:2: and wash your f.,
Gen 24:32: and water to wash his f., and the men's f. that were with him.
Gen 43:24: and they washed their f.;
Gen 49:10: nor a lawgiver from between his f.,
Gen 49:33: he gathered up his f. into the bed,
Ex 3:5: put off thy shoes from off thy f.,
Ex 4:25: and cast it at his f., and said,
Ex 12:11: your shoes on your f.,
Ex 24:10: was under his f. as it were a paved work ...
Ex 30:19: wash their hands and their f. thereat:
Ex 30:21: So they shall wash their hands and their f.,
Ex 40:31: washed their hands and their f. thereat:
Lev 8:24: the great toes of their right f.:
Lev 11:21: which have legs above their f.,
Lev 11:23: which have four f.,
Num 20:19: go through on my f.
Deut 2:28: I will pass through on my f.;
Deut 11:24: whereon the soles of your f. shall tread
Deut 28:57: that cometh out from between her f.,
Deut 33:3: they sat down at thy f.;
Josh 3:13: the soles of the f. of the priests that bear the ark
Josh 3:15: the f. of the priests that bare the ark
Josh 4:3: out of the place where the priests' f. stood firm,

Josh 4:9: where the f. of the priests which bare the ark

Josh 4:18: the soles of the priests' f. were lifted up unto the dry land,

Josh 9:5: And old shoes and clouted upon their f.,

Josh 10:24: put your f. upon the necks of these kings ... they came near, and put their f. upon the necks of them.

Josh 14:9: thy f. have trodden shall be thine inheritance

Judg 3:24: Surely he covereth his f. in his summer chamber.

Judg 4:15: and fled away on his f.

Judg 4:17: Sisera fled away on his f. to the tent of Jael

Judg 5:27: At her feet he bowed ... at her f. he bowed,

Judg 19:21: and they washed their f.,

Ruth 3:4: and uncover his f., and lay thee down;

Ruth 3:7: and uncovered his f., and laid her down.

Ruth 3:8: a woman lay at his f.

Ruth 3:14: she lay at his f. until the morning: another.

1 Sam 2:9: He will keep the f. of his saints

1 Sam 14:13: and upon his f.,

1 Sam 24:3: Saul went in to cover his f.:

1 Sam 25:24: And fell at his f.,

1 Sam 25:41: be a servant to wash the f.

2 Sam 3:34: nor thy f. put into fetters:

2 Sam 4:4: that was lame of his f.

2 Sam 4:12: cut off their hands and their f.,

2 Sam 9:3: which is lame on his f.

2 Sam 9:13: and was lame on both his f.

2 Sam 11:8: and wash thy f.

2 Sam 19:24: had neither dressed his f.,

2 Sam 22:10: and darkness was under his.

2 Sam 22:34: He maketh my feet like hinds' f:

2 Sam 22:37: so that my f did not slip.

2 Sam 22:39: they are fallen under my f.

1 Kgs 2:5: and in his shoes that were on his f.

1 Kgs 5:3: the LORD put them under the soles of his f.

1 Kgs 14:6: the sound of her f. as she came in at the door,

1 Kgs 14:12: when thy f. enter into the city,

1 Kgs 15:23: his old age he was diseased in his f.

2 Kgs 4:27: she caught him by the f.:

2 Kgs 4:37: and fell at his f.,

2 Kgs 6:32: the sound of his master's f. behind him?

2 Kgs 9:35: they found no more of her than the skull, and the f.,

2 Kgs 13:21: and stood up on his f.

2 Kgs 19:24and with the sole of my f ...

2 Kgs 21:8: Neither will I make the f. of Israel ...

1 Chron 28:2: David the king stood up upon his f.,

2 Chron 3:13: and they stood on their f.,

2 Chron 16:12: was diseased in his f.,

Neh 9:21: and their f. swelled not.

Esth 8:3: and fell down at his f.,

Job 12:5: ready to slip with his f. is as a lamp

Job 13:27: thou settest a print upon the heels of my f.,

Job 18:8: cast into a net by his own f.,

Job 18:11: and shall drive him to his f.

Job 29:15: and f. was I to the lame.

Job 30:12: they push away my f.,

Job 33:11: He putteth my f. in the stocks,

Ps 8:6: hast put all things under his f.:

Ps 18:9: and darkness was under his f.

Ps 18:33: He maketh my f. like hinds' f.,

Ps 18:36: that my f. did not slip.

Ps 18:38: they are fallen under my f.

Ps 22:16: pierced my hands and my f.

Ps 25:15: shall pluck my f. out of the net.

Ps 31:8: thou hast set my f. in a large room.

Ps 40:2: and set my f. upon a rock,

Ps 47:3: and the nations under our f.

Ps 56:13: wilt not thou deliver my f. from falling,

Ps 58:10: he shall wash his f. in the blood of the wicked.

Ps 66:9: and suffereth not our f. to be moved.

Ps 73:2: my f. were almost gone;

Ps 74:3: Lift up thy f. unto the perpetual desolations;

Ps 91:13: the dragon shalt thou trample under f.

Ps 105:18: Whose f. they hurt with fetters:

Ps 115:7: f. have they, but they walk not:

Ps 116:8: and my f. from falling.

Ps 119:59: turned my f. unto thy testimonies.

Ps 119:101: I have refrained my f. from every evil way,

Ps 119:105: Thy word is a lamp unto my f.,

Ps 122:2: Our f. shall stand within thy gates,

Prov 1:16: For their f. run to evil,

Prov 4:26: Ponder the path
of thy f.,
Prov 5:5: Her f. go down to
death;
Prov 6:13: he speaketh with
his f.,
Prov 6:18: f. that be swift in
running to mischief,
Prov 6:28: and his f. not be
burned?
Prov 7:11: her f. abide not in
her house:
Prov 19:2: he that hasteth
with his f. sinneth.
Prov 26:6: by the hand of a
fool cutteth off the f.,
Prov 29:5: his neighbour
spreadeth a net for his f.
Song 5:3: I have washed my f.;
Song 7:1: How beautiful are
thy f. with shoes,
Isa 3:16: making a tinkling
with their f.:
Isa 3:18: ornaments about
their f.,
Isa 6:2: and with twain he
covered his f.,
Isa 7:20: and the hair of the f.:
Isa 14:19: as a carcase
trodden under f.
Isa 23:7: her own f. shall carry
her afar off to sojourn.
Isa 26:6: even the f. of the poor,
Isa 28:3: shall be trodden
under f.:
Isa 32:20: that send forth
thither the f. of the ox and
the ass.
Isa 37:25: with the sole of my f.
have I dried ...
Isa 41:3: the way that he had
not gone with his f.
Isa 49:23: and lick up the dust
of thy f.;
Isa 52:7: are the f. of him that
bringeth good tidings,
Isa 59:7: Their f. run to evil,
Isa 60:13: I will make the
place of my f. glorious.
Isa 60:14: bow themselves
down at the soles of thy f.;

Jer 13:16: before your f.
stumble upon the dark
mountains,
Jer 14:10: they have not
refrained their f.,
Jer 18:22: and hid snares for
my f.
Jer 38:22: thy f. are sunk in
the mire,
Lam 1:13: he hath spread a
net for my f.,
Lam 3:34: To crush under his
f. all the prisoners of the earth,
Ezek 1:7: And their feet were
straight f.; and the sole of their
f. was like ...
Ezek 2:1: stand upon thy f.,
Ezek 2:2: and set me upon
my f.,
Ezek 3:24: and set me upon
my f.,
Ezek 16:25: hast opened thy f.
to every one that passed by,
Ezek 24:17: and put on thy
shoes upon thy f.,
Ezek 24:23: and your shoes
upon your f.:
Ezek 25:6: and stamped with
the f.,
Ezek 32:2: and troubledst the
waters with thy f.,
Ezek 34:18: tread down with
your f. the residue of your
pastures?
Ezek 34:19: they drink that
which ye have fouled with
your f.
Ezek 37:10: and stood up upon
their f.,
Ezek 43:7: the place of the
soles of my f.,
Dan 2:33: his f. part of iron
and part of clay.
Dan 2:34: which smote the
image upon his f ...
Dan 2:41: And whereas thou
sawest the f. and toes,
Dan 2:42: And as the toes of
the f. were part of iron,
Dan 2:33: his f. part of iron
and part of clay.

Dan 2:34: which smote the
image upon his f ...
Dan 2:41: whereas thou
sawest the f. and toes, part of
potters' clay,
Dan 2:42: the f. were part of
iron, and part of clay,
Dan 7:4: made stand upon the
f. as a man,
Dan 7:7: and stamped the
residue with the f. of it:
Dan 7:19: and stamped the
residue with his f.;
Dan 10:6: and his f. like in
colour to polished brass,
Nahum 1:3: and the clouds
are the dust of his f.
Nahum 1:15: the mountains
the f. of him that bringeth
good tidings,
Hab 3:5: and burning coals
went forth at his f.
Hab 3:19: will make my feet
like hinds' f.,
Zech 14:4: his f. shall stand
in that day upon the mount
of Olives,
Zech 14:12: they stand upon
their f.,
Mal 4:3: shall be ashes under
the soles of your f.
Mt 7:6: lest they trample them
under their f.,
Mt 10:14: shake off the dust
of your f.
Mt 15:30: cast them down at
Jesus' f.;
Mt 18:8: two f. to be cast into
everlasting fire.
Mt 18:29: And his
fellowservant fell down at
his f.,
Mt 28:9: And they came and
held him by the f.,
Mk 5:22: he fell at his f.,
Mk 6:11: shake off the dust
under your f.
Mk 7:25: and came and fell
at his f.:
Mk 9:45: than having two f. to
be cast into hell,

Lk 1:79: to guide our f. into the way of peace.
Lk 7:38: And stood at his f. behind him weeping, and began to wash his f. with tears, ... and kissed his f.,
Lk 7:44: thou gavest me no water for my f.: but she hath washed my f. with tears
Lk 7:45: hath not ceased to kiss my f.
Lk 7:46: this woman hath anointed my f. with ointment.
Lk 8:35: sitting at the f. of Jesus,
Lk 8:41: and he fell down at Jesus' f.,
Lk 9:5: f the very dust from your f ...
Lk 10:39: which also sat at Jesus' f.,
Lk 15:22: and shoes on his f.:
Lk 17:16: fell down on his face at his f.,
Lk 24:39: Behold my hands and my f.,
Lk 24:40: he shewed them his hands and his f.
Jn 11:2: and wiped his f. with her hair,
Jn 11:32: she fell down at his f.,
Jn 12:3: anointed the f. of Jesus, and wiped his f. with her hair:
Jn 13:5: began to wash the disciples' f.,
Jn 13:6: Lord, dost thou wash my f.?
Jn 13:8: Thou shalt never wash my f.
Jn 13:9: not my f. only, but also my hands and my head.
Jn 13:10: He that is washed needeth not save to wash his f.,
Jn 13:12: So after he had washed their f.
Jn 13:14: have washed your feet; ye also ought to wash one another's f.
Jn 20:12: and the other at the f.,

Acts 3:7: and immediately his f. and ankle bones received strength.
Acts 4:35: And laid them down at the apostles' f.:
Acts 4:37: and laid it at the apostles' f.
Acts 5:2: and laid it at the apostles' f.
Acts 5:9: the f. of them which have buried thy husband ...
Acts 5:10: Then fell she down straightway at his f.,
Acts 7:33: Put off thy shoes from thy f.:
Acts 7:58: laid down their clothes at a young man's f.,
Acts 10:25: and fell down at his f.,
Acts 13:25: whose shoes of his f. I am not worthy to loose.
Acts 13:51: But they shook off the dust of their f. against them,
Acts 14:8: a certain man at Lystra, impotent in his f.,
Acts 14:10: Stand upright on thy f.
Acts 16:24: and made their f. fast in the stocks.
Acts 21:11: bound his own hands and f.,
Acts 22:3: brought up in this city at the f. of Gamaliel,
Acts 26:16: rise, and stand upon thy f.:
Rom 3:15: Their f. are swift to shed blood:
Rom 10:15: How beautiful are the f. of them ...
Rom 16:20: shall bruise Satan under your f. shortly.
1 Cor 12:21: the head to the f., I have no need of you.
1 Cor 15:25: till he hath put all enemies under his f.
1 Cor 15:27: For he hath put all things under his f ...
Eph 1:22: And hath put all things under his f.,
Eph 6:15: And your f. shod with the preparation ...

1 Tm 5:10: she have washed the saints' f.,
Heb 2:8: Thou hast put all things in subjection under his f.
Heb 12:13: And make straight paths for your f.,
Rv 1:15: And his f. like unto fine brass,
Rv 1:17: when I saw him, I fell at his f. as dead.
Rv 2:18: and his f. are like fine brass;
Rv 3:9: come and worship before thy f.,
Rv 10:1: and his f. as pillars of fire:
Rv 11:11: and they stood upon their f.;
Rv 12:1: and the moon under her f.,
Rv 13:2: and his feet were as the f. of a bear,
Rv 19:10: And I fell at his f. to worship him.
Rv 22:8: I fell down to worship before the f. of the angel

Finger(s)

Ex 8:19: This is the f. of God:
Ex 29:12: put it upon the horns of the altar with thy f.,
Ex 31:18: written with the f. of God.
Lev 4:6: priest shall dip his f. in the blood,
Lev 4:17: the priest shall dip his f.
Lev 4:25: sin offering with his f.,
Lev 4:30: the blood thereof with his f.,
Lev 4:34: the sin offering with his f.,
Lev 8:15: altar round about with his f.,
Lev 9:9: he dipped his f. in the blood,
Lev 14:16: the priest shall dip his right f. in the oil
Lev 14:27: the priest shall sprinkle with his right f.

Lev 16:14: sprinkle it with his f.

Lev 16:19: the blood upon it with his f. seven times,

Num 19:4: take of her blood with his f.,

Deut 9:10: written with the f. of God;

1Kgs 2:10: My little f. shall be thicker than my father's loins.

1Chron 20:6: whose f. and toes were four and twenty,

2Chron 10:10: My little f. shall be thicker than my father's loins. 2Sam 21:20: that had on every hand six f.,

Ps 8:3: the work of thy f.,

Ps 144:1: and my f. to fight:

Prov 6:13: he teacheth with his f.;

Prov 7:3: Bind them upon thy f.,

Song 5:5: and my f. with sweet smelling myrrh,

Isa 2:8: that which their own f. have made:

Isa 17:8: which his f. have made,

Isa 58:9: the putting forth of the f.,

Isa 59:3: your f. with iniquity;

Jer 52:21: and the thickness thereof was four f.:

Dan 5:5: came forth f. of a man's hand,

Mt 23:4: will not move them with one of their f.

Mk 7:33: and put his f. into his ears,

Lk 11:20: if I with the f. of God cast out devils,

Lk 11:46: touch not the burdens with one of your f.

Lk 16:24: that he may dip the tip of his f. in water,

Jn 8:6: with his f. wrote on the ground,

Jn 20:25: and put my f. into the print of the nails,

Jn 20:27: Reach hither thy f.,

Foot

Gen 8:9: But the dove found no rest for the sole of her f.,

Gen 41:44: no man lift up his hand or f. in all the land of Egypt.

Ex 21:24: tooth for tooth, hand for hand, foot for f.,

Ex 29:20: and upon the great toe of their right f.,

Ex 30:18: a laver of brass, and his f. also of brass,

Ex 30:28: and the laver and his f.

Ex 31:9: and the laver and his f.,

Ex 35:16: the laver and his f.,

Ex 38:8: laver of brass, and the f. of it of brass,

Ex 39:39: the laver and his f.,

Ex 40:11: anoint the laver and his f.,

Lev 8:11: both the laver and his f.,

Lev 8:23: upon the great toe of his right f.

Lev 13:12: hath the plague from his head even to his f.,

Lev 14:14: and upon the great toe of his right f.:

Lev 14:17: the great toe of his right f.,

Lev 14:25: great toe of his right f.:

Num 22:25: and crushed Balaam's f. against the wall:

Deut 2:5: not so much as a f. breadth;

Deut 8:4: neither did thy f. swell, these forty years.

Deut 11:10: and wateredst it with thy f.,

Deut 19:21: hand for hand, foot for f.

Deut 25:9: loose his shoe from off his f.,

Deut 28:35: from the sole of thy f. unto the top of thy head.

Deut 28:56 to set the sole of her f. upon the ground

Deut 28:65: neither shall the sole of thy f. have rest:

Deut 29:5: thy shoe is not waxen old upon thy f.

Deut 32:35: their f. shall slide in due time:

Deut 33:24: and let him dip his f. in oil.

Josh 1:3: the sole of your f. shall tread upon,

Josh 5:15: Loose thy shoe from off thy f.;

2 Sam 2:18: and Asahel was as light of f. as a wild roe.

2 Sam 14:25: from the sole of his f. even to the crown of his head

2 Sam 21:20: and on every f. six toes,

2 Kgs 9:33: and he trode her under f.

1 Chron 20:6: and six on each f.:

2 Chron 33:8: I any more remove the f. of Israel from out of the land

Job 2:7: smote Job with sore boils from the sole of his f. unto his crown.

Job 23:11: My f. hath held his steps,

Job 28:4: the waters forgotten of the f.:

Job 31:5: or if my f. hath hasted to deceit;

Job 39:15: And forgetteth that the f. may crush them,

Ps 9:15: in the net which they hid is their own f. taken.

Ps 26:12: My f. standeth in an even place

Ps 36:11: Let not the f. of pride come against me,

Ps 38:16: when my f. slippeth,

Ps 66:6 they went through the flood on f.:

Ps 68:23: That thy f. may be dipped in the blood of thine enemies,

Ps 91:12: thou dash thy f. against a stone.

Ps 94:18: When I said, My f. slippeth;

Ps 121:3: He will not suffer thy f. to be moved:

Prov 1:15: refrain thy f. from their path:

Prov 3:23: and thy f. shall not stumble.

Prov 3:26: shall keep thy f. from being taken.

Prov 4:27: remove thy f. from evil.

Prov 25:17: Withdraw thy f. from thy neighbour's house;

Prov 25:19: and a f. out of joint.

Eccl 5:1: Keep thy f.when thou goest to the house of God,

Isa 1:6: From the sole of the f. even unto the head there is no soundness in it;

Isa 14:25: mountains tread him under f.:

Isa 18:7: a nation meted out and trodden under f.,

Isa 20:2: and put off thy shoe from thy f.

Isa 26:6: The f. shall tread it down,

Isa 41:2: called him to his f.,

Isa 58:13: If thou turn away thy f. from the sabbath,

Jer 2:25: Withhold thy f. from being unshod,

Jer 12:10: they have trodden my portion under foot,

Lam 1:15: The Lord hath trodden under foot

Ezek 6:11: and stamp with thy f.,

Ezek 29:11: No f. of man shall pass through it, nor foot of beast shall pass through it,

Ezek 32:13: neither shall the f. of man trouble them any more,

Dan 8:13: give both the sanctuary and the host to be trodden under f.?

Amos 2:15: he that is swift of f. shall not deliver himself:

Mt 4:6lest at any time thou dash thy f. against a stone.

Mt 5:13: and to be trodden under f. of men.

Mt 14:13: they followed him on f. out of the cities.

Mt 18:8: Wherefore if thy hand or thy f. offend thee,

Mt 22:13: Bind him hand and f.,

Mk 9:45: And if thy f. offend thee, cut it off:

Lk 4:11: thou dash thy f. against a stone.

Jn 11:44: bound hand and f. with graveclothes:

Acts 7:5: not so much as to set his f. on:

1 Cor 12:15: If the f. shall say, Because I am not the hand,

Heb 10:29: who hath trodden under f. the Son of God,

Rv 1:13: clothed with a garment down to the f.,

Rv 10:2: and his left f. on the earth,

Rv 11:2: they tread under f. forty and two months.

Forehead

Ex 28:38: And it shall be upon Aaron's f … and it shall be always upon his f.,

Lev 13:41: he is f. bald:

Lev 13:42: or bald f.,

1 Sam 17:49: smote the Philistine in his f.

2 Chron 26:19: the leprosy even rose up in his f …

2 Chron 26:20: he was leprous in his f.,

Jer 3:3: and thou hadst a whore's f.,

Ezek 3:8: and thy forehead strong against their f.

Ezek 3:9: As an adamant harder than flint have I made thy f.:

Ezek 9:4: and set a mark upon the f.

Ezek 16:12: And I put a jewel on thy f.,

Rv 14:9: and receive his mark in his f.,

Rv 17:5: upon her f. was a name written,

Foreskin(s)

Gen 17:11: And ye shall circumcise the flesh of your f.;

Gen 17:14: And the uncircumcised man child whose flesh of his f. is not circumcised,

Gen 17:23: and circumcised the flesh of their f.

Gen 17:24: And Abraham was ninety years old and nine, when he was circumcised in the flesh of his f.

Gen 17:25: And Ishmael his son was thirteen years old, when he was circumcised in the flesh of his f.

Ex 4:25: and cut off the f. of her son,

Lev 12:3: And in the eighth day the flesh of his f. shall be circumcised.

Deut 10:16: Circumcise therefore the f. of your heart,

Josh 5:3: and circumcised the children of Israel at the hill of the f.

1 Sam: 8:25: but an hundred f. of the Philistines,

1 Sam 18:27: and David brought their f.,

2 Sam 3:14: which I espoused to me for an hundred f. of the Philistines.

Jer 4:4: take away the f. of your heart,

Hab 2:16: and let thy f. be uncovered:

Hair

Lev 13:3: and when the h. in the plague is turned white,

Lev 13:4: the h. thereof be not turned white;

Lev 13:10: it have turned the h. white,

Lev 13:20: the h. thereof be turned white;

Lev 13:25: if the h. in the bright spot be turned white,
Lev 13:26: there be no white h. in the bright spot,
Lev 13:30: there be in it a yellow thin h.;
Lev 13:31: that there is no black h. in it;
Lev 13:32: there be in it no yellow h.,
Lev 13:36: not seek for yellow h.;
Lev 13:37: that there is black h. grown up therein;
Lev 13:40: And the man whose h. is fallen off his head,
Lev 13:41: he that hath his h. fallen off
Lev 14:8: shave off all his h.,
Lev 14:9: he shall shave all his h. off his head
Num 6:5: shall let the locks of the h. of his head grow.
Num 6:18: shall take the h. of the head of his separation,
Num 6:19: after the h. of his separation is shaven:
Judg 16:22: Howbeit the h. of his head began to grow again after he was shaven.
1 Sam 14:45: shall not one h. of his head fall to the ground;
2 Sam 14:11: shall not one h. of thy son fall to the earth.
2 Sam 14:26: the h. was heavy on him,
1 Kgs 1:52: shall not an h. of him fall to the earth:
Ezra 9:3: plucked off the h. of my head and of my beard,
Neh 13:25: plucked off their h.,
Job 4:15: the h. of my flesh stood up:
Song 4:1: thy h. is as a flock of goats,
Song 6:5: thy h. is as a flock of goats ...
Song 7:5: the h. of thine head like purple;
Isa 3:24: instead of well set h. baldness;
Isa 7:20: the h. of the feet:

Isa 50:6: to them that plucked off the h.:
Jer 7:29: Cut off thine h.,
Ezek 5:1: and divide the h.
Ezek 16:7: I and thine h. is grown,
Dan 3:27: nor was an h. of their head singed,
Dan 7:9: the h. of his head like the pure wool:
Mt 5:36: thou canst not make one h. white or black.
Lk 21:18: there shall not an h. of your head perish.
Jn 11:2: wiped his feet with her h.,
Jn 12:3: and wiped his feet with her h.:
Acts 27:34: there shall not an h. fall from the head of any of you.
1 Cor 11:14: if a man have long h.,
1Cor 11:15: But if a woman have long h.,
1 Tm 2:9: not with broided h.,
1 Pt 3:3: adorning of plaiting the h.,
Rv 6:12: the sun became black as sackcloth of h.,
Rv 9:8: they had hair as the h. of women,

Hand

Gen 3:22: lest he put forth his h.,
Gen 4:11: to receive thy brother's blood from thy h.;
Gen 8:9: then he put forth his h.,
Gen 9:2: into your h. are they delivered.
Gen 9:5: at the h. of every beast will I require it, and at the h. of man; at the h. of every man's brother will I require the life of man.
Gen 13:9: if thou wilt take the left h., then I will go to the right; or if thou depart to the right h., then I will go to the left.

Gen 14:15: which is on the left h. of Damascus.
Gen 14:20: delivered thine enemies into thy h.
Gen 14:22: I have lift up mine h. unto the LORD,
Gen 16:6: Behold, thy maid is in thy h.;
Gen 16:12: his h. will be against every man, and every man's h. against him;
Gen 19:10: But the men put forth their h.,
Gen 19:16: the men laid hold upon his h., and upon the h. of his wife, and upon the h. of his two daughters;
Gen 21:18: and hold him in thine h.;
Gen 21:30: For these seven ewe lambs shalt thou take of my h.,
Gen 22:6: and he took the fire in his h.,
Gen 22:10: And Abraham stretched forth his h.
Gen 22:12: And he said, Lay not thine h. upon the lad,
Gen 24:2: Put, I pray thee, thy h. under my thigh:
Gen 24:9: And the servant put his h. under the thigh of Abraham ...
Gen 24:10: for all the goods of his master were in his h.:
Gen 24:18: and let down her pitcher upon her h.,
Gen 24:49: that I may turn to the right h., or to the left.
Gen 25:26: and his h. took hold on Esau's heel
Gen 27:17: into the h. of her son Jacob.
Gen 30:35: and gave them into the h. of his sons.
Gen 31:29: It is in the power of my h. to do you hurt:
Gen 31:39: of my h. didst thou require it,
Gen 32:11: Deliver me, I pray thee, from the h. of my brother,

Gen 32:13: and took of that which came to his h.

Gen 32:16: And he delivered them into the h. of his servants,

Gen 33:10: receive my present at my h.:

Gen 33:19: at the h. of the children of Hamor,

Gen 35:4: ... all the strange gods which were in their h.,

Gen 37:22: and lay no h. upon him

Gen 37:27: and let not our h. be upon him;

Gen 38:18: thy staff that is in thine h.

Gen 38:28: that the one put out his h.:

Gen 38:29: as he drew back his h.,

Gen 38:30: that had the scarlet thread upon his h.:

Gen 39:3: the LORD made all that he did to prosper in his h.

Gen 39:4: that he had he put into his h.

Gen 39:6: And he left all that he had in Joseph's h.;

Gen 39:8: and he hath committed all that he hath to my h.;

Gen 39:12: he left his garment in her h.,

Gen 39:13: when she saw that he had left his garment in her h.,

Gen 39:22: And the keeper of the prison committed to Joseph's h ...

Gen 39:23: looked not to any thing that was under his h.;

Gen 40:11: And Pharaoh's cup was in my h ... and I gave the cup into Pharaoh's h.

Gen 40:13: and thou shalt deliver Pharaoh's cup into his h.,

Gen 40:21: and he gave the cup into Pharaoh's h.:

Gen 41:35: and lay up corn under the h. of Pharaoh,

Gen 41:42: And Pharaoh took off his ring from his h.,

Gen 41:44: without thee shall no man lift up his h. or foot.

Gen 42:37: if I bring him not to thee: deliver him into my h.,

Gen 43:9: of my h. shalt thou require him:

Gen 43:12: And take double money in your h.;

Gen 43:15: and they took double money in their h.,

Gen 43:21: and we have brought it again in our h.

Gen 43:26: they brought him the present which was in their h.

Gen 44:17: but the man in whose h. the cup is found,

Gen 46:4: and Joseph shall put his h. upon thine eyes.

Gen 47:29: thy h. under my thigh,

Gen 48:13: Ephraim in his right h. toward Israel's left hand, and Manasseh in his left hand toward Israel's right h.,

Gen 48:14: And Israel stretched out his right h. ... and his left h. upon Manasseh's head,

Gen 48:17: And when Joseph saw that his father laid his right h. upon the head of Ephraim,

Gen 48:18: put thy right h. upon his head.

Gen 48:22: which I took out of the h. of the Amorite

Gen 49:8: thy h. shall be in the neck of thine enemies;

Ex 2:19: An Egyptian delivered us out of the h. of the shepherds,

Ex 3:8: to deliver them out of the h. of the Egyptians,

Ex 3:19: not by a mighty h.

Ex 3:20: And I will stretch out my h.,

Ex 4:2: What is that in thine h.?

Ex 4:4: Put forth thine h.,

Ex 4:6: Put now thine h. into thy bosom. And he put his h. into his bosom ... his h. was leprous as snow.

Ex 4:7: Put thine h. into thy bosom again. And he put his h. into his bosom again;

Ex 4:13: by the h. of him whom thou wilt send.

Ex 4:17: And thou shalt take this rod in thine h.,

Ex 4:20: and Moses took the rod of God in his h.

Ex 4:21: which I have put in thine h.:

Ex 5:21: put a sword in their h. to slay us.

Ex 6:1: for with a strong h. shall he let them go, and with a strong h. shall he drive them out

Ex 7:4: that I may lay my h. upon Egypt,

Ex 7:5: when I stretch forth mine h. upon Egypt,

Ex 7:15: erpent shalt thou take in thine h.

Ex 7:17: I will smite with the rod that is in mine h.

Ex 7:19: stretch out thine h. upon the waters of Egypt,

Ex 8:5: Stretch forth thine h. with thy rod

Ex 8:6: And Aaron stretched out his h. over the waters ...

Ex 8:17: Aaron stretched out his h. with his rod,

Ex 9:3: Behold, the h. of the LORD ...

Ex 9:15: For now I will stretch out my h.,

Ex 9:22: Stretch forth thine h. toward heaven,

Ex 10:12: Stretch out thine h. over the land of Egypt

Ex 10:21: Stretch out thine h. toward heaven,

Ex 10:22: And Moses stretched forth his h. toward heaven;

Ex 12:11: and your staff in your h.;

Ex 13:3: by strength of h. the LORD

Ex 13:9: And it shall be for a sign unto thee upon thine h.,

Ex 13:14: By strength of h. the LORD

Ex 13:16: And it shall be for a token upon thine h. ... for by strength of h. the LORD

Ex 14:8: Israel went out with an high h.

Ex 14:16: stretch out thine h. over the sea,

Ex 14:21: Moses stretched out his h ...

Ex 14:22: and the waters were a wall unto them on their right h.,

Ex 14:26: Stretch out thine h. over the sea,

Ex 14:27: Moses stretched forth his h ...

Ex 14:29: and the waters were a wall unto them on their right h.

Ex 14:30: the LORD saved Israel that day out of the h. of the Egyptians;

Ex 15:6: Thy right h., O LORD, is become glorious in power: thy right h., O LORD, hath dashed in pieces the enemy.

Ex 15:9: I will draw my sword, my h.

Ex 15:12: stretchedst out thy right h.,

Ex 15:20: took a timbrel in her h.;

Ex 16:3: Would to God we had died by the h. of the LORD

Ex 17:5: take in thine h. and go.

Ex 17:9: with the rod of God in mine h.

Ex 17:11: And it came to pass, when Moses held up his h., that Israel prevailed: and when he let down his h.,

Ex 18:9: whom he had delivered out of the h. of the Egyptians.

Ex 19:13: There shall not an h. touch it,

Ex 21:13: but God deliver him into his h.;

Ex 21:16: or if he be found in his h., he shall surely be put to death.

Ex 21:20: and he die under his h.; he shall be surely punished.

Ex 21:24: Eye for eye, tooth for tooth, h. for h., foot for foot,

Ex 22:4: If the theft be certainly found in his h. alive,

Ex 22:8: to see whether he have put his h. unto his neighbour's goods.

Ex 22:11: that he hath not put his h. unto his neighbour's goods;

Ex 23:1: put not thine h. with the wicked

Ex 23:31 I will deliver the inhabitants of the land into your h.;

Ex 24:11: And upon the nobles of the children of Israel he laid not his h.:

Ex 25:25: And thou shalt make unto it a border of an h. breadth round

Ex 29:20: the thumb of their right h.,

Ex 32:4: And he received them at their h.,

Ex 32:11: and with a mighty h.?

Ex 32:15: and the two tables of the testimony were in his h.:

Ex 33:22: and will cover thee with my h.

Ex 33:23: And I will take away mine h.,

Ex 34:4: took in his h. the two tables ...

Ex 34:29: two tables of testimony in Moses' h.,

Ex 35:29: to be made by the h. of Moses.

Ex 38:15: on this hand and that h.,

Ex 38:21: by the h. of Ithamar,

Lev 1:4: And he shall put his h. upon the head of the burnt offering;

Lev 4:4: and shall lay his h. upon the bullock's head,

Lev 8:23: upon the thumb of his right h.,

Lev 9:22: And Aaron lifted up his h. toward the people,

Lev 10:11: spoken unto them by the h. of Moses.

Lev 14:14: and upon the thumb of his right h.

Lev 14:15: the palm of his own left h.:

Lev 14:16: right finger in the oil that is in his left h.,

Lev 14:17: And of the rest of the oil that is in his h.

Lev 14:25: and upon the thumb of his right h.

Lev 14:26: the palm of his own left h.:

Lev 14:32: whose h. is not able

Lev 22:25: Neither from a stranger's h.

Lev 25:14: thy neighbour's h.,

Lev 25:28: remain in the h. of him that

Lev 26:25: and ye shall be delivered into the h. of the enemy.

Lev 26:46: in mount Sinai by the h. of Moses.

Num 4:28: under the h. of Ithamar ...

Num 4:37: commandment of the LORD by the h. of Moses.

Num 5:25: jealousy offering out of the woman's h.,

Num 6:21: that that his h. shall get:

Num 7:8: under the h. of Ithamar ...

Num 10:13: the commandment of the LORD by the h. of Moses.

Num 11:15: I pray thee, out of h.,

Num 11:23: Is the LORD's h. waxed short?

Num 16:40: as the LORD said to him by the h. of Moses.

Num 20:11: And Moses lifted up his h.,

Num 20:17: we will not turn to the right h. nor to the left,

Num 20:20: Edom came out against him with much people, and with a strong h.

Num 21:2: deliver this people into my h.,

Num 21:26: all his land out of his h.,

Num 21:34: delivered him into thy h.,

Num 22:7: of divination in their h.;

Num 22:23: his sword drawn in his h.:

Num 22:26: no way to turn either to the right h. or to the left.

Num 22:29: were a sword in mine h.,

Num 22:31: his sword drawn in his h.:

Num 25:7: and took a javelin in his h.;

Num 27:18: and lay thine h. upon him;

Num 31:6: the trumpets to blow in his h.

Num 33:1: with their armies under the h. of Moses and Aaron.

Num 33:3: went out with an high h.

Num 35:18: Or if he smite him with an h. weapon of wood,

Num 35:21: Or in enmity smite him with his h.,

Num 35:25: deliver the slayer out of the h. of the revenger

Deut 1:27: to deliver us into the h. of the Amorites,

Deut 2:7: God hath blessed thee in all the works of thy h.:

Deut 2:15: the hand of the LORD was against them,

Deut 2:24: I have given into thine hand Sihon

Deut 2:27: I will neither turn unto the right h. nor to the left.

Deut 2:30: that he might deliver him into thy h.,

Deut 3:2: into thy h.;

Deut 3:8: out of the h. of the two kings

Deut 3:24: and thy mighty h.:

Deut 4:34: and by a mighty h.,

Deut 5:15: through a mighty h.

Deut 5:32: not turn aside to the right h. or to the left

Deut 6:8: a sign upon thine h.,

Deut 6:21: the LORD brought us out of Egypt with a mighty h.:

Deut 7:8: LORD brought you out with a mighty h.,

Deut 7:19: and the mighty h.,

Deut 7:24: into thine h.,

Deut 8:17: and the might of mine h.

Deut 9:26: thou hast brought forth out of Egypt with a mighty h.

Deut 10:3: the two tables in mine h.

Deut 11:2: his mighty h.,

Deut 11:18: and bind them for a sign upon your h.,

Deut 12:6: and heave offerings of your h.,

Deut 12:7: that ye put your h. unto,

Deut 12:11: heave offering of your h.,

Deut 13:9: thine h. shall be first upon him …

Deut 13:17: the cursed thing to thine h.:

Deut 14:25: up the money in thine h.,

Deut 14:29: bless thee in all the work of thine h. which thou doest.

Deut 15:3: with thy brother thine h. shall release;

Deut 15:7: nor shut thine h. from thy poor brother:

Deut 15:8: But thou shalt open thine h. wide unto him,

Deut 15:9: The seventh year, the year of release, is at h.;

Deut 15:10: and in all that thou puttest thine h. unto.

Deut 15:11: Thou shalt open thine h. wide unto thy brother,

Deut 16:10: a tribute of a freewill offering of thine h.,

Deut 17:11: they shall shew thee, to the right h., nor to the left.

Deut 17:20: to the right h., or to the left:

Deut 19:5: and his h. fetcheth a stroke with the axe

Deut 19:12: deliver him into the h. of the avenger

Deut 19:21: eye for eye, tooth for tooth, h. for h., foot for foot.

Deut 23:20: thou settest thine h. to in the land whither thou goest to possess it.

Deut 23:25: thou mayest pluck the ears with thine h.;

Deut 24:1: and give it in her h. and send her out of his house.

Deut 24:3: and giveth it in her h., and sendeth her out of his house;

Deut 25:11: and putteth forth her h., and taketh him by the secrets:

Deut 25:12: thou shalt cut off her h.,

Deut 26:4: take the basket out of thine h.,

Deut 26:8: And the LORD brought us forth out of Egypt with a mighty h.,

Deut 28:12: bless all the work of thine h.:

Deut 28:14: to the right h., or to the left,

Deut 28:20: settest thine h. unto for to do,

Deut 28:32: shall be no might in thine h.

Deut 30:9: God will make thee plenteous in every work of thine h.,

Deut 32:27: Our h. is high,
Deut 32:39: neither is there
any that can deliver out of
my h.
Deut 32:40: For I lift up my h.
to heaven,
Deut 33:2: from his right h.
went a fiery law for them.
Deut 33:3: all his saints are
in thy h.:
Deut 34:12: And in all that
mighty h.,
Josh 7: from it to the right h. or
to the left,
Josh 2:19: his blood shall
be on our head, if any h. be
upon him.
Josh 4:24: That all the people
of the earth might know the h.
of the LORD,
Josh 5:13: with his sword
drawn in his h.:
Josh 6:2: I have given into
thine h. Jericho,
Judg 1:2: delivered the land
into his h.
Judg 2:15: the h. of the LORD
was against them for evil,
Judg 2:16: delivered them out
of the h. of those that spoiled
them.
Judg 2:18: delivered them out
of the h. of their enemies
Judg 2:23: delivered he them
into the h. of Joshua.
Judg 3:8: and he sold
them into the h. of
Chushan-rishathaim
Judg 3:10: into his h.; and
his h. prevailed against
Chushan-rishathaim.
Judg 3:21: And Ehud put forth
his left h.,
Judg 3:28: delivered your
enemies the Moabites into
your h.
Judg 3:30: under the h. of
Israel.
Judg 4:7: I will deliver him
into thine h.

Judg 4:9: for the LORD shall
sell Sisera into the h. of a
woman.
Judg 4:14: the LORD hath
delivered Sisera into thine h.:
Judg 4:21: and took an
hammer in her h.,
Judg 4:24: And the h. of the
children of Israel prospered,
Judg 5:26: She put her h. to the
nail, and her right hand to the
workmen's hammer;
Judg 6:2: And the h. of Midian
prevailed against Israel:
Judg 6:9: And I delivered you
out of the h. of the Egyptians,
and out of the h. of all that
oppressed you,
Judg 6:21: angel of the LORD
put forth the end of the staff
that was in his h.,
Judg 6:36: you wilt save Israel
by mine h.,
Judg 6:37: save Israel by
mine h.,
Judg 7:6: putting their h. to
their mouth,
Judg 7:7: deliver the
Midianites into thine h.:
Judg 7:8: people took victuals
in their h.
Judg 7:9: I have delivered it
into thine h.
Judg 7:14: for into his h. hath
God delivered Midian,
Judg 7:15: for the LORD hath
delivered into your h. the host
of Midian.
Judg 7:16: a trumpet in every
man's h.,
Judg 8:7: delivered Zebah and
Zalmunna into mine h.,
Judg 8:22: for thou hast
delivered us from the h. of
Midian.
Judg 9:17: delivered you out of
the h. of Midian:
Judg 9:29: And would to God
this people were under my h.!
Judg 9:48: Abimelech took an
axe in his h.,

Judg 10:12: I delivered you out
of their h.
Judg 11:21: delivered Sihon
and all his people into the h.
of Israel,
Judg 13:1: and the LORD
delivered them into the h. of
the Philistines forty years.
Judg 13:5: deliver Israel out of
the h. of the Philistines.
Judg 14:6: and he had nothing
in his h.:
Judg 15:12: deliver thee into
the h. of the Philistines.
Judg 15:13: and deliver thee
into their h.:
Judg15:15: put forth his h.,
and took it,
Judg 15:17: that he cast away
the jawbone out of his h.,
Judg 15:18: deliverance into
the h. of thy servant:
Judg 16:18: brought money in
their h.
Judg 16:23: delivered Samson
our enemy into our h.
Judg 16:26: And Samson said
unto the lad that held him by
the h.,
Judg 16:29: of the one with his
right h., and of the other with
his left.
Judg 17:3: unto the LORD
from my h. for my son,
Judg 18:19: lay thine h. upon
thy mouth,
Judg 20:28 for tomorrow I will
deliver them into thine h.
Judg 20:48: and all that came
to h.:
Ruth1:13: for your sakes that
the h. of the LORD is gone out
against me.
Ruth 4:9: of the h. of Naomi.
1 Sam 2:13: with a fleshhook
of three teeth in his h.;
1 Sam 4:3: it may save us out
of the h. of our enemies.
1 Sam 4:8 who shall deliver
us out of the h. of these mighty
Gods?

1 Sam 5:6: But the h. of the LORD was heavy upon them ...

1 Sam 5:7: for his h. is sore upon us, and upon Dagon our god.

1 Sam 5:9: the h. of the LORD was against the city

1 Sam 5:11: the h. of God was very heavy there.

1 Sam 6:3: his h. is not removed from you.

1 Sam 6:5: will lighten his h. from off you,

1 Sam 6:9: we shall know that is not his h. that smote us;

1 Sam 6:12: and turned not aside to the right h. or to the left;

1 Sam 7:3: he will deliver you out of the h. of the Philistines.

1 Sam 7:8: that he will save us out of the h. of the Philistines.

1 Sam 7:13: and the h. of the LORD was against the Philistines

1 Sam 9:8: here at h. the fourth part

1Sam 9:16: save my people out of the h. of the Philistines:

1 Sam 10:18: and delivered you out of the h. of the Egyptians,

1 Sam 12:3: of whose h. have I received any bribe ...

1 Sam 12:4: neither hast thou taken ought of any man's h.

1Sam 12:5: that ye have not found ought in my h.

1 Sam 12:9: he sold them into the h. of Sisera,

1 Sam 12:10: but now deliver us out of the h. of our enemies,

1 Sam 12:11: and delivered you out of the h. of your enemies

1 Sam 12:15: then shall the h. of the LORD be against you,

1 Sam 13:22: neither sword nor spear found in the h

1 Sam 14:10: the LORD hath delivered them into our h.:

1 Sam 14:12: for the LORD hath delivered them into the h. of Israel.

1 Sam 14:19: Withdraw thine h.

1 Sam 14:26: but no man put his h. to his mouth

1 Sam 14:27: and put his h. to his mouth;

1 Sam 14:37: wilt thou deliver them into the h. of Israel?

1 Sam 14:43: the rod that was in mine h.,

1 Sam 16:16: he shall play with his h.,

1 Sam 16:23: David took an harp, and played with his h.:

1 Sam 17:22: And David left his carriage in the h. of the keeper ...

1 Sam 17:37: he will deliver me out of the h. of this Philistine.

1 Sam 17:40: and his sling was in his h.:

1 Sam 17:46: This day will the LORD deliver thee into mine h.;

1 Sam 17:49: David put his h. in his bag,

1 Sam 17:50: but there was no sword in the hand of David.

1 Sam 17:57: with the head of the Philistine in his h.

1 Sam 18:10: David played with his h.,

1 Sam 18:17: Let not mine hand be upon him, but let the h. of the Philistines be upon him.

1 Sam 18:21: and that the h. of the Philistines may be against him.

1 Sam 18:25: fall by the h. of the Philistines.

1 Sam 19:5: he did put his life in his h.,

1 Sam 19:9: with his javelin in his h.: and David played with his h.

1 Sam 20:16: Let the LORD even require it at the h. of David's enemies.

1 Sam 20:19: hide thyself when the business was in h.,

1 Sam 21:3: Now therefore what is under thine h.?

1 Sam 21:4: There is no common bread under mine h.,

1 Sam 21:8: And is there not here under thine h. spear or sword?

1 Sam 22:6: having his spear in his h.,

1 Sam 22:17: their h. also is with David,

1 Sam 23:4: I will deliver the Philistines into thine h.

1 Sam 23:6: that he came down with an ephod in his h.

1 Sam 23:7: God hath delivered him into mine h.;

1 Sam 23:11: Will the men of Keilah deliver me up into his h.?

1 Sam 23:12: my men into the h. of Saul?

1 Sam 23:14: but God delivered him not into his h.

1 Sam 23:16 strengthened his h. in God.

1 Sam 23:17: for the h. of Saul my father

1 Sam 23:20: shall be to deliver him into the king's h.

1 Sam 24:4: I will deliver thine enemy into thine h.,

2 Sam 1:14: stretch forth thine h. to destroy the LORD's anointed?

2 Sam 2:19: he turned not to the right h. nor to the left from following Abner.

2 Sam 2:21: Turn thee aside to thy right h. or to thy left,

2 Sam 3:8: and have not delivered thee into the h. of David,

2 Sam 3:12: my h. shall be with thee,

2 Sam 3:18: By the h. of my servant David

2 Sam 4:11: require his blood of your h.,
2 Sam 5:19: wilt thou deliver them into mine h.?
2 Sam 6:6: Uzzah put forth his h. to the ark of God,
2 Sam 8:1: and David took Metheg-ammah out of the h. of the Philistines.
2 Sam 10:2: comfort him by the h. of his servants for his father.
2 Sam 10:10: delivered into the h. of Abishai his brother
2 Sam 11:14: and sent it by the h. of Uriah.
2 Sam 12:7: and I delivered thee out of the h. of Saul;
2 Sam 12:25: And he sent by the h. of Nathan the prophet;
2 Sam 13:5: and eat it at her h.
2 Sam 13:6: that I may eat at her h.
2 Sam 13:10: that I may eat of thine h.
2 Sam 13:19: and laid her h. on her head,
2 Sam 14:19: Is not the h. of Joab with thee in all this?
2 Sam 15:5: he put forth his h., and took him,
2 Sam 16:6: on his right h. and on his left.
2 Sam 16:8: into the h. of Absalom thy son:
2 Sam 18:2: people under the h. of Joab … under the h. of Abishai … under the h. of Ittai
2 Sam 18:12: shekels of silver in mine h.,
2 Sam 18:14: And he took three darts in his h.,
2 Sam 18:28: that lifted up their h. against my lord the king.
2 Sam 19:9: out of the h. of our enemies, … out of the h. of the Philistines;
2 Sam 20:9: Joab took Amasa by the beard with the right h.

2 Sam 20:10: sword that was in Joab's h.:
2 Sam 20:21: hath lifted up his h. against the king,
2 Sam 21:20: that had on every h. six fingers,
2 Sam 21:22: and fell by the h. of David, and by the h. of his servants:
2 Sam 22:1: delivered him out of the h. of all his enemies, and out of the h. of Saul:
2 Sam 23:10: until his h. was weary, and his h. clave unto the sword:
2 Sam 23:21: had a spear in his h.;
2 Sam 24:14: let us fall now into the h. of the LORD;
2 Sam 24:16: And when the angel stretched out his h.
2 Sam 24:17: let thine h., I pray thee, be against me,
1 Kgs 2:19: and she sat on his right h.
1 Kgs 2:25: And king Solomon sent by the h. of Benaiah
1 Kgs 2:46: And the kingdom was established in the h. of Solomon.
1 Kgs 7:26: And it was an hand breadth thick,
1 Kgs 8:15: hath with his h. fulfilled it,
1 Kgs 8:24: fulfilled it with thine h.,
1 Kgs 8:42: of thy strong h.,
1 Kgs 8:53 as thou spakest by the h. of Moses
1 Kgs 8:56: which he promised by the h. of Moses
1 Kgs 11:12: I will rend it out of the h. of thy son.
1 Kgs 11:26: he lifted up his h. against the king.
1 Kgs 11:27: he lifted up his h. against the king:
1 Kgs 11:31: rend the kingdom out of the h. of Solomon,
1 Kgs 11:34: not take the whole kingdom out of his h.:

1 Kgs 11:35: But I will take the kingdom out of his son's h.,
1 Kgs 13:4: he put forth his h. from the altar, … And his h.,
1 Kgs 13:6: and the king's h. was restored him again,
1 Kgs 14:18: he spake by the h. of his servant Ahijah
1 Kgs 15:18: delivered them into the h. of his servants:
1 Kgs 16:7: And also by the h. of the prophet Jehu
1 Kgs 17:11: a morsel of bread in thine h.
1 Kgs 18:9: deliver thy servant into the h. of Ahab,
1 Kgs 18:44: like a man's h.
1 Kgs 18:46: And the h. of the LORD was on Elijah;
1 Kgs 20:6: they shall put it in their h., and take it away.
1 Kgs 20:13: I will deliver it in to thine h. this day;
1 Kgs 20:28: deliver all this great multitude into thine h.
1 Kgs 20:42: let go out of thy h. a man …
1 Kgs 22:3: take it not out of the h. of the king of Syria?
1 Kgs 22:6: for the Lord shall deliver it into the h. of the king.
1 Kgs 22:12: for the LORD shall deliver it into the king's h.
1 Kgs 22:15: for the LORD shall deliver it into the h. of the king.
1 Kgs 22:19: standing by him on his right h. and on his left.
1 Kgs 22:34: Turn thine h., and carry me out …
2 Kgs 3:10: deliver them into the h. of Moab!
2 Kgs 3:13: to deliver them into the h. of Moab.
2 Kgs 3:15: the h. of the LORD came upon him.
2 Kgs 3:18: deliver the Moabites also into your h.
2 Kgs 4:29: take my staff in thine h.

2 Kgs 5:11: and strike his h. over the place,

2 Kgs 5:18: and he leaneth on my h.,

2 Kgs 5:24: he took them from their h.,

2 Kgs 6:7: he put out his h., and took it.

2 Kgs 7:2: on whose h. the king leaned

2 Kgs 7:17: the lord on whose h. he leaned

2 Kgs 8:8: Take a present in thine h.,

2 Kgs 8:20: under the hand of Judah,

2 Kgs 8:22: from under the h. of Judah

2 Kgs 9:1: take this box of oil in thine h.,

2 Kgs 9:7: at the h. of Jezebel.

2 Kgs 10:15: give me thine h. And he gave him his h.;

2 Kgs 11:8: every man with his weapons in his h.:

2 Kgs 11:11: his weapons in his h.,

2 Kgs 12:15: into whose h. they delivered the money

2 Kgs 13:3: he delivered them into the h. of Hazael king of Syria

2 Kgs 13:5: under the h. of the Syrians:

2 Kgs 13:16: Put thine h. upon the bow. And he put his h. upon it:

2 Kgs 13:25: out of the h. of Ben-hadad

2 Kgs 14:5: was confirmed in his h.,

2 Kgs 14:25: which he spake by the h. of his servant Jonah,

2 Kgs 14:27: saved them by the h. of Jeroboam.

2 Kgs 15:19: his h. might be with him to confirm the kingdom in his h.

2 Kgs 16:7: save me out of the h. of the king of Syria

2 Kgs 17:7from under the h. of Pharaoh king of Egypt

2 Kgs 17:20: delivered them into the h. of spoilers,

2 Kgs 17:39: deliver you out of the h. of all your enemies.

2 Kgs 18:21: it will go into his h.,

2 Kgs 18:29: not be able to deliver you out of his h.:

2 Kgs 18:30: not be delivered into the h. of the king of Assyria.

2 Kgs 18:33: land out of the h. of the king of Assyria?

2 Kgs 18:34: have they delivered Samaria out of mine h.?

2 Kgs 18:35: the LORD should deliver Jerusalem out of mine h.?

2 Kgs 19:10: not be delivered into the h. of the king of Assyria.

2 Kgs 19:14: received the letter of the h. of the messengers,

2 Kgs 19:19: save thou us out of his h.,

2 Kgs 20:6: out of the h. of the king of Assyria;

2 Kgs 21:14: into the h. of their enemies;

2 Kgs 22:2: turned not aside to the right h. or to the left.

2 Kgs 22:5: deliver it into the h. of the doers of the work,

2 Kgs 22:7: was delivered into their h.,

2 Kgs 22:9: delivered it into the h. of them that do the work,

2 Kgs 23:8: which were on a man's left h. at the gate ...

2 Kgs 23:13: which were on the right h. of the mount of corruption,

1 Chron 4:10: and that thine h. might be with me,

1 Chron 5:10: they made war with the Hagarites, who fell by their h.:

1 Chron 4:10: and that thine h. might be with me,

1 Chron 5:10: they made war with the Hagarites, who fell by their h.:

1 Chron 5:20: and the Hagarites were delivered into their h.,

1 Chron 6:15: when the LORD carried away Judah and Jerusalem by the h. of Nebuchadnezzar.

1 Chron 6:39: And his brother Asaph, who stood on his right h.,

1 Chron 6:44: sons of Merari stood on the left h.:

1 Chron 11:23: and plucked the spear out of the Egyptian's h., and slew him ...

1 Chron 12:2: and could use both the right h. and the left

1 Chron 13:9: Uzza put forth his h. to hold the ark;

1 Chron 13:10: and he smote him, because he put his h. to the ark:

1 Chron 14:10: Go up; for I will deliver them into thine h.

1 Chron 14:11: God hath broken in upon mine enemies by mine h ...

1Chron 16:7: thank the LORD into the h. of Asaph

1 Chron 18:1: and took Gath and her towns out of the h. of the Philistines.

1 Chron 19:11: And the rest of the people he delivered unto the h. of Abishai

1 Chron 20:6: whose fingers and toes were four and twenty, six on each h.,

1 Chron 20:8: they fell by the h. of David, and by the h. of his servants.

1 Chron 21:13: let me fall now into the h. of the LORD ... but let me not fall into the h. of man

1 Chron 21:15: It is enough, stay now thine h.

1 Chron 21:16: having
a drawn sword in his h.
stretched out over Jerusalem.
1 Chron 21:17: let thine h., I
pray thee, O LORD my God,
be on me,
1 Chron 22:18: for he hath
given the inhabitants of the
land into mine h.;
1 Chron 26:28: it was under
the h. of Shelomith, and of his
brethren.
1 Chro 28:19: All this, said
David, the LORD made me
understand in writing by his
h. upon me,
1 Chron 29:8: by the h. of
Jehiel the Gershonite.
1 Chron 29:12: and in thine
h. is power and might; and in
thine h. it is to make great,
1 Chron 29:16: build thee an
house for thine holy name
cometh of thine h.,
2 Chron 3:17: one on the right
h., and the other on the left;
2 Chron 4:6: and put five on
the right h., and five on the
left,
2 Chron 4:7: five on the right
h., and five on the left.
2 Chron 6:15: and hast
fulfilled it with thine h., as it
is this day.
2 Chron 6:32: and thy mighty
h., and thy stretched out arm;
2 Chron 10:15: which he
spake by the h. of Ahijah the
Shilonite
2Chron 12:5: left you in the h.
of Shishak.
2 Chron 12:7: wrath shall not
be poured out upon Jerusalem
by the h. of Shishak.
2 Chron 13:8: in the h. of the
sons of David;
2 Chron 13:16: and God
delivered them into their h.
2 Chron 16:7: therefore is
the host of the king of Syria
escaped out of thine h.

2 Chron 16:8: delivered them
into thine h.
2 Chron 17:5: Therefore the
LORD stablished the kingdom
in his h.;
2 Chron 18:5: for God will
deliver it into the king's h.
2 Chron 18:11: for the LORD
shall deliver it into the h. of
the king.
2 Chron 18:14: and they shall
be delivered into your h.
2 Chron 18:18: and all the
host of heaven standing on his
right h. and on his left.
2 Chron 18:33: Turn thine h.,
that thou mayest carry me out
of the host;
2 Chron 20:6: and in thine h.
is there not power and might,
2 Chron 21:10: The same time
also did Libnah revolt from
under his h.;
2 Chron 23:7: every man with
his weapons in his h.;
2 Chron 23:10: every man
having his weapon in his h.,
2 Chron 23:18: by the h. of the
priests the Levites,
2 Chron 24:11: by the h. of the
Levites,
2 Chron 24:24: the LORD
delivered a very great host
into their h.,
2 Chron 25:15: which could
not deliver their own people
out of thine h.?
2 Chron 25:20: that he might
deliver them into the hand of
their enemies
2 Chron 26:11: by the h. of
Jeiel the scribe and Maaseiah
the ruler, under the h. of
Hananiah, one of the king's
captains.
2 Chron 26:13: And under
their h. was an army,
2 Chron 26:19: and had
a censer in his h. to burn
incense:
2 Chron 28:5: Wthe LORD his
God delivered him into the h.

of the king of Syria ... And he
was also delivered into the h.
of the king of Israel,
2 Chron 28:9: he hath
delivered them into your h.
2 Chron 30:6: that are
escaped out of the h. of the
kings of Assyria.
2 Chron 30:12: Also in Judah
the h. of God was to give them
one heart ...
2 Chron 30:16: which they
received of the h. of the
Levites.
2 Chron 31:13: were overseers
under the h. of Cononiah and
Shimei his brother,
2 Chron 32:11: God shall
deliver us out of the h. of the
king of Assyria?
2 Chron 32:13: to deliver their
lands out of mine h.?
2 Chron 32:14: that your God
should be able to deliver you
out of mine h.?
2 Chron 32:15: how much less
shall your God deliver you out
of mine h.?
2 Chron 32:17: the God of
Hezekiah deliver his people
out of mine h.
2 Chron 32:22: Jerusalem
from the h. of Sennacherib the
king of Assyria,
2 Chron 33:8: whole law
and the statutes and the
ordinances by the h. of Moses.
2 Chron 34:2: and declined
neither to the right h., nor to
the left.
2 Chron 34:9: kept the doors
had gathered of the h. of
Manasseh and Ephraim,
2 Chron 34:10: And they put it
in the h. of the workmen
2 Chron 34:17: and to the h. of
the workmen.
2 Chron 35:6: according to the
word of the LORD by the h. of
Moses.
2 Chron 36:17: gave them all
into his h.

Ezra 1:8: Cyrus king of Persia bring forth by the hand of Mithredath the treasurer,

Ezra 5:12 he gave them into the h. of Nebuchadnezzar

Ezra 6:12 that shall put to their h. and to alter and to destroy this house of God

Ezra 7:6 according to the h. of the LORD his God upon him.

Ezra 7:9 according to the good h. of his God upon him.

Ezra 7:14 according to the law of thy God which is in thine h.;

Ezra 7:25 that is in thine h.,

Ezra 7:28 I was strengthened as the h. of the LORD

Ezra 8:18: And by the good h. of our God

Ezra 8:22: The h. of our God is upon all them for good

Ezra 8:26: I even weighed unto their h. six hundred and fifty talents of silver,

Ezra 8:31: and the h. of our God was upon us,

Ezra 8:33: by the h. of Meremoth the son of Uriah the priest;

Ezra 9:2: the h. of the princes and rulers hath been chief in this trespass.

Ezra 9:7: been delivered into the h. of the kings of the lands

Neh 1:10: redeemed by thy great power, and by thy strong h.

Neh 2:8: according to the good h. of my God upon me.

Neh 2:18: Then I told them of the h. of my God

Neh 6:5: the fifth time with an open letter in his h.;

Neh 8:4: his right hand; and on his left h.,

Neh 9:14: and laws, by the h. of Moses thy servant:

Neh 9:27: who saved them out of the h. of their enemies.

Neh 9:28: therefore leftest thou them in the h. of their enemies,

Neh 9:30: therefore gavest thou them into the h. of the people ...

Neh 11:24: was at the king's h. in all matters

Neh 12:31: whereof one went on the right h. upon the wall

Esth 2:21: and sought to lay h. on the king Ahasuerus.

Esth 3:10: And the king took his ring from his h.,

Esth 5:2: the golden sceptre that was in his h.

Esth 6:2: who sought to lay h. on the king Ahasuerus.

Esth 6:9: And let this apparel and horse be delivered to the h.

Esth 8:7: because he laid his h. upon the Jews.

Esth 9:2: to lay h. on such as sought their hurt:

Esth 9:10: but on the spoil laid they not their h.

Esth 9:15: but on the prey they laid not their h.

Job 1:11: But put forth thine h. now,

Job 1:12: only upon himself put not forth thine h.

Job 2:5: But put forth thine h. now,

Job 2:6: Behold, he is in thine h.; but save his life.

Job 2:10: What? shall we receive good at the h. of God,

Job 5:15: and from the h. of the mighty.

Job 6:9: that he would let loose his h., and cut me off!

Job 6:23: Or, Deliver me from the enemy's h.? or, Redeem me from the h. of the mighty?

Job 9:24: The earth is given into the h. of the wicked:

Job 9:33: that might lay his h. upon us both.

Job 10:7: and there is none that can deliver out of thine h.

Job 11:14: If iniquity be in thine h.,

Job 12:6: into whose h. God bringeth abundantly.

Job 12:9: knoweth not in all these that the h. of the LORD hath wrought this?

Job 12:10: In whose h. is the soul of every living thing

Job 13:14: and put my life in mine h.?

Job 13:21: Withdraw thine h. far from me:

Job 15:23: he knoweth that the day of darkness is ready at his h..

Job 15:25: For he stretcheth out his h. against God,

Job 19:21: the h. of God hath touched me.

Job 20:22: every h. of the wicked shall come upon him.

Job 21:5: and lay your h. upon your mouth.

Job 21:16: their good is not in their h.:

Job 23:9: On the left h., where he doth work ... hideth himself on the right h ...

Job 26:13 his h. hath formed the crooked serpent.

Job 27:11: I will teach you by the h. of God:

Job 27:22: he would fain flee out of his h.

Job 28:9: He putteth forth his h. upon the rock;

Job 29:9: and laid their h. on their mouth.

Job 29:20: my bow was renewed in my h.

Job 30:12: Upon my right h. rise the youth;

Job 30:21: with thy strong h. thou opposest thyself against me.

Job 30:24: Howbeit he will not stretch out his h. to the grave,

Job 31:21: If I have lifted up my h. against the fatherless,

Job 31:25: mine h. had gotten much;

Job 31:27: my mouth hath kissed my h.:

Job 33:7: neither shall my h. be heavy upon thee.

Job 34:20: and the mighty shall be taken away without h.

Job 35:7: what receiveth he of thine h.?

Job 37:7: He sealeth up the h. of every man;

Job 40:4: I will lay mine h. upon my mouth.

Job 40:14: that thine own right h. can save thee.

Job 41:8: Lay thine h. upon him,

Ps 10:12: Arise, O LORD; O God, lift up thine h.:

Ps 10:14: to requite it with thy h.:

Ps 16:8: he is at my right h. I shall not be moved.

Ps 16:11: at thy right h. there are pleasures for evermore.

Ps 17:7: thou that savest by thy right h.

Ps 17:14: From men which are thy h., O LORD,

Ps 18:35: thy right h. hath holden me up,

Ps 20:6: with the saving strength of his right h.

Ps 21:8: Thine h. shall find out all thine enemies: thy right h. shall find out those that hate thee.

Ps 31:5: Into thine h. I commit my spirit:

Ps 31:8: And hast not shut me up into the h. of the enemy:

Ps 31:15: My times are in thy h.: deliver me from the hand of mine enemies,

Ps 32:4: For day and night thy h. was heavy upon me:

Ps 36:11: let not the h. of the wicked remove me.

Ps 37:24: for the LORD upholdeth him with his h.

Ps 37:33: The LORD will not leave him in his h.,

Ps 38:2: and thy h. presseth me sore.

Ps 39:10: I am consumed by the blow of thine h.

Ps 44:2: How thou didst drive out the heathen with thy h.

Ps 44:3: but thy right h., and thine arm,

Ps 45:4: and thy right h. shall teach thee terrible things.

Ps 45:9: upon thy right h. did stand the queen in gold of Ophir.

Ps 48:10: thy right h. is full of righteousness.

Ps 60:5: save with thy right h., and hear me.

Ps 63:8: thy right h. upholdeth me.

Ps 71:4: Deliver me, O my God, out of the h. of the wicked, out of the h. of the unrighteous

Ps 73:23: thou hast holden me by my right h.

Ps 74:11: Why withdrawest thou thy hand, even thy right h.?

Ps 75:8: For in the h. of the LORD there is a cup,

Ps 77:10: of the right h. of the most High.

Ps 77:20: Thou leddest thy people like a flock by the h. of Moses and Aaron.

Ps 78:42: They remembered not his h.,

Ps 78:54: which his right h. purchased.

Ps 78:61: his glory into the enemy's h.

Ps 80:15: And the vineyard which thy right h. hath planted,

Ps 80:17: Let thy hand be upon the man of thy right h.,

Ps 81:14: and turned my h. against their adversaries.

Ps 82:4: rid them out of the h. of the wicked.

Ps 88:5: and they are cut off from thy h.

Ps 89:13: strong is thy h., and high is thy right h.

Ps 89:21: With whom my h. shall be established:

Ps 89:25: I will set his h. also in the sea, and his right h. in the rivers.

Ps 89:42: Thou hast set up the right h. of his adversaries;

Ps 89:48: shall he deliver his soul from the h. of the grave?

Ps 91:7: and ten thousand at thy right h.;

Ps 95:4: In his h. are the deep places of the earth:

Ps 95:7: and the sheep of his h.

Ps 97:10: he delivereth them out of the h. of the wicked.

Ps 98:1: his right h., and his holy arm, hath gotten him the victory.

Ps 104:28: thou openest thine h., they are filled with good.

Ps 106:10: And he saved them from the h. of him that hated them,

Ps 106:26: Therefore he lifted up his h. against them,

Ps 106:41: And he gave them into the h. of the heathen;

Ps 106:42: they were brought into subjection under their h.

Ps 107:2: he hath redeemed from the h. of the enemy;

Ps 108:6: save with thy right h., and answer me.

Ps 109:6: let Satan stand at his right h.

Ps 109:27: That they may know that this is thy h.;

Ps 109:31: For he shall stand at the right h. of the poor,

Ps 110:1: Sit thou at my right h.,

Ps 110:5: The Lord at thy right h. shall strike through kings

Ps 118:15: the right h. of the LORD doeth valiantly.

Ps 118:16: The right h. of the LORD is exalted: the right h. of the LORD doeth valiantly.

Ps 119:109: soul is continually in my h.:

Ps 119:173: Let thine h. help me;

Ps 121:5: the LORD is thy shade upon thy right h.

Ps 123:2: Behold, as the eyes of servants look unto the h. of their masters,

Ps 127:4: As arrows are in the h. of a mighty man;

Ps 129:7: Wherewith the mower filleth not his h.;

Ps 136:12: With a strong h., and with a stretched out arm:

Ps 137:5: let my right h. forget her cunning.

Ps 138:7: thou shalt stretch forth thine h. against the wrath of mine enemies,

Ps 139:5: and laid thine h. upon me.

Ps 139:10: Even there shall thy h. lead me, and thy right h. shall hold me.

Ps 142:4: I looked on my right h.,

Ps 144:7: Send thine h. from above; rid me, and deliver me out of great waters, from the h. of strange children;

Ps 44:8: and their right h. is a right hand of falsehood.

Ps 144:11: and their right h. is a right h. of falsehood:

Ps 145:16: Thou openest thine h.,

Ps 149:6: a two edged sword in their h.;

Prov 1:24 I have stretched out my h.,

Prov 3:16: Length of days is in her right h.; and in her left h. riches and honour.

Prov 3:27: when it is in the power of thine h. to do it.

Prov 4:27: Turn not to the right h. nor to the left:

Prov 6:1: if thou hast stricken thy h. with a stranger,

Prov 6:3: when thou art come into the h. of thy friend; go,

Prov 6:5: Deliver thyself as a roe from the h. of the hunter,

Prov 10:4: He becometh poor that dealeth with a slack h.: but the h. of the diligent maketh rich.

Prov 11:21: Though h. join in h., the wicked shall not be unpunished:

Prov 12:24: The h. of the diligent shall bear rule:

Prov 16:5: though h. join in h., he shall not be unpunished.

Prov 17:16: Wherefore is there a price in the h. of a fool to get wisdom,

Prov 19:24: A slothful man hideth his h. in his bosom,

Prov 21:1: The king's heart is in the h. of the LORD,

Prov 26:6: He that sendeth a message by the h. of a fool cutteth off the feet,

Prov 26:9: As a thorn goeth up into the h. of a drunkard,

Prov 26:15: The slothful hideth his h. in his bosom;

Prov 27:16: the ointment of his right h., which bewrayeth itself.

Prov 30:32: if thou hast thought evil, lay thine h. upon thy mouth.

Prov 31:20: She stretcheth out her h. to the poor; yea, she reacheth forth her h.s to the needy.

Eccl 2:24: that it was from the h. of God.

Eccl 5:14: and there is nothing in his h.

Eccl 5:15: he may carry away in his h.

Eccl 7:18: also from this withdraw not thine h.:

Eccl 9:1: and the wise, and their works, are in the h. of God:

Eccl 9:10: Whatsoever thy h. findeth to do, do it …

Eccl 10:2: A wise man's heart is at his right h.;

Eccl 11:6: in the evening withhold not thine h.:

Song 2:6: His left h. is under my head, and his right h. doth embrace me.

Song 5:4: My beloved put in his h. by the hole of the door,

Song 8:3: His left hand should be under my h.,

Isa 1:12: who hath required this at your h., to tread my courts?

Isa 1:25: And I will turn my h. upon thee,

Isa 3:6: and let this ruin be under thy h.:

Isa 5:25: he hath stretched forth his h. against them.

Isa 6:6: having a live coal in his h.,

Isa 8:11: the LORD spake thus to me with a strong h.,

Isa 9:12: but his h. is stretched out still.

Isa 9:17: but his h. is stretched out still.

Isa 9:20: And he shall snatch on the right h., and be hungry; and he shall eat on the left h.,

Isa 9:21: but his h. is stretched out still.

Isa 10:4: but his h. is stretched out still.

Isa 10:5: the staff in their h. is mine indignation.

Isa 10:10: As my h. hath found the kingdoms of the idols,

Isa 10:13: By the strength of my h. I have done it,

Isa 10:14: my h. hath found as a nest the riches of the people:

Isa 10:32: he shall shake his h. against the mount of the daughter of Zion,

Isa 11:8: the weaned child shall put his h. on the cockatrice' den.

Isa 11:11: the Lord shall set his h. again the second time

Isa 11:14: they shall lay their h. upon Edom and Moab

Isa 11:15: he shake his h. over the river

Isa 13:2: shake the h., that they may go into the gates of the nobles.
Isa 13:6: for the day of the LORD is at h.;
Isa 14:26: this is the h. that is stretched out upon all the nations.
Isa 14:27: his h. is stretched out, and who shall turn it back?
Isa 19:4: the Egyptians will I give over into the h. of a cruel lord;
Isa 19:16: because of the shaking of the h. of the LORD of hosts,
Isa 22:21: I will commit thy government into his h.
Isa 23:11: He stretched out his h. over the sea,
Isa 25:10: For in this mountain shall the h. of the LORD rest,
Isa 26:11: LORD, when thy h. is lifted up, they will not see:
Isa 28:2: shall cast down to the earth with the h.
Isa 28:4: while it is yet in his h.
Isa 30:21: when ye turn to the right h., and when ye turn to the left.
Isa 31:3: When the LORD shall stretch out his h.,
Isa 34:17: his h. hath divided it unto them by line:
Isa 36:6: will go into his h., and pierce it:
Isa 36:15: this city shall not be delivered into the h. of the king of Assyria.
Isa 36:18: delivered his land out of the h. of the king of Assyria?
Isa 36:19: have they delivered Samaria out of my h.?
Isa 36:20: have delivered their land out of my h., that the LORD should deliver Jerusalem out of my h.?

Isa 37:10: Jerusalem shall not be given into the h. of the king of Assyria.
Isa 37:14: received the letter from the h. of the messengers,
Isa 37:20: save us from his h.,
Isa 38:6: deliver thee and this city out of the h. of the king of Assyria:
Isa 40:10: the Lord GOD will come with strong h.,
Isa 40:12: Who hath measured the waters in the hollow of his h.,
Isa 41:10: I will uphold thee with the right h. of my righteousness.
Isa 41:13: God will hold thy right h.,
Isa 41:20: that the h. of the LORD hath done this,
Isa 42:6: hold thine h., and will keep thee,
Isa 43:13: there is none that can deliver out of my h.:
Isa 44:5: and another shall subscribe with his h. unto the LORD,
Isa 44:20: Is there not a lie in my right h.?
Isa 45:1: whose right h. I have holden,
Isa 47:6: and given them into thine h.:
Isa 48:13: Mine h. also hath laid the foundation of the earth, and my right h. hath spanned the heavens:
Isa 49:2: shadow of his h. hath he hid me,
Isa 49:22: I will lift up mine h. to the Gentiles,
Isa 50:2: Is my h. shortened at all, that it cannot redeem
Isa 50:11: This shall ye have of mine h.;
Isa 51:16: I have covered thee in the shadow of mine h.,
Isa 51:17: which hast drunk at the h. of the LORD the cup of his fury;

Isa 51:18: neither is there any that taketh her by the h. of all the sons
Isa 51:22: I have taken out of thine h. the cup of trembling,
Isa 51:23: But I will put it into the h. of them that afflict thee;
Isa 53:10: and the pleasure of the LORD shall prosper in his h.
Isa 54:3: For thou shalt break forth on the right h. and on the left;
Isa 56:2: and keepeth his h. from doing any evil.
Isa 57:10: hast found the life of thine h.;
Isa 59:1: Behold, the LORD's h. is not shortened,
Isa 62:3: glory in the h. of the LORD,
Isa 62:8: The LORD hath sworn by his right h.,
Isa 63:12: That led them by the right h. of Moses
Isa 64:8: and we all are the work of thy h.
Isa 66:2: For all those things hath mine h. made,
Isa 66:14: and the h. of the LORD shall be known
Jer 1:9: Then the LORD put forth his h.,
Jer 6:9: turn back thine h. as a grape gatherer into the baskets.
Jer 6:12: I will stretch out my h. upon the inhabitants of the land,
Jer 11:21: that thou die not by our h.:
Jer 12:7: I have given the dearly beloved of my soul into the h.
Jer 15:6: therefore will I stretch out my h. against thee,
Jer 15:17: I sat alone because of thy h.:
Jer 15:21: And I will deliver thee out of the h. of the wicked, and I will redeem thee out of the h. of the terrible.

Jer: 6:21: I will cause them to know mine h. and my might;

Jer: 8:4: was marred in the h. of the potter:

Jer: 8:6: as the clay is in the potter's h., so are ye in mine h.

Jer: 0:4: and I will give all Judah into the h. of the king of Babylon,

Jer: 0:5: Judah will I give into the h. of their enemies,

Jer: 0:13: delivered the soul of the poor from the h. of evildoers.

Jer: 1:5: I myself will fight against you with an outstretched h ...

Jer: 1:7: and from the famine, into the h. of Nebuchadrezzar king of Babylon, and into the h. of their enemies, and into the h. of those that seek their life:

Jer: 1:10: it shall be given into the h. of the king of Babylon,

Jer: 1:12: and deliver him that is spoiled out of the h. of the oppressor,

Jer: 2:3: deliver the spoiled out of the h. of the oppressor:

Jer: 2:24: Jehoiakim king of Judah were the signet upon my right h.,

Jer: 2:25: And I will give thee into the h. of them that seek thy life,

Jer: 3:23: Am I a God at h., saith the LORD,

Jer: 5:15: Take the wine cup of this fury at my h.,

Jer: 5:17: Then took I the cup at the LORD's h.,

Jer: 5:28: if they refuse to take the cup at thine h. to drink,

Jer: 6:14: I am in your h.:

Jer: 6:24: Nevertheless the h. of Ahikam ... that they should not give him into the h. of the people

Jer: 27:3: by the h. of the messengers which come to Jerusalem

Jer: 27:6: I given all these lands unto the h. of Nebuchadnezzar

Jer: 27:8: I have consumed them by his h.

Jer: 29:3: By the h. of Elasah

Jer: 29:21: I will deliver them into the h. of Nebuchadrezzar

Jer: 31:11: and ransomed him from the h. of him that was stronger than he.

Jer: 31:32: I took them by the h. to bring them out of the land of Egypt

Jer: 32:3: I will give this city into the h. of the king of Babylon,

Jer: 32:4: but shall surely be delivered into the h. of the king of Babylon,

Jer: 32:21: and with a strong h.,

Jer: 32:24: the city is given into the h. of the Chaldeans,

Jer: 32:25: for the city is given into the h. of the Chaldeans.

Jer: 32:28: I will give this city into the h. of the Chaldeans,

Jer: 32:36: It shall be delivered into the h. of the king of Babylon

Jer: 32:43: it is given into the h. of the Chaldeans.

Jer: 34:2: I will give this city into the h. of the king of Babylon,

Jer: 34:3: And thou shalt not escape out of his h., but shalt surely be taken, and delivered into his h.;

Jer: 34:20: I will even give them into the h. of their enemies, and into the h. of them that seek their life:

Jer: 34:21: will I give into the h. of their enemies, and into the h. of them that seek their life, and into the h. of the king of Babylon's army,

Jer: 36:14: Take in thine h. the roll wherein thou hast read

Jer 37:17: thou shalt be delivered into the h. of the king of Babylon.

Lam 1:7: when her people fell into the h. of the enemy,

Lam 1:10: The adversary hath spread out his h. upon all her pleasant things:

Lam 1:14: The yoke of my transgressions is bound by his h.:

Lam 2:3: he hath drawn back his right h. from before the enemy,

Lam 2:4: he stood with his right h. as an adversary,

Lam 2:7: he hath given up into the h. of the enemy

Lam 2:8: he hath not withdrawn his h. from destroying:

Lam 3:3: he turneth his h. against me all the day.

Lam 5:6: We have given the h. to the Egyptians,

Lam 5:8: there is none that doth deliver us out of their h.

Lam 5:12: are hanged up by their h.:

Ezek 1:3: and the h. of the LORD was there upon him.

Ezek 2:9: an h. was sent unto me;

Ezek 3:14: but the h. of the LORD was strong upon me.

Ezek 3:18: but his blood will I require at thine h.

Ezek 3:20: but his blood will I require at thine h.

Ezek 3:22: And the h. of the LORD was there upon me;

Ezek 6:11: Smite with thine h., and stamp with thy foot,

Ezek 6:14: So will I stretch out my h. upon them,

Ezek 8:1: the h. of the Lord GOD fell there upon me.

Ezek 8:3: he put forth the form of an h.

Ezek 8:11: with every man his censer in his h.;

Ezek 9:1: every man with his destroying weapon in his h.
Ezek 9:2: and every man a slaughter weapon in his h.;
Ezek 10:2: fill thine h. with coals of fire
Ezek 10:7: And one cherub stretched forth his h.
Ezek 10:8: the form of a man's h. under their wings.
Ezek 12:7: I digged through the wall with mine h.;
Ezek 12:23: The days are at hand,
Ezek 13:9: And mine h. shall be upon the prophets ...
Ezek 13:21: deliver my people out of your h., and they shall be no more in your h.
Ezek 13:23: I will deliver my people out of your h.:
Ezek 14:9: I will stretch out my h. upon him,
Ezek 14:13: then will I stretch out mine h. upon it,
Ezek 16:27: Behold, therefore I have stretched out my h. over thee,
Ezek 16:39: And I will also give thee into their h.,
Ezek 16:46: that dwell at thy left hand ... that dwelleth at thy right h.,
Ezek 16:49: neither did she strengthen the h. of the poor and needy.
Ezek 17:18: he had given his h.,
Ezek 18:8: that hath withdrawn his h. from iniquity,
Ezek 18:17: That hath taken off his h. from the poor,
Ezek 20:5: and lifted up mine h. unto the seed of the house of Jacob,
Ezek 20:6: In the day that I lifted up mine h. unto them,
Ezek 20:15: I lifted up my h. unto them in the wilderness,
Ezek 20:22: Nevertheless I withdrew mine h.,

Ezek 20:23: I lifted up mine h. unto them
Ezek 20:28: I lifted up mine h. to give it to them,
Ezek 20:33: with a mighty h.,
Ezek 20:34: with a mighty h.,
Ezek 20:42: I lifted up mine h. to give it to your fathers.
Ezek 21:16: either on the right h., or on the left,
Ezek 21:22: At his right h. was the divination for Jerusalem
Ezek 21:24: ye shall be taken with the h.
Ezek 21:31: and deliver thee into the h. of brutish men,
Ezek 22:13: I have smitten mine h. at thy dishonest gain
Ezek 23:9: I have delivered her into the h. of her lovers,
Ezek 23:28: I will deliver thee into the h. of them
Ezek 23:31: I give her cup into thine h.
Ezek 25:7: therefore I will stretch out mine h. upon thee,
Ezek 25:13: I will also stretch out mine h. upon Edom,
Ezek 25:14: vengeance upon Edom by the h. of my people Israel:
Ezek 25:16: I will stretch out mine h. upon the Philistines,
Ezek 27:15: the merchandise of thine h.:
Ezek 28:9: in the h. of him that slayeth thee.
Ezek 28:10: uncircumcised by the h. of strangers:
Ezek 29:7: When they took hold of thee by thy h.,
Ezek 30:10: the multitude of Egypt to cease by the h. of Nebuchadrezzar,
Ezek 30:12: and sell the land into the h. of the wicked:
Ezek 30:22: cause the sword to fall out of his h.
Ezek 30:24: and put my sword in his h.:

Ezek 30:25: I shall put my sword into the h. of the king of Babylon,
Ezek 31:11: I have therefore delivered him into the h. of the mighty one ...
Ezek 33:6: but his blood will I require at the watchman's h.
Ezek 33:8: but his blood will I require at thine h.
Ezek 33:22: Now the h. of the LORD was upon me
Ezek 34:10: I will require my flock at their h.,
Ezek 35:3: I will stretch out mine h. against thee,
Ezek 36:7 I have lifted up mine h.,
Ezek 36:8: for they are at h. to come.
Ezek 37:1: The h. of the LORD was upon me,
Ezek 37:17: and they shall become one in thine h.
Ezek 37:19: which is in the h. of Ephraim,
Ezek 37:20: thou writest shall be in thine h. before their eyes.
Ezek 38:12: to turn thine h. upon the desolate places
Ezek 39:3: And I will smite thy bow out of thy left h., and will cause thine arrows to fall out of thy right h.
Ezek 39:21: and my h. that I have laid upon them.
Ezek 39:23: and gave them into the h. of their enemies:
Ezek 40:1: the h. of the LORD was upon me,
Ezek 40:3: with a line of flax in his h.,
Ezek 40:5: and in the man's h. a measuring reed
Ezek 40:43: an h. broad, fastened round about:
Ezek 43:13: and an h. breadth;
Ezek 44:12: I lifted up mine h. against them,
Ezek 46:7: according as his h. shall attain

Ezek 47:3: the line in his h. went forth eastward,
Ezek 47:14: I lifted up mine h. to give it unto your fathers:
Dan 1:2: And the Lord gave Jehoiakim king of Judah into his h.,
Dan 2:38: the fowls of the heaven hath he given into thine h.,
Dan 3:17: will deliver us out of thine h.,
Dan 4:35: none can stay his h.,
Dan 5:5: In the same hour came forth fingers of a man's h.,
Dan 5:23: and the God in whose h. thy breath is,
Dan 5:24: Then was the part of the hand sent from him;
Dan 7:25: they shall be given into his h.
Dan 8:4: neither was there any that could deliver out of his h.;
Dan 8:7 there was none that could deliver the ram out of his h.
Dan 8:25: he shall be broken without h.
Dan 9:15: with a mighty h., and hast gotten thee renown,
Dan 10:10: and upon the palms of my h.
Dan 11:11: but the multitude shall be given into his h.
Dan 11:16: which by his h. shall be consumed.
Dan 11:41: but these shall escape out of his h.,
Dan 11:42: He shall stretch forth his h ...
Dan 12:7: when he held up his right hand and his left h. unto heaven,
Hosea 2:10: none shall deliver her out of mine h.
Hosea 7:5: he stretched out his h. with scorners.
Hosea 12:7: the balances of deceit are in his h.:
Joel 1:15: the day of the LORD is at h.,

Joel 3:8 sell your sons and your daughters into the h. of the children of Judah,
Amos 1:8: and I will turn mine h. against Ekron:
Amos 5:19: and leaned his h. on the wall, and a serpent bit him.
Amos 7:7: with a plumbline in his h.
Amos 9:2: thence shall mine h. take them;
Jonah 4:11: that cannot discern between their right hand and their left h.;
Micah 2:1: because it is in the power of their h.
Micah 4:10: the LORD shall redeem thee from the h. of thine enemies.
Micah 5:9: Thine h. shall be lifted up upon thine adversaries
Micah 5:12: And I will cut off witchcrafts out of thine h.;
Micah 7:16: they shall lay their h. upon their mouth,
Hab 2:16: the cup of the LORD's right h. shall be turned unto thee,
Hab 3:4: had horns coming out of his h.:
Zeph 1:4: I will also stretch out mine h. upon Judah,
Zeph 2:13: And he will stretch out his h. against the north
Zeph 2:15: every one that passeth by her shall hiss, and wag his h.
Zech 2:1: behold a man with a measuring line in his h.
Zech 2:9: For, behold, I will shake mine h. upon them,
Zech 3:1: Satan standing at his right h. to resist him.
Zech 4:10: and shall see the plummet in the h. of Zerubbabel
Zech 8:4: and every man with his staff in his h. for very age.
Zech 11:6: I will deliver the men every one into his

neighbour's h., and into the h. of his king:
Zech 12:6: on the right h. and on the left:
Zech 13:7: and I will turn mine h. upon the little ones.
Zech 14:13: and his h. shall rise up against the h. of his neighbour.
Mal 1:10: neither will I accept an offering at your h.
Mal 1:13: should I accept this of your h.?
Mal 2:13: or receiveth it with good will at your h.
Mt 3:2: the kingdom of heaven is at h.
Mt 3:12: Whose fan is in his h.,
Mt 4:17: the kingdom of heaven is at h.
Mt 5:30: And if thy right h. offend thee, cut it off,
Mt 6:3: let not thy left hand know what thy right h. doeth:
Mt 8:3: And Jesus put forth his h., and touched him
Mt 8:15: And he touched her h.,
Mt 9:18: come and lay thy h. upon her,
Mt 9:25: and took her by the h., and the maid arose.
Mt 10:7: The kingdom of heaven is at h.
Mt 12:10: behold, there was a man which had his h. withered.
Mt 12:13: Then saith he to the man, Stretch forth thine h.
Mt 12:49: And he stretched forth his h. toward his disciples,
Mt 14:31: And immediately Jesus stretched forth his h.,
Mt 18:8: Wherefore if thy h. or thy foot offend thee,
Mt 20:21: the one on thy right h., and the other on the left,
Mt 20:23: but to sit on my right h., and on my left,

Mt 22:13: Bind him h. and foot, and take him away,
Mt 22:44: Sit thou on my right h.,
Mt 25:33: And he shall set the sheep on his right h.,
Mt 25:34: Then shall the King say unto them on his right h.,
Mt 25:41: Then shall he say also unto them on the left h.,
Mt 26:18: My time is at h.;
Mt 26:23: He that dippeth his h. with me in the dish,
Mt 26:45: behold, the hour is at h.,
Mt 26:46: behold, he is at h. that doth betray me.
Mt 26:51: stretched out his h., and drew his sword,
Mt 26:64: ye see the Son of man sitting on the right h. of power,
Mt 27:29: and a reed in his right h.:
Mt 27:38: one on the right h., and another on the left.
Mk 1:15: the kingdom of God is at h.:
Mk 1:31: And he came and took her by the h.,
Mk 1:41: put forth his h., and touched him,
Mk 3:1: there was a man there which had a withered h.
Mk 3:3: And he saith unto the man which had the withered h.,
Mk 3:5: Stretch forth thine h.
Mk 5:23: come and lay thy h. on her,
Mk 5:41: he took the damsel by the h.,
Mk 7:32: and they beseech him to put his h. upon him.
Mk 8:23: And he took the blind man by the h.,
Mk 9:27: But Jesus took him by the h., and lifted him up;
Mk 9:43: And if thy h. offend thee,

Mk 10:37: that we may sit, one on thy right h., and the other on thy left h.,
Mk 10:40: to sit on my right hand and on my left h. is not mine to give;
Mk 12:36: Sit thou on my right h.,
Mk 14:42: he that betrayeth me is at h.
Mk 14:62: ye shall see the Son of man sitting on the right h. of power,
Mk 15:27: the one on his right h., and the other on his left.
Mk16:19: and sat on the right h. of God.
Lk 1:1: Forasmuch as many have taken in h. to set forth in order ...
Lk 1:66: the h. of the Lord was with him.
Lk 1:71: from the h. of all that hate us;
Lk 1:74: being delivered out of the h. of our enemies
Lk 3:17: Whose fan is in his h.,
Lk 5:13: And he put forth his h., and touched him,
Lk 6:6: there was a man whose right h. was withered.
Lk 6:8: man which had the withered h.,
Lk 6:10: Stretch forth thy h.
Lk 8:54: and took her by the h.,
Lk 9:62: No man, having put his h. to the plough,
Lk 13:13: And he laid his h. on her:
Lk 15:22: and put a ring on his h.,
Lk 20:42: Sit thou on my right h.,
Lk 21:30: that summer is now nigh at h.
Lk 21:31: know ye that the kingdom of God is nigh at h.
Lk 22:21: behold, the h. of him that betrayeth me ...

Lk 22:69: the Son of man sit on the right h. of the power of God.
Lk 23:33: one on the right h., and the other on the left.
Jn 2:13: the Jews' passover was at h.,
Jn 3:35: hath given all things into his h.
Jn 7:2: Now the Jews' feast of tabernacles was at h.
Jn 10:28: neither shall any man pluck them out of my h.
Jn 10:29: no man is able to pluck them out of my Father's h.
Jn 10:39: but he escaped out of their h.,
Jn 11:44: bound h. and foot with graveclothes:
Jn 11:55: And the Jews' passover was nigh at h.:
Jn 18:22: with the palm of his h., saying,
Jn 19:42: for the sepulchre was nigh at h.
Jn 20:25: and thrust my h. into his side, I will not believe.
Jn 20:27: reach hither thy h., and thrust it into my side:
Acts 2:25: he is on my right h., that I should not be moved:
Acts 2:33: Therefore being by the right h. of God exalted,
Acts 2:34: Sit thou on my right h.,
Acts 3:7: he took him by the right h.,
Acts 4:28: For to do whatsoever thy h. and thy counsel determined
Acts 4:30: By stretching forth thine h. to heal;
Acts 5:31: Him hath God exalted with his right h. to be a Prince and a Saviour,
Acts 7:25: how that God by his h. would deliver them:
Acts 7:35: God send to be a ruler and a deliverer by the h. of the angel ...

Acts 7:50: Hath not my h. made all these things?

Acts 7:55: and Jesus standing on the right h. of God,

Acts 7:56: the Son of man standing on the right h. of God.

Acts 9:8: but they led him by the h.,

Acts 9:12: and putting his h. on him,

Acts 9:41: And he gave her his h.,

Acts 11:21: And the h. of the Lord was with them:

Acts 12:11: and hath delivered me out of the h. of Herod,

Acts 12:17: beckoning unto them with the h. to hold their peace,

Acts 13:11: And now, behold, the h. of the Lord is upon thee ... to lead him by the h.

Acts 13:16: Then Paul stood up, and beckoning with his h.

Acts 19:33: Alexander beckoned with the h.,

Acts 21:3: we left it on the left h., and sailed into Syria,

Rom 8:34: who is even at the right h. of God,

Rom 13:12: The night is far spent; the day is at h.:

1 Cor 12:15: Because I am not the h., I am not of the body;

1 Cor 12:21: And the eye cannot say unto the h.

1 Cor 16:21: The salutation of me Paul with mine own h.

2 Cor 6:7: by the armor of righteousness on the right h.

2 Cor 10:16: things made ready to our h.

Gal 3:19: and it was ordained by angels in the h. of a mediator.

Gal 6:11: I have written unto you with mine own h.

Eph 1:20: and set him at his own right hand in the heavenly places,

Phil 4:5: The Lord is at h.

Col 3:1: where Christ sitteth on the right h. of God.

Col 4:18: The salutation by the h. of me Paul.

2 Thes 2:2: that the day of Christ is at h.

2 Thes 3:17: The salutation of Paul with mine own h.,

2 Tm 4:6: the time of my departure is at h.

Phlm 1:19: I Paul have written it with mine own h.,

Heb 1:3: sat down on the right h. of the Majesty on high;

Heb 1:13: Sit on my right h.,

Heb 8:1: who is set on the right h. of the throne

Heb 8:9: I took them by the h. to lead them out of the land of Egypt

Heb 10:12 sat down on the right h. of God;

Heb 12:2: and is set down at the right h. of the throne of God.

1 Pt 3:22: and is on the right h. of God;

1 Pt 4:7: the end of all things is at h.:

1 Pt 5:6: Humble yourselves therefore under the mighty h. of God,

Rv 1:3 for the time is at h.

Rv 1:16: And he had in his right h. seven stars:

Rv 1:17: he laid his right h. upon me,

Rv 1:20: thou sawest in my right h.,

Rv 2:1: the seven stars in his right h.,

Rv 5:1: And I saw in the right h. of him that sat on the throne

Rv 5:7: and took the book out of the right h. of him that sat upon the throne.

Rv 6:5: and he that sat on him had a pair of balances in his h.

Rv 8:4: ascended up before God out of the angel's h.

Rv 10:2: And he had in his h. a little book open:

Rv 10:5: upon the earth lifted up his h. to heaven,

Rv 10:8: the little book which is open in the h. of the angel

Rv 10:10: And I took the little book out of the angel's h.,

Rv 13:16: to receive a mark in their right h.,

Rv 14:9: receive his mark in his forehead, or in his h.,

Rv 14:14: and in his h. a sharp sickle.

Rv 19:2: and hath avenged the blood of his servants at her h.

Rv 20:1: and a great chain in his h.

Rv 22:10: for the time is at h.

Hands

Gen 5:29: concerning our work and toil of our h.

Gen 16:9: submit thyself under her h.

Gen 20:5: in the integrity of my heart and innocency of my h. have I done this.

Gen 24:22: for her h. of ten shekels weight of gold;

Gen 24:30: he saw the earring and bracelets upon his sister's h.,

Gen 24:47: and the bracelets upon her h.

Gen 27:16: she put the skins of the kids of the goats upon his h.,

Gen 27:22: The voice is Jacob's voice, but the hands are the h. of Esau.

Gen 27:23: because his hands were hairy, as his brother Esau's h.:

Gen 31:42: seen mine affliction and the labour of my h.,

Gen 37:21: and he delivered him out of their h.;

Gen 37:22: that he might rid him out of their h.,

Gen 39:1: bought him of the h. of the Ishmeelites,

Gen 43:22: we brought down in our h. to buy food:
Gen 49:24: his hands were made strong by the h ...
Ex 9:29: I will spread abroad my h. unto the LORD;
Ex 9:33: and spread abroad his h. unto the LORD:
Ex 15:17: O Lord, which thy h. have established.
Ex 17:12: But Moses' h. were heavy;
Ex 29:10: and his sons shall put their h. upon the head of the bullock.
Ex 29:24: And thou shalt put all in the h. of Aaron, and in the h. of his sons;
Ex 29:25: And thou shalt receive them of their h.,
Ex 30:19: For Aaron and his sons shall wash their h.
Ex 30:21: So they shall wash their h.
Ex 32:19: he cast the tables out of his h.,
Ex 35:25: And all the women that were wise hearted did spin with their h.,
Ex 40:31: And Moses and Aaron and his sons washed their h.
Lev 4:15: the elders of the congregation shall lay their h.
Lev 7:30: His own h. shall bring the offerings
Lev 8:14: Aaron and his sons laid their h. upon the head of the bullock
Lev 8:18: Aaron and his sons laid their h. upon the head of the ram.
Lev 8:24: and upon the thumbs of their right h.,
Lev 8:27: And he put all upon Aaron's h.,
Lev 8:28: And Moses took them from off their h.,
Lev 15:11: hath not rinsed his h. in water,
Lev 16:12: and his h. full of sweet incense beaten small,

Lev 24:14: and let all that heard him lay their h. upon his head
Num 5:18: and put the offering of memorial in her h.,
Num 6:19: and shall put them upon the h. of the Nazarite,
Num 8:10: the children of Israel shall put their h. upon the Levites:
Num 8:12: And the Levites shall lay their h. upon the heads of the bullocks
Num 24:10: and he smote his h. together:
Num 27:23: And he laid his h. upon him,
Deut: :25: And they took of the fruit of the land in their h.,
Deut 3:3: the LORD our God delivered into our h. Og
Deut 4:28: And there ye shall serve gods, the work of men's h.,
Deut 9:15: and the two tables of the covenant were in my two h.
Deut 9:17: cast them out of my two h.,
Deut 12:18: rejoice before the LORD thy God in all that thou puttest thine h. unto.
Deut 16:15: in all the works of thine h.,
Deut 17:7: The h. of the witnesses shall be first upon him
Deut 20:13: thy God hath delivered it into thine h.,
Deut 21:6: shall wash their h. over the heifer
Deut 21:7: Our h. have not shed this blood,
Deut 21:10: the LORD thy God hath delivered them into thine h.,
Deut 24:19: the LORD thy God may bless thee in all the work of thine h.
Deut 27:15: the work of the h. of the craftsman

Deut 31:29: to provoke him to anger through the work of your h.
Deut 33:7: let his h. be sufficient for him;
Deut 33:11: accept the work of his h.:
Deut 34:9: Moses had laid his h. upon him
Josh 2:24: the LORD hath delivered into our h. all the land;
Judg 2:14: and he delivered them into the h. of spoilers.
Judg 6:13: and delivered us into the h. of the Midianites.
Judg 7:2: are too many for me to give the Midianites into their h.,
Judg 7:11: and afterward shall thine h. be strengthened
Judg 7:19: and brake the pitchers that were in their h.
Judg 7:20: and held the lamps in their left h., and the trumpets in their right h.
Judg 8:3: God hath delivered into your h. the princes of Midian,
Judg 8:6: Are the hands of Zebah and Zalmunna now in thine h.
Judg 8:34: who had delivered them out of the h
Judg 9:16: and have done unto him according to the deserving of his h.;
Judg 10:7: and he sold them into the h. of the Philistines, and into the h. of the children of Ammon.
Judg 11:30: the children of Ammon into mine h.,
Judg 11:32 and the LORD delivered them into his h.
Judg 12:2: delivered me not out of their h.
Judg 12:3: I put my life in my h.,
Judg 13:23: received a burnt offering and a meat offering at our h.,

Judg 14:9: And he took thereof in his h.,
Judg 15:14: and his bands loosed from off his h.
Judg 16:24: Our god hath delivered into our h. our enemy,
Judg 18:10: for God hath given it into your h.;
Judg 19:27: and her h. were upon the threshold.
1 Sam 5:4: both the palms of his h. were cut off upon the threshold;
1 Sam 7:14: did Israel deliver out of the h. of the Philistines.
1 Sam 10:4: which thou shalt receive of their h.
1 Sam 11:7: the coasts of Israel by the h. of messengers
1 Sam 14:13: And Jonathan climbed up upon his h.
1 Sam 14:48: and delivered Israel out of the h. of them that spoiled them.
1 Sam 17:47: he will give you into our h.
1 Sam 21:13: and feigned himself mad in their h.,
1 Sam 30:15: nor deliver me into the h. of my master,
2 Sam 2:7: let your h. be strengthened,
2 Sam 3:34: Thy h. were not bound,
2 Sam 4:1: his h. were feeble,
2 Sam 4:12: and cut off their h. and their feet,
2 Sam 16:21: then shall the h. of all that are with thee be strong.
2 Sam 21:9: And he delivered them into the h. of the Gibeonites,
2 Sam 22:21: according to the cleanness of my h. hath he recompensed me.
2 Sam 22:35: He teacheth my h. to war;
2 Sam 23:6: because they cannot be taken with h.:

1 Kgs 8:22: and spread forth his h. toward heaven:
1 Kgs 8:38: and spread forth his h. toward this house:
1 Kgs 8:54: with his h. spread up to heaven.
1 Kgs 14:27: and committed them unto the h. of the chief of the guard,
1 Kgs 16:7: provoking him to anger with the work of his h.
2 Kgs 3:11: which poured water on the h. of Elijah.
2 Kgs 4:34: and his hands upon his h.:
2 Kgs 5:20: in not receiving at his h ...
2 Kgs 9:23: And Joram turned his h.,
2 Kgs 9:35: and the palms of her h.
2 Kgs 10:24: I have brought into your h. escape,
2 Kgs 11:12: and they clapped their h.,
2 Kgs 11:16: And they laid h. on her;
2 Kgs 12:11: into the h. of them that did the work,
2 Kgs 13:16: and Elisha put his h. upon the king's h.
2 Kgs 19:18: but the work of men's h.,
2 Kgs 22:17: to anger with all the works of their h.;
1 Chron 12:17: seeing there is no wrong in mine h.,
1 Chron 25:2: the sons of Asaph under the h. of Asaph,
1 Chron 25:3: under the h. of their father Jeduthun,
1 Chron 25:6: All these were under the h. of their father
1 Chron 29:5: all manner of work to be made by the h. of artificers.
2 Chron 6:4: who hath with his h. fulfilled
2 Chron 6:12: and spread forth his h.:

2 Chron 6:4: who hath with his h. fulfilled that which he spake ...
2 Chron 6:12: and spread forth his h.:
2 Chron 6:13: and spread forth his h. toward heaven,
2 Chron 6:29: and shall spread forth his h. in this house:
2 Chron 8:18: And Huram sent him by the h. of his servants ...
2 Chron 12:10: committed them to the h. of the chief of the guard,
2 Chron 15:7: let not your h. be weak:
2 Chron 23:15: So they laid h. on her;
2 Chron 29:23: and they laid their h. upon them:
2 Chron 32:19: which were the work of the h. of man.
2 Chron 34:25: to anger with all the works of their h.;
2 Chron 35:11: the priests sprinkled the blood from their h.,
Ezra 1:6: strengthened their h. with vessels of silver,
Ezra 4:4: Then the people of the land weakened the h. of the people of Judah,
Ezra 5:8: and prospereth in their h.
Ezra 6:22: to strengthen their h. in the work of the house of God,
Ezra 9:5: and spread out my h. unto the LORD my God.
Ezra 10:19: And they gave their h. that they would put away their wives;
Neh 2:18: So they strengthened their h. for this good work.
Neh 4:17: every one with one of his h. wrought in the work,
Neh 6:9: Their h. shall be weakened from the work,
Neh 8:6: with lifting up their h.:

Neh 9:24: and gavest them into their h.,

Neh 13:21: I will lay h. on you.

Esth 3:6: And he thought scorn to lay h. on Mordecai alone;

Esth 3:9: ten thousand talents of silver to the h. of those that have the charge

Esth 9:16: but they laid not their h. on the prey,

Job 1:10: hast blessed the work of his h.,

Job 4:3: hast strengthened the weak h.

Job 5:12: so that their h. cannot perform their enterprise.

Job 5:18: and his h. make whole.

Job 9:30: and make my h. never so clean;

Job 10:3: that thou shouldest despise the work of thine h.,

Job 10:8: Thine h. have made me

Job 11:13: and stretch out thine h. toward him;

Job 14:15: thou wilt have a desire to the work of thine h.

Job 16:11: and turned me over into the h. of the wicked.

Job 16:17: for any injustice in mine h.:

Job 17:3: who is he that will strike h. with me?

Job 17:9: and he that hath clean h. shall be stronger and stronger.

Job 20:10: and his h. shall restore their goods.

Job 22:30: and it is delivered by the pureness of thine h.

Job 27:23: Men shall clap their hands at him,

Job 30:2: Yea, whereto might the strength of their h. profit me,

Job 31:7: and if any blot hath cleaved to mine h.;

Job 34:19: they all are the work of his h.

Job 34:37: he clappeth his h. among us,

Ps 7:3: if there be iniquity in my h.;

Ps 8:6: dominion over the works of thy h.;

Ps 9:16: snared in the work of his own h.

Ps 18:20: according to the cleanness of my h ...

Ps 18:34: He teacheth my h. to war,

Ps 22:16: they pierced my h. and my feet.

Ps 24:4: He that hath clean h.,

Ps 26:6: I will wash mine h. in innocency:

Ps 26:10: In whose h. is mischief,

Ps 28:2: I lift up my h. toward thy holy oracle.

Ps 28:4: after the work of their h.;

Ps 28:5: the operation of his h.,

Ps 44:20: or stretched out our h. to a strange god;

Ps 47:1: O clap your h., all ye people;

Ps 55:20: He hath put forth his h.

Ps 58:2: ye weigh the violence of your h. in the earth.

Ps 63:4: I will lift up my h. in thy name.

Ps 68:31: Ethiopia shall soon stretch out her h. unto God.

Ps 73:13: and washed my h. in innocency.

Ps 76:5: none of the men of might have found their h.

Ps 78:72: and guided them by the skilfulness of his h.

Ps 81:6: his h. were delivered from the pots.

Ps 88:9: I have stretched out my h. unto thee.

Ps 90:17: the work of our h. establish it.

Ps 91:12: shall bear thee up in their h.,

Ps 92:4: I will triumph in the works of thy h.

Ps 95:5: and his h. formed the dry land.

Ps 98:8: Let the floods clap their h.:

Ps 102:25: the heavens are the work of thy h.

Ps 111:7: The works of his h. are verity and judgment;

Ps 115:4: the work of men's h.

Ps 115:7: They have h., but they handle not:

Ps 119:48: My h. also will I lift up unto thy commandments,

Ps 119:73: Thy h. have made me and fashioned me

Ps 125:3: lest the righteous put forth their h. unto iniquity.

Ps 128:2: For thou shalt eat the labour of thine h.:

Ps 134:2: Lift up your h. in the sanctuary,

Ps 135:15: the work of men's h.

Ps 138:8: forsake not the works of thine own h.

Ps 140:4: from the h. of the wicked;

Ps 141:2: and the lifting up of my h. as the evening sacrifice.

Ps 143:5: I muse on the work of thy h.

Ps 143:6: I stretch forth my h. unto thee:

Ps 144:1: which teacheth my h. to war,

Prov 6:10: a little folding of the h. to sleep:

Prov 6:17: h. that shed innocent blood,

Prov 12:14: the recompence of a man's h. shall be rendered unto him.

Prov 14:1: the foolish plucketh it down with her h.

Prov 17:18: A man void of understanding striketh h.,

Prov 21:25: for his h. refuse to labour.

Prov 22:26: Be not thou one of them that strike h.,

Prov 24:33: a little folding of the h. to sleep:

Prov 30:28: The spider taketh hold with her h.,
Prov 31:13: worketh willingly with her h.
Prov 31:16: with the fruit of her h. she planteth a vineyard.
Prov 31:19: She layeth her h. to the spindle,
Prov 31:20: she reacheth forth her h. to the needy.
Prov 31:31: Give her of the fruit of her h.;
Eccl 2:11: Then I looked on all the works that my h. had wrought,
Eccl 4:5: The fool foldeth his h. together,
Eccl 4:6: than both the h. full with travail
Eccl 5:6: destroy the work of thine h.?
Eccl 7:26: and her h. as bands:
Eccl 10:18: through idleness of the h. the house droppeth through.
Song 5:5: and my h. dropped with myrrh,
Song 5:14: His h. are as gold rings set with the beryl:
Song 7:1 the work of the h. of a cunning workman.
Isa 1:15: when ye spread forth your h,
Isa 2:8: they worship the work of their own h.,
Isa 3:11: for the reward of his h. shall be given him.
Isa 5:12: neither consider the operation of his h.
Isa 13:7: Therefore shall all h. be faint,
Isa 17:8: the work of his h.,
Isa 19:25: and Assyria the work of my h.,
Isa 25:11: And he shall spread forth his h. in the midst of them,
Isa 29:23: the work of mine h.,
Isa 31:7: which your own h. have made unto you for a sin.
Isa 33:15: that shaketh his h. from holding of bribes,

Isa 35:3: Strengthen ye the weak h.,
Isa 37:19: but the work of men's hands,
Isa 45:9: or thy work, He hath no h.?
Isa 45:11: and concerning the work of my h. command ye me.
Isa 45:12: even my h., have stretched out the heavens,
Isa 49:16: Behold, I have graven thee upon the palms of my h.;
Isa 55:12: and all the trees of the field shall clap their h.
Isa 59:3: For your h. are defiled with blood,
Isa 59:6: the act of violence is in their h.
Isa 60:21: the work of my h., that I may be glorified.
Isa 65:2: I have spread out my h. all the day unto a rebellious people,
Isa 65:22: mine elect shall long enjoy the work of their h.
Jer 1:16: worshipped the works of their own h.
Jer 2:37: and thine h. upon thine head:
Jer 4:31: that spreadeth her h.,
Jer 6:24: our h. wax feeble:
Jer 10:3: the work of the h. of the workman,
Jer 10:9: and of the h. of the founder:
Jer 19:7: and by the h. of them that seek their lives:
Jer 21:4: weapons of war that are in your h.,
Jer 23:14: they strengthen also the h. of evildoers,
Jer 25:6: provoke me not to anger with the works of your h.
Jer 25:7: provoke me to anger with the works of your h.
Jer 25:14: according to the works of their own h.
Jer 30:6: wherefore do I see every man with his h. on his loins,

Jer 32:30: provoked me to anger with the work of their h.,
Jer 33:13: shall the flocks pass again under the h.
Jer 38:4: for thus he weakeneth the h. of the men of war
Jer 44:8: provoke me unto wrath with the works of your h.,
Jer 47:3: for feebleness of h.;
Jer 48:37: upon all the h. shall be cuttings,
Jer 50:43: and his h. waxed feeble:
Lam 1:14: the Lord hath delivered me into their h.,
Lam 1:17: Zion spreadeth forth her h.,
Lam 2:15: All that pass by clap their h. at thee;
Lam 2:19: lift up thy h. toward him for the life
Lam 3:41: Let us lift up our heart with our h.
Lam 3:64: according to the work of their h.
Lam 4:2: the work of the h. of the potter!
Lam 4:6: and no h. stayed on her.
Lam 4:10: The h. of the pitiful women have sodden their own children
Ezek 1:8: And they had the h. of a man under their wings
Ezek 7:17: All h. shall be feeble,
Ezek 7:21: And I will give it into the h. of the strangers for a prey,
Ezek 7:27: and the h. of the people of the land shall be troubled:
Ezek 10:7: and put it into the h. of him that was clothed with linen:
Ezek 10:12: And their whole body, and their backs, and their h.,
Ezek 10:21: and the likeness of the h. of a man was under their wings.

Ezek 11:9: and deliver you into the h. of strangers,

Ezek 13:22: and strengthened the h. of the wicked,

Ezek 16:11: I put bracelets upon thy h.,

Ezek 21:7: and all h. shall be feeble,

Ezek 21:14: and smite thine h. together,

Ezek 21:17: I will also smite mine h. together,

Ezek 22:14: or can thine h. be strong,

Ezek 23:37: and blood is in their h.,

Ezek 23:42: which put bracelets upon their h.,

Ezek 23:45: because they are adulteresses, and blood is in their h.

Ezek 25:6: Because thou hast clapped thine h.,

Dan 2:34: a stone was cut out without h.,

Dan 2:45: the stone was cut out of the mountain without h.

Dan 3:15: and who is that God that shall deliver you out of my h.?

Dan 10:10: and upon the palms of my h.

Hosea 14:3: neither will we say any more to the work of our h.,

Obad 1:13: nor have laid h. on their substance in the day of their calamity;

Jonah 3:8: and from the violence that is in their h.

Micah 5:13: and thou shalt no more worship the work of thine h.

Micah 7:3: That they may do evil with both h. earnestly,

Nahum 3:19: all that hear the bruit of thee shall clap the h. over thee:

Hab 3:10: and lifted up his h. on high.

Zeph 3:16: Let not thine h. be slack.

Hag 1:11: upon all the labour of the h.

Hag 2:14: and so is every work of their h.;

Hag 2:17: with hail in all the labours of your h.;

Zech 4:9: The h. of Zerubbabel have laid the foundation of this house; his h. shall also finish it;

Zech 8:9: Let your h. be strong,

Zech 8:13: but let your h. be strong.

Zech 13:6: What are these wounds in thine h.?

Mt 4:6: in their h. they shall bear thee up,

Mt 15:2: for they wash not their h. when they eat bread.

Mt 15:20: to eat with unwashen h. defileth not a man.

Mt 17:22: The Son of man shall be betrayed into the h. of men:

Mt 18:8: rather than having two h. or two feet to be cast into everlasting fire.

Mt 18:28: and he laid h. on him, and took him by the throat,

Mt 19:13: that he should put his h. on them, and pray:

Mt 19:15: And he laid his h. on them, and departed thence.

Mt 21:46: But when they sought to lay h. on him

Mt 26:45: the Son of man is betrayed into the h. of sinners.

Mt 26:50: laid h. on Jesus, and took him.

Mt 26:67: others smote him with the palms of their h.,

Mt 27:24: and washed his h. before the multitude,

Mk 5:23: come and lay thy hands on her,

Mk 6:2: that even such mighty works are wrought by his h.?

Mk 6:5: save that he laid his h. upon a few sick folk,

Mk 7:2: with unwashen, h., they found fault.

Mk 7:3: except they wash their h. oft,

Mk 7:5: but eat bread with unwashen h.?

Mk 8:23: and put his h. upon him, he asked him if he saw ought.

Mk 8:25: After that he put his h. again upon his eyes,

Mk 9:31: The Son of man is delivered into the h. of men,

Mk 9:43: than having two h. to go into hell,

Mk 10:16: put his h. upon them, and blessed them.

Mk 14:41 the Son of man is betrayed into the h. of sinners.

Mk 14:46: And they laid their h. on him, and took him.

Mk 14:58: I will destroy this temple that is made with h.,

Mk 14:65: the servants did strike him with the palms of their h.

Mk 16:18: they shall lay h. on the sick, and they shall recover.

Lk 4:11: And in their h. they shall bear thee up,

Lk 4:40: he laid his h. on every one of them, and healed them.

Lk 6:1: rubbing them in their h.

Lk 9:44: the Son of man shall be delivered into the h. of men.

Lk 13:13: And he laid his h. on her:

Lk 20:19: the chief priests and the scribes the same hour sought to lay h. on him;

Lk 21:12: they shall lay their h. on you,

Lk 22:53: stretched forth no h. against me:

Lk 23:46: Father, into thy h. I commend my spirit:

Lk 24:7: The Son of man must be delivered into the h. of sinful men,

Lk 24:39: Behold my h. and my feet,
Lk 24:40: he shewed them his h. and his feet.
Lk 24:50: he lifted up his h., and blessed them.
Jn 7:30: but no man laid h. on him,
Jn 7:44: but no man laid h. on him.
Jn 8:20: and no man laid h. on him;
Jn 13:3: the Father had given all things into his h.,
Jn 13:9: not my feet only, but also my h. and my head.
Jn 19:3: and they smote him with their h.
Jn 20:20: he shewed unto them his h. and his side.
Jn 20:25: Except I shall see in his h. the print of the nails
Jn 20:27: behold my h.;
Jn 21:18: thou shalt stretch forth thy h.,
Acts 2:23: and by wicked h. have crucified and slain:
Acts 4:3: And they laid h. on them,
Acts 5:12: And by the h. of the apostles were many signs
Acts 5:18: And laid their h. on the apostles,
Acts 6:6: they laid their h. on them.
Acts 7:41: and rejoiced in the works of their own h.
Acts 7:48: most High dwelleth not in temples made with h.;
Acts 8:17: laid they their h. on them,
Acts 8:18: through laying on of the apostles' h. the Holy Ghost was given,
Acts 8:19: that on whomsoever I lay h., he may receive the Holy Ghost.
Acts 9:17: and putting his h. on him ...
Acts 11:30: and sent it to the elders by the h. of Barnabas and Saul.

Acts 12:1: the king stretched forth his h. to vex certain of the church.
Acts 12:7: his chains fell off from his h.
Acts 13:3: and laid their h. on them,
Acts 14:3: and granted signs and wonders to be done by their h.
Acts 17:24: dwelleth not in temples made with h.;
Acts 17:25: Neither is worshipped with men's h.,
Acts 19:6: And when Paul had laid his h. upon them,
Acts 19:11: And God wrought special miracles by the h. of Paul:
Acts 19:26: which are made with h.:
Acts 20:34: that these h. have ministered unto my necessities,
Acts 21:11: and bound his own h. and feet ... and shall deliver him into the h. of the Gentiles.
Acts 21:27: stirred up all the people, and laid h. on him,
Acts 24:7: and with great violence took him away out of our h.,
Acts 27:19: we cast out with our own h. the tackling of the ship.
Acts 28:8: and laid his h. on him, and healed him.
Acts 28:17: yet was I delivered prisoner from Jerusalem into the h. of the Romans.
Rom 10:21: I have stretched forth my h.
1 Cor 4:12: d labour, working with our own h.:
2 Cor 5:1: an house not made with h.,
2 Cor 11:33: and escaped his h.
Gal 2:9: the right h. of fellowship;
Eph 2:11: the Circumcision in the flesh made by h.;

Eph 4:28: working with his h. the thing which is good,
Col 2:11: circumcision made without h.,
1 Thes 4:11: and to work with your own h., as we commanded you;
1 Tm 2:8: lifting up holy h., without wrath and doubting.
1 Tm 4:14: with the laying on of the h. of the presbytery.
1 Tm 5:22: Lay h. suddenly on no man,
2 Tm 1:6: by the putting on of my h.
Heb 1:10: are the works of thine h.:
Heb 2:7: and didst set him over the works of thy h.:
Heb 6:2: and of laying on of h.,
Heb 9:11: not made with h.,
Heb 9:24: For Christ is not entered into the holy places made with h.,
Heb 10:31: It is a fearful thing to fall into the h. of the living God.
Heb 12:12: Wherefore lift up the h. which hang down,
Jms 4:8: Cleanse your h., ye sinners;
1Jn 1:1: and our h. have handled, of the Word of life;
Rv 7:9: clothed with white robes, and palms in their h.;
Rv 9:20: yet repented not of the works of their h.,
Rv 20:4: neither had received his mark upon their foreheads, or in their h.;

Head
Gen 3:15: it shall bruise thy h.,
Gen 24:26: the man bowed down his h.,
Gen 24:48: And I bowed down my h.,
Gen 40:13: shall Pharaoh lift up thine h.,
Gen 40:16: I had three white baskets on my h.:

Gen 40:17: out of the basket upon my h.
Gen 40:19: shall Pharaoh lift up thy h. from off thee,
Gen 40:20: he lifted up the h. of the chief butler
Gen 47:31: Israel bowed himself upon the bed's h.
Gen 48:14: laid it upon Ephraim's h., who was the younger,
Gen 48:17: remove it from Ephraim's head unto Manasseh's h.
Gen 48:18: put thy right hand upon his h.
Gen 49:26: the crown of the h of him
Ex 12:27: the people bowed the h. and worshipped.
Ex 26:24: coupled together above the h.
Ex 29:6: shalt put the mitre upon his h.,
Ex 29:7: pour it upon his h., and anoint him.
Ex 34:8: bowed his h. toward the earth, and worshipped.
Lev 8:12: anointing oil upon Aaron's h.,
Lev 13:12: hath the plague from his h. even to his foot,
Lev 13:29: a plague upon the h. or the beard;
Lev 13:30: a leprosy upon the h. or beard.
Lev 13:40: the man whose hair is fallen off his h.
Lev 13:41: hair fallen off from the part of his h.
Lev 13:42: And if there be in the bald h.,
Lev 13:43: white reddish in his bald h.,
Lev 13:44: his plague is in his h.
Lev 13:45: and his h. bare,
Lev 14:9: shave all his hair off his h ...
Lev 14:18: pour upon the h. of him ...

Lev 14:29: upon the h. of him that is to be cleansed,
Lev 19:32: Thou shalt rise up before the hoary h.,
Lev 21:5: shall not make baldness upon their h.,
Lev 21:10: shall not uncover his h.,
Lev 24:14: lay their hands upon his h.,
Num 5:18: uncover the woman's h.,
Num 6:5: no razor come upon his h.:
Num 6:7: the consecration of his God is upon his h.
Num 6:9: hath defiled the h. of his consecration;
Num 6:18: Nazarite shall shave the h ...
Num 22:31: and he bowed down his h.,
Deut 21:12: and she shall shave her h.,
Deut 28:23: thy heaven that is over thy h. shall be brass,
Deut 28:35: from the sole of thy foot unto the top of thy h.
Deut 33:16: upon the top of the h. of him
Deut 33:20: teareth the arm with the crown of the h.
Josh 2:19: his blood shall be upon his h.,
Judg 5:26: she smote off his h.,
Judg 9:53: a millstone upon Abimelech's h.,
Judg 13:5: no razor shall come on his h.:
Judg 16:13: weavest the seven locks of my h ...
Judg 16:17: not come a razor upon mine h.;
Judg 16:19: to shave off the seven locks of his h.;
Judg 16:22: Howbeit the hair of his h ...
1 Sam 1:11: there shall no razor come upon his h.
1 Sam 4:12: and with earth upon his h.
1 Sam 5:4: the h. of Dagon

1 Sam 10:1: and poured it upon his h.,
1S am 14:45: not one hair of his h. fall to the ground;
1 Sam 17:5: helmet of brass upon his h.,
1 Sam 17:38: helmet of brass upon his h.;
1 Sam 17:46: and take thine h. from thee;
1 Sam 17:51: and cut off his h. therewith.
1 Sam 17:54: David took the h. of the Philistine,
1 Sam 17:57: with the h. of the Philistine in his hand.
1 Sam 25:39: wickedness of Nabal upon his own h.,
1 Sam 28:2: thee keeper of mine h. for ever.
1 Sam 31:9: And they cut off his h.,
2 Sam 1:2: and earth upon his h.:
2 Sam 1:10: I took the crown that was upon his h.,
2 Sam 1:16: Thy blood be upon thy h.;
2 Sam 2:16: caught every one his fellow by the h.,
2 Sam 3:29: Let it rest on the h. of Joab,
2 Sam 4:7: and took his h.,
2 Sam 4:8: Behold the h. of Ish-bosheth ...
2 Sam 4:12: But they took the h. of Ish-bosheth,
2 Sam 12:30: king's crown from off his h.,
2 Sam 13:19: Tamar put ashes on her h.,
2 Sam 14:25: even to the crown of his h.
2 Sam 14:26: And when he polled his h.,
2 Sam 15:30: and had his h. covered,
2 Sam 15:32: and earth upon his h.:
2 Sam 16:9: and take off his h.
2 Sam 18:9: his h. caught hold of the oak,

2 Sam 20:21: his head shall be thrown to thee over the wall.
2 Sam 20:22: they cut off the h. of Sheba
1 Kgs 2:32: return his blood upon his own h.,
1 Kgs 2:37: thy blood shall be upon thine own h.,
1 Kgs 2:32: his blood upon his own h.,
1 Kgs 2:44: thy wickedness upon thine own h.;
1 Kgs 8:32: to bring his way upon his h.;
1 Kgs 19:6: a cruse of water at his h.
2 Kgs 2:23: Go up, thou bald head; go up, thou bald h.
2 Kgs 4:19: My head, my h.
2 Kgs 6:31: the h. of Elisha the son of Shaphat
2 Kgs 6:32: sent to take away mine h.?
2 Kgs 9:3: and pour it on his h.,
2 Kgs 9:6: he poured the oil on his h.,
2 Kgs 9:30: and tired her h.,
2 Kgs 19:21: hath shaken her h. at thee.
1 Chron 10:9: they took his h.,
1 Chron 10:10: fastened his h. in the temple of Dagon.
1 Chron 20:2: it was set upon David's h.:
2 Chron 6:23: by recompensing his way upon his own h.;
2 Chron 20:18: And Jehoshaphat bowed his h
Ezra 9:3: plucked off the hair of my h ...
Ezra 9:6: our iniquities are increased over our h.,
Neh 4:4: their reproach upon their own h.,
Esth 2:17: he set the royal crown upon her h.,
Esth 6:8: the crown royal which is set upon his h.:
Esth 6:12: and having his h. covered.

Esth 9:25: should return upon his own h.,
Job 1:20: and shaved his h.,
Job 10:15: yet will I not lift up my h.
Job 16:4: and shake mine h. at you.
Job 19:9: taken the crown from my h.
Job 20:6: and his h. reach unto the clouds;
Job 29:3: When his candle shined upon my h.,
Job 41:7: or his h. with fish spears?
Ps 3:3: and the lifter up of mine h.
Ps 7:16: His mischief shall return upon his own h.,
Ps 21:3: thou settest a crown of pure gold on his h.
Ps 22:7: they shake the h. saying,
Ps 23:5: thou anointest my h. with oil;
Ps 24:7: Lift up your h.,
Ps 27:6: now shall mine h. be lifted up
Ps 38:4: mine iniquities are gone over mine h.:
Ps 40:12: they are more than the hairs of mine h.:
Ps 44:14: a shaking of the h. among the people.
Ps 60:7: Ephraim also is the strength of mine h.;
Ps 68:21: God shall wound the h. of his enemies,
Ps 69:4: more than the hairs of mine h.:
Ps 83:2: hate thee have lifted up the h.
Ps 108:8: Ephraim also is the strength of mine h.;
Ps 110:7: therefore shall he lift up the h.
Ps 133:2: precious ointment upon the h.,
Ps 140:7: thou hast covered my h. in the day of battle.
Ps 140:9: As for the h. of those that compass me about,

Ps 141:5: which shall not break my h.:
Prov 1:9: be an ornament of grace unto thy h.,
Prov 4:9: She shall give to thine h. an ornament of grace:
Prov 10:6: Blessings are upon the h. of the just:
Prov 11:26: blessing shall be upon the h. of him that selleth it.
Prov 16:31: The hoary h. is a crown of glory,
Prov 20:29: the beauty of old men is the gray h.
Prov 25:22: thou shalt heap coals of fire upon his h.,
Eccl 2:14: The wise man's eyes are in his h.;
Eccl 9:8: let thy h. lack no ointment.
Song 2:6: His left hand is under my h.,
Song 5:2: for my h. is filled with dew,
Song 5:11: His h. is as the most fine gold,
Song 7:5: Thine h. upon thee is like Carmel, and the hair of thine h. like purple;
Song 8:3: His left hand should be under my h.,
Isa 1:5: the whole h. is sick,
Isa 1:6: From the sole of the foot even unto the h.
Isa 3:17: smite with a scab the crown of the h.
Isa 7:20: the h, and the hair of the feet:
Isa 9:14: the LORD will cut off from Israel h. and tail,
Isa 9:15: he is the h.; and the prophet that teacheth lies, he is the tail.
Isa 19:15: which the h. or tail,
Isa 28:4: And the glorious beauty, which is on the h. of the fat valley,
Isa 37:22: the daughter of Jerusalem hath shaken her h. at thee.

Isa 51:11: everlasting joy shall be upon their h.:
Isa 58:5: is it to bow down his h. as a bulrush
Isa 59:1: helmet of salvation upon his h.;
Jer 2:16: have broken the crown of thy h.
Jer 2:37: thine hands upon thine h.:
Jer 9:1: Oh that my h. were waters,
Jer 18:16: and wag his h.
Jer 23:19: it shall fall grievously upon the h. of the wicked.
Jer 30:23: with pain upon the h. of the wicked.
Jer 48:37: For every h. shall be bald,
Jer 52:31: lifted up the h. of Jehoiachin king of Judah,
Lam 2:15: and wag their h. at the daughter of Jerusalem,
Lam 3:54: Waters flowed over mine h.;
Lam 5:16: crown is fallen from our h.:
Ezek 5:1: cause it to pass upon thine h …
Ezek 8:3: took me by a lock of mine h.;
Ezek 9:10: I will recompense their way upon their h.
Ezek 10:1: was above the h. of the cherubims
Ezek 10:11: to the place whither the h. looked they followed it;
Ezek 16:12: beautiful crown upon thine h.
Ezek 16:43: thy way upon thine h.,
Ezek 17:19: will I recompense upon his own h.
Ezek 24:17: bind the tire of thine h. upon thee,
Ezek 29:18: every h. was made bald,
Ezek 33:4: his blood shall be upon his own h.

Dan 1:10: make me endanger my h. to the king.
Dan 2:28: the visions of thy h. upon thy bed, are these;
Dan 2:32: This image's h. was of fine gold,
Dan 2:38: Thou art this h. of gold.
Dan 3:27: nor was an hair of their h. singed,
Dan 4:5: the visions of my h. troubled me.
Dan 4:10: Thus were the visions of mine h. in my bed;
Dan 4:13: I saw in the visions of my h. upon my bed,
Dan 7:1: visions of his h. upon his bed:
Dan 7:9 the hair of his h. like the pure wool:
Dan 7:15: the visions of my h. troubled me.
Dan 7:20: And of the ten horns that were in his h.,
Joel 3:4: recompence upon your own h.;
Joel 3:7: recompence upon your own h.:
Amos 8:10: and baldness upon every h.;
Amos 9:1: and cut them in the h.,
Obad 1:15: return upon thine own h.
Jonah 2:5: the weeds were wrapped about my h.
Jonah 4:6: that it might be a shadow over his h.,
Jonah 4:8: the sun beat upon the h. of Jonah,
Micah 2:13: on the h. of them.
Hab 3:13: thou woundedst the h. out of the house
Zech 1:21: that no man did lift up his h.:
Zech 3:5: Let them set a fair mitre upon his h. So they set a fair mitre upon his h,
Zech 6:11: set them upon the h. of Joshua
Mt 5:36: Neither shalt thou swear by thy h.,

Mt 6:17: anoint thine h.,
Mt 8:20: hath not where to lay his h.
Mt 10:30: the very hairs of your h. are all numbered.
Mt 14:8: Give me here John Baptist's h.in a charger.
Mt 14:11: And his h. was brought in a charger,
Mt 26:7: and poured it on his h.,
Mt 27:29: they put it upon his h.,
Mt 27:30: smote him on the h.
Mt 27:37: set up over his h. his accusation written,
Mk 6:24: The h. of John the Baptist.
Mk 6:25: the h. of John the Baptist.
Mk 6:27: commanded his h. to be brought:
Mk 6:28: And brought his h. in a charger,
Mk 12:4: wounded him in the h.,
Mk 14:3: and poured it on his h.
Mk 15:17: and put it about his h.,
Mk 15:19: And they smote him on the h. with a reed
Lk 7:38: wipe them with the hairs of her h.,
Lk 7:44: and wiped them with the hairs of her h.
Lk 7:46: My h. with oil thou didst not anoint:
Lk 9:58: the Son of man hath not where to lay his h.
Lk 12:7: the very hairs of your h. are all numbered.
Lk 21:18: there shall not an hair of your h. perish.
Jn 13:9: but also my hands and my h.
Jn 19:2: and put it on his h.,
Jn 19:30: he bowed his h.,
Jn 20:7: that was about his h.,
Jn 20:12: the one at the h.,
Acts 18:18: having shorn his h. in Cenchrea:

Acts 27:34: there shall not an hair fall from the h.
Rom 12:20: thou shalt heap coals of fire on his h.
1 Cor 11:3: the h. of the woman is the man; and the h. of Christ is God.
1Cor 11:4: having his h. covered, dishonoureth his h.
1 Cor 11:5: that prayeth or prophesieth with her head uncovered dishonoureth her h.:
1 Cor 11:7: For a man indeed ought not to cover his h.,
1 Cor 11:10: have power on her h. because of the angels.
1 Cor 12:21: nor again the h. to the feet,
Col 1:18: And he is the h. of the body,
Rv 1:14: His h. and his hairs were white like wool,
Rv 10:1: a rainbow was upon his h.,
Rv 12:1: upon her h. a crown of twelve stars:
Rv 14:14: having on his h. a golden crown
Rv 19:12: on his h. were many crowns;

Heart

Gen 6:5: that every imagination of the thoughts of his h. was only evil continually.
Gen 6:6: and it grieved him at his h.
Gen 8:21: the LORD said in his h., I will not again curse the ground
Gen 17:17: said in his h., Shall a child be born unto him that is an hundred years old?
Gen 20:5: in the integrity of my h.
Gen 20:6: thou didst this in the integrity of thy h.;
Gen 24:45: And before I had done speaking in mine h.,

Gen 27:41: and Esau said in his h. ... then will I slay my brother Jacob.
Gen 42:28: and their h. failed them,
Gen 45:26: And Jacob's h. fainted, for he believed them not.
Ex 4:14: and when he seeth thee, he will be glad in his h.
Ex 4:21: but I will harden his h.,
Ex 7:3: And I will harden Pharaoh's h.,
Ex 7:13: And he hardened Pharaoh's h.,
Ex 7:14: Pharaoh's h. is hardened,
Ex 7:22: and Pharaoh's h. was hardened,
Ex 7:23: And Pharaoh turned and went into his house, neither did he set his h. to this also.
Ex 8:15: he hardened his h.,
Ex 8:19: and Pharaoh's h. was hardened,
Ex 8:32: And Pharaoh hardened his h. at this time also,
Ex 9:7: the h. of Pharaoh was hardened,
Ex 9:12: And the LORD hardened the h. of Pharaoh,
Ex 9:14: For I will at this time send all my plagues upon thine h,
Ex 9:34: and hardened his h., he and his servants.
Ex 9:35: And the h. of Pharaoh was hardened,
Ex 10:1: for I have hardened his h., and the heart of his servants,
Ex 10:20: But the LORD hardened Pharaoh's h.,
Ex 10:27: But the LORD hardened Pharaoh's h.,
Ex 11:10: the LORD hardened Pharaoh's h.,
Ex 14:4: And I will harden Pharaoh's h.,

Ex 14:5: and the h. of Pharaoh and of his servants was turned against the people,
Ex 14:8: And the LORD hardened the h. of Pharaoh
Ex 15:8: and the depths were congealed in the h. of the sea.
Ex 23:9: for ye know the h. of a stranger,
Ex 25:2: of every man that giveth it willingly with his h.
Ex 28:29: in the breastplate of judgment upon his h.,
Ex 28:30: judgment of the children of Israel upon his h.
Ex 35:5: whosoever is of a willing h.,
Ex 35:21: And they came, every one whose h. stirred him up,
Ex 35:26: And all the women whose h. stirred
Ex 35:29: whose h. made them willing to bring
Ex 35:34: And he hath put in his h. that he may teach,
Ex 35:35: Them hath he filled with wisdom of h.,
Lev 19:17: Thou shalt not hate thy brother in thine h.:
Lev 26:16that shall consume the eyes, and cause sorrow of h.:
Num 15:39: and that ye seek not after your own h.
Num 32:7: And wherefore discourage ye the h. of the children of Israel
Num 32:9: they discouraged the h. of the children of Israel,
Deut 1:28: our brethren have discouraged our h.,
Deut 2:30: and made his h. obstinate,
Deut 4:9: lest they depart from thy h. all the days of thy life:
Deut 4:29: if thou seek him with all thy h. and with all thy soul.
Deut 4:39: consider it in thine h.,

Deut 5:29: O that there were such an h. i
Deut 6:5: love the LORD thy God with all thine h.,
Deut 6:6: shall be in thine h.:
Deut 7:17: If thou shalt say in thine h.,
Deut 8:2: to know what was in thine h.,
Deut 8:5: Thou shalt also consider in thine h.,
Deut 8:14: Then thine h. be lifted up,
Deut 8:17: And thou say in thine h.,
Deut 9:4: Speak not thou in thine h.,
Deut 9:5 for the uprightness of thine h.,
Deut 10:12: serve the LORD thy God with all thy h.
Deut 10:16: Circumcise therefore the foreskin of your h.,
Deut 11:13: serve him with all your h ...
Deut 11:16: that your h. be not deceived,
Deut 11:18: lay up these my words in your h.
Deut 13:3: love the LORD your God with all your h.
Deut 15:7: thou shalt not harden thine h.,
Deut 15:9: Beware that there be not a thought in thy wicked h.,
Deut 15:10: and thine h. shall not be grieved
Deut 17:17: that his h. turn not away:
Deut 17:20: That his h. be not lifted up above his brethren,
Deut 18:21: And if thou say in thine h.,
Deut 19:6: while his h. is hot,
Deut 20:8: lest his brethren's h. faint as well as his heart.
Deut 24:15: and setteth his h. upon it:
Deut 26:16: therefore keep and do them with all thine h.,

Deut 28:28: and astonishment of h.:
Deut 28:47: and with gladness of h.,
Deut 28:65: but the LORD shall give thee there a trembling h.,
Deut 28:67: for the fear of thine h. wherewith thou shalt fear,
Deut 29:4: Yet the LORD hath not given you an h. to perceive,
Deut 29:18: whose h. turneth away this day from the LORD our God,
Deut 29:19: that he bless himself in his h.,
Deut 30:2: thy children, with all thine h.,
Deut 30:6: thy God will circumcise thine h., and the h. of thy seed, to love the LORD thy God with all thine h.,
Deut 30:10: turn unto the LORD thy God with all thine h.,
Deut 30:14: and in thy h., that thou mayest do it.
Deut 30:17: But if thine h. turn away,
Josh 5:1: until we were passed over, that their h. melted,
Josh 14:7: and I brought him word again as it was in mine h.
Josh 14:8: made the h. of the people melt:
Josh 22:5: to serve him with all your h.
Josh 24:23: incline your heart unto the LORD God of Israel.
Judg 5:9: My h. is toward the governors of Israel,
Judg 5:15: For the divisions of Reuben there were great thoughts of h.
Judg 5:16: For the divisions of Reuben there were great searchings of h.
Judg 16:15: when thine h. is not with me?

Judg 16:17: That he told her all his h.,
Judg 16:18: And when Delilah saw that he had told her all his h.,
Judg 18:20: And the priest's h. was glad,
Judg 19:5: Comfort thine h. with a morsel of bread,
Judg 19:6: and let thine h. be merry.
Judg 19:8: Comfort thine h., I pray thee.
Judg 19:9: that thine h. may be merry;
Ruth 3:7: and his h. was merry,
1 Sam 1:8: and why is thy h. grieved?
1 Sam 1:13: Now Hannah, she spake in her h.;
1 Sam 2:1: My h. rejoiceth in the LORD,
1Sam 2:33: and to grieve thine h.:
1 Sam 2:35: according to that which is in mine h.
1Sam 4:13: for his h. trembled for the ark of God.
1 Sam 9:19: and will tell thee all that is in thine h.
1 Sam 10:9: God gave him another h.:
1 Sam 12:20: but serve the LORD with all your h.;
1 Sam 12:24: and serve him in truth with all your h.:
1 Sam 13:14: the LORD hath sought him a man after his own h.,
1 Sam 14:7: Do all that is in thine h.:
1 Sam 16:7: the LORD looketh on the h.
1 Sam 17:28: the naughtiness of thine h.;
1 Sam 17:32: Let no man's h. fail because of him;
1 Sam 21:12: And David laid up these words in his h.,
1 Sam 24:5: that David's h. smote him

1 Sam 25:31: nor offence of h. unto my lord,

1 Sam 25:36: and Nabal's h. was merry within him,

1 Sam 25:37: that his h. died within him,

1 Sam 27:1: And David said in his h.,

1 Sam 28:5: and his heart greatly trembled.

2 Sam 3:21: that thou mayest reign over all that thine h. desireth.

2 Sam 6:16: and she despised him in her h.

2 Sam 7:3: do all that is in thine h.;

2 Sam 7:21: according to thine own h.,

2 Sam 7:27: therefore hath thy servant found in his h. to pray this prayer ...

2 Sam 3:21: that thou mayest reign over all that thine h. desireth.

2 Sam 6:16: she despised him in her h.

2 Sam 7:3: do all that is in thine h.;

2 Sam 7:21 according to thine own h.,

2 Sam 7:27: therefore hath thy servant found in his h.to pray

2 Sam 13:28: Mark ye now when Amnon's h. is merry with wine,

2 Sam 13:33: take the thing to his h.,

2 Sam 14:1: the king's h. was toward Absalom.

2 Sam 17:10: whose h. is as the heart of a lion,

2 Sam 18:14: Tand thrust them through the h. of Absalom,

2 Sam 19:14: And he bowed the h. of all the men of Judah,

2 Sam 19:19: that the king should take it to his h.

2 Sam 24:10: And David's h. smote him after that he had numbered the people.

1 Kgs 2:4: to walk before me in truth with all their h.

1 Kgs 2:44: Thou knowest all the wickedness which thine h.

1 Kgs 3:6: and in uprightness of h. with thee

1 Kgs 3:9: Give therefore thy servant an understanding h.

1 Kgs 3:12: thee a wise and an understanding h.;

1 Kgs 4:29: and largeness of h.,

1 Kgs 8:17: And it was in the h. of David

1 Kgs 8:18: Whereas it was in thine h. to build

1 Kgs 8:23: walk before thee with all their h.:

1 Kgs 8:38: the plague of his own h.,

1 Kgs 8:39: whose h. thou knowest;

1 Kgs 8:48: And so return unto thee with all their h.:

1 Kgs 8:61: Let your h. therefore be perfect with the LORD ...

1 Kgs 8:66: and glad of h. for all the goodness that the LORD had ...

1 Kgs 9:3: mine h. shall be there perpetually.

1 Kgs 9:4: in integrity of h.,

1 Kgs 10:2: she communed with him of all that was in her h.

1 Kgs 10:24: which God had put in his h.

1 Kgs 11:2: for surely they will turn away your h. after their gods:

1 Kgs 11:3: his wives turned away his h.

1 Kgs 11:4: that his wives turned away his h. after other gods:

1 Kgs 11:9: because his h. was turned from the LORD

1 Kgs 12:26: Jeroboam said in his h.,

1 Kgs 12:27: then shall the h. of this people turn again unto their lord,

1 Kgs 12:33: even in the month which he had devised of his own h.;

1 Kgs 14:8: and who followed me with all his h.,

1 Kgs 15:3: and his h. was not perfect with the LORD

1 Kgs 15:14: nevertheless Asa's h. was perfect with the LORD

1 Kgs 18:37: that thou hast turned their h. back again.

1 Kgs 21:7: and let thine h. be merry:

2 Kgs 5:26: Went not mine h. with thee,

2 Kgs 6:11: the h. of the king of Syria was sore troubled

2 Kgs 9:24:t he arrow went out at his h.,

2 Kgs 10:15: Is thine h. right, as my h. is with thy h.?

2 Kgs 10:30: according to all that was in mine h.,

2 Kgs 10:31: walk in the law of the LORD God of Israel with all his h.:

2 Kgs 12:4: all the money that cometh into any man's h.

2 Kgs 14:10: thine h. hath lifted thee up:

2 Kgs 20:3: walked before thee in truth and with a perfect h.,

2 Kgs 22:19: Because thine h. was tender,

2 Kgs 23:3: and his statutes with all their h. and all their soul,

2 Kgs 23:25: that turned to the LORD with all his h.,

1 Chron 12:17: mine h. shall be knit unto you:

1 Chron 12:33: they were not of double h.

1 Chron 12:38: came with a perfect h. to Hebron,

1 Chron 15:29: and she despised him in her h.

1 Chron 16:10: let the h. of them rejoice that seek the LORD.

1 Chron 17:2: Do all that is in thine h.;

1 Chron 17:19: and according to thine own h.,
1 Chron 17:25: therefore thy servant hath found in his h. to pray before thee.
1 Chron 22:19: Now set your h. and your soul to seek the LORD
1 Chron 28:2: I had in mine h. to build an house
1 Chron 28:9: serve him with a perfect h.
1 Chron 29:9: because with perfect h. they offered willingly to the LORD:
1 Chron 29:17: that thou triest the h.,
1 Chron 29:18: the thoughts of the h. of thy people,
1 Chron 29:19: And give unto Solomon my son a perfect h.,
2 Chron 1:11: Because this was in thine h.,
2 Chron 6:7: Now it was in the h. of David my father
2 Chron 6:8: as it was in thine h. to build an house ... thou didst well in that it was in thine h.:
2 Chron 6:30: whose h. thou knowest;
2 Chron 6:38: If they return to thee with all their h.
2 Chron 7:10: glad and merry in h. for the goodness
2 Chron 7:11: and all that came into Solomon's h.
2 Chron 7:16: and mine h. shall be there perpetually.
2 Chron 9:1: she communed with him of all that was in her h.
2 Chron 9:23: that God had put in his h.
2 Chron 12:14: he prepared not his h. to seek the LORD.
2 Chron 15:12: with all their h. and with all their soul;
2 Chron 15:15: for they had sworn with all their h.,
2 Chron 15:17: the h. of Asa was perfect all his days.

2 Chron 16:9: behalf of them whose h. is perfect toward him.
2 Chron 17:6: And his h. was lifted up
2 Chron 19:3: and hast prepared thine h. to seek God.
2 Chron 19:9: and with a perfect h.
2 Chron 22:9: who sought the LORD with all his h.
2 Chron 25:2: but not with a perfect h.
2 Chron 25:19: thine h. lifteth thee up to boast:
2 Chron 26:16: his h. was lifted up to his destruction:
2 Chron 29:10: Now it is in mine h. to make a covenant
2 Chron 29:31: as many as were of a free h. burnt offerings.
2 Chron 29:34: for the Levites were more upright in h.
2 Chron 30:12: give them one h. to do the commandment
2 Chron 30:19: That prepareth his h. to seek God,
2 Chron 31:21: he did it with all his h.,
2 Chron 32:25: for his h. was lifted up:
2 Chron 32:26: Hezekiah humbled himself for the pride of his h.,
2 Chron 32:31: that he might know all that was in his h.
2 Chron 34:27: Because thine h. was tender
2 Chron 34:31: with all his h.,
2 Chron 36:13: and hardened his h. from turning unto the LORD ...
Ezra 6:22: and turned the heart of the king of Assyria
Ezra 7:10: For Ezra had prepared his h.
Ezra 7:27: as this in the king's h.,
Neh 2:2: is nothing else but sorrow of h.

Neh 2:12: God had put in my h. to do at Jerusalem:
Neh 6:8: but thou feignest them out of thine own h.
Neh 7:5: And my God put into mine h.
Neh 9:8: And foundest his h. faithful before thee,
Esth 1:10: when the h. of the king was merry with wine,
Esth 5:9: joyful and with a glad h.:
Esth 6:6: Now Haman thought in his h.,
Esth 7:5: that durst presume in his h. to do so?
Job 7:17: and that thou shouldest set thine h. upon him?
Job 8:10: utter words out of their h.?
Job 9:4: He is wise in h.,
Job 10:13: And these things hast thou hid in thine h.:
Job 11:13: If thou prepare thine h.,
Job 12:24: He taketh away the h. of the chief of the people
Job 15:12: Why doth thine h. carry thee away?
Job 17:4: For thou hast hid their h. from understanding:
Job 17:11: even the thoughts of my h.
Job 22:22: lay up his words in thine h.
Job 23:16: For God maketh my h. soft,
Job 27:6: my h. shall not reproach me so long as I live.
Ps 4:4: commune with your own h. upon your bed,
Ps 4:7: Thou hast put gladness in my h.,
Ps 7:10: which saveth the upright in h.
Ps 9:1: O LORD, with my whole h.;
Ps 10:3: wicked boasteth of his h. desire,
Ps 10:6: He hath said in his h.,

Ps 10:11: He hath said in his h.,

Ps 10:13: he hath said in his h.,

Ps 10:17: thou wilt prepare their h.,

Ps 11:2: that they may privily shoot at the upright in h.

Ps 12:2: and with a double h. do they speak.

Ps 13:2: having sorrow in my h. daily?

Ps 13:5: my h. shall rejoice in thy salvation.

Ps 14:1: The fool hath said in his h.,

Ps 15:2: and speaketh the truth in his h.

Ps 16:9: Therefore my h. is glad, and my glory rejoiceth:

Ps 17:3: Thou has proved mine h.;

Ps 19:8: rejoicing the h.:

Ps 19:14: and the meditation of my h.,

Ps 20:4: Grant thee according to thine own h.,

Ps 21:2: Thou hast given him his h.'s desire,

Ps 22:14my h. is like wax;

Ps 22:26: your h. shall live for ever.

Ps 24:4: and a pure h.;

Ps 25:17: The troubles of my h. are enlarged:

Ps 26:2: try my reins and my h.

Ps 27:3: my h. shall not fear:

Ps 27:8: my h. said unto thee,

Ps 27:14: he shall strengthen thine h.:

Ps 28:7: my h. trusted in him ... therefore my h. greatly rejoiceth;

Ps 31:24: he shall strengthen your h.,

Ps 32:11: all ye that are upright in h.

Ps 33:11: the thoughts of his h. to all generations.

Ps 33:21: For our h. shall rejoice in him,

Ps 34:18: The LORD is nigh unto them that are of a broken h.;

Ps 36:1: The transgression of the wicked saith within my h.,

Ps 36:10: and thy righteousness to the upright in h.

Ps 37:4: he shall give thee the desires of thine h.

Ps 37:15: Their sword shall enter into their own h.,

Ps 37:31: The law of his God is in his h.;

Ps 38:8: I have roared by reason of the disquietness of my h.

Ps 38:10: My h. panteth,

Ps 39:3: My h. was hot within me,

Ps 40:8: thy law is within my h.

Ps 40:10: I have not hid thy righteousness within my h.;

Ps 40:12: therefore my h. faileth me.

Ps 41:6: his h. gathereth iniquity to itself;

Ps 44:18: Our h. is not turned back,

Ps 44:21: he knoweth the secrets of the h.

Ps 45:1: My h. is inditing a good matter:

Ps 45:5: Thine arrows are sharp in the h. of the king's enemies;

Ps 49:3: and the meditation of my h. shall be of understanding.

Ps 51:10: Create in me a clean h.,

Ps 51:17: a broken and a contrite h.,

Ps 53:1: The fool hath said in his h.,

Ps 55:4: My h. is sore pained within me:

Ps 55:21: but war was in his h.:

Ps 57:7: My h. is fixed,

Ps 58:2: in h, ye work wickedness;

Ps 61:2: when my h. is overwhelmed:

Ps 62:8: pour out your h. before him:

Ps 62:10: if riches increase, set not your h. upon them.

Ps 64:6: and the h. is deep.

Ps 64:10: all the upright in h. shall glory.

Ps 66:18: If I regard iniquity in my h.,

Ps 69:20: Reproach hath broken my h.;

Ps 69:32: and your h. shall live that seek God.

Ps 73:1: even to such as are of a clean h.

Ps 73:7: they have more than h. could wish.

Ps 73:13: I have cleansed my h. in vain

Ps 73:21: Thus my h. was grieved,

Ps 73:26: My flesh and my h. faileth:

Ps 77:6: I commune with mine own h.:

Ps 78:8: a generation that set not their h. aright,

Ps 78:18: they tempted God in their h ...

Ps 78:37: For their h. was not right ...

Ps 78:72: according to the integrity of his h.;

Ps 84:2: my h. and my flesh crieth out for the living God.

Ps 84:5: in whose h. are the ways of them.

Ps 86:11: unite my h. to fear thy name.

Ps 86:12: with all my h.:

Ps 94:15: and all the upright in h. shall follow it.

Ps 95:8: Harden not your h.,

Ps 95:10: a people that do err in their h.,

Ps 97:11: gladness for the upright in h.

Ps 101:2: I will walk within my house with a perfect h.

Ps 101:4: A froward h. shall depart from me:

Ps 101:5: and a proud h. will not I suffer.

Ps 102:4: My h. is smitten,

Ps 104:15:and bread which strengtheneth man's h.

Ps 105:3: let the h. of them rejoice that seek the LORD.

Ps 105:25: He turned their h. to hate his people,

Ps 107:12: Therefore he brought down their h. with labour;

Ps 108:1: O God, my h. is fixed;

Ps 109:16: that he might even slay the broken in h.

Ps 109:22: my h. is wounded within me.

Ps 111:1: I will praise the LORD with my whole h.,

Ps 112:7: his h. is fixed, trusting in the LORD.

Ps 112:8: His h. is established,

Ps 119:2: that seek him with the whole h.

Ps 119:7: I will praise thee with uprightness of h.,

Ps 119:10: With my whole h. have I sought thee:

Ps 119:11: Thy word have I hid in mine h.,

Ps 119:32: when thou shalt enlarge my h.

Ps 119:34: I shall observe it with my whole h.

Ps 119:36: Incline my h. unto thy testimonies,

Ps 119:58: I intreated thy favour with my whole h.:

Ps 119:69: but I will keep thy precepts with my whole h.

Ps 119:70: Their h. is as fat as grease;

Ps 119:80: Let my h. be sound in thy statutes; that I be not ashamed.

Ps 119:111: for they are the rejoicing of my h.

Ps 119:112: I have inclined mine h. to perform thy statutes alway,

Ps 119:145: I cried with my whole h.;

Ps 119:161: but my h. standeth in awe of thy word.

Ps 131:1: LORD, my h. is not haughty,

Ps 138:1: praise thee with my whole h.:

Ps 139:23: Search me, O God, and know

Ps 140:2: Which imagine mischiefs in their h.;

Ps 141:4: Incline not my h. to any evil thing,

Ps 143:4: my h. within me is desolate.

Ps 147:3: He healeth the broken in h.,

Prov 2:2: and apply thine h. to understanding;

Prov 2:10: When wisdom entereth into thine h.,

Prov 3:1: but let thine h. keep my commandments:

Prov 3:3: write them upon the table of thine h.:

Prov 3:5: Trust in the LORD with all thine h.;

Prov 4:4: Let thine h. retain my words:

Prov 4:21: keep them in the midst of thine h.

Prov 4:23: Keep thy h. with all diligence;

Prov 5:12: and my h. despised reproof;

Prov 6:14: Frowardness is in his h.,

Prov 6:18: An h. that deviseth wicked imaginations,

Prov 6:21: Bind them continually upon thine h.,

Prov 6:25: Lust not after her beauty in thine h.;

Prov 7:3: write them upon the table of thine h.

Prov 7:10: and subtil of h.

Prov 7:25: Let not thine h. decline to her ways,

Prov 8:5: be ye of an understanding h.

Prov 10:8: The wise in h. will receive commandments:

Prov 10:20: the h. of the wicked is little worth.

Prov 11:20: They that are of a froward h. are abomination to the LORD:

Prov 11:29: and the fool shall be servant to the wise of h.

Prov 12:8: but he that is of a perverse h. shall be despised.

Prov 12:20: Deceit is in the h. of them that imagine evil:

Prov 12:23: but the h. of fools proclaimeth foolishness.

Prov 12:25: Heaviness in the h. of man maketh it stoop:

Prov 13:12: Hope deferred maketh the h. sick:

Prov 14:10: The h. knoweth his own bitterness;

Prov 14:13: Even in laughter the h. is sorrowful;

Prov 14:14: The backslider in h. shall be filled with his own ways:

Prov 14:30: A sound h. is the life of the flesh:

Prov 14:33: Wisdom resteth in the h. of him that hath understanding:

Prov 15:7: but the h. of the foolish doeth not so.

Prov 15:13: A merry h. maketh a cheerful countenance: but by sorrow of the h. the spirit is broken.

Prov 15:14: The h. of him that hath understanding seeketh knowledge:

Prov 15:15: he that is of a merry h. hath a continual feast.

Prov 15:28: The h. of the righteous studieth to answer:

Prov 15:30: The light of the eyes rejoiceth the h.:

Prov 16:1: The preparations of the heart in man,

Prov 16:5: Every one that is proud in h. is an abomination to the LORD:

Prov 16:9: A man's h. deviseth his way

Prov 16:21: The wise in h. shall be called prudent:

Prov 16:23: The h. of the wise teacheth his mouth,

Prov 17:16: seeing he hath no h. to it?

Prov 17:20: He that hath a froward h. findeth no good:

Prov 17:22: A merry h. doeth good like a medicine:

Prov 18:2: but that his h. may discover itself.

Prov 18:12: Before destruction the h. of man is haughty,

Prov 18:15: The h. of the prudent getteth knowledge;

Prov 19:3: and his h. fretteth against the LORD.

Prov 19:21: There are many devices in a man's h.;

Prov 20:5: Counsel in the h. of man is like deep water;

Prov 20:9: I have made my h. clean,

Prov 21:1: The king's h. is in the hand of the LORD, as the rivers of water:

Prov 21:4: An high look, and a proud h.,

Prov 22:11: He that loveth pureness of h.,

Prov 22:15: Foolishness is bound in the h. of a child; from him.

Prov 22:17: and apply thine h. unto my knowledge.

Prov 23:7: but his h. is not with thee.

Prov 23:12: Apply thine h. unto instruction

Prov 23:15: My son, if thine h. be wise,

Prov 23:17: Let not thine h. envy sinners:

Prov 23:19: and guide thine h. in the way.

Prov 23:26: My son, give me thine h.,

Prov 23:33: and thine heart shall utter perverse things.

Prov 24:2: For their h. studieth destruction,

Prov 24:12: doth not he that pondereth the h. consider it?

Prov 24:17: and let not thine h. be glad when he stumbleth:

Prov 25:3: and the h. of kings is unsearchable.

Prov 25:20: singeth songs to an heavy h.

Prov 26:23: Burning lips and a wicked h. are like a potsherd covered with silver dross.

Prov 26:25: for there are seven abominations in his h.

Prov 27:9: Ointment and perfume rejoice the h.:

Prov 27:11: and make my h. glad,

Prov 27:19: so the heart of man to man.

Prov 28:14: he that hardeneth his h. shall fall into mischief.

Prov 28:25: He that is of a proud heart stirreth up strife:

Prov 28:26: He that trusteth in his own h. is a fool:

Prov 31:11: The h. of her husband doth safely trust in her

Eccl 1:13: And I gave my h. to seek and search out by wisdom

Eccl 1:16: I communed with mine own h., ... my h. had great experience of wisdom

Eccl 1:17: And I gave my h. to know wisdom,

Eccl 2:1: I said in mine h., Go to now,

Eccl 2:3: I sought in mine h. to give myself unto wine,

Eccl 2:10: I withheld not my h.

Eccl 2:15: Then said I in my h., As it happeneth to the fool, ... Then I said in my h., that this also is vanity.

Eccl 2:20: Therefore I went about to cause my h. to despair.

Eccl 2:22: For what hath man of all his labour, and of the vexation of his h.,

Eccl 2:23: yea, his h. taketh not rest in the night.

Eccl 3:11: hath set the world in their h.,

Eccl 3:17: I said in mine h.,

Eccl 3:18: I said in mine h. concerning the estate of the sons of men,

Eccl 5:2: let not thine h. be hasty to utter any thing before God:

Eccl 5:20: because God answereth him in the joy of his h.

Eccl 7:2: the living will lay it to his h.

Eccl 7:3: for by the sadness of the countenance the h. is made better.

Eccl 7:4: The h. of the wise is in the house of mourning

Eccl 7:7: and a gift destroyeth the h.

Eccl 7:22: thine own h. knoweth that thou thyself likewise hast cursed others.

Eccl 7:25: I applied mine h. to know, and to search, and to seek out wisdom,

Eccl 7:26: whose h. is snares and nets,

Eccl 8:5: a wise man's h. discerneth both time and judgment.

Eccl 8:9: and applied my h. unto every work that is done under the sun:

Song 3:11: day of the gladness of his h.

Song 4:9: Thou hast ravished my h., ... my h. with one of thine eyes,

Song 5:2: I sleep, but my h. waketh:

Song 8:6: Set me as a seal upon thine h

Isa 1:5: and the whole h. faint.
Isa 6:10: Make the h. his
people fat,
Isa 7:2: and the h. of his
people,
Isa 9:9: pride and stoutness
of h.,
Isa 10:7: it is in his h. to
destroy
Isa 10:12: the fruit of the stout
h. of the king of Assyria,
Isa 13:7: every man's h. shall
melt:
Isa 14:13: For thou hast said
in thine h.,
Isa 15:5: My h. shall cry out
for Moab;
Isa 19:1: the h. of Egypt shall
melt
Isa 21:4: My h. panted,
Isa 29:13: but have removed
their h. far from me,
Isa 30:29: and gladness of h.,
Isa 32:4: The h. also of the
rash
Isa 32:6: and his h. will work
iniquity,
Isa 33:18: Thine h. shall
meditate terror.
Isa 35:4: to them that are of a
fearful h.,
Isa 38:3: in truth and with a
perfect h.,
Isa 42:25: yet he laid it not
to h.
Isa 44:19: none considereth
in his h.,
Isa 44:20: a deceived h.
turned him aside,
Isa 47:7: so that thou didst not
lay these things to thy h.,
Isa 47:8: that sayest in
thine h.,
Isa 47:10: thou hast said in
thine h., I am,
Isa 49:21: Then shalt thou say
in thine h.,
Isa 51:7: the people in whose h.
is my law;
Isa 57:1, and no man layeth
it to h.:
Isa 57:11: nor laid it to thy h.?

Isa 57:15: and to revive the h.
of the contrite ones.
Isa 57:17: and he went on
frowardly in the way of his h.
Isa 59:13: from the h. words of
falsehood.
Isa 60:5: and thine h. shall
fear,
Isa 63:4: day of vengeance is
in mine h.,
Isa 63:17: hardened our h.
from thy fear?
Isa 65:14: servants shall sing
for joy of h.,
Isa 66:14: And when ye see
this, your h. shall rejoice,
Jer :10: with her whole h.,
Jer 3:15: And I will give you
pastors according to mine h.,
Jer 3:17: the imagination of
their evil h.
Jer 4:4: take away the foreskins
of your h.,
Jer 4:9: and the h. of the
princes;
Jer 4:14: wash thine h. from
wickedness,
Jer 4:18: because it reacheth
unto thine h.
Jer 4:19: I am pained at my
very h.; my h. maketh a noise
in me;
Jer 5:23: a revolting and a
rebellious h.;
Jer 5:24: Neither say they in
their h.,
Jer 7:24: the imagination of
their evil h.,
Jer 7:31: neither came it into
my h.
Jer 8:18: my h. is faint in me.
Jer 9:8: but in h. he layeth his
wait.
Jer 9:14: walked after the
imagination of their own h.,
Jer 9:26: are uncircumcised
in the h.
Jer 11:8: the imagination of
their evil h.:
Jer 11:20: that triest the reins
and the h.,

Jer 12:3: and tried mine h.
toward thee
Jer 12:11: because no man
layeth it to h.
Jer 13:10: which walk in the
imagination of their h.,
Jer 13:22: And if thou say in
thine h.,
Jer 14:14: and the d eceit of
their h.
Jer 15:16: joy and rejoicing of
mine h.:
Jer 16:12: the imagination of
his evil h.,
Jer 17:1: graven upon the table
of their h.,
Jer 17:5: h. departeth from the
LORD.
Jer 17:9: The h. is deceitful
above all things,
Jer 17:10: I the LORD search
the h.,
Jer 18:12: we will every one do
the imagination of his evil h.
Jer 20:9: But his word was in
mine h. as a burning fire
Jer 20:12: and seest the reins
and the h.,
Jer 22:17: thine h. are not but
for thy covetousness,
Jer 23:9: Mine h. within me is
broken
Jer 23:16: speak a vision of
their own h.,
Jer 23:17: the imagination of
his own h.,
Jer 23:20: till he have
performed the thoughts of
his h.:
Jer 23:26: How long shall this
be in the h. of the prophets
Jer 24:7: give them an h. to
know me, ... return unto me
with their whole h.
Jer 29:13: when ye shall search
for me with all your h.
Jer 30:21: for who is this that
engaged his h. to approach
unto me?
Jer 30:24: performed the
intents of his h.:

Jer 31:21: set thine h. toward the highway,
Jer 32:39: And I will give them one h.,
Jer 32:41: will plant them in this land assuredly with my whole h.
Jer 48:29: and the haughtiness of his h.
Jer 48:31: mine h. shall mourn for the men of Kir-heres.
Jer 48:36: Therefore mine h. shall sound for Moab
Jer 49:16: and the pride of thine h.,
Jer 49:22: shall the h. of the mighty men of Edom be as the h. of a woman in her pangs.
Jer 51:46: And lest your h. faint,
Lam 1:20: mine h. is turned within me;
Lam 1:22: for my sighs are many, and my h. is faint.
Lam 2:18: Their h. cried unto the Lord;
Lam 2:19: pour out thine h. like water
Lam 3:41: Let us lift up our h. with our hands
Lam 3:51: Mine eye affecteth mine h.
Lam 3:65: Give them sorrow of h.,
Lam 5:15: The joy of our h. is ceased;
Lam 5:17: For this our h. is faint;
Ezek3:10: unto thee receive in thine h.,
Ezek 6:9: because I am broken with their whorish h.,
Ezek 11:19: And I will give them one h.,
Ezek 11:21: But as for them whose h. walketh after the h. of their detestable things
Ezek 13:17: which prophesy out of their own h.;
Ezek 13:22: Because with lies ye have made the h. of the righteous sad,

Ezek 14:3: these men have set up their idols in their h.,
Ezek 14:4: Every man of the house of Israel that setteth up his idols in his h.,
Ezek 14:5: That I may take the house of Israel in their own h.,
Ezek 14:7: setteth up his idols in his h.,
Ezek 16:30: How weak is thine h.,
Ezek 18:31: make you a new h.
Ezek 20:16: for their h. went after their idols.
Ezek 21:7: and every h. shall melt,
Ezek 21:15: that their h. may faint,
Ezek 22:14: Can thine h. endure,
Ezek 25:6: and rejoiced in h …
Ezek 25:15: and have taken vengeance with a despiteful h.,
Ezek 27:31: weep for thee with bitterness of h
Ezek 28:2: though thou set thine heart as the h. of God:
Ezek 28:5: thine h. is lifted up
Ezek 28:6: Because thou hast set thine h. as the heart of God;
Ezek 28:17: Thine h. was lifted up because of thy beauty
Ezek 31:10: his h. is lifted up in his height;
Ezek 33:31: but their h. goeth after their covetousness.
Ezek 36:5: the joy of all their h.,
Ezek 36:26: A new h. also will I give you … and I will give you an h. of flesh.
Ezek 40:4: and set thine h. upon all that I shall shew thee
Ezek 44:7: uncircumcised in h., and uncircumcised in flesh,
Ezek 44:9: uncircumcised in h.,
Dan 1:8: But Daniel purposed in his h.
Dan 2:30: that thou mightest know the thoughts of thy h.

Dan 4:16: Let his h. be changed from man's,
Dan 5:20: But when his h. was lifted up,
Dan 5:21: and his h. was made like the beasts,
Dan 5:22: hast not humbled thine h.,
Dan 6:14: and set his h. on Daniel to deliver him:
Dan 7:4: and a man's h. was given to it.
Dan 7:28: but I kept the matter in my h.
Dan 8:25: shall magnify himself in his h.,
Dan 10:12: set thine h. to understand,
Dan 11:12: his h. shall be lifted up;
Dan 11:28: his h. shall be against the holy covenant;
Hosea 4:8: and they set their h. on their iniquity.
Hosea 4:11: Whoredom and wine and new wine take away the h.
Hosea 7:6: they have made ready their h. like an oven,
Hosea 7:11: Ephraim also is like a silly dove without h.:
Hosea 7:14: they have not cried unto me with their h.,
Hosea 10:2: Their h. is divided;
Hosea 11:8: mine h. is turned within me,
Hosea 13:6: their h. was exalted;
Hosea 13:8: will rend the caul of their h.,
Joel 2:12: even to me with all your h.,
Joel 2:13: And rend your heart,
Obad 1:3: The pride of thine h. hath deceived thee … saith in his h.,
Nahum 2:10 and the h. melteth,
Zeph 1:12: that say in their h.,
Zeph 2:15: that said in her h.,

Zeph 3:14: rejoice with all the h.,

Zech 7:10: let none of you imagine evil against his brother in your h.

Zech 10:7: their h. shall rejoice in the LORD.

Zech 12:5: the governors of Judah shall say in their h.,

Mal 2:2: and if ye will not lay it to h. because ye do not lay it to h.

Mal 4:6: he shall turn the h. of the fathers to the children, and the h. of the children to their fathers,

Mt 5:8: Blessed are the pure in h.:

Mt 5:28: hath committed adultery with her already in his h.

Mt 6:21: there will your h. be also.

Mt 11:29: for I am meek and lowly in h.:

Mt 12:34: for out of the abundance of the h. the mouth speaketh.

Mt 12:35: A good man out of the good treasure of the h. bringeth forth good things:

Mt 12:40: shall the Son of man be three days and three nights in the h. of the earth.

Mt 13:15: For this people's h. is waxed gross ... and should understand with their h.,

Mt 13:19: and catcheth away that which was sown in his h.

Mt 15:8: but their h. is far from me.

Mt 15:18: those things which proceed out of the mouth come forth from the h.;

Mt 15:19: For out of the h. proceed evil thoughts,

Mt 22:37: love the Lord thy God with all thy h.,

Mt 24:48: evil servant shall say in his h.

Mk 6:52: for their h. was hardened.

Mk 7:6: but their h. is far from me.

Mk 7:19: it entereth not into his h.,

Mk 7:21: For from within, out of the h.

Mk 8:17: have ye your h. yet hardened?

Mk 10:5: For the hardness of your h. he wrote you this precept.

Mk 11:23: and shall not doubt in his h., but shall believe

Mk 12:30: love the Lord thy God with all thy h.,

Mk 12:33: to love him with all the h.,

Mk 16:14: with their unbelief and hardness of h.,

Lk 2:19: and pondered them in her h.

Lk 2:51: but his mother kept all these sayings in her h.

Lk 6:45: treasure of his h. bringeth forth that which is good;

Lk 8:15: which in an honest and good h.,

Lk 9:47: perceiving the thought of their h.,

Lk 10:27: love the Lord thy God with all thy h.,

Lk 12:34: there will your h. be also.

Lk 12:45: if that servant say in his h.,

Lk 24:25: O fools, and slow of h.

Lk 24:32: Did not our h. burn within us,

Jn 12:40: hardened their h.;

Jn 13:2: now put into the h. of Judas Iscariot,

Jn 14:1: Let not your h. be troubled:

Jn 14:27: Let not your h. be troubled,

Jn 16:6: sorrow hath filled your h.

Jn 16:22: and your h. shall rejoice,

Acts 2:26: Therefore did my h. rejoice,

Acts 2:37: they were pricked in their h.,

Acts 2:46: gladness and singleness of h.,

Acts 4:32: were of one h. and of one soul:

Acts 5:3: why hath Satan filled thine h.

Acts 5:4: why hast thou conceived this thing in thine h.?

Acts 5:33: they were cut to the h.,

Acts 7:23: it came into his h. to visit his brethren

Acts 7:51: Ye stiffnecked and uncircumcised in h.

Acts 7:54: they were cut to the h.,

Acts 8:21: for thy h. is not right in the sight of God.

Acts 8:22: the thought of thine h. may be forgiven thee.

Acts 8:37: If thou believest with all thine h.

Acts 11:23: that with purpose of h ...

Acts 13:22: a man after mine own h.,

Acts 16:14: whose h. the Lord opened,

Acts 21:13: What mean ye to weep and to break mine h.?

Acts 28:27: For the h. of this people is waxed gross,

Rom 1:21: and their foolish h. was darkened.

Rom 2:5: hardness and impenitent h ...

Rom 2:29: circumcision is that of the h.,

Rom 6:17: ye have obeyed from the h ...

Rom 9:2: I have great heaviness and continual sorrow in my h.

Rom 10:1: Brethren, my h. desire

Rom 10:6: Say not in thine h.,

Rom 10:8: and in thy h.: that is, the word of faith,
Rom 10:9: and shalt believe in thine h.
Rom 10:10: For with the h. man believeth unto righteousness;
1 Cor 2:9: neither have entered into the h. of man
1 Cor 7:37: Nevertheless he that standeth stedfast in his h.,
1 Cor 14:25: thus are the secrets of his h. made manifest;
2 Cor 2:4: out of much affliction and anguish of h.
2 Cor 3:3: but in fleshy tables of the h.
2 Cor 3:15: the vail is upon their h.
2 Cor 5:12: which glory in appearance, and not in h.
2 Cor 6:11: our h. is enlarged.
2 Cor 8:16: earnest care into the h.
2 Cor 9:7: Every man according as he purposeth in his h.,
Eph 4:18: of the blindness of their h.:
Eph 5:19: singing and making melody in your h.
Eph 6:5: in singleness of your h.,
Eph 6:6: doing the will of God from the h.;
Phil 1:7: because I have you in my h.;
Col 3:22: but in singleness of h.,
1 Thes 2:17: not in h.,
1 Tm 1:5: charity out of a pure h.,
2 Tm 2:22: out of a pure h.
Heb 3:10: They do always err in their h.;
Heb 3:12: any of you an evil h. of unbelief,
Heb 4:12: is a discerner of the thoughts and intents of the h.

Heb 10:22: having our h. sprinkled from an evil conscience
Heb 13:9: that the h. be established with grace;
Jms 1:26: but deceiveth his own h.,
1 Pt 1:22: love one another with a pure h. fervently:
1 Pt 3:4: let it be the hidden man of the h.,
2 Pt 2:14: an h. they have exercised with covetous practices;
1 Jn 3:20: For if our h. condemn us, God is greater than our h.,
1 Jn 3:21: if our h. condemn us not,
Rv 18:7: for she saith in her h,

Heel

Gen 3:15: and thou shalt bruise his h.
Gen 25:26: and his hand took hold on Esau's h.;
Job 18:9: The gin shall take him by the h.,
Ps 41:9: hath lifted up his h. against me.
Hosea 12:3: He took his brother by the h.
Jn 13:18: He that eateth bread with me hath lifted up his h. against me.

Hip

Judg 15:8: And he smote them h. and thigh

Jaw

Judg 15:19: But God clave an hollow place that was in the j.,
Job 41:2: or bore his j through with a thorn?
Prov 30:14: and their j. teeth as knives,

Joints

Song 7:1: the j. of thy thighs are like jewels,

Dan 5:6: so that the j. of his loins were loosed,
Col 2:19: from which all the body by j.
Heb 4:12: and of the joints and marrow,

Kidney/Liver

Ex 29:13: and the two k.,
Ex 29:22: the caul above the l., and the two k.,
Lev 3:4: And the two k ... the caul above the l., with the k., it shall he take away.
Lev 3:10: the two k., and the caul above the l., with the k., it shall he take away.
Lev 8:16: caul above the l., and the two k.,
Lev 8:25: and the caul above the l., and the two k., and their fat,
Prov 7:23: a dart strike through his l.;
Lam 2:11: my l is poured upon the earth,
Ezek 21:21: he looked in the l.

Knee(s)

Gen 30:3: she shall bear upon my k ...
Gen 41:43: Bow the k.:
Isa 45:23: That unto me every k. shall bow,
Gen 48:12: And Joseph brought them out from between his k.,
Gen 50:23: were brought up upon Joseph's k.
Deut 28:35: The LORD shall smite thee in the k.,
Judg 7:5: every one that boweth down upon his k. to drink.
Judg 7:6: the people bowed down upon their k. to drink water.
Judg 16:19: made him sleep upon her k.;
1Kgs 8:54: from kneeling on his k ...

1Kgs 18:42: put his face between his k.,
1Kgs 19:18: all the k. which have not bowed unto Baal,
2Kgs 1:13: and came and fell on his k.
2Kgs 4:20: he sat on her k. till noon,
2Chron 6:13: kneeled down upon his k.
Ezra 9:5: I fell upon my k.,
Job 3:12: Why did the k. prevent me?
Job 4:4: hast strengthened the feeble k.
Ps 109:24: My k. are weak through fasting;
Isa 35:3: and confirm the feeble k.
Isa 66:12: and be dandled upon her k.
Ezek 7:17: all k. shall be weak as water.
Ezek 21:7: all k. shall be weak as water:
Ezek 47:4: the waters were to the k.
Dan 5:6: his k. smote one against another.
Dan 6:10: he kneeled upon his k. three times a day,
Dan 10:10: which set me upon my k.
Nahum: 2:10: the k. smite together,
Mt 27:29: they bowed the k. before him,
Mk 15:19: and bowing their k. worshipped him.
Lk 5:8: he fell down at Jesus' k.,
Rom 11:4: who have not bowed the k. to the image of Baal.
Rom 14:11: every k. shall bow to me,
Eph 3:14: I bow my k. unto the Father of our Lord Jesus Christ,
Phil 2:10: at the name of Jesus every k. should bow,

Heb 12:12: Wherefore lift up the hands which hang down, and the feeble k.;

Leg(s)
Ex 12:9: his head with his l.,
Lev 8:21: And he washed the inwards and the l. in water;
Lev 11:21: which have l. above their feet,
Deut 28:35: The LORD shall smite thee in the knees, and in the l.,
1Sam 17:6: And he had greaves of brass upon his l.,
Ps 147:10: he taketh not pleasure in the l. of a man.
Prov 26:7: The l. of the lame are not equal:
Song 5:15: His l. are as pillars of marble,
Isa 3:20: and the ornaments of the l.
Isa 47:2: make bare the l.,
Dan 2:33: His l. of iron, his feet part of iron and part of clay.
Amos 3:12: out of the mouth of the lion two l.
Jn 19:31: that their l. might be broken,
Jn 19:32: and brake the l. of the first,
Jn 19:33: they brake not his l.:

Lips
Ex 6:12: how then shall Pharaoh hear me, who am of uncircumcised l.?
Ex 6:30: Behold, I am of uncircumcised l.
Lev 5:4: pronouncing with his l. to do evil,
Num 30:6: or uttered ought out of her l.,
Num 30:8: that which she uttered with her l.,
Num 30:12: then whatsoever proceeded out of her l. concerning her vows,
Deut 23:23: That which is gone out of thy l ...

1Sam 1:13: only her l. moved,
2Kgs 19:28: and my bridle in thy l.,
Job 2:10: In all this did not Job sin with his l.
Job 8:21: and thy l. with rejoicing.
Job 11:5: and open his l. against thee;
Job 13:6: hearken to the pleadings of my l.
Job 15:6: thine own l. testify against thee.
Job 16:5: the moving of my l. should asswage your grief.
Job 23:12: Neither have I gone back from the commandment of his l.;
Job 27:4: My l. shall not speak wickedness,
Job 32:20: I will open my l. and answer.
Job 33:3: and my l. shall utter knowledge clearly.
Ps 12:2: with flattering l. and with a double heart do they speak.
Ps 12:3: The LORD shall cut off all flattering l.,
Ps 12:4: our l. are our own: who is lord over us?
Ps 16:4: take up their names into my l.
Ps 17:1: that goeth not out of feigned l.
Ps 17:4: by the word of thy l. I have kept me from the paths of the destroyer.
Ps 21:2: and hast not withholden the request of his l.
Ps 31:18: Let the lying l. be put to silence;
Ps 34:13: and thy l. from speaking guile.
Ps 40:9: I have not refrained my l.,
Ps 45:2: grace is poured into thy l.:
Ps 51:15: O Lord, open thou my l.;
Ps 59:7: swords are in their l.:

Ps 59:12: the words of their l. let them even be taken in their pride …

Ps 63:3: my l. shall praise thee.

Ps 63:5: my mouth shall praise thee with joyful l.:

Ps 66:14: Which my l. have uttered, and my mouth hath spoken,

Ps 71:23: My l. shall greatly rejoice …

Ps 89:34: nor alter the thing that is gone out of my l.

Ps 106:33: so that he spake unadvisedly with his l.

Ps 119:13: With my l. have I declared all the judgments

Ps 119:171: My l. shall utter praise,

Ps 120:2: Deliver my soul, O LORD, from lying l.,

Ps 140:3: adders' poison is under their l.

Ps 140:9: let the mischief of their own l. cover them.

Ps 141:3: keep the door of my l.

Prov 4:24: Put away from thee a froward mouth, and perverse l. put far from thee.

Prov 5:2: and that thy l. may keep knowledge.

Prov 5:3: For the l. of a strange woman drop as an honeycomb,

Prov 7:21: with the flattering of her l. she forced him.

Prov 8:6: and the opening of my l. shall be right things.

Prov 8:7: and wickedness is an abomination to my l.

Prov 10:13: In the l. of him that hath understanding wisdom

Prov 10:18: He that hideth hatred with lying l.,

Prov 10:19: but he that refraineth his l. is wise.

Prov 10:21: The l. of the righteous feed many:

Prov 10:32: The l. of the righteous know what is acceptable:

Prov 12:13: The wicked is snared by the transgression of his l.:

Prov 12:22: Lying l. are abomination to the LORD:

Prov 13:3: he that openeth wide his l. shall have destruction.

Prov 14:3: the l. of the wise shall preserve them.

Prov 14:7: when thou perceivest not in him the l. of knowledge.

Prov 14:23: the talk of the l. tendeth only to penury.

Prov 15:7: The l. of the wise disperse knowledge:

Prov 16:10: A divine sentence is in the l. of the king:

Prov 16:13: Righteous l. are the delight of kings;

Prov 16:21: the sweetness of the l. increaseth learning.

Prov 16:23: and addeth learning to his l.

Prov 16:27: and in his l. there is as a burning fire.

Prov 16:30: moving his l. he bringeth evil to pass.

Prov 17:4: A wicked doer giveth heed to false l.;

Prov 17:7: much less do lying l. a prince.

Prov 17:28: he that shutteth his l. is esteemed a man of understanding.

Prov 18:6: A fool's l. enter into contention,

Prov 18:7: his l. are the snare of his soul.

Prov 18:20: and with the increase of his l. shall he be filled.

Prov 19:1: he that is perverse in his l.,

Prov 20:15: therefore meddle not with him that flattereth with his l.

Prov 22:11: for the grace of his l. the king shall be his friend.

Prov 22:18: they shall withal be fitted in thy l.

Prov 23:16: when thy l. speak right things.

Prov 24:2: and their l. talk of mischief.

Prov 24:26: Every man shall kiss his l. that giveth a right answer.

Prov 24:28: and deceive not with thy l.

Prov 26:23: Burning l. and a wicked heart are like

Prov 26:24: He that hateth dissembleth with his l.,

Prov 27:2: and not thine own l.

Eccl 10:12: the l. of a fool will swallow up himself.

Song 4:3: Thy l. are like a thread of scarlet,

Song 4:11: Thy l., O my spouse, drop as the honeycomb:

Song 5:13: his l. like lilies,

Song 7:9: causing the l. of those that are asleep to speak.

Isa 6:5: I am a man of unclean l.,

Isa 6:7: this hath touched thy l.;

Isa 11:4: with the breath of his l. shall he slay the wicked.

Isa 28:11: For with stammering l. and another tongue

Isa 29:13: and with their l. do honour me,

Isa 30:27: his l. are full of indignation,

Isa 37:29: and my bridle in thy l.,

Isa 57:19: I create the fruit of the l.;

Isa 59:3: your l. have spoken lies,

Jer 17:16: that which came out of my l. was right before thee.

Lam 3:62: The l. of those that rose up against me,

Ezek 24:17: cover not thy l., and eat not the bread of men.

Ezek 24:22: ye shall not cover your l.,

Ezek 36:3: ye are taken up in the l. of talkers,

Dan 10:16: the sons of men touched my l.:
Hosea 14:2: so will we render the calves of our l.
Micah 3:7: they shall all cover their l.;
Hab 3:16: my l. quivered at the voice:
Mal 2:6: iniquity was not found in his l.:
Mal 2:7: For the priest's l. should keep knowledge,
Mt 15:8: and honoureth me with their l.;
Mk 7:6: This people honoureth me with their l.,
Rom 3:13: the poison of asps is under their l.:
1 Cor 14:21: With men of other tongues and other l. will I speak
Heb 13:15: the fruit of our l. giving thanks to his name.
1 Pt 3:10: and his l. that they speak no guile:

Mouth

Gen 8:11: in her m. was an olive leaf pluckt off:
Gen 24:57: We will call the damsel, and enquire at her m.
Gen 45:12: that it is my m. that speaketh unto you.
Ex 4 11: Who hath made man's m.?
Ex 4:12: I will be with thy m.,
Ex 4:15: and put words in his m.: and I will be with thy m., and with his m., and will teach you what ye shall do.
Ex 4:16: he shall be to thee instead of a m.,
Ex 13:9: that the LORD's law may be in thy m.:
Ex 23:13: let it be heard out of thy m.
Num 12:8: With him will I speak mouth to m.,
Num 22:28: And the LORD opened the m. of the ass,
Num 22:38: the word that God putteth in my m.,

Num 23:5: the LORD put a word in Balaam's m.,
Num 23:12: which the LORD hath put in my m.?
Num 23:16: and put a word in his m.,
Num 30:2: he shall do according to all that proceedeth out of his m.
Num 32:24: do that which hath proceeded out of your m.
Deut 8:3: but by every word that proceedeth out of the m. of the LORD doth man live.
Deut 18:18: will put my words in his m.;
Deut 23:23: which thou hast promised with thy m.
Deut 30:14: the word is very nigh unto thee, in thy m.,
Deut 32:1: hear, O earth, the words of my m.
Josh 1:8: This book of the law shall not depart out of thy m.;
Josh 6:10: neither shall any word proceed out of your m.,
Josh 9:14: asked not counsel at the m. of the LORD.
Judg 7:6: putting their hand to their m.,
Judg 9:38: Where is now thy m.,
Judg 11:35: I have opened my m. unto the LORD,
Judg: 11:36: if thou hast opened thy m. unto the LORD,
Judg 18:19: lay thine hand upon thy m.,
1 Sam 1:12: that Eli marked her m.
1 Sam 2:1: my m. is enlarged over mine enemies;
1 Sam 2:3: let not arrogancy come out of your m.:
1 Sam 14:26: but no man put his hand to his m.:
1 Sam 14:27: and put his hand to his m.;
1 Sam 17:35: delivered it out of his m.:
2 Sam 1:16: for thy m. hath testified against thee,

2 Sam 14:3: Joab put the words in her m.
2 Sam 14:19: he put all these words in the m. of thine handmaid:
2 Sam 18:25: there is tidings in his mouth.
2 Sam 22:9: and fire out of his m. devoured:
1 Kgs 8:15: which spake with his m. unto David my father,
1 Kgs 8:24: thou spakest also with thy m.,
1 Kgs 13:21: Forasmuch as thou hast disobeyed the m. of the LORD,
1 Kgs 17:24: that the word of the LORD in thy m. is truth.
1 Kgs 19:18: and every m. which hath not kissed him.
1 Kgs 22:13: declare good unto the king with one m.:
1 Kgs 22:22: I will be a lying spirit in the m. of all his prophets.
1 Kgs 22:23: lying spirit in the m. of all these thy prophets,
2 Kgs 4:34: put his mouth upon his m.,
1 Chron 16:12: the judgments of his m.;
2 Chron 6:4: that which he spake with his m. to my father David,
2 Chron 6:15: and spakest with thy m.,
2 Chron 18:21: be a lying spirit in the m. of all his prophets.
2 Chron 18:22: a lying spirit in the m. of these thy prophets,
2 Chron 35:22: the words of Necho from the m. of God,
2 Chron 36:12: speaking from the m. of the LORD.
2 Chron 36:21: the word of the LORD by the m. of Jeremiah,
2 Chron 36:22: by the m. of Jeremiah might be accomplished,
Ezra 1:1: by the m. of Jeremiah might be fulfilled,

Neh 9:20: withheldest not thy manna from their m.,

Esth 7:8: As the word went out of the king's m.,

Job 3:1: After this opened Job his m.,

Job 5:15: he saveth the poor from the sword, from their m.,

Job 5:16: and iniquity stoppeth her m.

Job 7:11: I will not refrain my m.;

Job 8:2: how long shall the words of thy m. be like a strong wind?

Job 8:21: Till he fill thy m. with laughing,

Job 9:20: mine own m. shall condemn me:

Job 12:11: and the m. taste his meat?

Job 15:5: For thy m. uttereth thine iniquity,

Job 15:6: Thine own m. condemneth thee,

Job 15:13: and lettest such words go out of thy m.?

Job 15:30: by the breath of his m. shall he go away.

Job 16:5: But I would strengthen you with my m.

Job 16:10: They have gaped upon me with their m.;

Job 19:16: I intreated him with my m.

Job 20:12: Though wickedness be sweet in his m.,

Job 20:13: but keep it still within his m.:

Job 21:5: lay your hand upon your m.

Job 22:22: the law from his m.,

Job 23:4: and fill my m. with arguments.

Job 23:12: I have esteemed the words of his m ...

Job 29:9: and laid their hand on their m.

Job 29:10: their tongue cleaved to the roof of their m.

Job 29:23: they opened their m. wide as for the latter rain.

Job 31:27: or my m. hath kissed my hand:

Job 31:30: Neither have I suffered my m. to sin

Job 32:5: When Elihu saw that there was no answer in the m.

Job 33:2: now I have opened my m.,

Job 34:3: as the m. tasteth meat.

Job 35:16: Therefore doth Job open his m. in vain;

Job 37:2: sound that goeth out of his m.

Job 40:4: will lay mine hand upon my m.

Job 40:23: can draw up Jordan into his m.

Job 41:19: Out of his m. go burning lamps,

Job 41:21: and a flame goeth out of his m.

Ps 5:9: there is no faithfulness in their m.;

Ps 8:2: Out of the m. of babes and sucklings

Ps 10:7: His m. is full of cursing and deceit and fraud:

Ps 17:3: I am purposed that my m. shall not transgress.

Ps 17:10: with their m. they speak proudly.

Ps 18:8: and fire out of his m. devoured:

Ps 19:14: Let the words of my m.,

Ps 22:21: Save me from the lion's m.:

Ps 32:9: whose m. must be held in with bit and bridle,

Ps 33:6: the host of them by the breath of his m.

Ps 34:1: his praise shall continually be in my m.

Ps 35:21: Yea, they opened their m. wide against me,

Ps 36:3: The words of his m. are iniquity and deceit:

Ps 37:30: The m. of the righteous speaketh wisdom,

Ps 38:13: as a dumb man that openeth not his m.

Ps 38:14: and in whose m. are no reproofs.

Ps 39:1: I will keep my m. with a bridle,

Ps 39:9: I opened not my m.;

Ps 40:3: he hath put a new song in my m.

Ps 49:3: My m. shall speak of wisdom;

Ps 50:16: thou shouldest take my covenant in thy m.?

Ps 50:19: Thou givest thy m. to evil,

Ps 51:15: my m. shall shew forth thy praise.

Ps 54:2: give ear to the words of my m.

Ps 55:21: The words of his m. were smoother than butter,

Ps 58:6: in their m.: break out the great teeth

Ps 59:7: they belch out with their m.:

Ps 59:12: For the sin of their m ...

Ps 62:4: they bless with their m.,

Ps 63:5: my m. shall praise thee with joyful lips:

Ps 63:11: but the m. of them that speak lies shall be stopped.

Ps 66:14: my m. hath spoken, when I was in trouble.

Ps 66:17: I cried unto him with my m.,

Ps 71:8: Let my m. be filled with thy praise

Ps 71:15: My m. shall shew forth thy righteousness

Ps 73:9: They set their m. against the heavens,

Ps 78:1: incline your ears to the words of my m.

Ps 78:2: I will open my m. in a parable:

Ps 78:36 did flatter him with their m.,

Ps 81:10: open thy m. wide,

Ps 89:1: with my m. will I make known

Ps 103:5: Who satisfieth thy
m. with good things;
Ps 105:5: the judgments of
his m.;
Ps 107:42: all iniquity shall
stop her m.
Ps 109:2: For the m. of the
wicked and the m. of the
deceitful are opened
Ps 109:30: I will greatly praise
the LORD with my m.; yea,
Ps 119:13: I declared all the
judgments of thy m.
Ps 119:43: take not the word of
truth utterly out of my m.;
Ps 119:72: The law of thy m.
is better
Ps 119:88: so shall I keep the
testimony of thy m.
Ps 119:103: sweeter than
honey to my m.!
Ps 119:108: freewill offerings
of my m.,
Ps 119:131: I opened my m.,
and panted:
Ps 126:2: Then was our m.
filled with laughter,
Ps 137:6: let my tongue cleave
to the roof of my m.;
Prov 2:6: out of his m.
cometh knowledge and
understanding.
Prov 4:5: neither decline from
the words of my m.
Prov 4:24: Put away from thee
a froward m.,
Prov 5:3: her m. is smoother
than oil:
Prov 5:7: depart not from the
words of my m.
Prov 6:2: Thou art snared with
the words of thy m., thou art
taken with the words of thy m.
Prov 6:12: a wicked man,
walketh with a froward m.
Prov 7:24: attend to the words
of my m.
Prov 8:7: For my m. shall
speak truth;
Prov 8:8: All the words of my
m. are in righteousness;

Prov 8:13: the froward m., do
I hate.
Prov 10:6: violence covereth
the m. of the wicked.
Prov 10:11: The m. of a
righteous man is a well of life:
but violence covereth the m. of
the wicked.
Prov 10:14: the m. of the
foolish is near destruction.
Prov 10:31: The m. of the just
bringeth forth wisdom:
Prov 10:32: the m. of the
wicked speaketh frowardness.
Prov 11:9: An hypocrite
with his m. destroyeth his
neighbour:
Prov 11:11: it is overthrown by
the m. of the wicked.
Prov 12:6: the m. of the
upright shall deliver them.
Prov 12:14: A man shall be
satisfied with good by the fruit
of his m.:
Prov 13:2: A man shall eat
good by the fruit of his m.:
Prov 13:3: He that keepeth his
m. keepeth his life:
Prov 14:3: In the m. of the
foolish is a rod of pride:
Prov 15:2: the m. of fools
poureth out foolishness.
Prov 15:14: the m. of fools
feedeth on foolishness.
Prov 15:23: A man hath joy by
the answer of his m.:
Prov 15:28: the m. of the
wicked poureth out evil things.
Prov 16:10: his m.
transgresseth not in judgment.
Prov 16:23: The heart of the
wise teacheth his m.,
Prov 16:26: for his m. craveth
it of him.
Prov 18:4: The words of a
man's m. are as deep waters,
Prov 18:6: and his m. calleth
for strokes.
Prov 18:7: A fool's m. is his
destruction,

Prov 18:20: A man's belly
shall be satisfied with the fruit
of his m.;
Prov 19:24: and will not so
much as bring it to his m.
again.
Prov 19:28: the m. of the
wicked devoureth iniquity.
Prov 20:17: but afterwards his
m. shall be filled with gravel.
Prov 21:23: Whoso keepeth his
m. and his tongue keepeth his
soul from troubles.
Prov 22:14: The m. of strange
women is a deep pit:
Prov 24:7: he openeth not his
m. in the gate.
Prov 26:7: so is a parable in
the m. of fools.
Prov 26:9: so is a parable in
the m. of fools.
Prov 26:15: it grieveth him to
bring it again to his m.
Prov 26:28: a flattering m.
worketh ruin.
Prov 27:2: and not thine
own m.;
Prov 30:20: she eateth, and
wipeth her m.,
Prov 30:32: lay thine hand
upon thy mo.
Prov 31:8: Open thy m. for the
dumb ...
Prov 31:9: Open thy m., judge
righteously,
Prov 31:26: She openeth her
m. with wisdom;
Eccl 5:2: Be not rash with
thy m.,
Eccl 5:6: Suffer not thy m. to
cause thy flesh to sin;
Eccl 6:7: the labour of man is
for his m.,
Eccl 10:12: The words of a wise
man's mouth are gracious;
Eccl 10:13: The beginning
of the words of his m. is
foolishness:
Song 1:2: kiss me with the
kisses of his m.:
Song 5:16: His m. is most
sweet:

Song 7:9: the roof of thy m. like the best wine

Isa 1:20: the m. of the LORD hath spoken it.

Isa 5:14: and opened her m. without measure:

Isa 6:7: And he laid it upon my m.,

Isa 9:12: they shall devour Israel with open m.

Isa 9:17: and every m. speaketh folly.

Isa 10:14: or opened the m. or peeped.

Isa 11:4: he shall smite the earth with the rod of his m.,

Isa 19:7: by the m. of the brooks,

Isa 29:13: this people draw near me with their m.,

Isa 30:2: have not asked at my m.;

Isa 34:16: for my m. it hath commanded,

Isa 40:5: for the m. of the LORD hath spoken it.

Isa 45:23: the word is gone out of my m. in righteousness,

Isa 48:3: they went forth out of my m.,

Isa 49:2: he hath made my m. like a sharp sword;

Isa 51:16: I have put my words in thy m.,

Isa 53:7: yet he opened not his m ... and as a sheep before her shearers is dumb, so he openeth not his m.

Isa 53:9: neither was any deceit in his m.

Isa 55:11: So shall my word be that goeth forth out of my m.:

Isa 57:4: against whom make ye a wide m.,

Isa 58:14: for the m. of the LORD hath spoken it.

Isa 59:21: my words which I have put in thy m.,

Isa 62:2: which the m. of the LORD shall name.

Jer 1:9: and touched my m.

Jer 5:14: I will make my words in thy m. fire,

Jer 7:28: and is cut off from their m.

Jer 9:8: one speaketh peaceably to his neighbour with his m.,

Jer 9:12: the m. of the LORD hath spoken,

Jer 9:20: let your ear receive the word of his m.,

Jer 12:2: thou art near in their m.,

Jer 15:19: thou shalt be as my m.:

Jer 23:16: and not out of the m. of the LORD.

Jer 32:4: speak with him m. to m.,

Jer 34:3: he shall speak with thee m. to m.,

Jer 36:4: and Baruch wrote from the m. of Jeremiah

Jer 36:6: thou hast written from my m.,

Jer 36:17: How didst thou write all these words at his m.?

Jer 36:18: He pronounced all these words unto me with his m.,

Jer 36:27: the words which Baruch wrote at the m. of Jeremiah,

Jer 36:32: who wrote therein from the m. of Jeremiah

Jer 44:17: whatsoever thing goeth forth out of our own m.,

Jer 44:26: my name shall no more be named in the m. of any man of Judah ...

Jer 45:1: written these words in a book at the m. of Jeremiah,

Jer 48:28: the dove that maketh her nest in the sides of the hole's m.

Jer 51:44: I will bring forth out of his m ...

Lam 2:16: All thine enemies have opened their m. against thee:

Lam 3:29: He putteth his m. in the dust:

Lam 3:38: Out of the m. of the most High proceedeth not evil and good?

Lam 4:4: The tongue of the sucking child cleaveth to the roof of his m. for thirst:

Ezek 2:8: open thy m. and eat ...

Ezek 3:2: So I opened my m.,

Ezek 3:3: and it was in my m. as honey for sweetness.

Ezek 3:17: hear the word at my m.,

Ezek 3:26: I will make thy tongue cleave to the roof of thy m.,

Ezek 3:27: But when I speak with thee, I will open thy m.,

Ezek 4:14: neither came there abominable flesh into my m.

Ezek 16:56: For thy sister Sodom was not mentioned by thy m ...

Ezek 16:63: never open thy m. any more because of thy shame,

Ezek 21:22: to open the m. in the slaughter,

Ezek 24:27: In that day shall thy m. be opened to him

Ezek 29:21: I will give thee the opening of the m. in the midst of them;

Ezek 33:7: shalt hear the word at my m.,

Ezek 33:22: and had opened my m.,

Ezek 33:31: for with their m. they shew much love,

Ezek 34:10: I will deliver my flock from their m,

Ezek 35:13: with your m. ye have boasted against me,

Dan 4:31: While the word was in the king's m.,

Dan 7:5: and it had three ribs in the m. of it between the teeth of it:

Dan 7:8: and a m. speaking great things.

Dan 7:20: *a m. that spake very great things,*
Dan 10:3: *neither came flesh nor wine in my m.,*
Dan 10:16: *then I opened my mouth,*
Hosea 2:17: *I will take away the names of Baalim out of her m.,*
Hosea 6:5: *I have slain them by the words of my m.:*
Hosea 8:1: *Set the trumpet to thy m.*
Joel 1:5: *for it is cut off from your m.*
Amos 3:12: *As the shepherd taketh out of the m. of the lion two legs,*
Micah 4:4: *for the m. of the LORD of hosts hath spoken it.*
Micah 6:12: *and their tongue is deceitful in their m.*
Micah 7:5: *keep the doors of thy m. from her that lieth*
Micah 7:16: *they shall lay their hand upon their m.,*
Nahum 3:12: *they shall even fall into the m. of the eater.*
Zeph 3:13: *a deceitful tongue be found in their m.:*
Zech 8:9: *hear in these days these words by the m. of the prophets,*
Zech 9:7: *I will take away his blood out of his m.,*
Zech 14:12: *their tongue shall consume away in their m.*
Mal 2:6: *The law of truth was in his m.,*
Mal 2:7: *should seek the law at his m.:*
Mt 4:4: *but by every word that proceedeth out of the m. of God.*
Mt 5:2: *And he opened his m., and taught them, saying,*
Mt 12:34: *out of the abundance of the heart the m. speaketh.*
Mt 13:35: *I will open my m. in parables;*

Mt 15:8: *This people draweth nigh unto me with their m.,*
Mt 15:11: *but that which cometh out of the m.,*
Mt 15:17: *whatsoever entereth in at the m. goeth into the belly,*
Mt 15:18: *those things which proceed out of the m.*
Mt 18:16: *that in the m. of two or three witnesses*
Mt 21:16: *Out of the m. of babes and sucklings*
Lk 1:64: *And his m. was opened immediately,*
Lk 1:70: *As he spake by the m. of his holy prophets,*
Lk 4:22: *gracious words which proceeded out of his m.*
Lk 6:45: *for of the abundance of the heart his m. speaketh.*
Lk 11:54: *seeking to catch something out of his m.,*
Lk 19:22: *Out of thine own m. will I judge thee,*
Lk 21:15: *For I will give you a m. and wisdom*
Lk 22:71: *we ourselves have heard of his own m.*
Jn 19:29: *and put it to his m.*
Acts 1:16: *by the m. of David spake before concerning Judas,*
Acts 3:18: *had shewed by the m. of all his prophets,*
Acts 3:21: *God hath spoken by the m …*
Acts 4:25: *Who by the m. of thy servant David hast said,*
Acts 8:32: *so opened he not his m.:*
Acts 8:35: *Then Philip opened his m.,*
Acts 10:34: *Then Peter opened his m.,*
Acts 11:8: *at any time entered into my m.*
Acts 15:7: *that the Gentiles by my m. should hear*
Acts 15:27: *tell you the same things by m.*
Acts 18:14: *when Paul was now about to open his m.,*

Acts 22:14: *and shouldest hear the voice of his m.*
Acts 23:2: *to smite him on the m.*
Rom 3:14: *Whose m. is full of cursing and bitterness:*
Rom 3:19: *that every m. may be stopped,*
Rom 10:8: *even in thy m., and in thy heart:*
Rom 10:9: *That if thou shalt confess with thy m. the Lord Jesus,*
Rom 10:10 *with the m. confession is made unto salvation.*
Rom 15:6: *one mind and one m. glorify God,*
2 Cor 6:11: *O ye Corinthians, our m. is open unto you,*
2 Cor 13:1: *In the m. of two or three witnesses*
Eph 4:29: *Let no corrupt communication proceed out of your m.,*
Eph 6:19: *that I may open my m. boldly,*
Col 3:8: *filthy communication out of your m.*
2 Thes 2:8: *with the spirit of his m.,*
Jms 3:10: *Out of the same m. proceedeth blessing and cursing.*
1 Pt 2:22: *neither was guile found in his m.:*
Jude 1:16: *their m. speaketh great swelling words,*
Rv 1:16: *and out of his m. went a sharp two-edged sword:*
Rv 2:16: *will fight against them with the sword of my m.*
Rv 3:16: *I will spew thee out of my m.*
Rv 9:19: *For their power is in their m.,*
Rv 10:9: *it shall be in thy m. sweet as honey.*
Rv 10:10: *it was in my m. sweet as honey:*
Rv 11:5: *fire proceedeth out of their m.,*

Rv 12:15: the serpent cast out of his m. water as a flood
Rv 13:5: there was given unto him a m. speaking great things
Rv 13:6: he opened his m. in blasphemy against God,
Rv 14:5: in their m. was found no guile:
Rv 16:13: like frogs come out of the m. of the dragon, and out of the m. of the beast, and out of the m. of the false prophet.
Rv 19:15: And out of his m. goeth a sharp sword,
Rv 19:21: which sword proceeded out of his m.:

Muscle (Sinew)
Gen 32:32: because he touched the hollow of Jacob's thigh in the s. that shrank.
Job 10:11: and hast fenced me with bones and s.
Job 30:17: and my s. take no rest.
Job 40:17: the s. of his stones are wrapped together.
Isa 48:4: and thy neck is an iron s.
Ezek 37:6: And I will lay s. upon you,
Ezek 37:8: lo, the s. and the flesh came up upon them,

Nails (finger and toe)
Deut 21:12: she shall shave her head, and pare her n.;
Dan 4:33: his hairs were grown like eagles' feathers, and his n. like birds' claws.
Dan 7:19: whose teeth were of iron, and his n. of brass;
Neck
Gen 27:16: upon the smooth of his n.:
Gen 27:40: that thou shalt break his yoke from off thy n.
Gen 33:4: fell on his n., and kissed him:
Gen 41:42: put a gold chain about his n.;

Gen 45:14: he fell upon his brother Benjamin's n.,
Gen 46:29: and he fell on his n.,
Gen 49:8: thy hand shall be in the n. of thine enemies;
Ex 13:13: then thou shalt break his n.:
Ex 34:20: then shalt thou break his n.
Lev 5:8: wring off his head from his n.,
Deut 21:4: shall strike off the heifer's n. there in the valley:
Deut 28:48: he shall put a yoke of iron upon thy n.,
Deut 31:27: I know thy rebellion, and thy stiff n.:
1 Sam 4:18: his n. brake, and he died:
2 Chron 36:13: but he stiffened his n.,
Neh 9:29: and hardened their n.,
Job 15:26: He runneth upon him, even on his n.,
Job 16:12: he hath also taken me by my n.,
Job 39:19: hast thou clothed his n. with thunder?
Job 41:22: In his n. remaineth strength,
Ps75:5: speak not with a stiff n.
Prov 1:9: and chains about thy n.
Prov 3:3: bind them about thy n.;
Prov 3:22: and grace to thy n.
Prov 6:21: and tie them about thy n.
Prov 29:1: He, that being often reproved hardeneth his n.,
Song 1:10: thy n. with chains of gold.
Song 4:4: Thy n. is like the tower of David
Song 4:9: with one chain of thy n.
Song 7:4: Thy n. is as a tower of ivory;
Isa 8:8: he shall reach even to the n.;

Isa 10:27: and his yoke from off thy n.,
Isa 30:28: reach to the midst of the n.,
Isa 48:4: and thy n. is an iron sinew,
Isa 52:2: loose thyself from the bands of thy n.,
Jer 17:23: but made their n. stiff,
Jer 27:2: and put them upon thy n.,
Jer 27:8: not put their n. under the yoke of the king of Babylon,
Jer 27:11: nations that bring their n. under the yoke of the king of Babylon,
Jer 28:10: took the yoke from off the prophet Jeremiah's n.,
Jer 28:11: the yoke of Nebuchadnezzar king of Babylon from the n.
Jer 28:12: the prophet had broken the yoke from off the n
Jer 28:14: I have put a yoke of iron upon the n. of all these nations,
Jer 30:8: break his yoke from off thy n.,
Lam 1:14: and come up upon my n.:
Ezek 16:11: and a chain on thy n.
Dan 5:7: and have a chain of gold about his n.,
Dan 5:16: a chain of gold about thy n.,
Dan 5:29: put a chain of gold about his n.,
Hosea 10:11: passed over upon her fair n.:
Hab: 3:13: by discovering the foundation unto the n.
Mt 18:6: that a millstone were hanged about his n.,
Mk 9:42: that a millstone were hanged about his n.,
Lk 15:20: fell on his n. and kissed him.
Lk 17:2: that a millstone were hanged about his n.,

Acts 15:10: to put a yoke upon the n. of the disciples,
Acts 20:37: and fell on Paul's n., and kissed him,

Nostrils
Gen 2:7: breathed into his n. the breath of life;
Gen 7:22: whose nostrils was the b. of life,
Ex 15:8: with the blast of thy n. the waters were gathered together,
Num 11:20: until it come out at your n.,
2Sam 22:9: went up a smoke out of his n.,
2Sam 22:16: blast of the breath of his n.
Job: 4:9: by the breath of his n. are they consumed.
Job 27:3: the spirit of God is in my n.;
Job 39:20: the glory of his n. is terrible.
Job 41:20: Out of his n. goeth smoke,
Ps 18:8: went up a smoke out of his n.,
Ps 18:15: the blast of the breath of thy n.
Isa 2:22: whose breath is in his n.:
Lam 4:20: The breath of our n.,
Amos 4:10: stink of your camps to come up unto your n.:

Shoulder
Gen 21:14: and gave it unto Hagar, putting it on her s.,
Gen 24:15: Abraham's brother, with her pitcher upon her s.
Gen 24:45: Rebekah came forth with her pitcher on her s.;
Gen 24:46: and let down her pitcher from her s.,
Gen 49:15: bowed his s. to bear,

Ex 29:22: and the right s.; for it is a ram of consecration:
Ex 29:27: s. of the heave offering,
Lev 7:32: And the right s. shall ye give unto the priest
Lev 7:33: the right s. for his part.
Lev 7:34: the heave s. have I taken of the children of Israel
Lev 8:25: their fat, and the right s.:
Lev 8:26: and upon the right s.
Lev 9:21: breasts and the right s.
Lev 10:14: And the wave breast and heave s. shall ye eat
Lev 10:15: The heave s. and the wave breast shall they
Num 6:19: And the priest shall take the sodden s. of the ram,
Num 6:20: with the wave breast and heave s.:
Num 18:18: as the wave breast and as the right s. are thine.
Deut 18:3: give unto the priest the s.,
Josh 4:5: man of you a stone upon his s.,
Judg 9:48: and laid it on his s.,
1Sam 9:24: And the cook took up the s.,
Neh 9:29: and withdrew the s., and hardened their neck,
Job 31:22: Then let mine arm fall from my s. blade,
Job 31:36: I would take it upon my s.,
Ps 81:6: I removed his s. from the burden:
Isa 9:4: and the staff of his s.,
Isa 9:6: government shall be upon his s.:
Isa 10:27: his burden shall be taken away from off thy s.
Isa 22:22: the key of the house of David will I lay upon his s.;
Isa 46:7: They bear him upon the s.,

Ezek 12:7: and I bare it upon my s. in their sight.
Ezek 12:12: shall bear upon his s. in the twilight,
Ezek 24:4: every good piece, the thigh, and the s.;
Ezek 29:7: and rend all their s.
Ezek 29:18: and every s. was peeled:
Ezek 34:21: ye have thrust with side and with s.,
Zech 7:11: and pulled away the s.,

Skin
Ex 22:27: it is his raiment for his s.:
Ex 29:14: his s., and his dung, shalt thou burn with fire
Ex 34:29: Moses wist not that the s. of his face shone
Ex 34:30: the s. of his face shone;
Ex 34:35: the s. of Moses' face shone:
Lev 4:11: And the s. of the bullock,
Lev 7:8: the priest shall have to himself the s.
Lev 11:32: whether it be any vessel of wood, or raiment, or s., or sack,
Lev 13:2: a man shall have in the s ...
Lev 13:3: the plague in the s. of the flesh:
Lev 13:4: If the bright spot be white in the s. of his flesh,
Lev 13:5: the plague spread not in the s.;
Lev 13:6: the plague spread not in the s.;
Lev 13:7: But if the scab spread much abroad in the s.,
Lev 13:8: the scab spreadeth in the s.,
Lev 13:10: if the rising be white in the s.,
Lev 13:11: It is an old leprosy in the s. of his flesh,
Lev 13:12: And if a leprosy break out abroad in the s.,

Lev 13:18: even in the s. thereof,
Lev 13:20: it be in sight lower than the s.,
Lev 13:21: if it be not lower than the s.,
Lev 13:22: And if it spread much abroad in the s.,
Lev 13:24: if there be any flesh, in the s.
Lev 13:25: be in sight deeper than the s.;
Lev 13:26: it be no lower than the other s.,
Lev 13:27: spread much abroad in the s.,
Lev 13:28: and spread not in the s.,
Lev 13:30: be in sight deeper than the s.;
Lev 13:31: in sight deeper than the s.,
Lev 13:32: and the scall be not in sight deeper than the s.;
Lev 13:34: scall be not spread in the s.,
Lev 13:35: scall spread much in the s ...
Lev 13:36: if the scall be spread in the s.,
Lev 13:38: have in the s. of their flesh bright spots,
Lev 13:39: if the bright spots in the s. of their flesh be darkish white;
Lev 13:43: as the leprosy appeareth in the s. of the flesh;
Lev 13:48: or of woollen; whether in a s., or in any thing made of s.;
Lev 13:49: either in the warp, or in the woof, or in any thing of s.;
Lev 13:51: either in the warp, or in the woof, or in a s.,
Lev 13:52: in woollen or in linen, or any thing of s.;
Lev 13:53: either in the warp, or in the woof, or in any thing of s.;
Lev 13:56: rend it out of the garment, or out of the s.,

Lev 13:57: either in the warp, or in the woof, or in any thing of s.
Lev 13:58: or whatsoever thing of s. it be,
Lev 15:17: every garment, and every s.,
Num 19:5: her s., and her flesh, and her blood, with her dung, shall he burn:
Job 2:4: And Satan answered the LORD, and said, S. for s.,
Job 7:5: my s. is broken, and become loathsome.
Job 10:11: Thou hast clothed me with s. and flesh,
Job 16:15: I have sewed sackcloth upon my s.,
Job 18:13: It shall devour the strength of his s.:
Job 19:20: My bone cleaveth to my s ...
Job 19:26: And though after my s. worms destroy this body,
Job 30:30: My s. is black upon me,
Job 41:7: Canst thou fill his s. with barbed iron?
Ps 102:5: my groaning my bones cleave to my s.
Jer 13:23: Can the Ethiopian change his s.,
Lam 3:4: my s. hath he made old;
Lam 4:8: their s. cleaveth to their bones;
Lam 5:10: Our s. was black
Ezek 16:10: shod thee with badgers' s.,
Ezek 37:6: cover you with s.,
Ezek 37:8: and the s. covered them above:
Micah 3:2: who pluck off their s. from off them,
Micah 3:3: and flay their s. from off them;
Mk 1:6: a girdle of a s. about his loins;

Skull
Judg 9:53: and all to brake his s.

2Kgs 9:35: no more of her than the s.,
Mt 27:33: a place of a s.,
Mk 15:22: The place of a s.
Jn 19:17: called the place of a s.,

Stomach
1 Tm 5:23: but use a little wine for thy s. sake
Thigh
Gen 24:2: thy hand under my t.:
Gen 24:9: the servant put his hand under the t. of Abraham
Gen 32:25: he touched the hollow of his thigh; and the hollow of Jacob's t. was out of joint,
Gen 32:31and he halted upon his t.
Gen 32:32: which is upon the hollow of the t.,
Gen 47:29: thy hand under my t.,
Num 5:21: when the LORD doth make thy t. to rot,
Num 5:22: and thy t. to rot:
Num 5:27: and her thigh shall rot:
Judg 3:16: he did gird it under his raiment upon his right t.
Judg 3:21: took the dagger from his right t.,
Judg 15:8: And he smote them hip and t.
Ps 45:3: Gird thy sword upon thy t.,
Song 3:8: every man hath his sword upon his t.
Isa 47:2: uncover the t., pass over the rivers.
Jer 31:19: I smote upon my t.:
Ezek 21:12: smite therefore upon thy t.
Ezek 24:4: even every good piece, the t., and the shoulder;
Rv 19:16: and on his t. a name written, KING OF KINGS, AND LORD OF LORDS.

Throat

Ps 5:9: *their t. is an open sepulchre; they flatter with their tongue.*
Ps 69:3: *I am weary of my crying: my t. is dried:*
Ps 115:7: *neither speak they through their t.*
Prov 23:2: *And put a knife to thy t.,*
Jer 2:25: *and thy t. from thirst:*

Thumb

Ex 29:20: *upon the t. of their right hand,*
Lev 8:23: *upon the t. of his right hand,*

Toe(s)

Lev 8:24: *and upon the great t. of their right feet:*
Judg 1:6: *and cut off his thumbs and his great t.*
Judg 1:7: *having their thumbs and their great t. cut off,*
2 Sam 21:20: *and on every foot six t.*
1 Chron 20:6: *whose fingers and t. were four and twenty*
Dan 2:41: *And whereas thou sawest the feet and t.*
Dan 2:42: *And as the toes of the feet were part of iron,*

Tongue

Gen 10:5: *every one after his t. after their families, in their nations.*
Ex 4:10: *slow of speech, and of a slow t.*
Ex 11:7: *But against any of the children of Israel shall not a dog move his t.,*
Deut 28:49: *a nation whose t. thou shalt not understand;*
Josh 10:21: *none moved his t. against any of the children of Israel.*
Judg 7:5: *Every one that lappeth of the water with his t.,*
2Sam 23:2: *and his word was in my t.*

Ezra 4:7: *and interpreted in the Syrian t.*
Esth 7:4: *I had held my t.,*
Job 5:21: *Thou shalt be hid from the scourge of the t.:*
Job 6:24: *Teach me, and I will hold my t.:*
Job 6:30: *Is there iniquity in my t.?*
Job 13:19: *if I hold my t., I shall give up the ghost.*
Job 15:5 *and thou choosest the t. of the crafty.*
Job 20:12: *though he hide it under his t.;*
Job 20:16: *the viper's t. shall slay him.*
Job 27:4: *nor my t. utter deceit.*
Job 29:10: *and their t. cleaved to the roof of their mouth.*
Job 33:2: *my t. hath spoken in my mouth.*
Job 41:1: *or his t. with a cord which thou lettest down?*
Ps 5:9: *they flatter with their t.*
Ps 10:7: *under his t. is mischief and vanity.*
Ps 12:3: *and the t. that speaketh proud things:*
Ps 12:4: *With our t. will we prevail;*
Ps 15:3: *He that backbiteth not with his t.,*
Ps 22:15: *and my t. cleaveth to my jaws;*
Ps 34:13: *Keep thy t. from evil,*
Ps 35:28: *And my t. shall speak of thy righteousness*
Ps 37:30: *and his t. talketh of judgment.*
Ps 39:1: *that I sin not with my t.:*
Ps 39:3: *then spake I with my t.,*
Ps 45:1: *my t. is the pen of a ready writer.*
Ps 50:19: *and thy t. frameth deceit.*
Ps 51:14: *my t. shall sing aloud of thy righteousness.*

Ps 52:2: *Thy t. deviseth mischiefs;*
Ps 52:4: *O thou deceitful t.*
Ps 57:4: *and their t. a sharp sword.*
Ps 64:3: *Who whet their t. like a sword,*
Ps 64:8: *their own t. to fall upon themselves:*
Ps 66:17: *and he was extolled with my t.*
Ps 68:23: *the t. of thy dogs in the same.*
Ps 71:24: *My t. also shall talk of thy righteousness all the day long:*
Ps 73:9: *their t. walketh through the earth.*
Ps 109:2: *they have spoken against me with a lying t.*
Ps 119:172: *My t. shall speak of thy word:*
Ps 120:2: *and from a deceitful t ...*
Ps 120:3: *thou false t.?*
Ps 126:2: *our t. with singing:*
Ps 137:6: *let my t. cleave to the roof of my mouth;*
Ps 139:4: *For there is not a word in my t.,*
Prov 6:17: *A proud look, a lying t.,*
Prov 6:24: *from the flattery of the t. of a strange woman.*
Prov 10:20: *The t. of the just is as choice silver:*
Prov 10:31: *the froward t. shall be cut out.*
Prov 12:18: *but the t. of the wise is health.*
Prov 12:19: *but a lying t. is but for a moment.*
Prov 15:2: *The t. of the wise useth knowledge aright:*
Prov 15:4: *A wholesome t. is a tree of life:*
Prov 16:1: *the answer of the t., is from the LORD.*
Prov 17:4: *a liar giveth ear to a naughty t.*

Prov 17:20: he that hath a perverse t. falleth into mischief.
Prov 18:21: Death and life are in the power of the t.:
Prov 21:6: The getting of treasures by a lying t. is a vanity
Prov 21:23: Whoso keepeth his mouth and his t. keepeth his soul from troubles.
Prov 25:15: and a soft t. breaketh the bone.
Prov 25:23: so doth an angry countenance a backbiting.
Prov 26:28: A lying t. hateth those that are afflicted by it;
Prov 28:23: than he that flattereth with the t.
Prov 31:26: and in her t. is the law of kindness.
Song 4:11: honey and milk are under thy t.;
Isa 3:8: because their t. and their doings are against the LORD
Isa 11:15: And the LORD shall utterly destroy the t. of the Egyptian sea;
Isa 28:11: with stammering lips and another t. will he speak to this people.
Isa 30:27: his t. as a devouring fire:
Isa 32:4: the t. of the stammerers shall be ready to speak plainly.
Isa 33:19: of a stammering t., that thou canst not understand.
Isa 35:6: the t. of the dumb sing:
Isa 41:17: and their t. faileth for thirst,
Isa 45:23: That unto me every knee shall bow, every t. shall swear.
Isa 50:4: The Lord GOD hath given me the t. of the learned,
Isa 54:17: every t. that shall rise against thee in judgment
Isa 57:4: and draw out the t.?

Isa 59:3: your t. hath muttered perverseness.
Jer 9:5: they have taught their t. to speak lies,
Jer 9:8: Their t. is as an arrow shot out;
Jer 18:18: let us smite him with the t.,
Lam 4:4: The t. of the sucking child
Ezek 3:26: And I will make thy t. cleave to the roof of thy mouth,
Dan 1:4: they might teach the learning and the t. of the Chaldeans.
Hosea 7:16: their princes shall fall by the sword for the rage of their t.:
Amos 6:10: Then shall he say, Hold thy t.:
Micah 6:12: and their t. is deceitful in their mouth.
Hab 1:13: and holdest thy t. when the wicked devoureth ...
Zeph 3:13: neither shall a deceitful t. be found in their mouth:
Zech 14:12: and their t. shall consume away in their mouth.
Mk 7:33: and he spit, and touched his t.;
Mk 7:35: and the string of his t. was loosed,
Lk 1:64: and his t. loosed,
Lk 16:24: and cool my t.;
Jn 5:2: which is called in the Hebrew t. Bethesda,
Acts 1:19: that field is called in their proper t.,
Acts 2:8: And how hear we every man in our own t.,
Acts 2:26: and my t. was glad;
Acts 21:40: he spake unto them in the Hebrew t.,
Acts 22:2: (And when they heard that he spake in the Hebrew t. to them,
Acts 26:14: saying in the Hebrew t.,

Rom 14:11: every knee shall bow to me, and every t. shall confess to God.
1 Cor 14:2: For he that speaketh in an unknown t.
1 Cor 14:4: He that speaketh in an unknown t. edifieth himself;
1 Cor 14:9: except ye utter by the t. words easy to be understood,
1 Cor 14:13: let him that speaketh in an unknown t ...
1 Cor 14:14: if I pray in an unknown t.,
1 Cor 14:19: than ten thousand words in an unknown t.
1 Cor 14:26: hath a doctrine, hath a t., hath a revelation,
1 Cor 14:27: If any man speak in an unknown t.,
Phil 2:11: every t. should confess that Jesus Christ is Lord,
Jms 1:26: and bridleth not his t.,
Jms 3:5: Even so the t. is a little member
Jms 3:6: And the t. is a fire,
Jms 3:8: But the t. can no man tame;
1Pt: 3:10: let him refrain his t. from evil,
1Jn 3:18: neither in t.; but in deed and in truth.
Rv 5:9: and t., and people, and nation;
Rv 9:11: whose name in the Hebrew t. is Abaddon, but in the Greek t. hath his name Apollyon.
Rv 14:6: and to every nation, and kindred, and t., and people,
Rv 16:16: into a place called in the Hebrew t. Armageddon.

Tooth (Teeth)
Gen.49:12: and his t. white with milk.

Ex.21:24: Eye for eye, tooth for tooth,
Ex.21:27: he shall let him go free for his t. sake,
Lev 24:20: Breach for breach, eye for eye, t. for t.:
Num.11:33: And while the flesh was yet between their t.,
Deut 19:21: eye for eye, tooth for t., hand for hand,
Deut 32:24: I will also send the t. of beasts upon them,
1 Sam 2:13: with a fleshhook of three t. in his hand;
Job 4:10: the t. of the young lions, are broken.
Job 13:14: Wherefore do I take my flesh in my t.
Job 16:9: he gnasheth upon me with his t.;
Job 19:20: the skin of my t.
Job 29:17: plucked the spoil out of his t.
Job 41:14: his t. are terrible round about.
Ps 3:7: thou hast broken the t. of the ungodly.
Ps 35:16: they gnashed upon me with their t.
Ps 37:12: and gnasheth upon him with his t.
Ps 57:4: whose t. are spears and arrows,
Ps 58:6: Break their t., O God,
Ps 112:10: he shall gnash with his t.,
Ps 124:6: who hath not given us as a prey to their t.
Prov 10:26: As vinegar to the t.,
Prov 25:19: is like a broken t., and a foot out of joint.
Prov 30:14: There is a generation, whose t. are as swords, and their jaw t. as knives,
Song 4:2: Thy t. are like a flock of sheep ...
Song 6:6: Thy t. are as a flock of sheep

Isa: 41:15: a new sharp threshing instrument having t.:
Jer 31:29: the children's t. are set on edge.
Jer 31:30: his t. shall be set on edge.
Lam 2:16: and gnash the t.:
Lam 3:16: He hath also broken my t. with gravel stones,
Ezek 18:2: the children's t. are set on edge?
Dan 7:5 in the mouth of it between the t. of it:
Dan 7:7: and it had great iron t.:
Dan 7:19: whose t. were of iron,
Joel 1:6: whose t. are the teeth of a lion, and he hath the cheek t. of a great lion.
Amos 4:6: And I also have given you cleanness of t.
Micah 3:5: that bite with their t., and cry,
Zech 9:7: and his abominations from between his t.:
Mt 5:38: eye for an eye, and a t. for a t.:
Mt 8:12: there shall be weeping and gnashing of t.
Mt 13:42: there shall be wailing and gnashing of t.
Mt 13:50: there shall be wailing and gnashing of t.
Mt 22:13: there shall be weeping and gnashing of t.
Mt 24:51: there shall be weeping and gnashing of t.
Mt 25:30: there shall be weeping and gnashing of t.
Mt 27:44: cast the same in his t.
Mt 9:18: and gnasheth with his t.,
Lk 13:28: There shall be weeping and gnashing of t.
Acts 7:54: gnashed on him with their t.
Rv 9:8: and their t. were as the t. of lions

Womb
Gen 25:23: Two nations are in thy w.,
Gen 25:24: there were twins in her w.
Gen 29:31: he opened her w.:
Gen 30:2: who hath withheld from thee the fruit of the w.?
Gen 30:22: and opened her w.
Gen 38:27: behold, twins were in her w.
Gen 49:25: blessings of the breasts, and of the w.:
Ex 13:2: whatsoever openeth the w. among the children of Israel,
Num 8:16: instead of such as open every w.,
Num 12:12: half consumed when he cometh out of his mother's womb.
Deut 7:13: he will also bless the fruit of thy w.,
Judg 13:5: for the child shall be a Nazarite unto God from the w.:
Judg 13:7: for the child shall be a Nazarite to God from the w. to the day of his death.
Judg 16:17: for I have been a Nazarite unto God from my mother's w.
Ruth 1:11: are there yet any more sons in my w.,
1 Sam 1:5: the LORD had shut up her w.
1 Sam 1:6: because the LORD had shut up her w.
Job 1:21: Naked came I out of my mother's w.,
Job 3:10: Because it shut not up the doors of my mother's w.,
Job 3:11: Why died I not from the w.?
Job 10:18: Wherefore then hast thou brought me forth out of the w.?
Job10:19: I should have been carried from the w. to the grave.

Job 24:20: The w. shall
forget him;
Job 31:15: Did not he that
made me in the w. make him?
and did not one fashion us in
the w.?
Job 31:18: and I have guided
her from my mother's w.;
Job 38:8: as if it had issued out
of the w.?
Job 38:29: Out of whose w.
came the ice?
Ps 22:9: But thou art he that
took me out of the w.:
Ps 22:10: I was cast upon thee
from the w.:
Ps 58:3: The wicked are
estranged from the w.:
Ps 71:6: By thee have I been
holden up from the w.:
Ps 110:3: in the beauties of
holiness from the w. of the
morning:
Ps 127:3: and the fruit of the
w. is his reward.
Ps 139:13: thou hast covered
me in my mother's w.
Prov 30:16: The grave; and the
barren w.;
Prov 31:2: and what, the son
of my w.?
Eccl 5:15: As he came forth of
his mother's w.
Eccl 11:5: nor how the bones
do grow in the w. of her that is
with child:
Isa 13:18: they shall have no
pity on the fruit of the w.;
Isa 44:2: and formed thee
from the w.,
Isa 44:24: he that formed thee
from the w.,
Isa 46:3: which are carried
from the w.:
Isa 48:8: and wast called a
transgressor from the w.
Isa 49:1: The LORD hath
called me from the w.;
Isa 49:5: And now, saith the
LORD that formed me from
the w. to be his servant,

Isa 49:15: she should not have
compassion on the son of
her w.?
Isa 66:9: and shut the w.?
Jer 1:5: and before thou
camest forth out of the w. I
sanctified thee,
Jer 20:17: Because he slew me
not from the w.;
Jer 20:18: Wherefore came I
forth out of the w.
Ezek 20:26: to pass through
the fire all that openeth the w.,
Hosea 9:11: and from the w.,
and from the conception.
Hosea 9:14: give them a
miscarrying w. and dry
breasts.
Hosea 9:16: yet will I slay even
the beloved fruit of their w.
Hosea 12:3: He took his
brother by the heel in the w.,
Mt 19:12: which were so born
from their mother's w.:
Lk 1:15: even from his
mother's w.
Lk 1:31: And, behold, thou
shalt conceive in thy w.,
Lk 1:41: the babe leaped in
her w.;
Lk 1:42: and blessed is the
fruit of thy w.
Lk 1:44: the babe leaped in my
w. for joy.
Lk 2:21: which was so named
of the angel before he was
conceived in the w.
Lk 2:23: Every male that
openeth the w. shall be called
holy to the Lord;
Lk 11:27: Blessed is the w. that
bare thee,
Jn 3:4: can he enter the second
time into his mother's w., and
be born?
Acts 3:2: And a certain man
lame from his mother's w. was
carried,
Acts 14:8: being a cripple from
his mother's w.,

Rom 4:19: neither yet the
deadness of Sara's w.:
Gal 1:15: who separated me
from my mother's w.,

CPSIA information can be obtained
at www.ICGtesting.com
Printed in the USA
BVHW071920260619
552017BV00006B/90/P